DATE DUE
Unless Recalled Earlier

JUN _ 4 1993

DEMCO 38-297

Literature on the Threshold

Literature on the Threshold
The German Novel in the 1980s

Edited by
Arthur Williams
Stuart Parkes
and
Roland Smith

BERG
New York / Oxford / Munich
Distributed exclusively in the US by
St Martin's Press, New York

First published in 1990 by
Berg Publishers Limited
Editorial Offices:
165 Taber Avenue, Providence R.I. 02906, USA
150 Cowley Road, Oxford OX4 1JJ, UK
Westermühlstraße 26, 8000 München 5, FRG

© Arthur Williams, Stuart Parkes and Roland Smith 1990

All rights reserved.
No part of this publication may
be reproduced in any form
or by any means without the permission of
Berg Publishers Limited.

Library of Congress Cataloging-in-Publication Data

Literature on the threshold: The German novel in the 1980's / edited by Arthur Williams, Stuart Parkes, Roland Smith.
 p. cm.
 ISBN 0-85496-616-1
 1. German fiction—20th century—History and criticism.
 I. Williams, Arthur, 1940 June 5– II. Parkes, K. Stuart, 1943–
 III. Smith, Roland, 1926– .
 PT772.L59 1989
 833'.91409—dc20   89-35880
                                                              CIP

British Library Cataloguing in Publication Data
Literature on the threshold: the German novel in the 1980s.
 1. Fiction in German, 1945– — Critical studies
 I. Williams, Arthur II. Parkes, Stuart III. Smith, Roland
 833'.914'09
 ISBN 0-85496-616-1

Printed in Great Britain by
Billing & Sons Ltd, Worcester

Contents

Preface ix

Introduction 1
Stuart Parkes

1 History in the Contemporary German Novel
  Ralf Schnell 9

2 'Ein Junge aus dem "Dreikaiserjahr"': Uwe
  Johnson's *Versuch, einen Vater zu finden*
  Norbert Mecklenburg 29

3 'The Purpose of my Life seems to be to Learn about
  the Purpose of my Life': Erwin Strittmatter's
  Two-Part Novel *Der Laden*
  Christa Hartwig 49

4 The Recent Historical Novel in the GDR
  J. H. Reid 61

5 Günter de Bruyn and *Neue Herrlichkeit*
  Roland Smith 77

6 Christoph Hein: The Novelist as Dramatist Manqué
  Gisela Shaw 91

7 'Was da ist, das ist [nicht] mein': The Case of Peter
  Schneider
  Gordon Burgess 107

8 Peter Handke's *Der Chinese des Schmerzes*: The
  Threshold as a Place of Waiting
  Peter Pütz 123

9 The German Academic Novel of the 1980s, or a
  Tale of Four Hetero-Academic Novels
  Brian Keith-Smith 135

Contents

10 Themes in the German–Swiss Novel of the 1980s: Beat Sterchi's *Blösch* and Gertrud Leutenegger's *Kontinent*
Malcolm Pender — 153

11 Beyond Reality: Theory and Practice of Austrian Prose in the 1980s
Hubert Lengauer — 169

12 Thomas Bernhard's 'Musical Prose'
Andrea Reiter — 187

13 Power, Politics and Pornography: Elfriede Jelinek's Satirical Exposés
Juliet Wigmore — 209

14 Culpabilities of the Imagination: The Novels of Monika Maron
Martin Kane — 221

15 Loyalty and its Limits: Christa Wolf's *Kassandra* as a 'Schlüsselerzählung'
David Jenkinson — 235

16 Myth in Contemporary Women's Literature
Ricarda Schmidt — 253

17 'Das Kapitel Mann ist beendet': 'Female texts' by Male Authors as Critiques of Patriarchy? Stefan Schütz and Botho Strauß
Moray McGowan — 263

18 Botho Strauß and the Land of his Fathers: From *Rumor* to *Der junge Mann*
Arthur Williams — 279

19 The Novels of Patrick Süskind: A Phenomenon of the 1980s
Stuart Parkes — 309

20 Literature and the End of the World: Günter Grass's *Die Rättin*
Julian Preece — 321

21 German Literature on the Threshold of the Twenty-First Century: A Critic's Perspective
Martin Lüdke — 335

Contents

Notes on the Contributors 349
Select Bibliography 353
Index 359

Preface

The majority of the papers in this volume were written originally for a colloquium on *The German Novel in the 1980s* held in the University of Bradford in March 1988. The colloquium would not have been possible without the support of the Austrian Cultural Institute, London, the Goethe-Institut, Manchester, and the German Academic Exchange Service, London, to whose Directors the editors wish to record their profound gratitude. Heartfelt thanks, too, to Liz Williams, who gave unstintingly of her time, typing and computing skills, and to Sarah Brickwood, whose contribution to this volume has gone far beyond the translations accredited to her.

Arthur Williams
Stuart Parkes
Roland Smith

Introduction

STUART PARKES

'Who is worth reading after Grass and Böll?' This is the kind of question posed by those eager to keep up-to-date with contemporary German literature. It is hoped that this volume of essays, most of which were originally papers given at a conference on the German novel in the 1980s held at the University of Bradford in March 1988, can provide some answers. There can be little doubt that the question is justified; as Martin Lüdke points out, a generational change is taking place in German literature.

Böll died in 1985. Other members of what might be called the postwar generation of German writers do feature in this collection but often in a context that suggests that they no longer hold the prominent position they once enjoyed. Grass's *Die Rättin*, discussed by Julian Preece, may well be that author's last major work; in any case, there are good reasons for applying the adjective 'valedictory' to it. Wolfgang Hildesheimer, as Ralf Schnell notes, is one writer who has specifically stated that he no longer considers it appropriate to write works of literature, although it is interesting that both he and Grass are now largely devoting themselves to their other talent – fine art. As for others in this age-group, Martin Walser, whose *Brandung* is considered here under the heading of the academic novel, continues to be prolific; it is held by some though, possibly a little harshly, that his portrayals of largely nondescript failures from the lower middle classes increasingly resemble one another. There is, however, a new departure in his most recent novel, *Jagd* (1988), where a long section is devoted to the psychology of a female character. Siegfried Lenz, too, is to some degree taken to task here by Ralf Schnell for his traditionalism.

Before leaving this generation of novelists, it is worth recalling what, in general terms, they stood for. After the national catastrophe of the Third Reich, these writers were committed – and the term is used deliberately – to a new democratic society that would represent a total break with the past. 'Overcoming the past' – often a cliché in the mouths of politicians – was a deadly serious matter to a writer like Heinrich Böll, much of whose own youth had been squandered in the service of an odious regime. Moral indignation about this fact, coupled with strong protest against the re-emergence of forces and individuals discredited by their behaviour under the Nazis, remained the seminal feature of his work right down to the posthumously published *Frauen vor Flußlandschaft*. In relation to the past and the developing postwar world, West German writers like Böll can be said to have stood for the values of the Enlightenment – values that in Germany had frequently been swamped by the forces of irrationalism. Their concern for humanity and tolerance was shared by others from outside the Federal Republic, Max Frisch for example. But it was Günter Grass, with his unfailing support for Western pluralist democracy, who saw himself as the defender of Enlightenment values against all forms of extremism. *Die Rättin* has changed that. That human society is incapable of realizing such values and is more likely to destroy itself in a nuclear catastrophe is the message he now appears to be conveying, as he, along with other members of his generation, vacates centre stage.

'Who is worth reading in 1988?' Twenty years ago, at the height of student unrest in the Federal Republic and other European states, such a question might well have been thought absurd. For it was then that a debate was taking place under the heading of the 'death of literature'. Many prominent writers and intellectuals led by Hans Magnus Enzensberger seemed to be saying that literature had no place in a world where revolutionary political change was at the top of the agenda. Lyric poetry was weighed in the balance against political manifestos and found wanting. All that might possibly be acceptable was writing that largely reproduced document or fact. Half a decade later, however, the relieved cry 'Jetzt dichten sie wieder' was to be heard. 'Neue Subjektivität' was the term used to describe much of the literature of the 1970s. Both this term and the slogan 'death of literature' are misleading. As usual, Enzensberger, who never ceased his own literary production, was hedging his bets, whilst the subjectivity of the 1970s had a social and political dimension. In particular, in largely autobiographical novels like Nicolas Born's *Die erdabgewandte Seite der Geschichte* or Bernward Vesper's *Die Reise*, writers sought to come to terms with the political events of the 1960s and their role within them.

From this, it is only a relatively short step to the themes of the 1980s that emerge from the essays in this collection: namely history and myth. 'Emerge' is the appropriate word, since in their original conception of the Bradford conference, the organizers (and editors of this volume) did not seek to impose any themes or subjects on contributors. The themes simply presented themselves. Neither 'history' nor 'myth' is a clear-cut term either in itself or in relation

Introduction

to literature. Not only do the two areas overlap but it could also be argued that any novel which is narrated in the past tense – and with the exception of those that rely on a stream-of-consciousness technique, nearly all novels are – is in some sense historical. Conversely, the term 'historical novel' can be restricted to those works which, in the manner of Walter Scott, seek to retell, more or less realistically, events of previous generations or centuries.

In the Federal Republic, history is at present in the forefront of public attention. A – if not the – major intellectual debate of the past two years has been the *Historikerstreit*, with the point of contention being whether Nazi genocide represented a unique act of barbarism or just one example of 'man's inhumanity to man'. Chancellor Kohl is putting his weight behind a new museum of German history in West Berlin. In addition, the GDR, already in possession of such a museum, now seems anxious to claim for itself an increasing number of historical figures who had previously been rejected on ideological grounds, such as Luther, Bismarck and Frederick II of Prussia, recently restored to the title 'Frederick the Great'. In the case of Austria, it is only necessary to mention the name of Kurt Waldheim.

This is said to be the postmodern age. Architects, for instance, have abandoned the stern requirement of Le Corbusier that buildings be machines; instead they have introduced decorative features that seem arbitrarily to take over aspects of all previous architectural periods. If there is a literary equivalent to this development, it might be in works like Eco's *The Name of the Rose* or, in a German context, Süskind's *Das Parfum*, which is discussed below by Stuart Parkes, pp. 311–19. Whatever the merits of works like these – and it is far from certain that they will be read in twenty years time – most of the novels of the 1980s discussed here are anything but fashionable indulgences against the colourful background of a romanticized past. What is more, in structural terms they hardly ever take the form of a linear narrative.

It is a truism that in most cases historical novels are not solely concerned with the past. The Joseph novels of Thomas Mann, for example, were inspired by Roosevelt's New Deal, whilst elder brother Heinrich used the figure of Henry IV of France to show an ideal of government relevant to his own time. Equally, in many novels of the 1980s the past is narrated for more than its own sake. This gives the lie to any suggestion that the contemporary novel has lapsed into a kind of historicism that disregards controversial issues. That past, present and future stand in a dynamic, fluctuating relationship is pointed out by Martin Lüdke, with reference to comments by Günter Grass. Equally, within this relationship, the past cannot be regarded as something fixed and available like electronically stored information. The works of two authors in particular stress the uncertainties surrounding the past: Gisela Shaw shows how the narrative technique used by Christoph Hein in *Horns Ende* reflects the difficulties of 'overcoming the past' in the GDR, in this case the Stalinism of the 1950s, whilst Norbert Mecklenburg points to the 'open' and 'tentative' narrative form of Uwe Johnson's *Versuch, einen Vater zu finden*. In two other novels that are not ostensibly historical novels at all, the past plays a different role. Alois Brandstetter's *Die Burg*, discussed by Brian Keith-Smith, has as its main character a struggling academic named Arthur whose field is appropriately medieval studies. Peter Handke's hero in *Der Chinese des Schmerzes* – the subject of Peter Pütz's essay – is a teacher and archaeologist. In this novel, three time-levels are important: the distant past that is the subject of archaeology, the recent past (in the form of the Third Reich) and the present, as represented by the featureless modern suburb of Salzburg where the hero lives.

From the time of his first spectacular appearance at the 1966 gathering of the *Gruppe 47*, Handke has often been accused of being a writer with scant social and political concern. If this was ever true, which must be doubted, it cannot be maintained in the face of *Der Chinese des Schmerzes*. The same charge is often levelled at Botho Strauß, who is frequently regarded as the epitome of a non-committed writer. It is not intended here to go into a detailed examination of the term 'commitment'; suffice it to say that Arthur Williams manages to show how wrong this cliché is. What is shown in Williams's essay is that Strauß's concerns range from the German language to the prevention of the re-emergence of any form of neo-Nazism. Moreover, Strauß is shown to be steeped in the work of the first generation of postwar writers like Grass and Böll.

It has already been pointed out how the Nazi past cast its shadow over this first generation of postwar writers. That the shadow remains for writers other than Handke and Strauß can be seen in a work like Peter Schneider's *Vati*, even if in Gordon Burgess's view the result is extremely disappointing. Another novel in which the past dominates a father–son relationship is Jurek Becker's *Bronsteins Kinder* (1986). Here the question is how should a son react when his Jewish father reverses the roles of the past by helping to keep a former concentration camp guard imprisoned in the family's weekend cottage. What is possibly different in these and other novels of the 1980s is that they – continuing the interest in the subjective that emerged in the 1970s – may often stress the personal element within major historical events. Individual family history in its relationship to the wider historical perspective is the subject of Strittmatter's *Der Laden*, discussed by Christa Hartwig, and Johnson's *Versuch, einen Vater zu finden*. Elsewhere, history and myth are used to illustrate more general, though still far from abstract, social issues, for instance the role of women in society in Renate Feyl's academic novel *Idylle mit Professor* and in the works considered by Ricarda Schmidt.

To sum up: the claim that history and myth have come to the fore in the contemporary German novel must not be taken to imply that the traditional historical novel has returned in either content or form. The term 'history' in particular has to be used to cover references to both ancient myths and events that come into the category of contemporary history (*Zeitgeschichte*). In aesthetic terms, there is a wide variety of styles and approaches. Nevertheless, the two concepts of history and myth provide some kind of common denominator for many of the novels discussed in this volume. As Hubert Lengauer points out, novelists are confronting an age in which reality has become so bizarre that a one-dimensional mimetic approach seems wholly inappropriate. Multi-dimensionality is literally the order of the day. A specific example that reflects this multi-dimensionality can be given. The work that receives most attention in this collection is undoubtedly Christa Wolf's *Kassandra*. On the one hand, this may have something to do with the reputation of the author; on the other hand, it also suggests that the novel has a wider relevance. Ralf Schnell considers it in the context of the historical novel, Ricarda Schmidt sees it as an example of the use of myth in women's literature, whilst for David Jenkinson it is to be regarded to a large extent as a 'Schlüsselerzählung' portraying Christa Wolf's relationship to the GDR. It is not intended here to assess these different approaches to the book, which in any case should not be regarded as mutually exclusive. The relevant point is surely that *Kassandra* denies simple categorization as either 'GDR literature', 'women's literature' or 'historical novel'. In this, it is a paradigm for so many of the works discussed in this collection.

The problem of categorization recurs in relation to a term like 'women's literature'. In the 1970s, it was applied to largely confessional or semi-autobiographical works like Verena Stefan's *Häutungen* (1975) or Karin Struck's *Klassenliebe* (1973). At the same time, Irmtraud Morgner was introducing a historical and non-realistic dimension into her picture of the lot of women in the GDR, as is indicated in the lengthy title of the novel in question: *Leben und Abenteuer der Trobadora Beatriz nach Zeugnissen ihrer Spielfrau Laura* (1974). In this collection, Ricarda Schmidt shows how the use of myth has extended and developed the historical aspect. Equally significantly, the changed role of women in today's society has become a topic of interest for male writers, as Moray McGowan's essay indicates. Since he concludes that on the 'ground where certain male writers are laboriously pitching their tents, many women writers are decamping', it is possibly premature to speak of such men being at the forefront of feminist literature. Nevertheless, 'women's literature' can no longer be considered as an exclusive or esoteric domain by diehards of either sex.

What this collection of essays shows particularly is that neat compartmentalization is no longer possible. It would be a bold person who, after reading them, would still insist that there are four distinct national literatures matching the four major German-speaking states. The propaganda term 'Sozialistische Nationalliteratur der DDR' appears ludicrous in the light of a work like *Kassandra*, whilst there is the increasingly difficult problem of labelling those writers who have moved permanently to the West or chosen to stay there for lengthy periods. (Monika Maron is the latest to take extended leave from the GDR since Martin Kane completed his essay.) Even some who stay in the GDR are only published abroad. Equally, it is hard to regard Peter Handke simply as an Austrian writer when he and Botho Strauß are often mentioned in the same breath as the leading postmodernists. It is interesting to note that the academic novels chosen by Brian Keith-Smith come from three of the German-speaking states; moreover, the recent prevalence of this kind of novel seems to signify a general internationalization of German literature. It is not surprising that two of the works discussed in detail by Keith-Smith have an American dimension. Even some of the barriers between different art-forms seem less rigid after one has read Andrea Reiter on the musical dimension to Thomas Bernhard's prose!

Admittedly, it might seem at first sight that the two Swiss novels discussed in detail by Malcolm Pender have a peculiarly Swiss dimension. However, Pender is at pains to point out that such a description would be a gross simplification. In his essay, he points out how, at the very least, the relationship between Switzerland and the rest of the world has become a major literary theme and how in any comparison it is by no means axiomatic that Switzerland will appear in a favourable light. That Swiss writers may look

Introduction

to other countries in their efforts to find an answer to the question of what constitutes a worthwhile society is shown by Adolf Muschg's *Baiyun oder die Freundschaftsgesellschaft*, a novel referred to by Pender. It was Muschg who in 1980 questioned the idea that there was anything like a discrete Swiss literature, and there is much evidence to support this view.[1] Swiss society, if marked by the degree of intolerance that Otto F. Walter portrays in *Die Verwilderung* (1977), cannot provide in itself a model for novelists of international stature.

'Anything goes'. That well-known phrase was used – in English – by both Norbert Mecklenburg and Martin Lüdke in their original manuscripts. Despite its usual undertones, it need not be an expression of bewilderment or despair in the context of the German novel of the 1980s. Moreover, another recurring German term 'gleich-gültig' with its implication that in the 'postmodern' era nothing matters is shown, particularly by Ralf Schnell, to be a false description of many writers' attitudes to both present and past. It is much more appropriate to speak of a variety of responses to the provocations of a complex age and of fruitful interrelationships between various authors and types of work. At a technical level, the editors of this volume have attempted to take cognizance of these interrelationships by providing a detailed index and by trying to order the contributions so that connections become more apparent. On a different and – dare one say – more elevated plane, those with an interest in German literature can be pleased that it has widened its scope so much. It might just be possible in the late 1980s to apply J. H. Reid's thesis that the historical novel in the GDR has come of age to the postwar German novel as a whole.

Editors' postscript
All of the articles in this book were completed several months before the momentous events in Berlin and the GDR in autumn 1989, yet it is fascinating to note how often these events, the underlying explanation of their inevitability and the revelations consequent upon them are prefigured in the literature discussed in this volume.

1. For a more detailed discussion see: Malcolm Pender, 'The German–Swiss Novel since 1945', in Keith Bullivant (ed.), *The Modern German Novel*, Leamington Spa, 1987, pp. 19–35.

–1–

History in the Contemporary German Novel

RALF SCHNELL

The title of my paper – let me confess immediately – works on set concepts about which only one thing can at present be said with any certainty: they function in a sphere of indeterminacy to which there is no easily defined approach. With the current polyphonic chorus of postmodern voices – our minds with Marx, our hearts with Benjamin, Derrida in our eyes and Baudrillard breathing down our necks – there might well be problems in reaching agreement on the question of how history should be defined today in material terms. Nor should we expect a categorical solution to the problem of the 'form of the novel': 'Die Variabilität dieser Form war immer schon sehr groß. Heute aber sieht es beinahe so aus, als ob auf dem Gebiet des Romans nur noch das in Betracht käme, was kein Roman mehr ist.'[1] This observation was made by Thomas Mann in a lecture in 1942, and as you are aware his verdict has been borne out and reaffirmed countless times since then, from Arno Schmidt to Jürg Laederach, with the result that while the literary scholar can still attempt to describe and account for the development of the novel, he can no longer hope to establish definitions. Finally, I wish to disregard entirely the question of how many German literatures there are, not only to avoid repeating myself but also owing to the obvious sterility of qualifying and disqualifying literature by the demarcation of state boundaries.

Nor is it necessary, however, to justify this paper's approach by performing prodigious feats of definition. As Wittgenstein rightly emphasized, it is perfectly possible for concepts to operate 'mit verschwommenen Rändern', and an 'unscharfes Bild' is 'oft gerade

---

Translation by Sarah Brickwood.
1. Thomas Mann, 'Joseph und seine Brüder. Ein Vortrag', *Schriften und Reden zur Literatur, Kunst und Philosophie*, vol. 2, Frankfurt/Main, 1968, p. 386.

das, was wir brauchen'.[2] It is in this sense that I should like to call to mind a scene, in a literary setting, which may illuminate the relationship between 'history' and 'novel' and may form a kind of 'Relaisstation', to use Alexander Kluge's term, which, if it promises no certainties, at least promises to guarantee an approach to the uncertainties.

In 1838 two men meet in Paris who are immediately drawn together by a mutual liking and also, very rapidly, the endeavour to collect, penetrate and assimilate all the knowledge available to them, in order – from the highest state of awareness possible in their time – to be able to work both successfully and practically with the knowledge thus accumulated. History constitutes one of the spheres of their thirst for encyclopaedic learning. But how deceived and disappointed in their high expectations they are when they uncover the vicissitudes and contradictions, the platitudes and mundaneness of what they have hitherto understood as history, and especially the lies, forgeries, distortions, and inconsistencies of historiography.

Bouvard and Pécuchet – for it is to Gustave Flaubert's heroes that I refer – now discover in their quest for historical truth that all historians have had in mind:

> a special cause, a religion, a nation, a party or a system, or else wished to denigrate kings, give advice to people, and offer moral examples. The others, who claim only to narrate, are no better, for it is impossible to say everything; a choice has to be made. But in the choice of documents, a certain attitude will prevail, and since this varies according to the author's conditions, history will never be clearly determined. They thought this sad.[3]

The reason for their sadness is not unfamiliar to us today. Documents and dates, facts and interpretations – nothing is more dubious! Whatever is stored in the memories and archives of the historical consciousness, and whatever the documentary accounts, historiographic tomes, and monumental collections of facts may preserve and reveal – all this in truth constitutes nothing but continual and virtually interminable variations on that one, neverending tale called 'history'. The devastating discovery made by Bouvard and Pécuchet leads them to the recognition that 'the

---

2. Ludwig Wittgenstein, *Philosophische Untersuchungen*, Werkausgabe, vol. 1, Frankfurt/Main, 1984, § 71, p. 280.
3. Gustave Flaubert, *Bouvard et Pécuchet*, in *Œuvres*, eds. A. Thibaudet and R. Dumesnil, vol. 2, Paris, 1952, p. 820.

outward facts are not everything'.⁴ This enables literature to enter the scene. They procure 'some historical novels':⁵ 'First they read Walter Scott. It was the surprise of an entirely new world.'⁶ Admittedly, this new sense of the world only remains with them as long as their preferred novels by Walter Scott do not lose themselves in 'repetition of the same effects'.⁷ And this is precisely why it only lasts for a limited amount of time. 'Bric-à-brac' is the judgement which Flaubert's heroes immediately pass on the principal witness for the theory of the historical novel – and turn to George Sand.

The light thus cast on the mid-nineteenth century by Flaubert's flashes of malice could also illuminate our discussion of history in the contemporary German novel. For it is also possible to read Flaubert's sketch as constituting an implicit, negative poetics of the modern historical novel. The 'boredom' which the 'entirely new world' of Walter Scott immediately produces in the heroes of Gustave Flaubert does not simply indicate the constant pleasure in criticism which we all know makes up the carper's paradise. Rather, it is precisely what, from Gutzkow and Alexis and Fontane right through to Georg Lukács, it has been customary to praise in Walter Scott: objectivity, verisimilitude, naturalness, *description* of lives and *depiction* of crises, variety and sensitivity – all these categories from the arsenal of both bourgeois and socialist realism are found guilty when measured against the code of Flaubertian *impassibilité* of being outmoded. For Flaubert hands down a judgement which, in the sharper forms of his poetic ruthlessness, is negative and figurative: the historical novel, if it were on a level with its period, should adopt this period in its use of forms, in such a way that it would not merely *tell of* history and, in telling, *make use of* history, but would primarily place itself in a conscious relationship to history and would embody this relationship throughout, both in its structure and its form of expression. 'There is no "True"! There are only ways of perceiving', wrote Flaubert in a letter of 1880.⁸ The poetic consequence of this dictum is obvious: the different perceptions of history in the novel may be read as mutually competing interpretations of the historical process. There is no abstract criterion of truth by which they may be evaluated and

4. Ibid., p. 826.
5. Ibid.
6. Ibid.
7. Ibid., p. 828.
8. *The Letters of Gustave Flaubert 1857–1880*, ed. and trans. by Francis Steegmuller, London, 1982, p. 266.

assessed. Its place is taken by the question of how the novel manages to accommodate this loss of 'the True'.

Hence I should like to suggest an interpretation of the forms in which history is used in the contemporary German novel – as 'ways of perceiving'. Here it will not, perhaps, come as a surprise that the diversity involves an element of consensus; from Ernst Jünger to Christa Wolf, from Wolfgang Hildesheimer to Uwe Johnson, from Peter Weiss and Günter Grass to Alexander Kluge and Alfred Andersch, there prevails a unanimous view that the path of history has taken a disastrous turn. Christa Wolf, for instance, talks of a 'Wahndenken' to which the historical process has led.[9] In Peter Weiss we read: 'Immer hatten sich die Oberen ihre Rechte geholt, und immer hatten sie auf ihrer Hegemonie bestanden, bis andre Mächtige zur Ablösung kamen, und wir hatten es nie weitergebracht, als nachzugeben und uns zu fügen, und wieder einmal verharrten wir angesichts auflebender Tyrannei, die wir nicht kommen gesehn hatten.'[10] The 'früheste Wurzel' of his archetypal historical 'disaster' – Stalingrad – is sought by Alexander Kluge 'mindestens tausend Jahre zurück'.[11] It was not without reason that Günter Grass followed *Der Butt* (1977), the novel of the Hegelian *Weltgeist*, with *Die Rättin* (1986), the complementary novel about the end of the world. And Wolfgang Hildesheimer in particular depicts in the darkest conceivable colours the state which history has currently reached: 'Der Trost, den wir bisher aus der uns umgebenden Natur geschöpft haben, wird zu Untröstlichkeit angesichts der systematischen Zerstörung, der Einengung und Entwürdigung, die ihr überall zuteil wird. In den jahreszeitlichen Wandlungen treten ominöse Verschiebungen auf, sie erschüttern die Gewißheit der ewigen zyklischen Wiederkehr.'[12] Consensus, therefore, in a dark and pessimistic view of things. However, in order to confirm this judgement with regard to history and to assess its significance with regard to the present, we should refrain from yet again invoking Walter Benjamin's 'Engel der Geschichte', whose exegetical function has long since worn thin and who sees 'eine einzige Katastrophe, die unablässig Trümmer auf Trümmer

9. Christa Wolf, *Voraussetzungen einer Erzählung: Kassandra*, Darmstadt, 1983, p. 78.
10. Peter Weiss, *Die Ästhetik des Widerstands*, 3 vols., Frankfurt/Main, 1975–81, vol. 1 p. 9.
11. Alexander Kluge, *Schlachtbeschreibung. Der organisatorische Aufbau eines Unglücks*, Munich, 1978, p. 296.
12. Wolfgang Hildesheimer, 'Endzeit – nur ein Gerede? Zu einem Satz Peter Handkes', *Die Zeit*, 5 December 1986, p. 51.

häuft'.[13] For this obvious consensus is not inherently undifferentiated: *what* is perceived as the catastrophe and *how* it is handled, *why* attention is devoted to it and *for what purpose* it is used in literature – these are the elements which constitute the 'ways of perceiving' and which also challenge us, the readers, critics, and literary scholars, to identify with different positions.

In other words, the perception of the historical process as a chain of disasters is suddenly transformed, at its culmination, into the quintessence of poetic counter-action and thus opens up – precisely by virtue of radical disillusionment – an area of literary freedom which makes it possible to offer reflections, draft out plans, develop new perspectives and test models: for the sake of an alternative history. Literature as the subjunctive mood of history – this is the perception from which contemporary German literature proceeds when assimilating and adapting history.

Alfred Andersch's novel *Winterspelt* (1974) exemplifies this use of the subjunctive mood: 'Das Vergangene ist nie tot; es ist nichteinmal vergangen'[14] and 'Geschichte berichtet, wie es gewesen. Erzählung spielt eine Möglichkeit durch'.[15] It is between these two precepts that Alfred Andersch unfolds the panorama of his great 'Sandkastenspiel'[16] in a style which is at once essayistic, documentary and fictional. In October 1944, Joseph Dincklage, a major in the *Wehrmacht* and holder of the *Ritterkreuz*, plans the peaceful surrender of his battalion to the Americans: a sort of mental exercise on the major's part – and on that of Andersch. A number of characters are involved – an old communist, a schoolmistress, an art historian, a US army major, a US army captain, and a fascist – who, in a constantly changing pattern of new moves and variations, test out possibilities of converting the mental exercise into a reality which it can never become. For the narrative premise of the novel is paradoxical enough: nothing like this was ever attempted let alone carried out successfully in the Second World War. Thus the ultimate failure of the undertaking is its precondition – which is admitted and at the same time reflected with utter consistency and conveyed formally through the self-reflexive structure of the novel. It is a self-reflexivity which emerges from the reality of the war and which finds expression in the novel's structure in total concentra-

13. Walter Benjamin, 'Über den Begriff der Geschichte', *Gesammelte Schriften*, eds. Rolf Tiedemann and Hermann Schweppenhäuser, Frankfurt/Main, 1974, vol. 1, pt 2, p. 697.
14. Alfred Andersch, *Winterspelt*, Zurich, 1974, p. 7.
15. Ibid., p. 22.
16. Ibid., *passim*.

tion on the methods of narration – to the extent of dividing the latter into 'fictional' and 'documentary' sections and heading one chapter, 'Was nicht mehr erzählt wird'. Precisely because such an operation did not occur in the Second World War, the novel can concentrate on its fictional possibilities, developing and playing out their intrinsic credibility.

But what is the intention behind this 'Sandkastenspiel' which the narrator Alfred Andersch has a German army major by the name of Dincklage perform in 1944? One of the characters, the old communist Wenzel Hainstock, makes a pronouncement which holds good for the novel as a whole: '"Wenn man darauf verzichtet, sich vorzustellen, wie etwas hätte sein können, verzichtet man auf die Vorstellung einer besseren Möglichkeit überhaupt. Dann nimmt man die Geschichte eben hin, wie sie eben kommt."'[17] Andersch's *Winterspelt* recounts an 'unerhörte Begebenheit'[18] whose implausibility springs from the very fact that although it did not take place, it could have taken place. Herein lies the intention behind the mental exercise of the narrative. The course of history seems unsatisfactory to Alfred Andersch, the moralist and political educator, and consequently he sets about rewriting it. He shares this idea with the history teacher Gabi Teichert, a character from Alexander Kluge's film *Die Patriotin*. She goes to an SPD conference, since she finds the 'Ausgangsmaterial für den Geschichtsunterricht an den Höheren Schulen . . . nicht verbreitungswürdig'.[19] She therefore wishes to influence history at its inception. It is not the fact that both characters – Major Dincklage as much as Gabi Teichert – ultimately fail which creates the common ground between them; it is the fact that they risk the attempt of confronting an impossible reality with the unreality of its possibility. However, all this is not a political and certainly not a historical programme but (much more modestly and also much more dangerously) a literary programme, drawn up with an eye on the past and an eye to the present – for the benefit of the future.

If Alfred Andersch's *roman d'essai* is taken as a basic model of the literary forms of history in the subjunctive mood, Ernst Jünger's novel *Eumeswil* (1977) may be described as its counter-model, or even as a reply: the tense affinity of Andersch to Jünger is well known. Jünger's novel is a historical novel in ahistorical time, or, to be more precise, a novel which presupposes the end of history as

17. Ibid., pp. 99f.
18. Johann Wolfgang von Goethe, *Gespräche mit Eckermann*, in *Hamburger Ausgabe*, vol. 6, Munich, 1973, p. 726 (29 January 1827).
19. Alexander Kluge, *Die Patriotin. Texte/Bilder 1–6*, Frankfurt/Main, 1979, p. 79.

a condition of being able to contemplate history. The divinatory view enjoyed by his first-person narrator (called Venator, for he is at once an explorer and a hunter in the realms of history), which allows him to exercise sovereign power over historical figures and the events of history, is due to the realization, 'die Geschichte ist tot'. Through boundless variations and ramifications, through twists and turns which in the end exhaust themselves, and ultimately lacking any life of its own, lacking substance, history has, so to speak, reached a stalemate within itself and has come to a standstill, a fatal paralysis: *Eumeswil* is 'geschichtslos'. What once occurred – whether murder or power struggle, historical movement or the dream-like lists of secret associations – may be perceived from the point of view now achieved, a point of view both heightened and distanced, as a model or collection of models whose substratum, the material breeding-ground for a sequence of events and generations, has in each case disappeared. The energetic principle of history – and with it the spirit of history – has evaporated into the extratemporal and the atemporal.

The advantage of this ahistorical situation for the first-person narrator is clearly apparent. 'Die Geschichte ist tot; das erleichtert den historischen Rückblick und hält ihn von Vorurteilen frei, jedenfalls für jene, die den Schmerz erlitten und ihn hinter sich gebracht haben.'[20] He, the historian, who considers himself an 'Anarch' – the converse of an 'Anarchist' – is now able, with the help of the 'Luminar', an omniscient piece of equipment resembling a computer, to see history in perspective. He always has available for study what he requires in order to exercise his true occupation of 'Geschicht[!]-schreiber': history as the material for the thoroughly distanced view of the historian, who moves through history as through a picture gallery. For this very reason he is able to assimilate his subject totally – as the actor does his role.

This novel might be described as the historical novel of postmodern thought were it not for the danger that this might only detract from discussion of the novel itself. Obviously the elements of etiolation, variation and repetition which Jünger filters from the course of an imaginary dead history are related in structure to Jean Baudrillard's concept of 'simulation'. However, I do not wish the course of my presentation to be determined by evidence of this nature but rather by the consequences inherent in and generated by Jünger's picture of history. For if history is dead, it is not, however, at an end. 'Andererseits,' we read in *Eumeswil*, 'kann nicht gestorben sein, was die

20. Ernst Jünger, *Eumeswil*, Stuttgart, 1977, p. 382.

Geschichte mit Inhalt füllte und in Gang setzte. Es muß sich aus der Erscheinung in die Reserve verlagert haben – auf die Nachtseite. Wir hausen auf fossilem Grunde, der unvermutet Feuer speien kann. Wahrscheinlich ist alles Brennstoff, bis zum Mittelpunkt.'[21] What kind of an assumption is this, which is here pursued into a certainty – what kind of a certainty which is pursued into speculation? If we weigh Jünger's picture in its exact meaning, then dead history is seen obviously to be transformed into a type of prehistory, a state of freedom from history which unfolds in a mythological, cosmological and organological sphere. The image of fire, of fuel, is a reminder of the mythical, cosmic, organicistic visions of *Auf den Marmorklippen*: 'Die Menschenordnung gleicht dem Kosmos darin, daß sie von Zeit zu Zeiten, um sich von neuem zu gebären, ins Feuer tauchen muß.'[22] Ernst Jünger has remained true to himself, and yet he has altered. History is no longer categorized – as in the era of fascism – as being shaped by natural and intrinsically inexorable forces, but has died through withdrawal of its substance. At the same time, however, it continues to exist in the prehistoric suspense of the myth, awaiting that which one day will afford it some content and set it in motion once again.

Jünger's novel leads, it seems to me, to a remythicizing of history. It is as a kind of riposte to this narrative strategy that I view Christa Wolf's novel *Kassandra*: a historicizing of the myth and the attempt to shed some illumination on the present with the aid of a mythological subject. Kassandra is the Trojan princess who was granted the gift of prophecy by Apollo at the price of having to sleep with him. Because she refuses to submit to him, he denies her the ability to convince other people of the truth of her prophecies. Kassandra, the archetypal female victim, is doubly a victim: of men and of objective reality, from which she is, so to speak, progressively excluded. Having reached the end of the path she has to pursue as a double victim, she is struck dead and that which previously went unheeded is definitively silenced. It is in Mycenae that she meets her end – and it is with this end that Christa Wolf's novel begins.

> Hier war es. Da stand sie. Diese steinernen Löwen, jetzt kopflos, haben sie angeblickt. Diese Festung, einst uneinnehmbar, ein Steinhaufen jetzt, war das letzte, was sie sah. Ein lange vergessener Feind und die Jahrhunderte, Sonne, Regen, Wind haben sie geschleift. Unverändert der Him-

---

21. Ibid.
22. Ernst Jünger, *Auf den Marmorklippen*, Stuttgart, 1960, p. 64.

mel, ein tiefblauer Block, hoch, weit. Nah die zyklopisch gefügten Mauern, heute wie gestern, die dem Weg die Richtung geben: zum Tor hin, unter dem kein Blut hervorquillt. Ins Finstere. Ins Schlachthaus. Und allein.[23]

What begins now is poetry as an attempt to brush history against the grain (as Walter Benjamin put it) – an alternative to the heroic epic of classical times and the accounts given in the *Iliad*, the *Odyssey* and the *Oresteia*, an alternative constructed with a detailed knowledge of all the important accounts of the myths recorded by Robert Graves, Schwab and Kerényi. As may be gathered from her lectures on poetics entitled *Voraussetzungen einer Erzählung: Kassandra*, Christa Wolf has used as subject matter for her narrative all the facts which have been handed down to us, recasting them to form a literary inner perspective. While the epic strives after objectivity and the poetic creation of a self-contained and comprehensive whole, a self-sufficient and rounded narrative cosmos, Christa Wolf's *Kassandra* aims to sketch a subjectivity which, conveyed through the technique of interior monologue, goes against the 'Linie des männlichen Handelns'[24] and the glorification of 'Geschichte als Heldengeschichte'.[25] Thus Christa Wolf in no way endeavours to distil a type of interlinear version of the myths surrounding Cassandra from the diversity of the traditions and variants. On the contrary, in the myths which have come down to us she seeks out structures which indicate a recurrent pattern of domination and force, victory and downfall, power and masculinity. And it is the subjectivized perception of this dominating pattern of human evolution which lends it its archetypal significance: Kassandra, the archetypal female victim, relates the archetypal fall of Troy in such a way that an arc may easily be traced to the present day. 'Wann Krieg beginnt,' runs the now famous central sentence which announces the transfer, 'das kann man wissen, aber wann beginnt der Vorkrieg. Falls es da Regeln gäbe, müßte man sie weitersagen. In Ton, in Stein eingraben, überliefern.'[26] This handing down is the task of this novel.

The narration is based on a *vision par derrière*, which results in a radical difference between narrative time, an afternoon in Mycenae, and narrated time, a life in Troy. From this difference there springs the tension which is the primary factor in allowing scope for a

23. Christa Wolf, *Kassandra*, Darmstadt, 1983, p. 5.
24. Wolf, *Voraussetzungen*, p. 91.
25. Ibid., p. 117.
26. Wolf, *Kassandra*, pp. 76f.

subjectivizing introspection – between the self as narrator and the self as a receptacle of experience. This is a tension which encourages reflection instead of chronology, which allows for criticism, comment and correction, and which leads to rearrangements and displacements within the structural continuity of time. It is an inner tension which also characterizes the narrating self as a modern self which can view itself as an object and has remained alien to both the gods and society. It is a self which enlists neither the gods nor the souls of the dead to account for the course of the action but which is able to analyse psychological, political and pragmatic factors. This is a historical and not a mythical self: it demythologizes mythical material by illuminating it through rational interpretation. The social structures, the interdependence and manipulation, the economic and technocratic mechanisms, the interconnections between politics and media, economics and science are plainly apparent to this self. Thus it is not only able to differentiate between the world of men and that of women but is also able to distinguish the two within its own self and draw upon them for alternative lines of action. This self takes a path which leads it from the quest for itself via self-knowledge to the finding of itself in death. A path which begins with alienation from the self and undying love of the father, continues with a flight into madness and exile in the caves ('Da endlich hatte ich mein "Wir"'),[27] and is completed by the process of life reflecting itself – at the price of death: 'Gescheitert das Wagnis, der Eiseskälte der Außerirdischen unsere kleine Wärme entgegenzusetzen.'[28]

And yet Christa Wolf writes, 'Das Troia, das mir vor Augen steht, ist – viel eher als eine rückgewandte Beschreibung – ein Modell für eine Art von Utopie.'[29] A contradiction? If *Kassandra* is compared to such works as *Nachdenken über Christa T.* and *Kein Ort. Nirgends*, it may be seen as a logical continuation of the poetic protest against a life which is unlivable, an expression both of criticism and disillusionment, and also a space for reflection in a 'Zwischenzeit' (Ernst Bloch) in which that which has not yet occurred is at the same time continually endangered.

At this point let us once more trace an arc back to Alfred Andersch's *Winterspelt*. In Ernst Jünger we have the remythicizing of history; in Christa Wolf, the historicizing of myth. This means, just as in Alfred Andersch, a hermeneutic appropriation of history, history as the material for poetic construction and reconstruction,

27. Ibid., p. 141.
28. Ibid., p. 5.
29. Wolf, *Voraussetzungen*, p. 83.

as a substratum of counter-history and counter-histories. However, this possible way of utilizing history does not leave unaffected or unchanged the objective reality of the historical material itself. Dates and facts no longer conflict with poetic invention but are dissolved in it and with this transformed into its instrument. The consequences for the relationship between literature and history are as significant as the degrees of stratification are indicative of its dissolution.

If Alfred Andersch had already created a rich interplay of tensions in the relationship between 'Bericht' and 'Fiktion' mediated by the technique of narrative self-reflexivity, in his *Schlachtbeschreibung* Alexander Kluge took this process even further for the relationship between document and fiction mediated by the technique of montage. Where Andersch addresses the question of whether it might not have been possible for history to take a different course, Kluge, in his reconstruction of Stalingrad, addresses the problem of why history had of necessity to take this particular course. This question, too, can only be treated in the subjunctive mood, that is, it cannot be answered from one single isolated perspective, and the answer only carries weight if it gives rise to more questions. '"Ein Unglück wie Stalingrad hat den Vorteil, daß es unmöglich mit zwei Augen zu sehen ist. So sah keiner von uns alles . . .",'[30] reads a fictitious quotation from the preface, which Kluge has entitled 'Nachricht' in allusion to Clausewitz's *Vom Kriege*. The multiperspectivity which is the natural consequence of this insight brings together and contrasts the most varied documents and sources, evidence and testimonies, materials and facts, stories and anecdotes, fictions and fantasies, in the form of a montage of conflicting elements, rich in tension. Through this montage the status of the material is altered: the documentary record loses authenticity in the measure that the fiction gains objective reality.

A 'postscript' gives as sources the Institut für Zeitgeschichte in Munich, the Bundesarchiv in Koblenz, accounts of those who came back, documents made available privately, radio messages and memoranda. However, by referring to such records, Kluge effectively relativizes the quality of any act of authentication made in the name of any reality. In other words, Alexander Kluge, the narrator, is enough of a realist to distrust reality. He knows that to get hold of reality you need more than the evidence gleaned from it aurally and visually. What he said is true, namely that it is the 'schärfste Ideologie: daß sich dei Realität auf ihren realistischen

---

30. Kluge, *Schlachtbeschreibung*, p. 7.

Charakter beruft'.[31] This is precisely why the ingredient of fiction is needed: particularly in its most authentic form of the invisible and yet effective montage, it sets the seal of genuineness on a historical authenticity endorsed by the interest in understanding on the part of the perceiving subject who is interpreting history. But this narrative subject receives life and identity only through his own deconstruction. Kluge elevates documentary record to the status of fiction and lends fiction the quality of documentary record. As a narrator he is invisible, albeit present, in both processes, and he is also invisible in the assembly of the entire collection: the narrator as arranger of the material.

The element of re-creating and re-inventing history which thus comes into play also secretly imparts energies which oppose history 'wie sie wirklich war' and oppose reality 'wie sie einmal ist'. 'Das Motiv für Realismus', according to Alexander Kluge, 'ist nie Bestätigung der Wirklichkeit, sondern Protest.'[32] Such protest has been carried even further and radicalized by a different author who in the end, logically enough, stopped writing – Wolfgang Hildesheimer. His novel *Marbot* (1981) presents the biography of a fictitious figure of art history, a figure whose breaking of the incest taboo with his mother lends him an aura of erotic sensationalism. It also enhances his particular talent since, by concentrating on an empathetic reconstruction of technique and emotion, the language of colour and form in nineteenth-century art, Marbot is foreshadowing the possibilities of psychological interpretation in art and painting. Hildesheimer has very carefully given life and authenticity to his completely fictional-character by appearing to authenticate his existence with records and photographs. It was in *Marbot* that Hildesheimer created what he was able to take for granted in his biography of Mozart: a life, psychological identity, statements worthy of being handed down, a definable historical and social setting and, not least, theoretical work which generates such a high degree of authenticity or, rather, internal credibility within itself that the author is later able to quote from it as he would have from a historical source.

Hildesheimer's novel is a hypertrophying of the technique already evolved in Alfred Andersch and Alexander Kluge: not simply turning documentary record into fiction, nor fiction into documentary record, nor yet the oscillating interplay of fiction and record, but rather a fictionalization of fiction, which itself becomes

---

31. Alexander Kluge, *Gelegenheitsarbeit einer Sklavin. Zur realistischen Methode*, Frankfurt/Main, 1975, p. 214.
32. Ibid., p. 216.

a record, a source, a solid and manageable object. This technique passes sentence on history and indicates the boundaries of literature. Only where these boundaries are overstepped can literature still assert its right to exist. However, such an overstepping of boundaries is only possible on condition that what has become the historicity of history is cast off and that channels for a new counter-history are driven through it, a counter-history which, in addition to all its energy of protest, also communicates a movement of rejection. On this basis, however, literature is hardly possible any longer: it has rendered itself impossible by denying its premise – history – and its target – reality. It is not only the 'end of fiction' (Hildesheimer) but also the end of literature. 'Das war mein letztes Buch', said Wolfgang Hildesheimer in 1982 and – sad to say – he has kept his word. He added, 'Es ist mir rätselhaft, wie Leute überhaupt noch ein Werk reiner Fiktion schreiben können, weil – wie ich es sehe – sämtliche Konstellationen des Romans schon dagewesen sind.'[33]

Against this background we may ask whether, faced with the multiplicity of extremely varied forms in which history has been reworked, it is still possible to find and establish criteria for criticism, appraisal and judgement. 'There is no "True"! There are only ways of perceiving.' Does this mean retreat to an aconceptual relativism, an admission of flat in-difference (*Gleich-Gültigkeit*)? I shall attempt to answer this question indirectly through the medium of Siegfried Lenz's novel *Exerzierplatz* (1985). Lenz tells the story of a somewhat simple young man by the name of Bruno, whose boss, the owner of a large tree nursery, once saved his life shortly before the end of the Second World War and has built up the tree nursery jointly with him. Now, the boss's potential heirs have him certified *non compos mentis* because he wants to bequeath a large part of his property to his limited colleague. In this story, Lenz is also telling the story of the appropriation of land. The military training ground – 'wo früher Verteidigungsnester gewesen waren', 'wo die Soldaten sich vielleicht zum Überraschungsangriff gesammelt hatten'[34] – becomes the seed of what later becomes the extensive property that is to be disputed. Thus here we have a historical novel from which, paradoxically, Lenz has exorcized all historicity – the story of what is, so to speak, an 'ursprüngliche Akkumulation' which totally lacks social and economic dimensions. Thus Lenz recounts history, recounts his story, from a

33. Wolfgang Hildesheimer in an interview with Hanjo Kesting, Norddeutscher Rundfunk, Drittes Programm, 29 June 1987.
34. Siegfried Lenz, *Exerzierplatz*, Hamburg, 1985, p. 35.

consistently maintained first-person perspective which, even though thoroughly limited in both senses of the word, has to authenticate all historicity. While it was still the case in Lenz's earlier novel *Heimatmuseum* (1978) that the first-person narrator Zygmunt Rogalla was able constantly to interrupt himself and his narrative flow with the perplexed question of whether it was actually at all possible for him to recount history, his own history and that of his Masurian homeland (yet then go on to do it: dreamily, in love with the landscape and lost in legend), in *Exerzierplatz* there is no room even for doubt such as this. Lenz narrates as if this unquestioned 'Konstitution des Romans' (Hildesheimer) did not yet exist. In other words, Lenz narrates in the 'classic' manner, as if 'the true' still existed. Since Flaubert, however, this can only be done – as I see it – at the price of that refraction of the narrative perspective which in Thomas Mann is known as 'irony'. Even this only constitutes a kind of narrative self-rescue, and by now we will have to regard even this as itself belonging to history.

Of course, Siegfried Lenz is not the only one to have this problem in the works to which we have referred. The narrative of Ernst Jünger's *Eumeswil* is also based on a single perspective, albeit one which is a model of alienation and inherent pointillist fragmentation (that of the 'Anarch' Venator). And Ernst Jünger has admitted this problem, craftily enough, by having his first-person narrator disappear without trace at the end of the book and having his records 'preserved' by his brother. This is a circumspect refraction of possible identifications – it is in keeping with a novel which is open to various interpretative approaches.

Christa Wolf is also aware of this problem – which is basically one of narrative theory – when she confesses: 'Empfinde die geschlossene Form der Kassandra-Erzählung als Widerspruch zu der fragmentarischen Struktur, aus der sie sich für mich eigentlich zusammensetzt. Der Widerspruch kann nicht gelöst, nur benannt werden.'[35] It may also be possible to account for this contradiction. With Christa Wolf's *Kassandra* – in the approving judgement of feminist-inspired literary criticism – the oppressed voice of women, usually divided and dispersed amidst the chorus of suffering that is human history, has made itself heard both eloquently and emphatically. It has indeed done this, but at the price of aesthetic affirmation, which is compensated for neither by the lectures on poetics that appeared at the same time, nor by the story's modest framing. As a character, Kassandra is drawn in such

---

35. Wolf, *Voraussetzungen*, p. 120.

a way that we may identify with her. The use of interior monologue is very instructive in this respect. It does, after all, permit a narrative openness – we have only to think of the final chapter of *Ulysses* – through a montage of fragmentary, open-ended and eruptive thoughts. In Christa Wolf this openness is found in the form of a complex movement, an associative, vortical narrative which proceeds in strides – not in counterpoint; and it is also found in the form of past and present as a fusion – not as a montage – of narrative and reflexion. The characteristic style of the narrative is not marked by discontinuities but rather by gently associative transitions executed almost imperceptibly, which are linguistically very dense: 'Erzähltechniken, die ja in ihrer jeweiligen Geschlossenheit oder Offenheit auch Denk-Muster transportieren', as Christa Wolf knows only too well.[36] The dense net of this prose, its planar texture, whose inner tension never ruptures and whose smooth sweeps are never breached, baulks at all openness in order to ensure the rigorous maintenance of the subjectivized perspective. Precisely because the fictional figure of Kassandra is portrayed as archetypal with regard to the history of female oppression and female suffering, in Christa Wolf she must regain her voice, which must now be heard. Form must succeed where history has failed. Although the process of suffering is pursued to the mortal end, instead of allowing the marks of derangement, of suffering and of oppression in themselves to become form, form itself heals the open wound.

The criticism I have levelled at Siegfried Lenz, Ernst Jünger and Christa Wolf is substantiated when seen against the light of the two outstanding monuments to the literary reworking of history in our time, that is, Peter Weiss's *Die Ästhetik des Widerstands* (1975, 1978, 1981) and Uwe Johnson's *Jahrestage* (1970, 1971, 1973, 1983). And here I am sure you will understand if, in the present context, I discuss these two colossi of the epic solely from one particular aspect of narrative theory, the one we are here concerned with: epic self-reflexivity. The uniqueness of these two works does not spring solely from their obvious monumentality – Peter Weiss's is over a thousand pages long; two thousand in the case of Uwe Johnson's – but, conversely, the epic massif, which in each case invites and challenges us to scale it, owes its dimensions to the method which seeks to maintain constant transparency with regard to its own procedures. Here, too, with what are once again two very different 'ways of perceiving', we have history in the subjunctive mood, but

36. Ibid.

a subjunctive mood which in addition reflects upon its own preconditions and consequences.

Uwe Johnson has organized the epic self-reflexivity of his tetralogy as a dialogue between narrator and character, a dialogue which is the product of a double refraction. The story is that of Gesine Cresspahl, living in New York with her daughter Marie, who recounts her own story for the benefit of her daughter and by means of a constant exchange with people, places and events from her past in the town of Jerichow in Mecklenburg. The frequent change from the first-person to the third-person perspective reflects the double outlook of this narrative thread. In contrast, the narrator is for his part divided within himself or, perhaps we should say, switches between different identities. On the one hand, he gives an account of the character Gesine Cresspahl; on the other, he functions as a voice for Johnson the author, and here too there are points of intersection. Each of these refractions gives rise not only to a fascinating interplay between author and character, a shattering of the illusion in the Romantic tradition, but – more importantly still – to the possibility of understanding and writing history as a 'draft' (*Entwurf*).

'Hier bei den *Jahrestagen*', Johnson once said, 'habe ich von einer zugegebenermaßen erfundenen Person quasi den Auftrag, oder ich habe mit ihr den Vertrag, ihr Leben wiederzufinden und aufzuschreiben in einer Form, die sie billigen würde.'[37] This 'Auftrag' gives rise to a whole host of discussions and controversies between the 'character' and the narrator which serve not merely to entertain the reader but above all to authenticate the narrative technique. 'Wer erzählt hier eigentlich', we may read in one passage from the first volume, and the answer runs: 'Wir beide. Das hörst du doch Johnson.'[38] And in another passage, in the last volume: 'Ein Jahr hab ich dir gegeben. So unser Vertrag. Nun beschreibe das Jahr.'[39] And in the third volume they all but come to blows: 'Es ist uns schnuppe', scolds Gesine Cresspahl, 'ob dir das zu deftig beladen ist, Genosse Schriftsteller! Du schreibst das hin! Wir können auch heute noch aufhören mit deinem Buch. Dir sollte erfindlich sein, wie wir uns etwas vorgenommen haben für den Tod.'[40] This is, as I have already said, the shattering of an illusion within the course of the narrative itself, entirely in the tradition familiar to us from the

---

37. 'Gespräch mit Uwe Johnson', in Manfred Durzak, *Gespräche über den Roman. Formbestimmungen und Analysen*, Frankfurt/Main, 1976, p. 429.
38. Uwe Johnson, *Jahrestage*, 4 vols., Frankfurt/Main, 1970–83, vol. 1, p. 256.
39. Ibid., vol. 4, Frankfurt/Main, 1983, p. 1426.
40. Ibid., vol. 3, Frankfurt/Main, 1973, p. 1259.

Romantic comedies. The characters talk with the author about the play, its plot and themselves, in order thus to rend asunder the veil of aesthetic appearance – which admittedly they then restore in a different way. Johnson makes use of this tradition, but with a different aim. He sees himself as the narrating co-organizer of a literary cosmos which possesses sufficient reality and inherent laws of its own to develop its own existence. *Jahrestage* is intended as a draft which draws its substance from history and yet at the same time is summoned against it. 'Dies hab ich dir aufgeschrieben', notes Gesine Cresspahl in a letter to her daughter Marie, 'damit du nicht raten mußt, wie ich.'[41] From the narrative present of his 'character' and with her 'licence' (Johnson), the author records the previous history of this present, in order to sketch an outline of Gesine's hopes for the benefit of the daughter Marie, to whom the future will belong – 'für wenn ich tot bin', as Johnson puts it. This is a draft of history which serves 'Wahrheitsfindung' (Johnson) without however on that account claiming to be 'the True' itself.

Such self-denial links Johnson's work, the differences notwithstanding, to Peter Weiss's *Die Ästhetik des Widerstands*. 'Wie könnte dies alles geschildert werden?'[42] is the question which recurs here like a leitmotif and which reveals the organizing principle of his narration as a principle stemming from his self-reflexivity, an energetic principle of drafting out, questioning and emphasizing the problematic elements. This question brings together in a nutshell the rifts and contradictions, hopes and doubts, objectives and problems of the German labour movement before projecting them, from a dominant perspective of resistance, onto the extensive historical backdrop of western civilization and art. 'Wie könnte dies alles geschildert werden?' This is both a political and historical question, a question of ethics and a question of literary theory. And the answer – no matter what disparaging remarks the critics may have let drop – certainly does not turn out to be affirmative since Peter Weiss has incorporated the self-doubt of this question in the work's structural form: both in the variety of its layering (description, historical and political excursus, aesthetic analysis) and in the formal multiplicity of its registers (report, essay, analysis, reflection). Precisely because the narrating subject takes and must take sides in the era of fascism, it is beset with questions, doubts and reservations. Precisely because it has doubts, it must unearth its personal assumptions and reflect these in the work. Precisely

---

41. Ibid., vol. 2, Frankfurt/Main, 1971, p. 690.
42. Weiss, *Die Ästhetik des Widerstands*, vols. 1–3, *passim*.

because it is bound to its time in this way, it should outlast its time – our time. In this respect the style in the final section, determined by the use of the conditional, is both programme and provocation: it poses the question of the possibilities of narration, also demanding that the conditions for narrative possibilities be narrated at the same time.

'Doch im Frühjahr Fünfundvierzig, als die Aufteilung Deutschlands in Besatzungszonen bevorstand, gab es nur noch den Wettlauf, um rechtzeitig an bestimmten Plätzen zu sein'[43] – this is the disillusioned assessment at the end of the war. But it does not lead to a resigned abandonment of former desires and objectives:

> Und wenn es auch nicht so werden würde, wie wir es erhofft hatten, so änderte dies doch an den Hoffnungen nichts. Die Hoffnungen würden bleiben. Die Utopie würde notwendig sein. Auch später würden die Hoffnungen unzählige Male aufflammen, vom überlegnen Feind erstickt und wieder neu erweckt werden. Und der Bereich der Hoffnungen würde größer werden, als er es zu unserer Zeit war, er würde sich über alle Kontinente erstrecken. Der Drang zum Widerspruch, zur Gegenwehr würde nicht erlahmen.[44]

The conditional style is the grammar of hope, traces of which have been detected by *Die Ästhetik des Widerstands* in petrified history, the memorials of art, and the ruins of culture. This, too, is literary historiography for the sake of the future.

It is the disastrous course of history, as I said at the beginning, which constitutes the common point of departure for the works under discussion here. The answers they give and the solutions they put forward are as varied as the perspectives whose choice precedes them. However, this choice is anything but arbitrary. It expresses the historical state of an aesthetic practice whose implicit roots in the philosophy of history – as Rainer Rother has recently expounded in his thesis[45] – are revealed in the medium of their self-reflexivity. This suggests the loss of all certainties. There no longer exists the possibility of reading history – in the spirit of the Enlightenment – as the continuous chain-reaction of progress. It is impossible to see the present – in the Hegelian sense – as the self-fulfilment of the spirit which realizes itself in history. And it is certainly impossible to recall the past, following the maxim of

---

43. Ibid., vol. 3, Frankfurt/Main, 1981, p. 257.
44. Ibid., p. 265.
45. Rainer Rother, *Die Gegenwart der Geschichte. Ein Versuch über Film und zeitgenössische Literatur*, Stuttgart, 1990.

historicism, completely and graphically through the faithful rendering of detail and scale.

But even the perception of history which is now common currency cannot apply: that cultural syndrome of citing history which has literally taken root in the last few years. Everything has to be commemorated — and just because some date has reached round figures! Whether Berlin, East *and* West, is 750 years old, or Jean Paul 225, or fascism seized power 50 years ago: the fixation with commemorating dates has replaced a historical consciousness which would still be able to perceive itself as part of a historical continuity. We commemorate the Hohenstaufens and we commemorate the Prussians. We celebrate Karl Marx Year and we celebrate Luther Year. We build museum villages and we build windmill parks. Art exhibitions, retrospectives, gospel-books, fashions and faces: everything is now equally important, only providing it serves the conservation and consumption of history. We may — with Hermann Lübbe — interpret such a presentation of history as the attempt to put an end to the rapid increase in the speed of change in our time through conscious acts to preserve history. That such endeavours remain ineffective is connected with the fact that they are in essence in-different (*gleich-gültig*). Because of their structure, they are neutral with respect to the objects and events with which they deal. Basically, everything can be adapted and made topical without distinction: the operation is a well-oiled machine.

The perception of history in the contemporary German novel spurns this way of going about things. In its reworking of history, it places the determining of its own position first: the conscious perception of a present time which, marked by disaster, turns to the past in order to understand itself. What literature performs is the recalling of history in the medium of a self-reflexive aesthetics. This gives expression to the alienation of the aesthetic subject and to its alienation from itself. But at the same time it also works against the preconditions for alienation and alienation from the self both in history and in the present. This is an interminable and possibly futile task, a task in the subjunctive mood, a 'nonetheless'. It is undertaken in the spirit of an ancient maxim of historiography: lest, as Herodotus suggested, posterity might forget what once happened among men — a task for the future.

–2–

'Ein Junge aus dem "Dreikaiserjahr"': Uwe Johnson's *Versuch, einen Vater zu finden*

NORBERT MECKLENBURG

> Wohl dem, der sagen kann 'als', 'ehe' und 'nachdem'!
> Robert Musil, *Der Mann ohne Eigenschaften*

> Nur soll die jeweils erzählte Vergangenheit uns unsere gegenwärtigen Verhältnisse erklären.
> Uwe Johnson, 'Vorschläge zur Prüfung eines Romans'

> Geschichte ist ein Entwurf
> Heinrich Cresspahl, in Johnson, *Jahrestage*

I

In this paper I wish to examine the presentation of history in the work of Uwe Johnson with the aid of one specific text. To this end I have chosen *Versuch, einen Vater zu finden*, a text which may be described as historical, since the interval between the narrated time and the time of narration is relatively great. The text recounts the childhood and youth of Heinrich Cresspahl, one of the main characters in *Mutmassungen über Jakob* and *Jahrestage*, in the period between 1888 and 1914. Thus, of all Johnson's work, this is the text which goes back furthest into the past. It constitutes the first part of a more extensive narrative project linked very closely to *Jahrestage* in both theme and content. The author intended to publish it under the title of *Heute neunzig Jahr*, but owing to his premature death it has remained unfinished. In 1975 Johnson read the first part of his manuscript on Norddeutscher Rundfunk as a separate, self-contained narrative entitled *Versuch, einen Vater zu finden*. A cassette recording

---

Translation by Sarah Brickwood. The text observes Johnson's use of 'ss' for 'ß' in quotations and titles.

of this reading, together with the script, was published in 1988.¹

The time of narration is left open in the text, as is the fictitious narrative situation as a whole. However, with the help of certain clues, it is possible to locate it as being 1967–8 – the narrative time of *Jahrestage*.² This maintains the degree of temporal distance which has been so readily used as a criterion of historical narrative ever since Walter Scott's ''tis sixty years since'.³ I do not wish to enter the discussion over the historical novel as a genre with this reference to a rather arbitrary measure,⁴ nor do I in any way wish to deny that Johnson's œuvre, which depicts human lives throughout the twentieth century, occupies an eminent literary position as a presentation of history: German contemporary history between 1930 and 1960. It is in order to examine this particular, outstanding, aspect of Uwe Johnson's narrative œuvre, and especially the great main work *Jahrestage*, that I am pursuing an indirect approach via a short, marginal text, which does, however, have the peculiar characteristic of being classifiable as a historical story in the narrow and traditional sense. My interpretational approach to this text concerns the question: What does Uwe Johnson the narrator achieve as a historian, and how does he achieve it? To this end it is necessary to place the text within a critical frame of reference, and I believe the current academic and literary debates on history are eminently suited to this purpose.

This debate has a variety of focal points, even if ultimately it always comes back to the same problem: the 'public use of history'.⁵ One point of focus is the argument over methods and concepts in the study of history and another is the question of feasibility and forms of the historical novel in the modern and postmodern age. An area of contact between these two fields is to be found in the theoretical and critical debate on history and poetics – on history as discourse.⁶

1. Uwe Johnson, *Versuch, einen Vater zu finden. Marthas Ferien*, ed. Norbert Mecklenburg, Frankfurt/Main, 1988. All page references in the text are to this edition.
2. Uwe Johnson, *Jahrestage*, 4 vols., Frankfurt/Main, 1970–83. For its connection, at its inception, with *Jahrestage*, see my epilogue in Johnson, *Versuch*, pp. 73–6.
3. See Ina Schabert, *Der historische Roman in England und Amerika*, Darmstadt, 1981, p. 4.
4. See Harro Müller, *Geschichte zwischen Kairos und Katastrophe. Historische Romane im 20. Jahrhundert*, Frankfurt/Main, 1988, pp. 11–20.
5. Jürgen Habermas, *Eine Art Schadensabwicklung. Kleine Politische Schriften IV*, Frankfurt/Main, 1987, p. 145.
6. Dominick LaCapra, *Geschichte und Kritik*, Frankfurt/Main, 1987; Hayden White, 'The Question of Narrative in Contemporal Historical Theory', *History and Theory*, vol. 23, 1984, pp. 1–33; Eberhard Lämmert, 'Geschichten von der

Uwe Johnson's Versuch, einen Vater zu finden

The debates on history and historiography have taken on topical public form in the Federal Republic with the so-called *Historikerstreit*, a form governed in this case by theoretical and methodological considerations when determining the primacy of either modern social history or the postmodern history of daily life. The *Historikerstreit*, which first came to the fore in 1986, relates on the surface to the assessment of genocide and the conduct of war in Nazi Germany, but also, on a deeper level, to the 'historische Interpretation und die politische Bedeutung der neueren deutschen Geschichte'.[7] Here we have, once again, the old problem of an 'Aufarbeitung der Vergangenheit',[8] a problem which for decades has been regarded by many German writers and intellectuals as one of their most important tasks. Uwe Johnson was among them from the very beginning. As I shall show, his *Versuch, einen Vater zu finden* is influenced by the same central question as modern academic studies on German history over the past hundred years. The fact that the *Historikerstreit* was also sparked off, amongst other things, by metaphors and similes – or, in more general terms, by the relationship between the knowledge, presentation and judgement of history – shows how the current public controversy coincides with the subtle theoretical discussions on the connections between history and poetics. This controversy does not solely concern the cognitive insight and communication afforded by narration but also its linguistic manifestations in the shape of historiographic and literary texts. How legitimate are rhetorical and poetic elements in academic texts? On the other hand, what specific insights can literary methods provide with regard to history? This latter question I shall relate to Uwe Johnson's text with the aid of a case study.

Questions of historical knowledge and questions of literary presentation and style again coincide in the methodological controversy surrounding the new 'postmodern' studies of the history of daily life, the history of civilization, regional history and oral

---

   Geschichte', *Poetica*, vol. 17, 1985, pp. 228–54; Paul Michael Lützeler, 'Geschichtsschreibung und Roman. Aspekte ihrer Interdependenzen', *Zeitschrift für Ästhetik und allgemeine Kunstwissenschaft*, vol. 30, 1985, pp. 138–57; Dietrich Harth, 'Fiktion, Erfahrung, Gewißheit. Second Thoughts', in Reinhart Koselleck, W. J. Mommsen, Jörn Rüsen and Heinrich Lutz (eds.), *Formen der Geschichtsschreibung*, Munich, 1982, pp. 621–30; Karlheinz Stierle, 'Erfahrung und narrative Form', in J. Kocka and Th. Nipperdey (eds.), *Theorie und Erzählung in der Geschichte*, Munich, 1979, pp. 85–118; S. Quandt and H. Süssmuth (eds.), *Historisches Erzählen. Formen und Funktionen*, Göttingen, 1982.
7. Hans-Ulrich Wehler, *Entsorgung der deutschen Vergangenheit?*, Munich, 1988, p. 7.
8. Theodor W. Adorno, 'Was bedeutet: Aufarbeitung der Vergangenheit', in *Eingriffe*, Frankfurt/Main, 1963, pp. 125–46.

history. The history of daily life, which incorporates the experiences and way of life of 'ordinary people' in a manner both critical and involved and which frequently uses documentary methods (interviews, life stories) in the process, meets with approval among supporters of modern social history in so far as it does not isolate its micro-studies made 'from below' and 'from the inside', but is able to assimilate them into the macro-history of processes and structures. As far as critical reappraisal of the German past is concerned, the current history of daily life manifests an interest in discovery and presentation which is in some degree similar to that in German novels since the early 1960s, including Johnson's fictional works. In order to identify some features which link his *Versuch, einen Vater zu finden* to historiography, I have devised an extremely simplified table (see Figure 1) which compares and contrasts three types of historiography with the historical novel. This enables us to ask how the modern (and postmodern) historical novel and how Johnson's text relate to these types and categories.

Historical narration in the shape of novels, those hybrids of fact and fiction, has been a legitimate object of criticism ever since the great historical novels proved that *realist* literature can successfully take as its subject the reality of *history*. However, the illusory realism of the traditional and popular historical novel has become obsolete in the modern age, a period of disastrous political experiences, aesthetic avant-gardes and radical criticism. Forms and methods for a 'different' historical novel[9] have been tried out from Döblin's *Wallenstein* to Alexander Kluge's *Schlachtbeschreibung*.[10] But after the modern in literature has, in its turn, become history and its claim to set the norm has been put into perspective, new 'postmodern' forms are appearing even in the field of the historical novel, irritatingly mixing illusionistic tricks, ironic adaptation of popular models and reference to historical facts. Viewed from this angle, a narrative technique such as Uwe Johnson's, which is distinguished equally by its quest for truth, its moral commitment and its style of dialectical realism, seems at first to be thoroughly old-fashioned. But what do we mean by old-fashioned? In the postmodern epoch such a value judgement has lost its importance, and in an age when 'anything goes', the virtue of old-fashioned literary criticism has gained a new importance in that judgement is not passed on an individual work according to one of many

---

9. Hans Vilmar Geppert, *Der 'andere' historische Roman*, Tübingen, 1976.
10. Müller, *Geschichte zwischen Kairos und Katastrophe*.

Figure 1

Traditional political history	Modern social history	'Postmodern' history of daily life	Historical novel
'public' events	social processes	'public' and 'private' events	'public' and 'private' events
'important' individuals	social structures	'ordinary' individuals	'important' and 'ordinary' individuals
history of political ideas	modes of discourse and states of mind	collective and individual experience	collective and individual experience
political system	social system	culture of daily life	culture of daily life and personal histories
objective, 'pure' narration	critical, theory-orientated narration	critical, sympathetic and documentary narration (life-stories)	mimetic and alienating narration

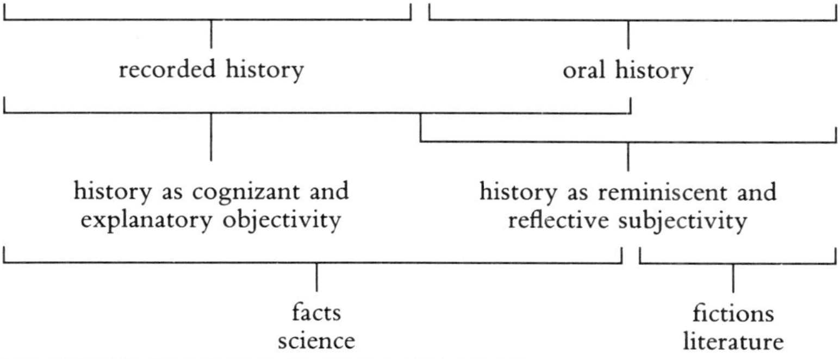

```
└─────────────┬─────────────┘ └─────────────┬─────────────┘
        recorded history              oral history
└─────────────────────┬─────────────┘ └─────────────┬─────────────┘
   history as cognizant and           history as reminiscent and
    explanatory objectivity             reflective subjectivity
└─────────────────────────────┬─────────────┘ └──────┬──────┘
                           facts                  fictions
                          science               literature
```

competing aesthetic doctrines but is rather evolved from a careful balancing of textual analysis and contextualization within a framework of critical theory. This is what I shall now undertake using Uwe Johnson's *Versuch, einen Vater zu finden* as an example.[11]

11. Section II, which follows, is a revised and expanded version of sections of my epilogue in Johnson's *Versuch*.

II

One particular region (Mecklenburg) and one particular set of people (the Cresspahl family) form the epic core of Johnson's work. Numerous threads from previous or projected texts come together in *Jahrestage*, the principal work, which, as the subtitle suggests, recounts passages from the life of Gesine Cresspahl. The fictitious narrative situation in *Jahrestage* – described metaphorically as a 'pact' between Gesine and Johnson – consists of a fairly complex interweaving of authorial and first-person narrative.[12] Gesine, who was born in 1933, grew up in Nazi Germany and the GDR and later moved from West Germany to New York, endeavours through daily acts of reminiscence to acquaint her growing daughter, Marie, with her origins and at the same time to find the inner logic of her own life. The fictional framework of *Jahrestage* is not developed any further in *Versuch, einen Vater zu finden*, which is based on the same interest in understanding the past. Gesine here appears throughout much more as a soliloquizing first-person narrator without an interlocutor. If one views the whole text as a single act of speech, it is a monologue.

As in *Jahrestage*, Gesine cannot get away from the attempt to understand her dead father: his life is inextricably mixed up with German history and all its catastrophic changes. Above all, in 1933 he took what was a momentous decision for his family and himself by moving from England to the 'Third Reich', in spite of being very politically aware and, as a socialist, an opponent of the Nazis. Gesine wants to know from her father's life why he remained in Germany after 1933. Why did he leave Mecklenburg and Germany for the Netherlands and England in 1920? What kind of background and circumstances shaped Cresspahl's life before 1920 that might explain his behaviour? It is this last question which underlies *Versuch, einen Vater zu finden*.

In her 'Spurensuche',[13] Gesine, therefore, has to look for her father where he is most difficult to find, that is, beyond the reach of her recollection: in his childhood and youth under the German Empire before the First World War. For this reason the daughter must of necessity become a biographer and Johnson himself be-

---

12. See on this subject the thesis by Ulrich Fries, *Uwe Johnsons 'Jahrestage'*, Göttingen, 1990.
13. Uwe Johnson (blurb for *Heute neunzig Jahr*), quoted from Siegfried Unseld, 'Uwe Johnson als Partner seiner Figuren. Anmerkungen zur Poetologie', in H. D. Schlosser and H. D. Zimmermann (eds.), *Poetik*, Frankfurt/Main, 1988, pp. 81–92; here p. 82.

comes an investigative historian, for Gesine's 'Versuch', which he narrates, cannot be based on direct access to the past. Johnson shows us how Gesine carefully attempts to reconstruct the first phase of her father's life from 1888 to 1914 and how at the same time she ponders the dangers and difficulties of this attempt.

Although for her this is a laborious jigsaw puzzle with many gaps, for us Johnson's paradoxical narrative technique builds up an impressive picture of an individual life in the nineteenth century, a life from a lost age: the birth of Heinrich Cresspahl, a cartwright's son, on a nobleman's estate in the Grand Duchy of Mecklenburg-Schwerin, childhood and school years in the country, a joinery apprenticeship in the town of Malchow, young love, involvement in organizations, military service, years as a travelling journeyman, master craftsman's diploma and call-up for the First World War. The Cresspahls belonged to the lower classes, the 'ordinary people'. Thus the biographical insight into Heinrich's youth also becomes an insight into the way 'ordinary people' were inextricably caught up in Germany's disastrous history. What were the lives of these people, the everyday lives, really like a hundred years ago? None of the history books has told Gesine anything about this, not even the Marxist ones from which she was taught in the GDR and to which she repeatedly refers in the text. Modern social history and the history of daily life were only just beginning to emerge as disciplines in 1967–8.

Consequently, in her role of a 'private historian' who is not governed by a specialist interest in discovery but rather by a personal interest, Gesine has to tread her own path between knowledge and conjecture. This path can be discerned in the structure of the text. Just as two points of focus define an ellipse, so the narrative style is defined by two basic features: tabulation and modality (as the grammar of conjectures). From a superficial reading, the text seems like a chronological table in narrative form. It is built on a simple framework consisting of the individual years from 1888 onwards, the 'Kette der Jahre', and their respective political events as Gesine has committed them to memory from her school books. However, for her this is only the 'äussere Kruste des Gewesenen'.[14] But how is it possible to get from the crust to the core, from political history to the history of an individual, from the facts to the truth? Gesine attempts to get closer by supplementing simple memorized facts with research and reflection, not only in order to accumulate as many facts and as much definite knowledge

---

14. Johnson, *Versuch*, p. 7.

as possible, but also in order to 'see' and, perhaps eventually, 'understand' her father and his history (p. 22).

The text is structured accordingly. The dates mark first of all the events of the broader history of Europe and the Wilhelmine Empire, from 100 years ago – the year of the three kaisers – up until the shots at Sarajevo. To this is added the narrower history of the Mecklenburg region with all the peculiarities of a late-feudal corporative state. Also mentioned are symptomatic manifestations of cultural, social and economic history at both regional and national level, from rural households to the guilds and associations of small towns, from railway construction to the working world east of the Elbe. It is into this general history, both the broad sweeps and narrow bands, that the individual, extremely confined history, the life of the young Heinrich Cresspahl, is inserted. However, this story can only be narrated in a fragmentary and hypothetical manner.

This is the second basic feature of the narrative technique: modality as an antithesis to the concatenation of dates and facts. The frequent recurrence, wide variety, and stylistic highlighting of modal structures are among the prevalent linguistic features of the text. 'Modality is the grammar of explicit comment, the means by which people express their degree of commitment to the truth of the propositions they utter.'[15] Gesine's commentary relates amongst other things to the degree to which her conjectures concerning her father's life are valid. Since she knows so little about his youth, she cannot set it down in one simple linear narrative. She has constantly to pause and reflect on the degree of truth in her evidence and the value as evidence of the materials she has furnished. Here we have 'Mutmassungen über Heinrich', a mosaic of facts and signs, dates and sources, documents and oral evidence processed into hypotheses, episodes and images, and all with a strong degree of personal involvement.

Within the modal structures of the text a complex narrative subject finds expression, unable to disown factual accuracy and exactitude on the one hand or emotional factors such as love, desires and grief on the other. Gesine must stimulate her imagination in order to 'see' anything of Cresspahl, but then critical self-reflection must draw the boundaries between legitimate hypothesis and groundless invention. 'Ein Kind in schwarzen, knielangen Hosen, einem zerschlissenen Hemd ohne Bund; das darf ich sehen. Uneben geschnittene weisse Haare, fest gegen den Boden

---

15. Roger Fowler, *Linguistic Criticism*, Oxford, 1986, pp. 131f.

gestemmte Beine; es wäre ja erfunden' (p. 12). Johnson's fictional narrator Gesine has little feeling for fictions. Of course, for the reader Heinrich Cresspahl's personal history nonetheless remains a poetic fiction whose aura of realism is only intensified by the narrator's manifest self-doubt. But the poetic element in Johnson's story must obviously be sought beyond an illusionistic and fictional 'amplification' of established history in the style of the classic historical novel.

In the *Versuch*, Johnson does not simply show how, with the aid of deduction and reflection, a narrator handles the material she comes across in the course of her biographical researches. Rather, he allows the narrator herself to reveal the origin of this material, her sources and resources. For the purposes of extending the already considerable historical knowledge acquired at school, she refers to commonly available literature which she occasionally even cites by title and year of publication. The encyclopaedia she uses is the 1889 *Großer Meyer*, of which Thomas Mann made such good use.[16] She uses other reference books as well: diaries, historical treatises, writings on folklore, regional works, memoirs and even literary texts. Many of the titles in her fictitious library might well be found in Johnson's own library, which numbered among its 4,000 volumes a great many works on German history and an extensive collection of Mecklenburgiana (650 volumes).[17] It would be worth analysing more closely exactly *how* Johnson used this literature: which passages caught his attention (many of the books contain his marks); the various ways in which he integrated such passages into his own text as regards content and language; how the type of integration can also mark a critically ironic distancing; how dialogic qualities are developed, giving a many-voiced tension between the narrator's 'own' speech and that of 'others'; and how

16. *Meyers Konversations-Lexikon. Eine Encyklopädie des allgemeinen Wissens*, 4th edn, Leipzig, 1889.
17. Eberhard Fahlke, 'Bücher: gesammelt und geschrieben, um die Geschichte aufzuheben. Uwe Johnsons Bibliothek', in Schlosser and Zimmermann, *Poetik*, pp. 110–32; here p. 126. Among the books used repeatedly but *not* cited in the text are the following: *Großherzoglich Mecklenburg-Schwerinscher und Mecklenburg-Strelitzscher Kalender*, Wismar, 1888– ; Otto Vitense, *Geschichte von Mecklenburg*, Gotha, 1920; Richard Wossidlo, *Mecklenburgische Volksüberlieferungen*, vols. 1–3, Wismar, 1897–1906, vol. 4, Rostock, 1931; Friedrich Mager, *Geschichte des Bauerntums und der Bauernkultur im Lande Mecklenburg*, Berlin (GDR), 1955; Hans Bernitt, *Vom alten und vom neuen Mecklenburg*, Schwerin, 1954; Joachim Dissow, *Adel im Übergang*, 2nd edn, Stuttgart, 1962; *Geschichte der deutschen Arbeiterbewegung. Chronik*, 2 vols., Berlin (GDR), 1965; *Sachwörterbuch der Geschichte Deutschlands und der deutschen Arbeiterbewegung*, 2 vols., Berlin (GDR), 1969.

references to other texts through quotation or allusion function. The way in which narrator and author handle these 'foreign' texts not only tells us something about how they interpret *history* but also constitutes part of the *poetic* structure of Johnson's text.

Thematically, the underlying design principle of *Versuch* consists in the relating of history to a biography and the description of a period in the life of one person from the individual perspective of another person. However, history is not reduced to biography in the process, and the duality of a figure who narrates and one who is the object of the narration prevents a one-sided subjectivization of the narrative. By seeking out an individual in the circumstances of his life in time and place, history and landscape, the very structures of these circumstances themselves become apparent. The circumstances shape the man, but the man is unable, as an individual, to shape the circumstances. It is upon this materialist insight that Johnson bases his narrative dialectic, which is far removed from that 'mediation' of 'individual and society' so dear to the biographical genre. That which is presented – Cresspahl's life – is decentred, having no *roter Faden* of its own, and the presentation – Gesine's narrative – is similarly decentred. This is apparent from the paratactic, montage-like style, which I shall consider in greater detail shortly.

The young Heinrich Cresspahl's circumstances can most briefly be described by the word 'Mecklenburg'. This is the German territorial state which in the nineteenth century was regarded as the 'komische Figur' of Europe on account of its backwardness (p. 28). Johnson combines critical satire on the political and social conditions under which Heinrich grows up, with a painstaking reconstruction of a way of life against a historical landscape, and a loving imagination of the child whose life unfolds in this landscape. Like the landscape, the language also establishes a common sphere between the character narrating and the character who is the object of the narration – it is the Low German of popular sayings and nursery rhymes, which Johnson has taken in part from Richard Wossidlo's book on folklore.[18]

The broadest framework for the story of the young Cresspahl is formed by German history during the Wilhelmine era, with the inevitable forays into imperialist world politics. It is amazing how many dimensions of history Johnson manages to accommodate as he steers his course between the dates of history on a grand scale

---

18. Wossidlo, *Mecklenburgische Volksüberlieferungen*; See Norbert Mecklenburg, *Erzählte Provinz*, Königstein, 1982, pp. 211f; Mecklenburg, *Die grünen Inseln*, Munich, 1986, pp. 134ff.

and those of Cresspahl's own personal history. In addition to the chain of political events traditionally taught in schools, reference is made to overarching structures, such as the constitution of the *Land* Mecklenburg, and long-term trends, such as are discernible from the figures for Reichstag elections and the increase in votes for the SPD. Mention is made of global developments such as imperialism and accumulation of arms side by side with everyday life – from sanitation on a noble estate to the skills involved in lifting potatoes – and with the fund of everyday knowledge expressed in popular belief, the education of the lower classes, and proverbs. Manifestations of social and regional history are meticulously noted: rural conditions, agricultural machinery, migration trends.

Yet, however petty many of the data with which Gesine experimentally surrounds her father may appear, her private investigation is nevertheless characterized by breadth of horizon and a high level of reflection. It is the level of a modern, critical historiography which under no circumstances evades social history by ducking into the recesses of the history of culture and daily life. Thus Johnson's historical description of this province east of the Elbe with all the latter's strange 'chronological displacement' does not solely convey idyllic, nostalgic impressions but, much more, an exemplary view of one of the structural conditions of modern German history, namely the dominance of preindustrial power élites of big landowners, which was a factor in determining the disastrous political 'special path' of the Germans. The epic return to the time of the Empire is not a simple result of the biographical narrative structure or the fact that Cresspahl is 'ein Junge aus dem "Dreikaiserjahr"',[19] or even simply of the 'grandmother principle' prized by both Johnson and Günter Grass as narrators; rather, this procedure is exactly in keeping with a historical insight which even the recent *Historikerstreit* could not seriously question: the fact that many of the conditions which made the Third Reich possible had their roots in the German Empire.[20] The year of the three kaisers – 1888 – when Heinrich was born, can be interpreted symbolically as the beginning of a fateful continuity. To reappraise this continuity critically in epic form is one of the goals which Uwe Johnson the historian has set himself.

Naturally Johnson is not vying with historical research proper, without whose aid Gesine would not have been able to discover any details about her father's youth. He is, however, remarkably

19. See Unseld, 'Uwe Johnson als Partner', p. 82.
20. Hans-Ulrich Wehler, *Das Deutsche Kaiserreich: 1871–1918*, Göttingen, 1973, p. 16.

close to the forms of contemporary historiography. Yet he proceeds according to his own specifically literary principles. Thus modality, emphasizing the problematic nature of what can be told, does not so much follow the objective criteria of validation or the issues of the modern study of history as, rather, the private impulses of a narrator who links the roles of both daughter and a member of the present generation, and who combines the quest for truth and the quest for her father in one single project. By reappraising history in terms of 'previous history', Gesine is focusing on the way both society and the individual have become what they are. She does not confine herself to interrogating – from an undogmatic left-wing position which she has partly 'inherited' from her father and partly acquired through her own discoveries and experience – the social and political errors in Germany up to 1933: a perspective she shares with modern historians. At the same time she interrogates her father's personal history and the turning points in it which have had important consequences for her own life. Like the quest for truth and the quest for her father, an understanding of history and an understanding of the self are also bound up in Gesine's attempt. However, Johnson does not blend political and private history (the historiographic and the fictional narrative) by means of a cleverly contrived plot as in the traditional historical novel, but unfolds them in parallel, as it were, as two voices. However persuasively Gesine's scrupulous research, in particular, may reinforce the 'effect of the real' (Roland Barthes), the difference, the hiatus between fiction and history, nonetheless always remains clearly discernible to the reader. This discernible difference is due to the elements of poetic structure in the text.

The poetic structure is marked essentially by a process of quotation and montage. This process, which forms part of Johnson's 'paratactic narrative technique',[21] does not dissolve the outlines of the individual discoveries of historical research into a continuous narrative flow but sets them off in sharp definition by use of abrupt cuts. The juxtaposition of documentary material and commentary[22] allows the reader scope to adopt his own position. Critical, ironic or satirical alienation effects emerge from the way in which syntactic units are ordered and combined in the form of confrontations and short circuits, points, parallels and correspondences.

The narrative voice does not disappear amidst the montage of materials, nor does it in any way confine itself to the subjective,

21. Mecklenburg, *Erzählte Provinz*, pp. 192ff.
22. See Siegfried Kracauer's theory of the novel; on this subject, Dietrich Scheunemann, *Romankrise*, Heidelberg, 1978, pp. 199f.

personal and private spheres, and to modality, but emerges with a clear propensity for evaluative statements and ideological criticism of the 'authoritarian word' (Mikhail Bakhtin) mentioned in the text and is distinguished by the epigrammatic laconicism so characteristic of Johnson's style: 'Das Hauptfach war die Furcht des Herrn und seines Stellvertreters von Bobzin' (p. 12). In its context of the story of the schoolboy Cresspahl, this sentence takes the place of long explanations concerning conditions in country schools east of the Elbe. Even the smallest stylistic elements are overdetermined in the dense text. When the Queen of England is called 'Oma Victoria' (p. 15), this is (1) a correct statement of her relationship to 'Willy Zwo', (2) an ironic play on the name of the Boer president 'Onkel Paulus Krüger', (3) an imitation of the 'humorous' tone of the history teacher, (4) the expression of an intentionally irreverent view of the ruling figures 'from below' and (5) a use of satirical contrast: the familiarity between representatives of states which are in mortal imperialist rivalry is a mere pretence.

There is satire also in the indication of the date of the notorious 'Huns' speech of Wilhelm II: 'im selben Jahr, in dem das Bürgerliche Gesetzbuch in Kraft tritt' (p. 16). Bismarck's famous remark, 'Wir Deutsche fürchten Gott, aber sonst nichts auf der Welt' (p. 10), referred to Russo-German tension and not to the recently accomplished strengthening of the army or (as the text has it) 'Wehrvorlage'. Here it is changed by a contextual distortion which in history would be a falsification but which here, by means of a Brechtian alienation technique, is a change 'bis zur Kenntlichkeit': ideological criticism occurs in the juxtaposition of arms policy and fear of God. That the rural population of Mecklenburg were 'germanisierte Slawen' (p. 7) is what we may originally read in the 1889 *Großer Meyer*, but the use of the verb 'hausen' in connection with them adds an element of exaggeration and discrimination which satirically pinpoints social and national resentments in an apparently objective encyclopaedia, and the use of the term *germanisieren* recalls the Prussian policy of Germanization with regard to the Poles in the Empire.[23]

The deliberately pointed ending of *Versuch* is typical of Johnson's historical narrative technique, the effects of which are often the result of minimal changes to the material. In the following example a list of 1914 war-aims taken from a reference work is satirically pointed up by readjusting the order and slightly varying the words. At the same time a transition is made, by means of a narrative and

---

23. See also Fahlke on this point: 'Bücher: gesammelt und geschrieben', p. 122.

syntactic short circuit, from politics on a grand scale, as practised by the European powers, to the young master joiner who in 1914 stepped – against his will – out of history on a small scale into history on a large scale: into the war. I have set source and reworking side by side.

'Rußland erhoffte sich die Aufteilung der Türkei zu seinen Gunsten und die Erweiterung seines Einflusses auf dem Balkan.'	Russland wünschte die Aufteilung der Türkei zu seinen Gunsten, wollte auch mehr das Sagen haben auf dem Balkan;
'Frankreich strebte nach der Rückgewinnung Elsaß-Lothringens und der Erweiterung seines Kolonialbesitzes in Afrika.'	Frankreich gedachte sich Elsass-Lothringen zurückzuholen, auch in Afrika etwas zu gewinnen;
'Großbritannien wollte das imperialistische Dtschl. als Hauptkonkurrenten bei der Erlangung der Weltherrschaft ausschalten, dessen Kolonialreich annektieren und sich Teile der Türkei aneignen.'	Grossbritannien benötigte das Sagen auf den Weltmeeren für sich allein, konnte die deutschen Kolonien gut brauchen, auch paar Stücke Türkei;
'Dem mit Dtschl. verbündeten Österreich-Ungarn ging es um die Vorherrschaft auf dem Balkan und die Annexion russischer Gebiete.'	Österreich hoffte zuversichtlich auf russischen Boden und darauf, das Sagen zu bekommen auf dem Balkan;
'Der dt. Imperialismus besaß das abenteuerlichste und aggressivste Kriegszielprogramm. Er strebte nach der Vorherrschaft über Europa und der "Neuaufteilung der Welt".'[24]	Willy Zwo bedurfte all dessen auch, sowie des deutschen Sagens in Europa, weiterhin des Kanoniers Heinrich Cresspahl an der Barbarastrasse in Güstrow. (p. 33)

Another of the special qualities of Johnson's poetic alienation of historical narration is the use of allusion, elliptically abbreviated to the point of being enigmatic, which tries to encourage the reader to find out more, as for example when an SPD conference is mentioned: 'da hatte eine Frau namens Luxemburg nicht ausreden dürfen' (p. 29).[25] Then there are the echo effects within the text (also scattered beyond our particular fragment into the rest of *Heute neunzig Jahr*), as when, for example, the harsh working conditions of servants are recounted early on (p. 9) and then several pages later

---

24. *Sachwörterbuch der Geschichte Deutschlands*, vol. 2, pp. 805f.
25. At the SPD conference in Magdeburg (18–24 September 1910) Rosa Luxemburg was forced to break off her speech due to provocation and noise from right-wing party members.

the 'Abschaffung der Gesindeordnung' is mentioned as an item in the SPD programme (p. 11). Finally, there is a stylistic feature which might be described as 'semantic rhyme'. Syntactic units different in theme and not connected paratactically are combined by means of a striking common semantic element. Thus 'vierzig goldene Mark', which the apprentice Cresspahl has saved up during his first year, is placed in juxtaposition to the Deutsche Bank as the builder of the Baghdad railway (p. 23). Thus after the political catchword of *Entente Cordiale* there comes the cordial understanding between Heine Cresspahl and the love of his youth, Gesine Redebrecht (p. 24). It is precisely through unexpected, artificial consonance that such 'semantic rhymes' mark the hiatus which divides general history from that of the individual.

Versuch, einen Vater zu finden forms a mosaic of amazing denseness and complexity, a narrative arc which extends from dry statistics to almost lyrical evocation of countryside, from the insight of satirical documentary keenly focused on the revealing detail to a lovingly sensitive re-creation of a human life which no longer exists. However, the most surprising feature of this text which appears to consist mainly of monologue and soliloquy is its constant and systematic use of dialogic qualities and its openness to what Mikhail Bakhtin has called the variety of social discourse.[26] The voice of the narrator does not drown out the many voices which speak in the story from the historical, social and regional spheres, but allows them to preserve their own identity. Thus the whole text becomes a score whose virtuosity can only be fully appreciated when read aloud. When you hear Uwe Johnson reading the text then you can *hear* this linguistic and ideological polyphony.

III

In conclusion, I should like to incorporate the results of my analysis of *Versuch* in an assessment of what Uwe Johnson has achieved as a historical narrator. For a critical frame of reference I shall take my previous outline of the current academic and literary debates on history.

The analysis of structure has shown how far removed Uwe Johnson the narrator is from the traditional or popular form of the historical narrative. The comfortable thread of 'als', 'ehe' and 'nachdem' is rejected by Johnson as it is by the authors of the classic

---

26. Mikhail Bakhtin, *Die Ästhetik des Wortes*, Frankfurt/Main, 1979.

modern novels: his text consists of a richly varied spectrum of speech forms and polyphonically contrasting voices.

The thematic analysis has shown how close Uwe Johnson the historian stands to forms of modern historiography. If we refer to Figure 1 above (p. 33), it is easy to see that Johnson's text integrates all three types of historiography. On the whole, traditional political history is used here only as a framework. The interest lies more in the narrative balance between social history and the history of daily life. Once again, as in *Jahrestage*,[27] Johnson endeavours to outline structures and processes as a backcloth for the presentation of the culture of daily life and individual life stories. He shares with modern German historiography both the interest in enlightening people by uncovering and understanding the roots of modern German history and the moral desire not to suppress the disastrous German past. In common with the new history of daily life, his view 'from below' is in sympathy with the 'ordinary people', the victims of large-scale history. At the same time, the poetic dialectic of mimesis and alienation together with the unfolding of a history based on reminiscence and reflective subjectivity produces a distinctive achievement of its own as compared with historiographic presentation.

But how, as a poetic text, does *Versuch, einen Vater zu finden* make a specific contribution to understanding? Its complexity probably results in its being able to contain more information – for the non-academic reader – than many academic texts on the same period: a conclusion which would be in keeping with one of the findings of modern poetics and the theory of history.[28] However, this information is not so much in the nature of the 'narrative explanation' or 'explanatory narrative' which marks historiographic discourse.[29] Explanatory syntagmata are rare in *Versuch*. The underlying character of Johnson's narrative technique tends rather to correspond to the type of 'investigative account' described by Droysen, which allows the reader to 'gleichsam mitsuchen und mitfinden', so that the 'gefundene Geschichte' is based less in the text than in the imagination of its recipient.[30] By imparting qualities of dialogue to the narrative voice and developing a variety of

---

27. Lämmert, 'Geschichten von der Geschichte', p. 251.
28. Yuri M. Lotman, *Die Struktur literarischer Texte*, Munich, 1972, pp. 42f, 420; White, 'The Question of Narrative', p. 19.
29. Werner Schiffer, *Theorien der Geschichtsschreibung und ihre erzähltheoretische Relevanz*, Stuttgart, 1980.
30. Johann Gustav Droysen, *Historik*, ed. R. Hübner, 7th edn, Darmstadt, 1972, p. 278; see Lämmert, 'Geschichten von der Geschichte', pp. 239, 247.

Uwe Johnson's Versuch, einen Vater zu finden

voices, Johnson's text is articulating an element of historical narration which the historians themselves tend to suppress and whose significance has only been revealed by the modern theory of history.[31]

Johnson's narrative projects share with modern, critical historiography the interest in intervening in the public use of history in such a way as to enlighten. *Unlike* historiography in general and also unlike the modern type of 'archival novel',[32] he is at the same time concerned with the individual's acquisition of a *personal* sense of history, as typically demonstrated by Gesine. Gesine the historian not only risks her own draft of history, but, as a character, she herself also represents an – extremely unfashionable – alternative scheme in the face of the current wasting away of historical experience. On the one hand, as a first-person narrator, she takes historical facticity, the 'tiresome facts',[33] far more seriously than is usually the case in the historical novel; on the other, her discourse incorporates reflective, emotional, critical, ethical and political factors, which enable history to become first and foremost an experience, as opposed to its scientific reification as specialized historical knowledge. Johnson's text articulates and demonstrates an approach to history which could also insure against the abuse of history for the purposes of ideological planning.

However, this also focuses attention on a problematic element in Johnson's method of narration. The fictitious narrative situation alone, in which the author's real method of work – the unity of reading, collecting and writing[34] – shows through all too clearly, undoubtedly exhibits a certain fragility: unlike *Jahrestage*, a pragmatic foundation for Gesine's narrative project is barely discernible. The *process* of her quest for historical truth, for her father and for herself, is not narrated per se but appears suspended in relation to a text which has been artistically worked out to the last detail, which presents *results*, and in which, strictly speaking, the insistent conjectures constitute an alien element, since they tend to form part of the *process*. Moreover, they relate only to Cresspahl's personal history. This alone contains elements not yet determined; broader history by comparison seems to be clearly established. The portrayal of a nascent historical awareness in the narrator herself, taken in conjunction with her authorial stance in the narrative, constitutes a latent contradiction. Gesine's historical awareness in

---

31. LaCapra, *Geschichte und Kritik*, pp. 30, 33.
32. Harth, 'Fiktion, Erfahrung, Gewißheit', p. 628.
33. See Bernd W. Seiler, *Die leidigen Tatsachen*, Stuttgart, 1983.
34. Fahlke, 'Bücher: gesammelt und geschrieben', p. 113.

the text is 'finished' – no longer in movement. If this was the narrative form originally contemplated for *Jahrestage*, then it explains why Johnson ultimately gave the fictitious narrative situation in his main work a very much more complex and subtly differentiated form – although this too was not without its contradictions.

What I should like to term a 'contemplative element' in Johnson's narrative technique can be detected in equal degree in both *Jahrestage* and *Versuch, einen Vater zu finden*. On the one hand, Johnson's *critical* materialist view prevents him from representing history according to an orthodox Marxist superstructure–substructure model such as was still used by Brecht, and provides what tends to be an open, tentative, polyperspectival illumination of sociohistorical reality. Yet on the other hand, basic assumptions of historical materialism and the corresponding interpretation of German history which Gesine and Johnson learnt at school, however much they may be doubted and criticized in detail, are as a whole neither called into question nor developed further. The lead which, in the Western context, Johnson had over 'bourgeois' conceptions of history in the 1960s, now appears from today's point of view much less significant. Johnson's critical moral commitment seems oddly backward-looking. His manner of clinging to a view of history which has not been significantly revised for a long time is a clear reflection of resignation and helplessness on the Left.

The very fact that things continue in the same vein is the disaster: this is a view which Johnson shares with Walter Benjamin, but he does not share the latter's 'messianic' standpoint. In the spirit of Benjamin, Johnson the historian endeavours to brush history against the grain and take up the tradition of the oppressed. But instead of the famous 'tiger's leap' into the past,[35] in Johnson we find lots of little jumps – made by the 'Katze Erinnerung' (p. 7), who in spite of all our efforts very seldom allows herself to be caught. 'Geschichte ist ein Entwurf':[36] this somewhat enigmatic pronouncement of Cresspahl's is indeed appropriate to the experimental character of Johnson's historical and narrative discourse, but it is not appropriate to the picture of history which he draws. To conceive and to narrate history as a plan, a project, or actual practice was not something Johnson attempted. Forces which have the potential to change the course of history – such as enlightenment and understanding, solidarity and the experience of happiness – and to which we have to commit ourselves if we are not to fall

---

35. Walter Benjamin, 'Geschichtsphilosophische Thesen', VII and XIV, in *Illuminationen. Ausgewählte Schriften*, ed. Siegfried Unseld, Frankfurt/Main, 1961.
36. *Jahrestage*, vol. 4, p. 1891.

prey to premodern fatalism or postmodern cynicism, are withdrawn in Johnson's work from the sphere of narrated history into the attitude of the narrator. Enlightenment is what the text of the narrative provides, solidarity is the relationship between narrator and character, and the experience of happiness occurs in the success of remembering.

To the accusation of being contemplative, Johnson might perhaps have replied that for the narration of history to change, history itself must first change. This is open to argument. As far as the presentation of history in his narrative work is concerned, we should in particular study his main work, *Jahrestage*, to see how the elements revealed by this analysis of *Versuch, einen Vater zu finden* are differentiated there. Again Johnson combines a realist stance and a modern approach to writing. The result is a work which has no equal as an epic reworking of modern German history.

–3–

'The Purpose of my Life seems to be to Learn about the Purpose of my Life': Erwin Strittmatter's Two-Part Novel *Der Laden*

CHRISTA HARTWIG

The novels I intend to consider are put by some literary critics on a par with Gorki's, Proust's and Nexø's investigations of their childhoods. Klaus Jarmatz writes:

> Man muß sich den *Laden*-Romanen gegenüber verhalten wie gegenüber dem wirklichen Leben: Man muß immer wieder 'hineinhorchen', ohne Voreingenommenheit, und man wird stets neue Entdeckungen machen. In einem Gang sind diese Bücher kaum auszuschöpfen, da sie aus einem universalistischen Blickpunkt geschrieben sind, haben sie selbst etwas von der Universalität des Lebens.[1]

Thus my paper can deal only with a few aspects and should be understood as an invitation to make personal acquaintance with the work.

In 1987 Erwin Strittmatter celebrated his seventy-fifth birthday.[2]

---

1. Klaus Jarmatz, 'Erwin Strittmatters *Laden*-Romane', *Weimarer Beiträge*, vol. 33, no. 11, 1987, p. 1796.
2. Erwin Strittmatter was born in Spremberg on 8 August 1912, the son of a baker and smallholder. He learned the baker's trade, worked as a waiter, chauffeur, zoo-keeper and unskilled worker. He deserted from Hitler's *Wehrmacht* towards the end of the war. After the Second World War he became administrative head of seven rural districts, later a newspaper editor. He was encouraged by Brecht and lives now as a freelance author. Novels: *Ochsenkutscher* (1951), *Tinko* (1955), *Der Wundertäter* (3 vols., 1957, 1973, 1980), *Ole Bienkopp* (1963), *Der Laden* (2 vols., 1983, 1987, all volume and page references in the text are to this edition). Short stories: *Pony Pedro* (1959), *Schulzenhofer Kramkalender* (1966), *Ein Dienstag im September* (1969), *3/4 hundert Kleingeschichten* (1971), *Die blaue Nachtigall* (1972), *Meine Freundin Tina Babe* (1977), *Selbstmunterungen* (1981), *Wahre Geschichten aller Ard(t)* (1982), *Grüner Juni* (1985). Plays: *Katzgraben* (1953), *Die Holländerbraut* (1959). (All published in Berlin (GDR).)

All the essays written and published for this event have at least two things in common: the authors mention both the distinctive nature of Strittmatter's style and the poetry in his works. Strittmatter is one of the most outstanding and most translated of authors from the German Democratic Republic; he has been awarded five State Prizes for Art and Literature (1953, 1955, 1964, 1976, 1984). Strittmatter's wife, Eva, for many years a literary critic before she made a name for herself as a poet, writes in her *Briefe aus Schulzenhof* that no medals, prizes and honours can help an author in his work. Each new book marks the new beginning.[3] What is more, medals say nothing about a book's public appeal. Of Strittmatter it can be said that he is 'ausgezeichnet' in both senses of the word, a distinguished and decorated author whose books are a public success.

After such important milestones in GDR literature as *Ochsenkutscher* (1951), *Tinko* (1955) and *Ole Bienkopp* (1963), the 1970s brought a reorientation and a new beginning for Strittmatter. This can be put down to the fact that the development of a new society was much more complicated than it had first appeared to be.

> Die Beiträge meiner Schriftstellerkollegen, die in den heutigen Lesebüchern stehen, will ich nicht schmähen, aber laßt mich wenigstens über meine Beiträge etwas spotten und ein wenig süßsauer lächeln. Nicht, daß sie sprachlich geschludert wären, aber da sind einige, die handeln vom *Neuen Menschen*, den ich vor Jahrzehnten glaubte aus der Zukunft heraustreten zu sehen. Aber ists, daß meine Augen inzwischen schlechter wurden, oder ists, daß ich kein Utopist mehr bin, der *Neue Mensch*, wenn es ihn gibt, hält sich noch immer hinter den blauen Schleiern der Zukunft versteckt. Na, mäg! (1, 470)

And in 1973 Strittmatter said in an interview with Heinz Plavius:

> Wenn ihre äußerliche Versorgung gesichert ist, beginnen die Menschen zu fragen: Wo komme ich her? Weshalb bin ich hier? Welches sind meine wirklichen gesellschaftlichen Verpflichtungen? Das liegt in der Natur des Menschen, das zeichnet ihn aus. Wer antwortet auf solche Fragen? Die Kirche versuchts unzulänglich, wie ich meine. Die Ökonomen und die Politiker antworten oft zu einseitig. Also müssen die Künstler zu antworten versuchen, was ihres Amtes eigentlich immer war.[4]

Strittmatter is in a period of reorientation, the period of *Der Wundertäter II* (1973) and *Der Wundertäter III* (1980). In 1972 Stritt-

---

3. See Eva Strittmatter, *Briefe aus Schulzenhof*, Berlin (GDR), 1979, p. 45.
4. Helga Panoke, *Erwin Strittmatter. Lebenszeit*, Berlin (GDR), 1987, p. 26.

matter published a cycle of four reminiscences under the title *Die blaue Nachtigall oder der Anfang von etwas*. These stories are both recollections and *Novellen*, they are biographical stories without sentimentality.

In these stories Strittmatter turns to childhood. He writes: 'Als ich den Scheitelpunkt meines Lebens erreicht zu haben glaubte, fing ich an, es von hinten zu betrachten.'[5] What he intends to achieve by this method is explained in the epilogue to the nightingale stories: 'Ich versuche seit Jahren einer Sache nachzuspüren, und die Sache ist: Woher kam jener Zustand von Poesie und Schwerelosigkeit in der Kindheit und in der Jugend, der uns so unwiederbringlich erscheint? Ist er nicht zurückholbar? Soll man ihn als endgültig verloren gelten lassen? Kann man ihn wieder herbeilisten, herbeitrotzen?'[6] The results of his efforts to find his way back into this condition of poetry and weightlessness form the two parts of his novel *Der Laden*. This novel can be seen as his best work to date. Hans Richter says of it that Strittmatter surpasses Strittmatter.[7]

It is impossible to retell the plot of the novel. The only fixed points are the place of action, the time and the ensemble of characters; the latter is unique in GDR literature. The rest consists of interconnections between the childhood reminiscences of the first-person narrator, comments on them, reflections on present-day events, dialogues with the reader – all of which produces a complex epic structure. Although the geographical context and the periods of time presented are restricted, the scope of the questions posed by the text is very wide. This does not mean, however, that the two volumes are difficult to read, quite the reverse. They are full of wit and roguishness, which prevents Strittmatter from falling into nostalgia and sentimentalizing the hard life of common people. In his dialogue with the reader the narrator is never omniscient. His aim is not to teach his reader. He would be proud, 'wenn einige Leser, die auf das stoßen, was ich aufschrieb, ganz für sich sagen würden: Das ists, was ich auch dachte, ohne es ausdrücken zu können; der da hats mir abgenommen'.[8] Thus the reader's opinion can differ from the narrator's.

In *Der Laden* Strittmatter lets a first-person narrator, speaking in the present tense, narrate parts of the life of a boy called Esau Matt. The first volume starts when the family of the baker Heinrich Matt

---

5. *Selbstermunterungen*, p. 113.
6. *Die blaue Nachtigall*, p. 139.
7. Hans Richter, 'Ein Romangedicht vom Menschen', *Kritik 84*, Halle, 1985, p. 157.
8. Panoke, *Erwin Strittmatter*, p. 113.

moves from Grauschteen to Bossdom (both are villages in the moorland of Niederlausitz) and ends four years later when Esau's grandfather brings him in a covered wagon to Grodk (Spremberg), where Esau is looking forward to attending the boys' grammar school. Bossdom and Grodk are worlds apart. Most people from Grodk do not even know that there is a village called Bossdom. Their town is at the centre of the German Empire. The second volume reports on Esau's life in Grodk, where he is offered a scholarship at school and ends when Esau hits a teacher in the face for humuliating him. The last sentence is: 'Und damit fängt mein absonderliches Mannsleben an, von dem ich erst jetzt weiß, was es *ganzes von mir gewollt hat*' (2, 496).

Some of the characters are already familiar from other stories and Strittmatter makes reference to this fact, assuming that his readers are familiar with all his works. Some motifs from *Die blaue Nachtigall* and from *Meine Freundin Tina Babe* (1977) are taken up again.

The dustcovers of both books show photographs of places important at certain times in Esau's life: the front of volume 1 shows Heinrich Matt's bakery and the grocer's shop, while on the back we find the Bossdom school building and above it the words that form the title of my paper: 'Der Sinn meines Lebens scheint mir darin zu bestehen, hinter den Sinn meines Lebens zu kommen.' They are already familiar from *Selbstermunterungen*.[9] On the back of volume 2 is the *Realreformgymnasium* Esau attended and the girls' grammar school, in the cellar of which he lived with the janitor Juro Baltin and his wife Mina, acquaintances of his mother's; the front shows Esau and his brothers Heinjak and Tinko sitting on a horse. At the head of the horse is the mother, at the hindquarters the father in his baker's apron. These photographs give the impression of authenticity and it is thus not surprising that readers from Lower Lusatia (Niederlausitz) look for and expect authenticity in the novels. With regard to this response the author says in the second volume:

> Seit mein Buch *Der Laden* erschien, wird in meiner Heimat nachgeforscht: Wer ist wer? Und man kommt dabei zu falschen Schlüssen und behauptet, ich hätte diesem und jenem und solchen etwas angedichtet, was sie nicht getan haben. Und sie bestehen darauf, daß sie die im Roman vorkommenden Leute erkennen, vor allem sich selber. Und es kommen Leserbriefe, in denen angefragt wird, wieviel Prozent von dem, was ich aufschrieb, auf Wahrheit beruhe, und wieviel Prozent erdichtet, um zu sagen erlogen sind. Ich antworte diesen Lesern hiermit:

9. P. 7.

Wahrlich, ich sage euch, dieses Buch da und dieses Buch hier enthalten neunzig Prozent Wahrheit und zehn Prozent Erlogenes. Ich sage absichtlich Erlogenes, weil jene Leser den Unterschied zwischen Dichtung und Lüge nicht erkennen.(2, 406)

'Dichtung und Lüge' reminds one of Goethe's *Dichtung und Wahrheit*. Esau is required by one of his teachers to read this work and to retell it for his schoolmates. He interpreted the title as: 'In Wahrheit ist alles erdichtet, was im Buche steht' (1, 470), whilst the teacher had the opposite opinion; thus Esau never became the propagandist for Goethe the teacher had wished him to become. While this might prompt some people, critics included, to ask whether or not Esau Matt, whom we meet again in *Grüner Juni* (1985), is Erwin Strittmatter, it is more important to know what is narrated and how.

Because the novels deal with reminiscences there is no division into chapters. Relatively independent episodes are simply divided by a break in the text. Sometimes episodes or thematic complexes form discrete sections of the book, sometimes they are taken up again later. Often one story follows on from another; sometimes it is necessary to tell some past stories first before the one announced follows: 'Aus jeder Lebens-Ecke unserer Eltern und Großeltern drängen Geschichten heran. Wie soll ich alle bändigen und ordnen, damit sie wenigstens Kulissen in meinem kleinen Tautropfen-Welt-Theater abgeben!' (1, 97). Repeatedly the author–narrator apologizes to the reader or warns those who are used to linear narrative: 'Eine Nebengeschichte drängt sich auf. Wer sie nicht hören will, soll umblättern' (1, 372). The point is not objective time but the reminiscences, their location in Esau Matt's boyhood and the moment when they come back into the old Esau Matt's mind. He says: 'Es gibt keine Zeit, in der nichts geschieht, denn geschähe nichts, gäbe es keine Zeit, aber beim Erzählen wird Chronologie zum Mistbeet für Langeweile. Ich will euch nicht langweilen und verzichte auf Chronologie. Ich durchforsche jene meiner Erlebnisse, die mir zu erklären scheinen, wer ich bin' (2, 159).

The village of Bossdom, where, in June 1919, Heinrich Matt bought the bakery with the help of a loan from Esau's grandfather, is a half-Sorbian village. The 511 inhabitants are Germans, Sorbs and half-Sorbs. Poland is not far away. The grandfather, the grandmother, called the one-and-a-half-metre grandmother because of her height, Esau's mother, his great-aunt Maika, a Wendish wise-woman and the teacher are all Sorbs, although the teacher does not want to be one, 'er ist eine Achse, um die sich das

Dorfleben dreht' (1, 47). Esau's father is German; in family quarrels he regrets marrying into a Wendish bunch. Esau, his brothers and his sister are half-Sorbs, and classmates in Grodk, sons of better-off parents, mostly textile factory owners, call him 'Wendish Kito'. It is his great-aunt Maika who teaches him to be proud of his ancestry. The Germans think they are better than the Sorbs and the Sorbs think themselves superior to the Poles. Although there is no express allusion to fascism's racist theory, the preconditions for its development are clearly delineated in the novel. The people from the neighbouring village, Friedensrain, 'halten sich für echte Deutsche. An ihren Familiennamen ist das zu erkennen. Sie heißen Sasowski, Wischinski, Kowalski, Nymschiski, und was du willst. Alle ihre Arbeitskollegen aus den umliegenden Dörfern sind für sie *wendsche Kitos*' (1, 389). There are well-off farmers in another neighbouring village, Gulitzscha, and their sons, with whom Esau comes into contact, 'werden demnächst tapfere Arier sein' (1, 237). Like Heinrich Matt, the cottagers, miners and smallholders of Bossdom are mostly Social Democrats. Matt is for the November Revolution in theory and he will later be taken in by fascism just as Esau's friends Erwin Koalik and Wullo Kanin are, but this goes beyond the framework of these two novels and is mentioned only briefly by the narrator.

Esau's mother would have liked to attend a school for young ladies, but her father, at that time a brewer's drayman, had no money for the fees. Six weeks as a maid in Berlin-Schöneberg remain her only trip into the wide world. 'Was sich sonst noch an Weltverständnis in ihr anfand, gelangte über *Vobachs Modenzeitung fürs deutsche Haus* und durch eine Anzahl Bücher von unterschiedlicher Güte, vor allem durchs Leben in sie hinein' (1, 195). She tries in vain to turn Esau, his brother and sister into urban petty bourgeois children. Esau learns a lot from his grandfather, how to handle horses, horse-trading and other things. About those times the narrator writes: 'Wenn mein Sohn mich fragen würde: Erkanntest du damals, daß dein Großvater ein abgefeimter Händler war? müßte ich ihm antworten: Nein, ich erkannte es damals nicht. Großvater war gut zu mir, und mein Gefühl versperrte mir die Sicht auf den wirklichen Großvater' (1, 327).

It is the same with his parents. His father and mother occasionally out-do each other in illogical actions. One expression for this is, 'daß die kindischen Eltern Geldhäufchen, die aus dem Laden kommen, als ihren blanken Verdienst betrachten und keinen Augenblick daran denken, daß sie mit diesem Geld wieder Waren einkaufen müssen, daß ihnen keiner der Geldscheine eigentlich gehört' (1, 437). Things are not looking too good when an auditor finds out that Esau's mother, who has established a post office in her living room, 'borrows' money from the post office cashbox. Only another loan from his grandfather to discharge the debt saves her from impending punishment. The post office is given to a member of the Nazi party.

Strittmatter portrays the characters around the young Esau Matt with a mixture of sympathy and detachment. All of them are contradictory and none afford the reader the possibility of identification with them. Even the boy Esau Matt has nobody he can identify with or orientate himself by. He is influenced by different people from the family or from outside, all of whom contribute to the development of his own personality. The strongest influence on Esau is the shop: 'Ich sehe, was ich sehe, aber Mutters Laden macht mich zum Parteigänger, ich soll nur sehen, was dem Geschäft nicht schadet. Diese Nötigung verfolgt mich mein Leben lang: Andere verlangen von mir, daß ich sehe, was sie wünschen' (1, 175). On the other hand, the shop gives him a good opportunity to watch the customers and to study their characters. Great-aunt Maika's wisdom could be regarded as Esau's only guide through life, although sometimes he understands it only later as an old man.

In *Der Laden* the author is in search of his *Kindheitsmuster* – to use the term made famous by Christa Wolf's novel. He does not turn to his childhood to avoid the present and the problems of today. Through the old Esau Matt the problems of today are always present: 'Von dem Buchschreiber, der ich bin, weiß ich, daß die von mir geschaffenen Figuren Versuche sind, zu ergründen, wie es mit mir ausgegangen wäre, wenn dieser oder jener meiner schwach ausgebildeten Charakterzüge ausgeformter und kräftiger mein Leben beherrscht hätte' (2, 28).

But the novel is more than a family saga; it is a homage to the *Kraft der Schwachen*. Important events in the 1920s in Germany are not at the centre of *Der Laden*.

> Möglich, daß der Vorsitzende des sozialdemokratischen Ortsvereins Erich Schinko, auch ein paar andere eifrige Sozialdemokraten, wissen, was in Berlin und sonstwo vor sich geht, möglich, daß sie den Generalstreik zum Sturz eines Regierenden, der sich Kuno nennt, bewußt unterstützen, möglich, daß sie etwas vom Hitler–Ludendorff–Putsch in München wissen, aber sie tragen ihre Erregung, sofern sie erregt sind, nicht ins Dorf. (1, 508)

Thus these events make their way as 'Pipatzchen [Kleinigkeiten] . . . zu uns in die Kleine Republik der Selbstversorger, abseits aller Straßen' (1, 508). With the help of their 'Heidephilosophie', a combination of native wit and superstition, the people of Bossdom try simply to survive the various crises which influence their small world: for example, inflation.

> Es schleicht sich etwas nach Bossdom hinein, was die Reisenden *Inflation* nennen . . . Leute reden, der vertrackte Zustand kommt aus Berlin. Aus Berlin kam auch die Grippe. Sie verdrängte die Influenza, die Menschenstaupe, wie Großvater sie nennt. Die *Inflation* ist so etwas wie eine Geldgrippe, scheint mir. Großvater, der *brain trust* der Familie, sitzt oben in der Großelternstube und rechnet, rechnet. Bald keen Steen vom Grundstück is mehr eire, sagt er. Da wir nach Großvaters Berechnungen so gut wie nichts mehr haben und doch leben, schweben wir wohl. Paßt man uff, wenn ihr runterknallt, sagt Großvater. Ich warte auf den Knall, nicht allzu ängstlich, mehr neugierig. Damals weiß ich nicht, daß dieser Schwebezustand in der Welt der Wirtschaft häufig vorkommt, daß zuweilen ganze Regierungen mit ihren Ländern und Leuten durch die Zeiten schweben. (1, 383)

This passage also provides a good example of Strittmatter's narrative style in *Der Laden*. The time in which the reminiscences take place is fused with the time in which they are told. Here a distance of more than 60 years between the boy Esau Matt and the narrator is bridged by the use of '*brain trust*', which came into German very recently, or 'damals weiß ich nicht'. The perspective of the mature narrator is used to relativize his own intellectual and political horizons as a youth. None the less Dietrich Sommer fears that, 'die Begrenzungen des unmittelbaren Geschehens und die Reflexionsweisen der Figuren manche Leser daran hindern könnten, die Handlung und die erzählten Geschichten uneingeschränkt als ein – wenn auch verkleinertes – exemplarisch wirkendes Welttheater zu registrieren'.[10] As far as the boy's reminiscences are concerned the narrator reports a dialogue with his son: 'Das schreibst du heute, sagt mein Sohn, aber hast dus damals so gesehen? Ich habe es damals so gesehen, aber ich sagte es nicht, ich fürchtete mich vor dem Ausgelächter' (1, 9).

The same question is put again in volume 2, and the answer then is: 'Ich habe es so gesehen, doch damals beobachtete ich nur und

---

10. Dietrich Sommer, 'Erzählerische Selbstverständigung und poetisches Selbstverständnis in Strittmatters Roman *Der Laden*', in *DDR-Literatur '83 im Gespräch*, Berlin (GDR), 1984, p. 182.

formulierte nicht. Heute drängt es mich mitzuteilen, was ich beobachtete; vielleicht der krankhafte Drang eines alternden Mannes. Und die Innigkeit damals, mit der ich beobachtete, das Verschmelzen mit dem, was ich beobachtete, war die richtigere und die glücklichere Art zu leben' (2, 135). The narrator is not lamenting over his lost childhood, but he is thinking about what would have been the happier way of living a fulfilled life and what makes any particular life special. 'Ich bewundere manche meiner Lebensgenossen, die mit vorgeburtlicher Reinheit ins Dasein treten, in die Schule gehen, die Universität besuchen, alles, alles, ohne Anstoß zu erregen. Sie lösen willig und ohne zu zweifeln alle Aufgaben, die man ihnen stellt, haben nie Schwierigkeiten, werden Tugendwächter, beobachten zum Beispiel die Worte, die ich von mir gebe' (1, 115). According to the narrator:

> [verläuft] unser Leben nach einem Plan, nach einer Linie, die sich uns verborgen hält; sie verläuft von oben nach unten, falls man meint, oben und unten gäbe es wirklich. Es ist eine gezackte Linie. Die Zacken entstehen, wenn wir selbstherrlich in unser Leben eingreifen und meinen, wir hätten seinen Verlauf korrigiert. Das Leben läßt sich unsere Eingriffe geschmeidig geschehen und geht dann wieder auf seine Linie zurück. (1, 213)

An important means of characterizing the people in the novel quite precisely is the use of the dialect spoken in Lower Lusatia which shows differences in morphology and syntax from village to village. 'Die Sprache, die wir in den halbwendischen Dörfern sprechen, ist ein sogenanntes Ponaschemu, eine Unter-Uns-Sprache, eine Zwischensprache. Die Kleinstädter belächeln und verspotten sie, und in den halbwendischen Dörfern wird belächelt und verspottet, wer kein Ponaschemu spricht' (1, 19f). This is enriched by other linguistic peculiarities: Heinrich Matt's mother left Hamburg with her first husband for North America and came back with a smattering of English which was also adopted by other members of her family. Esau's mother and her friend Mina Baltin, who want something better for themselves and their families, have difficulty with standard High German when they try to speak like urban ladies. Sometimes the narrator himself uses expressions or single words of his native dialect.

'Nach Grodk bin ich mehrstenteils geworden, weil mir zu Hause das Gezänk um Geschäfte, Geld und Zinsen das Leben vergällte. Auf die *hoche Jungsenschule* bin ich aufgemacht, weil es geheißen hat, ich kann dort mehr lernen als bei Rumposchen in Bossdom'

(2, 7) is an example of German which would make any German teacher's hair stand on end. The narrator's justification for this is: 'ich kann . . . nicht verstehen, weshalb man nur so reden und so schreiben soll, wie der Herr Duden es bestimmte. Das Leben verschmälert sich, wenn man nur mit Worten über es redet, die einem vorgeschrieben sind' (2, 61). He gives us the following example, to show how Sorbian appropriates foreign words into a kind of half-Sorbian. When electricity came to Bossdom 'Installationsmaterial' was turned into 'Stallationsmaterial'.

> Einen Stall kennt jeder. Nachträglich verschafft mir die Ankunft dieses Fremdwortes in Bossdom, die ich miterlebte, einen schmalen Einblick in die Entstehung der halbsorbischen Sprache, mit der ich aufwuchs: Sie sträubt sich, Fremdworte aufzunehmen, oder sie ebnet sie ein, sie anerkennt keine Worte, die sich auf noch unbekannte Dinge oder gar auf Abstraktes beziehen, und sie modelt sie, bis sie in etwa ein bekanntes Ding bezeichnen. (1, 340)

And the narrator admits: 'Ich habe es noch heute schwer mit jenen Vereinbarungen, die die Grammatiker *die Fälle* nennen. Beim schnellen Sprechen, wenn ich keine Zeit für Nebenrechnungen, das heißt, fürs Deklinieren habe, verschlucke ich lieber einen halben Satz, damit ich nicht auf Rümpfnasen stoße, wenn ich *mir* sage, wo es *mich* heißen muß' (1, 527).

Another striking feature of Strittmatter's style is his linguistic innovation, which contributes greatly to the poetic charm of his novels. Such formulations as the following are most striking: 'Spiegel *zerscherbt* – sieben Jahre Pech' (1, 8); 'Großmutter *pantoffelt* von der Küche durch die dunkle Wohnstube in den Laden' (1, 85); 'mal riecht es *zwiebelig*, mal *gewürzkörnig*, mal *lorbeerblätterig* oder *sauermilchig*' (1, 104f); 'der darf nur *strümpflich* in die Oberstube' (1, 258), to mention only a few. Strittmatter responds to a reader who asks:

> Sie schreiben, es herbstelte. Haben Sie das bewußt gemacht? Ich muß ihm sagen, ich habe es nicht bewußt gemacht, aber ich spürte, daß man mit diesem einen Wort zehn Sätze sparen kann. Man kann auch einen Herbst, einen Herbsttag, so beschreiben, daß man sagt: die Sonne steht schräg, die Blätter fallen von den Bäumen, das Gras ist grau, der Himmel ist blau usw. Das sind alles abgenutzte poetische Requisiten. Ich kann aber auch voraussetzen, daß viele meiner Leser diese poetischen Requisiten kennen, und wir einigen uns darauf, ganz unter uns, ich schreibe: es herbstelte, und überlasse meinem Leser, hinzuzufügen, was

ich nicht geschrieben habe in den anderen zehn Sätzen, mit denen ich sonst eine Herbststimmung hätte beschreiben müssen. Eine gewisse Ökonomie steckt dahinter. Außerdem ist zu bedenken, daß die Sprache etwas mit Musik zu tun hat.[11]

Some readers, however, object to this as affected and forced. Linguistic innovation creates difficulties for translators. Thus translation of *Der Laden* into Russian shows that there is no equivalent for the dialect, but other characteristics are translated astonishingly well – including innovation in Russian.

Finally, one has to mention the vividness of Strittmatter's language, the discovery of poetry in everyday life. He wonders, 'Strömt Poesie aus den Dichtern oder aus den Dingen? Spürt der Dichter die Poesie, die in den Dingen liegt, auf, oder ruft die Poesie der Dinge den Dichter heran?' (2, 480). It is a question without an answer, and there are a lot of them in the novels. Though the distinctive elements in his language seem to come easily to him and are an important component of his style, his style is in fact anything but easy. In his *Selbstermunterungen* we read: 'Es gibt ein landläufiges Formulieren, das sich mir beim Schreiben hartnäckig anbietet, weil ich viel landläufig Geschriebenes gelesen habe. Das Formulieren aus eigener Sicht, also das, was das Geschriebene unverwechselbar macht, muß ich täglich üben'.[12] Being distinctive has nothing to do with vanity, it is Strittmatter's justification as a writer. A good novel should not be overtaken by the events of the next day, it should be timeless. *Der Laden* seems likely to stand the test of time in the literature of the GDR.

---

11. *Schriftsteller der Gegenwart: Erwin Strittmatter. Analysen, Erörterungen, Gespräche*, 3rd edn, Berlin (GDR), 1984, p. 248.
12. p. 116.

–4–

The Recent Historical Novel in the GDR

J. H. REID

Over the past twenty years plays and novels with historical themes have taken on central significance in the GDR's literature. It has perhaps been most marked in the theatre. Volker Braun, Heiner Müller, Christoph Hein have all made their contributions, and the dearth of plays on contemporary topics has been bemoaned on many occasions.[1] But in the field of the novel too, especially in the past decade, history has become a major preoccupation. Important examples include Christa Wolf's *Kein Ort. Nirgends* (1979) on Heinrich von Kleist and Karoline von Günderrode, Martin Stade's *Der närrische Krieg* (1981) on a minor eighteenth-century war, Joachim Walther's *Bewerbung bei Hofe* (1982) set at the court of August the Strong of Saxony, and Waldtraut Lewin's *Federico* (1984) on Emperor Frederick II of Sicily. Other works which tend more to fictional biography than to the historical novel proper include Renate Feyl's *Idylle mit Professor* (1986), a novel about the life of Luise Adelgunde Victoria Gottsched and Volker Ebersbach's *Caroline* (1987), about Caroline Böhmer-Schlegel-Schelling, actually subtitled 'historischer Roman'. Hans-Peter Jaeck's *Kammerherr und König. Voltaire in Preußen* (1987) is a novel by a professional historian, who in a postscript discusses the advantages of *Belletristik* over conventional history-writing and describes his work as 'eine realistische Fiktion'.[2] Sigrid Damm's *Vögel, die verkünden Land* (1985), on the life and times of J. M. R. Lenz, might also be mentioned here: although strictly speaking historical biography, it is related to fiction through its subject-matter – a writer – and its questioning, tentative narrative technique.

One striking feature of this interest in history is the way in which

1. Gottfried Fischborn, 'Umgehen mit Geschichte', *neue deutsche literatur*, vol. 32, no. 11, 1984, pp. 64–77.
2. Hans-Peter Jaeck, *Kammerherr und König. Voltaire in Preußen*, Berlin (GDR), 1987, p. 323.

a number of the writers mentioned appear to be taking up each other's motifs, building on and developing them. A whole 'family' of novels can be traced to the influence of Martin Stade's *Der König und sein Narr* of 1975 on the relation between the philosopher Gundling, the 'fool' of the title, and King Frederick William I of Prussia. The very title of Jaeck's novel implies the reference, although Voltaire, whom Frederick II of Prussia tried to make into his 'Affe' as his father had done with Gundling, was, unlike Gundling, able to free himself from the ignominy of life at a philistine Prussian court. In Renate Feyl's novel the arbiter of literary taste, Victoria's husband Gottsched, is less independent than Voltaire; his repressive insistence on the 'rules' of poetry is the literary pendant to Frederick II's Prussian discipline and he is rewarded with a poem from the king's own pen. Walther's *Bewerbung bei Hofe* takes as its starting point the same event as Stade's novel: the advent of Frederick William as King of Brandenburg-Prussia; the new king's favouring of the army at the expense of culture leads to the dismissal of court poet and master of ceremonies Johann von Besser, who subsequently goes to Dresden and whose 'diary' forms the novel. In Walther's novel, Besser's protégé, the poet Johann Günther, is also his principal antagonist; Günther also plays a minor role in Feyl's novel. In a different genre, the first part of Heiner Müller's play *Leben Gundlings Friedrich von Preußen Lessings Schlaf Traum Schrei* (1977) must similarly have been influenced by Stade's novel.

All the works I have mentioned are concerned to a greater or lesser extent with the relation between writers and society. They are also all set in the more or less remote past; but the term 'historical' can justifiably apply to the Third Reich and indeed to the beginnings of the GDR's own history in the 1950s. Novels such as *Kindheitsmuster* (1976) and *Der Aufenthalt* (1977) are historical in this sense, as are Erwin Strittmatter's *Der Wundertäter*, the third volume of which, set in the early years of the GDR, appeared in 1980, Erik Neutsch's mammoth *Der Frieden im Osten*, a novel devoted to the history of the GDR, of which four volumes have so far appeared, the latest in 1987, and also Christoph Hein's *Horns Ende* (1985). All of these recent works confront the question of Stalinism in their very different ways.

Traditionally the GDR's official view of history was reminiscent of that of Goethe's Wagner:

> Verzeiht! Es ist ein groß Ergetzen,
> Sich in den Geist der Zeiten zu versetzen,

The Recent Historical Novel in the GDR

> Zu schauen, wie vor uns ein weiser Mann gedacht,
> Und wie wir's dann zuletzt so herrlich weit gebracht.

In 1976 Walter Scheel suggested that the West Germans were in danger of becoming 'ein geschichtsloses Volk';[3] since then there has been the *Historikerstreit* and the controversy over the new museum of German history to be created in West Berlin. By contrast the GDR has always insisted on the importance of a clear grasp of history. Its essence was expressed by Erich Honecker in his preface to the standard GDR compendium *Klassenkampf–Tradition–Sozialismus* where the GDR is described as 'die staatliche Verkörperung der besten Traditionen der deutschen Geschichte . . . Als sozialistische Arbeiter- und Bauernmacht ist sie das gesetzmäßige Ergebnis und die Krönung des jahrhundertelangen Kampfes der Volksmassen für den gesellschaftlichen Fortschritt.'[4] But in the past decade this monolithic view of history has been giving way to a more differentiated one. Since 1978 the GDR has been revising its official image of Prussia, emphasizing the 'progressive' traditions as well as the reactionary ones.[5] Of especial interest is the new view of Martin Luther developed during the run-up to the quincentenary celebrations of 1983;[6] the early GDR historical novel was dominated by Luther's antagonist Thomas Müntzer, who was presented as the progressive forerunner of Marx and Lenin.[7] Official biographies have reassessed not only Frederick II of Prussia, now sometimes re-christened Frederick the Great, but even Otto von Bismarck.[8] This is a quite remarkable reversal of the view expressed in 1947:

---

3. Address to a historians' conference in Mannheim, quoted by Sven Papcke, 'Gibt es eine kulturelle Einheit der Deutschen?', in Werner Weidenfeld (ed.), *Die Identität der Deutschen*, Munich, 1983, p. 248.
4. Quoted by Wilfried von Bredow, 'Geschichte als Element der deutschen Identität?', in Weidenfeld (ed.), *Die Identität*, pp. 108f.
5. Horst Bartel, Ingrid Mittenzwei and Walter Schmidt, 'Preußen und die deutsche Geschichte', *Einheit*, vol. 34, 1979, pp. 637–46; see Johannes Rogalla von Bieberstein, 'Preußentum und Sozialismus', in Paul Gerhard Klussmann and Heinrich Mohr (eds.), *Deutsche Misere einst und jetzt: Die deutsche Misere als Thema der Gegenwartsliteratur: Das Preußensyndrom in der Literatur der DDR*, Bonn, 1982, pp. 227–42.
6. Horst Bartel *et al.*, 'Thesen über Martin Luther. Zum 500. Geburtstag', *Einheit*, vol. 36, 1981, pp. 890–903; see also Mark Brayne, 'Luther: "One of the Greatest Sons of the German People"', *GDR Monitor*, no. 3, Summer 1980, pp. 35–43.
7. Jay Rosellini, 'Zur Funktionsbestimmung des historischen Romans in der DDR-Literatur', *Amsterdamer Beiträge zur neueren Germanistik*, nos. 11–12, 1981, pp. 61–101, esp. pp. 79ff.
8. Ingrid Mittenzwei, *Friedrich II. von Preußen. Eine Biographie*, Berlin (GDR), 1980; Ernst Engelberg, *Bismarck: Urpreuße und Reichsgründer*, Berlin (GDR), 1985.

'Historisch betrachtet führt eine gerade Linie von Luther über den Großen Kurfürsten, über Friedrich II. und seine Nachfolger, über Bismarck und die wilhelminische Zeit bis zu Hitler.'[9]

This modification of the official view on history has implications for the historical novel, although writers have not been content to follow political fashion. In an address to the presiding body of the Writers' Union in 1981, Helmut Sakowski declared:

> Wir, die Deutschen in der DDR, sind aus der ganzen deutschen Geschichte gewachsen und haben nicht nur jene Bereiche geerbt, mit denen wir uns identifizieren können, die Bauernkriege zum Beispiel. Wir haben jetzt sogar begonnen, unser Verhältnis gegenüber Preußen differenzierter zu bestimmen. Warum sollte es dann nicht auch möglich sein, daß wir uns mit den Umständen oder Zeugnissen der frühmittelalterlichen Staatsgründung befassen, die Grundlagen geschaffen hat oder Vorbedingungen für die Herausbildung der deutschen Nation?[10]

Sakowski himself, however, is more sceptical of the rehabilitation of Prussia than these words imply; the original version of his novel *Wie ein Vogel im Schwarm* (1984) was serialized in *Wochenpost* and contained some critical remarks on the 'Preußen-Renaissance' which were excised from the book version.[11] In Günter de Bruyn's *Neue Herrlichkeit* (1984) the continuity (in the bad sense) of German history from Prussia to the GDR is symbolized in the villa of the title – class privileges are as prevalent now as then. In *Hinze-Kunze-Roman* Volker Braun's 'Herr' and 'Knecht' ride out into the 'preußische Prärie' as Diderot's eighteenth-century characters had done before them.[12] Renate Feyl's *Idylle mit Professor* makes no concessions to the new affection for Frederick II and his Prussians, who invade Saxony, march into Leipzig and cause untold misery to thousands. Gottsched, the Prussian, is delighted; but Victoria, who is from Danzig, hates 'alles Preußische, Maßvolle, Abgezirkelte, haßt diesen sturen, engbrüstigen Verstand, haßt diesen Dünkel und vor allem die Karabiner, mit denen zwar Macht demonstriert wird, aber doch kein einziges freundschaftliches Gefühl erobert werden

---

9. W. von Hanstein, *Von Luther bis Hitler*, Dresden, 1947, quoted by Bieberstein, 'Preußentum und Sozialismus', p. 230.
10. Helmut Sakowski, 'Von Sachsenkaisern, Robotern und dem Sinn für Realitäten', *neue deutsche literatur*, vol. 29, no. 7, 1981, p. 11.
11. See Harald Kleinschmidt, 'Tapferkeit und Vorsicht. Unklarheiten in der Kulturpolitik der DDR', *Deutschland Archiv*, vol. 18, 1985, p. 117.
12. Volker Braun, *Hinze-Kunze-Roman*, Halle, 1985, p. 35.

kann'.[13] Wolfgang Harich has associated recent attempts to rehabilitate Nietzsche in the GDR with the revision of views on Luther, Frederick the Great and Bismarck, which he regards as the imitation of 'Westmoden' and the 'Aushöhlung kulturpolitischer Grundsätze',[14] accusations which led Hermann Kant to accuse him in turn of 'Polpotterien'. Kant's ironic comment 'Man sehe in unsere Literatur – die hält von Preußen nicht übermäßig viel' is, in the light of the examples I have given, nothing but the truth.[15]

History-writing is important for the establishment of national legitimacy.[16] The historical novel or drama can also be used to this end. The GDR critic Henryk Keisch tries to explain the turning to historical drama by reference to the GDR's development of a national identity and compares the situation with that of Shakespeare in Elizabethan England and Schiller in revolutionary Germany: 'Es mag mit dem Entstehen historisch neuer staatlicher Strukturen, mit der Festigung und Vertiefung eines neuen Staatsbewußtseins in der DDR zusammenhängen, daß sich hier die Literaturwerke, insbesonders die dramatischen Werke mit historischem Stoff (oder auch mit indirektem Bezug auf einen solchen) mehren.'[17] It is precisely this, however, which is called into question in many of the novels I am discussing.

The function of the GDR's historical novel was described as follows in 1979 by one of the GDR's establishment authors, Wolfgang Joho: 'Als die vornehmste Aufgabe des geschichtlichen Romans sehe ich es an, gerade bei den jüngeren Generationen Geschichtsbewußtsein zu wecken, sie die sozialistische Gegenwart, in die sie geboren sind, als das folgerichtige Ergebnis früherer Geschehnisse begreifen zu lehren, sie sich als Erben der Geschichte wie als ihre Vollstrecker fühlen zu lassen.'[18] But just as the conception of history has been modified, so too has the historical novel. In

13. Renate Feyl, *Idylle mit Professor*, Berlin (GDR), 1986, pp. 231–2.
14. Wolfgang Harich, '"Revision des marxistischen Nietzschebildes?"', *Sinn und Form*, vol. 39, 1987, p. 1054; Harich was responding to Heinz Pepperle's article with the same title, ibid., vol. 38, 1986, pp. 934–69.
15. Hermann Kant, 'Rede auf dem X. Schriftstellerkongreß der Deutschen Demokratischen Republik', *neue deutsche literatur*, vol. 36, no. 2, 1988, pp. 27f. See also the articles in Klussmann and Mohr (eds.), *Deutsche Misere einst und jetzt*, esp. Wolfgang Emmerich, 'Der Alp der Geschichte. "Preußen" in Heiner Müllers *Leben Gundlings Friedrich von Preußen Lessings Schlaf Traum Schrei*', 1982, pp. 115–58.
16. See von Bredow, 'Geschichte', p. 107.
17. Henryk Keisch, 'Geschichte auf dem Theater', *neue deutsche literatur*, vol. 29, no. 6, 1981, p. 93.
18. Wolfgang Joho, in 'Möglichkeiten des Historischen', *neue deutsche literatur*, vol. 27, no. 11, 1979, p. 74.

a sense *all* socialist-realist literature is historical: socialist realism is 'die wahrheitsgetreue, historisch konkrete Darstellung der Wirklichkeit in ihrer revolutionären Entwicklung'.[19] Literature of this kind is embedded in the movement of history, embracing both past and future, so that in a paradigmatic work of socialist realism like Erik Neutsch's *Drei Tage unseres Lebens* (1969) the building of a motorway is related both to the moment when man broke away from the animal kingdom by developing tools, and to the socialist future when he will have landed on Venus. A proper historical consciousness in the Marxist sense involves the 'Aneignung' of works of the classical heritage – on one famous occasion Walter Ulbricht claimed that the GDR was writing the third part of Goethe's *Faust*.[20] In recent years this appropriation of history has taken on unorthodox forms, as with Plenzdorf's *Die neuen Leiden des jungen W.* or Irmtraud Morgner's feminist adaptation of Goethe's *Faust* in her *Amanda*. Conversely *Geschichtspessimismus* is one of the supreme heresies of which writers such as Günter Kunert and Volker Braun have at various times been accused. Socialist-realist writing of the kind represented by Neutsch is no longer central to the GDR's literary production, although it continues to be written and although critics from time to time bemoan the inability of young writers nowadays to tell 'Geschichte in Geschichten'.[21]

The historical novel is popular for many reasons. Action literature and romance are favourite reading in the GDR as in the rest of the world, and the subtitle 'historischer Roman' is said to guarantee sales.[22] The historical novel has always given scope for the erotic,[23] and novels such as *Bewerbung bei Hofe* and *Federico* have their fair share of erotic scenes. The genre satisfies a craving for facts, for authenticity, and this has been a preoccupation of the GDR's literature for many years now. But there may also be something escapist about it, and from Feuchtwanger onwards the writers of historical novels have always had to defend themselves against this accusation. In an authoritarian society like the GDR this 'escapism'

---

19. Hans-Jürgen Schmitt and Godehard Schramm (eds.), *Sozialistische Realismuskonzeptionen. Dokumente zum 1. Allunionskongreß der Sowjetschriftsteller*, Frankfurt/Main, 1974, p. 390.
20. Walter Ulbricht, 'An alle Bürger der DDR! An die ganze deutsche Nation', *Neues Deutschland*, 28 March 1962, pp. 3–5.
21. Klaus Kändler, 'Uwe Saeger: *Nöhr*', *Weimarer Beiträge*, vol. 27, 1981, p. 157; see also Fischborn, 'Umgehen mit Geschichte', p. 64.
22. Martina and Detlef Langermann, 'Greifswalder Kolloquium zur Historischen Belletristik', *Weimarer Beiträge*, vol. 32, 1986, p. 1393.
23. Rosellini, 'Zur Funktionsbestimmung des historischen Romans', gives examples of erotic scenes in the early GDR historical novel.

may not be purely self-imposed: contemporary topics are inclined to be problematic, leading to difficulties with the censor.[24] The past is safer: after the events of June 1953 the proportion of published novels dealing with the present dropped from 26 per cent to 11 per cent in two years, and in 1955 historical novels made up 24 per cent of total output.[25] The current revival of the genre may imply similar problems; the depoliticization of East German literature which many critics have diagnosed in recent years finds its reflection in a turning to historical themes. Conversely it may be possible to infringe taboos by putting on the mask of history.

The theoretical basis for historical novels in the socialist-realist mode is Georg Lukács's *Der historische Roman*, first published in Moscow in 1937, in Berlin in 1955. History was for Lukács the 'Schicksal des Volkes'.[26] The historical novel was to portray 'solche individuellen Schicksale . . ., in denen die Lebensprobleme der Epoche *unmittelbar* und zugleich typisch zum Ausdruck gelangen' (p. 347). By the term 'typisch' Lukács understood what was significant in the Marxist view of historical development. In fact he refused to regard the historical novel as a genre separate from the contemporary social novel, observing 'daß die Beziehung des Schriftstellers . . . zur historischen Wirklichkeit prinzipiell keine andere sein kann als die zur Wirklichkeit überhaupt' (p. 202). The historical novel presented the 'Vorgeschichte der Gegenwart':

> Ohne eine erlebbare Beziehung zur Gegenwart ist eine Gestaltung der Geschichte unmöglich. Aber diese Beziehung besteht für die wirklich große historische Kunst nicht in Anspielungen auf zeitgenössische Ereignisse . . ., sondern in dem Lebendigmachen der Vergangenheit als Vorgeschichte der Gegenwart, in der dichterischen Verlebendigung jener geschichtlichen, sozialen und menschlichen Kräfte, die im Laufe einer langen Entwicklung unser heutiges Leben zu dem geformt haben, was es ist, als was wir selbst es erleben. (p. 64)

Novels which merely used the past as 'Illustrationsmaterial für die Probleme der Gegenwart' (p. 352) were inferior products. Other influential features of Lukács's work relate to his view of the relation between the fictitious hero and the 'world-historical indi-

---

24. See Christoph Hein, 'Ein Interview', in *Öffentlich arbeiten. Essais und Gespräche*, Berlin (GDR), 1987, p. 100.
25. See Rosellini, 'Zur Funktionsbestimmung des historischen Romans', p. 77.
26. Georg Lukács, *Der historische Roman*, in *Werke. Probleme des Realismus III*, vol. 6, Darmstadt, 1965, pp. 14–429, here p. 347. Page references in the text are to this edition.

vidual', and his rejection of the biographical novel. The historical novel preferred as its subject-matter transitional ages, the crises of history; Walter Scott's success lay in his ability to find 'mediocre' heroes, 'historical-social types' who could embody the totality of certain transitional stages of history (p. 42); the 'world-historical personage', on the other hand, was best treated as a more subsidiary figure, assisting the writer to relate popular movements to the actual events of history (p. 254). By concentrating on the world-historical individual, the biographical novel falsely displaced the emphasis from the social to the psychological: 'Diese Schwäche der biographischen Form des Romans läßt sich verallgemeinernd so aussprechen, daß die privatpersönlichen, rein psychologisch-biographischen Züge eine proportional unrichtige Breite, ein falsches Übergewicht erhalten. Dadurch kommen die großen historisch treibenden Kräfte zu kurz' (p. 393).

Add to these points Lukács's insistence on the omniscient, authoritative narrator, and it is clear that many of these theses no longer apply to a GDR literature which over the past twenty years has been so concerned with subjective authenticity. The biographical novel, in particular, has enjoyed increasing favour. And yet the notion that the historical novel presents the 'prehistory of the present' has been extraordinarily fruitful, if not necessarily in the way intended by Lukács. It is the central question of Christa Wolf's *Kindheitsmuster*, 'Wie sind wir so geworden, wie wir heute sind?'[27] the answer to which is a non-standard presentation of the relation between fascism and postwar socialism, but it also applies to more recent GDR novels set in the 1950s. A work like Christoph Hein's *Der fremde Freund* (1982) can be read as an answer to Wolf's question: the Stalinism of the GDR's early years is the cause of the distortions of consciousness in the present. And if this seems to be widening the scope of 'historicity' unduly, then I should point to Martin Stade's *Der König und sein Narr* (1975) as a very respectable example of a historical novel which fulfils some of Lukács's demands, while at the same time going beyond them. As its title suggests, the novel confronts the 'mediocre hero', the obscure philosopher Gundling, best known for his funeral in a wine barrel, with the 'world-historical individual', Frederick William I, the architect of modern Prussia. But it is Gundling's story; the king remains a figure whom we see only from without. Both characters are caught up in and ultimately frustrated by the transition between feudalism and capitalism. And although Gundling is an intellectual

---

27. Christa Wolf, *Kindheitsmuster*, Darmstadt, 1977, pp. 246, 375, 428.

and not sufficiently in tune with the populace at large, it is precisely this failure on his part which is implicitly criticized in the novel, whose central topic is the *trahison des clercs*. It is, however, when one tries to see the events of Stade's novel in terms of the 'Vorgeschichte der Gegenwart' that the Lukácsian model is subverted, since the GDR claims to have overcome the contradictions of Frederick William's Prussia. Instead it is the analogies which come to mind, especially the situation of the intellectual in the contemporary GDR. The pattern of the novel's events resembles that of plays such as *Großer Frieden* by Volker Braun, in which the idealism of an early revolution, in the time of Frederick William I, gives way, under the forces of external circumstances and subjective weaknesses, to pragmatism, brutality and defeat. It is a pattern repeated in Waldtraut Lewin's *Federico* in the career of Emperor Frederick II. In both novels the historical models reflect by implication the fate of the socialist revolution in the twentieth century.

There is an alternative model to Lukács's and today it is perhaps more important: that of Lion Feuchtwanger, in whose name an annual prize for historical fiction or biography is awarded (both Waldtraut Lewin and Sigrid Damm have been its recipients). In an essay of 1935, Feuchtwanger admitted that the accusation of escapism was sometimes a valid one, but pointed out that from its earliest beginnings great literature had used historical themes.[28] Like the author of contemporary fiction, the writer of historical fiction is expressing his own '(zeitgenössisches) Lebensgefühl, sein subjektives Weltbild'.[29] Feuchtwanger's own historical novels had the same subject-matter as his other works: 'Ich habe nie daran gedacht, Geschichte um ihrer selbst willen zu gestalten, ich habe im Kostüm, in der historischen Einkleidung immer nur ein Stilisierungsmittel gesehen, ein Mittel, auf die einfachste Art die Illusionen der Realität zu erzielen.'[30]

Waldtraut Lewin has described her own outlook in very similar terms: 'Mein Interesse an den wechselnden Formen der Historie ist, grob gesprochen, das des Schauspielers an seinem Kostüm. Der Mensch in seinem Verhalten zur Gesellschaft, das sich ständig erneuernde Kontinuum seines Kampfes um Würde, Freiheit und Glück ist der ewige Gegenstand meiner Neugier.' But she also saw the historical mode as one which produced 'Verfremdung'.[31]

28. Lion Feuchtwanger, 'Vom Sinn und Unsinn des historischen Romans', *Internationale Literatur*, vol. 5, no. 9, 1935, p. 19.
29. Ibid., p. 20.
30. Ibid.
31. Waldtraut Lewin, in 'Möglichkeiten des Historischen', *neue deutsche literatur*,

Under the mask of history she introduces topics of contemporary social interest: the bisexuality of Federico, presented as something totally natural, the active involvement of women in history, and inasmuch as Federico unites Christians and Moslems among his advisers, one may even detect a contemporary international dimension in the novel. In *Federico* history and myth are linked, as they are in Christa Wolf's *Kassandra* and Irmtraud Morgner's *Amanda* (both 1983), to which latter it is heavily indebted. It begins with an unorthodox creation myth. Eating of the fruit of the Tree of Knowledge was not forbidden by God, but rather encouraged. Three races of beings proceeded from the act of Creation: the first was the children of God, a languid, decadent race, too lazy to eat the fruit; the second was the descendants of Adam and Eve, diligent and inventive; the third race, however, was the product of the direct union of God and Eve, and they call this race 'Unruhvollen Stamm . . . oder Salz der Erde.'[32] Irritation, provocation, nonconformism, curiosity are supreme human virtues down the centuries. The historian herself, inquisitive and provocative, is an embodiment of these values, which may not be those of the authorities of her own society.

Feuchtwanger's most famous novel, *Jud Süß*, is, on the author's own account, the presentation of the career of Walter Rathenau transposed into the eighteenth century.[33] While recognizing Feuchtwanger's impeccable socialist and humanist intentions, Lukács disapproved of this technique, which he regarded as dangerously close to a decadent Nietzscheanism, since the use of historical parallels implied that things did not change.[34] But this seems to be precisely the message of many of the GDR's recent historical novels. The setting in the past is a mask; these novels are not describing merely the 'prehistory of the present' but the 'present' itself. The opening of Christa Wolf's *Kein Ort. Nirgends*, like that of her later *Kassandra*, makes plain the relation between past and present: Kleist and Günderrode are 'Vorgänger' of the narrator; 'we,' she says, 'immer noch vergebend unsern Schuldigern . . . immer noch gierig auf den Aschegeschmack der Worte. Immer noch nicht, was uns anstünde, stumm.'[35] In an essay on Karoline von Günderrode, Wolf went so far as to speak of the 'wheel of history', a phrase

---

    vol. 27, no. 11, 1979, p. 78.
32. Waldtraut Lewin, *Federico*, Berlin (GDR), 1984, p. 11.
33. Feuchtwanger, 'Vom Sinn und Unsinn des historischen Romans', p. 21.
34. Lukács, *Der historische Roman*, pp. 286, 352–62.
35. Christa Wolf, *Kein Ort. Nirgends*, Berlin, 1979, p. 5.

closer to Nietzsche than to Marx.[36] *Kein Ort. Nirgends* was written under the impact of the Biermann affair and reflects the atmosphere of isolation experienced by writers like Christa Wolf at the time. It also raises the questions of patriarchal social structures and male–female relationships which its author believed had not yet been resolved by the socialist GDR. In Nees von Esenbeck it ironizes the GDR's confidence in science's ability to solve humanity's problems and create a paradise on earth. Moreover the image which it presents of the relation between the writer and the Prussian state does not altogether correspond to the new view of Prussia propagated by the politicians.[37]

The old Prussia is one half of the geographical area of the present-day GDR; the other half is Saxony,[38] the setting of Walther's *Bewerbung bei Hofe*, in which the broad Saxon accent of August the Strong himself[39] has its especial irony for GDR readers, who will remember the voice of Walter Ulbricht and other political leaders of their own times. Walther's novel has its echoes of the Lukácsian model, inasmuch as its centre of interest, the poet Johann Christian Günther, has strong sympathies with the *Volk*, downtrodden and exploited as they are.[40] His fate, however, that of being ignored in favour of a now-forgotten nonentity, mirrors that of the GDR's writers in 1982, many of whom had been driven into exile. Saxony is a place of surveillance and opportunism, where the court lives in luxury at the expense of ordinary people and where literature is supposed to be written according to certain conventions – all features which have their counterparts in the contemporary GDR. Martin Stade's *Der närrische Krieg* takes place in another part of Saxony. It appeared at the height of the rearmament debates and is an impressively anti-militarist statement. This is one aspect of the historical novel which is perhaps peculiar to the GDR: the relatively monolithic nature of its society and ideological basis makes the historical model attractive, enables the drawing of parallels between earlier social structures and those of the present in a way which would not apply to liberal democracies like West Germany.

36. 'Der Schatten eines Traumes. Karoline von Günderrode – ein Entwurf', in *Fortgesetzter Versuch. Aufsätze, Gespräche, Essays*, 2nd edn, Leipzig, 1980, p. 294.
37. Dennis Tate includes *Kein Ort* in the group of works of the 1970s he considers to invoke the 'spectre of the Deutsche Misere': *The East German Novel. Identity, Community, Continuity*, Bath, 1984, pp. 215–21.
38. See Marlies Menge, *Die Sachsen – das Staatsvolk der DDR*, Munich, 1985.
39. A recent East German biography is Georg Piltz, *August der Starke: Träume und Taten eines deutschen Fürsten*, Berlin (GDR), 1986.
40. Joachim Walther, *Bewerbung bei Hofe*, Berlin (GDR), 1982, p. 80.

Feuchtwanger declared that history-writing was no less fiction than the writing of historical novels, since it too implied selectivity in accordance with subjective or ideological considerations,[41] and a major aspect of the East German novel has been the questioning of historiography itself. This has an old and honourable tradition. In Hermann Kant's novel *Die Aula* (1965) there is an account of the Arbeiter- und Bauernfakultät (ABF) freshers' first history lesson. What is history? The lecturer Riebenlamm responds with Brecht's 'Fragen eines lesenden Arbeiters'. They have all been taught to see history through middle-class spectacles: 'Das Bild von der Welt, so wie man es uns dort gemalt hat, steht zu großen Teilen auf dem Kopf. Hier wollen wir ihm wieder auf die Beine helfen.'[42] The ABF was founded among other things to counteract false bourgeois conceptions of history. Brecht's own fragmentary novel *Die Geschäfte des Herrn Julius Cäsar* constitutes a debunking of history as written by bourgeois historians. But while the early East German novel was concerned with 'standing history on its feet again', stressing the role of the masses rather than that of the rulers, more recent works have been questioning this too, seeking a more differentiated, dialectical approach to history.[43] They have also been questioning official GDR premises on history-writing. Stefan Heym's *Der König David Bericht* (1972) is perhaps the most famous example of a work which unmasks the Stalinist rewriting of history. More recently the story 'Das Duell' in Franz Fühmann's *Saiäns-Fiktschen* (1981) describes the rewriting and reinterpretation of history in similar terms in the year 3456. In Waldtraut Lewin's *Federico* Clio, the muse of history, is a bored, untidy, browbeaten secretary with a typewriter: 'Offenbar hatte man sie schon öfter zum Weglaufen genötigt, um die Prozesse neu aufzurollen und Heiligsprechung oder Fluch zu überprüfen'.[44] Christa Wolf's *Kassandra* questions male-oriented history-writing in the name of the unheard female voice.

The other interesting feature of the contemporary historical novel is the self-conscious attention paid to form and technique. In 1979 Inge von Wangenheim criticized the old-fashioned historical novel for its attempt to keep up the fiction that the author had 'really been there': 'Das "Dabeigewesensein" läßt sich nicht mehr

---

41. Feuchtwanger, 'Vom Sinn und Unsinn des historischen Romans', p. 22.
42. Hermann Kant, *Die Aula*, Berlin (GDR), 1965, p. 80.
43. This point was made by Gunner Müller-Waldeck at a conference on the historical novel in Greifswald – see Martina and Detlef Langermann, 'Greifswalder Kolloquium zur Historischen Belletristik', p. 1394.
44. Lewin, *Federico*, p. 24.

vorspiegeln . . . Der Künstler im Schriftsteller muß es schaffen, Konzeptionen, Methoden und Mittel (auch Techniken) einzubringen, die das "Dabeigewesensein", auf das es nach meiner Meinung nun unter den veränderten Bedingungen unserer gesellschaftlichen Gegenwart entscheidend ankommt, als Kunsterlebnis zu bewerkstelligen.'[45] One does still find the authoritative omniscient narrator: Klaus Hoffmann-Reicker's *Teufelsbünder* (1982), about the Jesuits in late sixteenth-century Saxony, makes no pretence at modernist sophistication. Jaeck's *Kammerherr und König*, although it too introduces a debate on historiography, is conventionally narrated. But the liberal and libertarian novels by Wolf, Stade, Walther and Lewin all are marked by a rejection of authoritative, therefore authoritarian, narrative standpoints. Stade and Walther solve the problem described by Inge von Wangenheim in a relatively traditional way. *Der König und sein Narr* is Gundling's (fictitious) autobiography, his 'letztes Buch'; although a first-person narrative, there is little attempt to create the illusion of reality, in that Gundling is still writing as he dies and in places fulfils the function of the old-fashioned omniscient narrator; but the appending of authentic historical documents to Gundling's own account is one way in which history-writing itself is thematized. The novel's message is conveyed through the self-criticism of its narrator. *Der närrische Krieg* is comparatively unliterary; it is in diary form and is based on the real diary from 1747 of one Lieutenant Rauch, which had also been used earlier by Gustav Freytag.[46] Stade's invention is the figure of a sceptical, humanist doctor who accompanies Rauch and reasons with him; in the end Rauch dies in an absurd duel, the doctor finds his diary and appends a brief epilogue, commenting: 'Eines muß man zugeben: Er hatte angefangen nachzudenken. Das Denken ist das wichtigste. Das Denken und der Zweifel.' [47] Walther's *Bewerbung bei Hofe*, on the other hand, is a wholly fictitious diary, that of Johann von Besser, poet and master of ceremonies at the court of August the Strong; its author is supposed to have left instructions that his diary should be published 250 years after his death, by which time not only will his rival Günther be wholly forgotten and he himself have become immortal, but the citizens of the twentieth century will no longer know 'Kriege, Ungerechtigkeit, Wortklauberei, Verrat, Speichel-

---

45. Inge von Wangenheim, in 'Möglichkeiten des Historischen', *neue deutsche literatur*, vol. 27, no. 11, 1979, pp. 75f.
46. *Bilder aus der deutschen Vergangenheit*, Vollständige Ausgabe, vol. 2, Berlin, n.d. (1927), pp. 556–82.
47. Stade, *Der närrische Krieg*, Berlin (GDR), 1981, p. 205.

leckerei, Ruhmredigkeit, Lüge, Heuchelei, Korruption, Gewalt, Haß, Stumpfsinn, Neid, Dummheit' and all the other ills to which his world was still subject;[48] none of these prophecies has in fact come to pass – again the inference is that history does not bring change.

Christa Wolf's *Kein Ort. Nirgends* and Waldtraut Lewin's *Federico* are much more complex in their narration. The former covers the events of a single day; its extensive use of flashback and memory creates an atmosphere of timelessness to imply a relation to the present-day GDR,[49] and its inner monologues, *erlebte Rede* and narratorial voice merge imperceptibly to the point where one is on occasion not sure who is speaking – indeed 'Wer spricht?' is the question posed (by whom we cannot be certain) at the beginning of the narrative.[50] *Federico* is more monumental in scale. It is yet another novel on the writing of a novel, a kind of '*Nachdenken über Federico*', an '*Auf der Suche nach Federico*', a '*Mutmaßungen über Federico*' or even a '*Gruppenbild mit Federico*'. For the story of the emperor is embedded in the story of Truda, the narrator (alter ego of Waldtraut Lewin), who descends to the underworld in search of her subject-matter and is guided there by various figures from Federico's own times. There are thus several first-person narrators, whose varying accounts balance and illuminate one another. The explicit model is Dante's *Divine Comedy*, appropriately enough, as Dante was almost a contemporary of Federico. In this respect we have in Lewin's novel yet another example of an 'Aneignung des klassischen Kulturerbes', but it is a work which also quotes, among other things, Hans Magnus Enzensberger's *Der Untergang der Titanic* and Pink Floyd's *The Wall*. Truda herself is a mythical figure, who plays a part in the events of Federico's life, for example, guiding him across the Alps on his way to Germany. Her search for the truth about her hero is inconclusive; the search itself is more important than the finding. This in itself is an emancipatory feature of the novel: the reader is not fed with unquestioned facts but is encouraged to join the 'Unruhvoller Stamm', to eat of the Tree of Knowledge.

Kein Ort. Nirgends, *Bewerbung bei Hofe* and *Federico* all in their very different ways use the historical mode with a high degree of sophistication. They are novels which confront the reader with no simple answers. They deal with topics of contemporary interest. They also call in question some of the official platitudes on German

---

48. Walther, *Bewerbung bei Hofe*, p. 7.
49. Tate, *The East German Novel*, p. 219.
50. Wolf, *Kein Ort. Nirgends*, p. 6.

history and its relation to the present. In her investigation of the GDR's early historical novel Jay Rosellini concluded: 'Die Weiterentwicklung des Genres in der DDR hängt vor allem davon ab, inwiefern die analytischen Methoden des Materialismus in Zukunft über das *Historische* hinaus auf die *bestehende* Gesellschaft angewandt werden können.'[51] Precisely this has come to pass. The 1980s could be said to have seen the historical novel in the GDR come of age.

---

51. Rosellini, 'Zur Funktionsbestimmung des historischen Romans', p. 101.
    Note Some of the material in this article has already appeared in my book *Writing Without Taboos: The New East German Literature*, Oxford, 1990.

–5–

Günter de Bruyn and *Neue Herrlichkeit*

ROLAND SMITH

I

Günter de Bruyn is not as well known as Christa Wolf, as prolific as Erik Neutsch nor as fashionable as Christoph Hein, but he has produced a body of work which makes up in sensitivity what it lacks in quantity. He was born in Berlin in 1926 (the same year as Hermann Kant) and has lived in the capital and in the Mark Brandenburg all his life, apart from a short spell as a soldier during the Second World War. Until 1961 he worked as a librarian in Berlin, since then he has been an independent writer.

His major works include: *Der Hohlweg* (1963), *Buridans Esel* (1968), *Preisverleihung* (1972), *Das Leben des Jean Paul Friedrich Richter* (1976), *Märkische Forschungen* (1978) and *Neue Herrlichkeit* (1984). In addition he has written a number of short stories, essays and reviews, many of them gathered together in *Frauendienst*, published in 1986.[1]

What, then, are his qualities as an author? First, he is a realist, secondly, an acute observer of the human scene, thirdly, a humorist, fourthly, a moralist, fifthly, a social critic, sixthly, a Prussian and lastly, a man of literature.

To take these points in order, more than any other writer currently at work in the German Democratic Republic, de Bruyn presents us with pictures of everyday life there. He, more than any other, is the poet of the myriad of minor things which go to make up ordinary lives and can thus communicate the flavour of everyday existence.

What de Bruyn does not do is give us socialist realism, still the officially prescribed mode in the GDR, though admittedly these days more honoured in the breach than the observance. Thus the hero of his third novel, *Preisverleihung*, the university lecturer, Teo

---

1. Published in Halle/Saale; *Neue Herrlichkeit* was first published by Fischer, Frankfurt/Main.

Overbeck, has come to realize that his earlier enthusiasm for this genre was misplaced: 'Er war damals von einer Literatur beeindruckt, die den Zugang zur Wirklichkeit mehr verbaute als eröffnete, umgab sich mit Leuten, die wie er Wunschvorstellungen für Realität, Realität für Schönheitsfehler hielten und mit uneingestandenem Hochmut auf Leute herabsahen, die ihnen unterentwickelt waren.'[2]

One of de Bruyn's greatest strengths is his portrayal of relationships, particularly those between the sexes, and of the emotions these engender. Nowhere is this more the case than in his second novel, *Buridans Esel*, the story of an extra-marital affair and of its impact upon the three lives involved. It is in this work rather than the unsuccessful first novel *Der Hohlweg* that his power as a writer is first fully revealed, his ability to convey genuine emotion and to register the hopes and disappointments, the awakenings and betrayals which are involved in human relationships. What is impressive about *Buridans Esel* is the way in which de Bruyn enters into not only the 'hero's' inner life but also those of his wife and mistress, who are depicted so sympathetically that one can talk of a feminine sensibility at work. These are fully rounded characters who are well able to face up to life's challenges; often in contrast to their male counterparts, who tend to be anti-heroes.

Unlike lesser writers, de Bruyn is able by means of humour to resist any temptation to slip into the maudlin, though it is a humour which, for the most part, eschews overtly comical situations and which concentrates on the discrepancy between human aspiration and human achievement, such as the undignified situation Karl Erp finds himself in, when, emerging from the block in which the object of his affections, Frl. Broder (whose Christian name is never given), lives, he is subjected to a 'citizen's arrest' by Anita (who has been spurned by Erp) and her teenage accomplices and has to explain himself at the local police station, which involves a telephone call to his wife.

A further example of situation comedy is provided by the third novel, *Preisverleihung*. In this, the hero, Teo Overbeck, has to deliver a speech in honour of the recipient of a literary prize, Paul Schuster. He is extremely reluctant to do this because, not only does he think Paul unworthy of such an honour, he also bitterly regrets his own part in making the author what he is. He nevertheless agrees and is then dumb-founded by the sudden realization, at the last moment, that, while correctly dressed for such a formal

---

2. *Preisverleihung*, p. 41.

occasion in every other respect, he is still wearing his bedroom slippers. There is no time to change, so he goes onto the platform as he is; the result is a total disaster as he lurches on through an incoherent speech, unable to extricate himself from the thicket of verbiage. The students show their disapproval by scraping their feet.

The parallel with *Lucky Jim* is close but, whereas Jim Dixon has an essentially anarchic role, Teo Overbeck really believes in what he is doing and is utterly cast down by his failure. The point is that he feels responsible in a way that Kingsley Amis's youthful hero never can, and this sense of responsibility is an indication of the moral dimension which all de Bruyn's novels display.

In *Buridans Esel* this does not yet seem too highly developed: it is the convenience of Berlin and the comfort of life in their villa by the Spree which induces Karl Erp to return to his wife instead of going off to the provinces with his mistress. In *Preisverleihung*, however, the moral sense of the hero is much more prominent; he feels guilt at having played a part in the culpable behaviour of the GDR provincial press: 'Man meldete nicht, was war, sondern was gewünscht wurde, war an guten Statistiken mehr interessiert als an guten Taten, duldete Schönfärber eher als Kritiker.'[3]

He feels responsible for having encouraged the writer, Paul Schuster, to take the wrong (socialist-realist) road, he feels keenly the unwillingness of his students to venture their own opinions (ironically, when a group does for once get started he has to cut it short himself because of his forthcoming speech) and he is unwilling to use his influence to help his daughter, who gets bad *Abitur* results, gain entrance to University.

In the case of Ernst Pötsch, the hero of *Märkische Forschungen*, this strong moral sense is still more marked. He becomes convinced that the Romantic poet and novelist, Max von Schwedenow, did not provide a role model for the GDR by dying a hero's death on the battlefield in 1813, fighting for his republican beliefs against Napoleonic tyranny, but in fact survived until the 1820s, becoming, true to his class origins, a supporter of Metternich and the notorious Karlsbad Decrees of 1819. Since this runs exactly counter to the thesis of the only other Schwedenow scholar, the celebrated Professor Menzel, that his subject would be a splendid specimen for GDR historiography, it means that there must be war between them.

In such a conflict between an established professor and an

---

3. Ibid., p. 42.

unknown provincial schoolmaster it is apparent that the latter can stand no chance, every outlet available to him being blocked by Menzel, who is utterly ruthless in defence of his own position and reputation. Pötsch however is equally determined to get at the truth and displays the persistence of a Michael Kohlhaas in proving he is right. It may, however, be doubted whether such a stance is in fact ultimately moral, for in the end he, too, sacrifices everything, his job, his wife, children and friends, in the pursuit of his obsession.

The social criticism inherent in both *Buridans Esel* and *Preisverleihung* is perhaps most clearly expressed by Pötsch's wife when she and her husband visit the Menzels to celebrate the professor's fiftieth birthday. She finds herself in a glittering assembly of leading personalities from many walks of life but she is not overawed, taking due note of the ostentation and display on the one hand and of a persistent note of cynicism on the other.[4] She reflects on the contrast of life-style between the assembled company, the self-styled leaders of the people, with all their attendant privileges, and the great mass of ordinary folk.

> Sie waren die Missionare, die den Ureinwohnern raten konnten, ihnen kostenlos auch die nötige Kultur noch brachten, die stolz waren auf diese pflichttreuen Menschen, die nachts in Schnee und Regen ins übernächste Dorf zur Frühschicht in den modernsten aller Rinderställe fuhren, die morgens in den Bussen, die sie ins Kombinat beförderten, fest schliefen. Elke wurde immer ungerechter. Sie fragte sich, ob das süße Kind, von dem die übergroße Frau dort erzählte, auch so süß wäre, wenn es im Winter täglich unausgeschlafen mit dem überfüllten Sechs-Uhr-Zug zum Kindergarten befördert würde.[5]

This theme of contrast between the lives of those in power and the rest is developed still more starkly in *Neue Herrlichkeit*.

Mention of people doing their duty reminds us that de Bruyn is nothing if not representative of Prussian virtues. They are embodied in the hero of *Preisverleihung* of whom it is said: 'Teo Overbeck gehört nicht zu den Genialen, sondern zu den Tüchtigen. Alles, was er ist und kann, ist und kann er durch Fleiß und Hartnäckigkeit. In ihm ist nichts, als was er durch mühsame Kleinarbeit hineinge-

---

4. When he is presented with a picture of himself as a youthful member of the FDJ, standing in front of the ruins of Berlin in the late 1940s, Professor Menzel makes the comment, ' "Das Lächeln der Sieger der Geschichte" ', which gives rise to prolonged merriment among the assembled company (*Märkische Forschungen*, p. 101).
5. Ibid., p. 98.

bracht hat. Ihm fliegt nichts zu, er muß es sich holen.'⁶ In *Buridans Esel*, these virtues of hard work, economy, self-reliance and unpretentiousness appear in the figure of Karl Erp's father, Friedrich Wilhelm Erp, a former teacher, now seventy-nine. He advises his son to give up the liaison with Frl. Broder: 'Das Wort Pflicht hörst du nicht gern und redest mit dergleichen Ausdauer, wie ich von ihr, vom Glück. Ich denke über derlei schon länger nach als du und finde, es steht damit so wie mit der Freiheit, die man auch nur hat, wenn man auf sie verzichtet.'⁷

Erp himself finds this too absolute, too 'Prussian', we are informed, but it does seem to make some impression on him, and when, a little later, he is summoned to the old man's death-bed it is significant that he does not even consider taking Frl. Broder with him, whereas his wife does appear and gives comfort to the old man in his final hours.

Although Erp has moved away from his father, there can be no doubt that he has taken over many of the latter's values, not least his attitude towards Prussia: 'Das Deutschland, von dem man dauernd redet, hat 75 Jahre bestanden, Preußen Jahrhunderte.'⁸ And this reminds us that, while for foreigners the word 'Prussia' often brings with it undertones of war, the associations for the inhabitants of those parts are much richer. For de Bruyn they are predominantly personal, but also literary, and this is not surprising in one who reveres Fontane.

De Bruyn is nothing if not a literary writer. He has written about a number of authors and his study of Jean Paul, published in 1976, must be reckoned one of his major achievements. The heroes of his novels are intellectuals – a librarian, a university lecturer and a schoolteacher – and there are many references to literature in his work. In his essay, 'Wie ich zur Literatur kam', he describes how in 1933, at the age of seven, the discovery of Karl May led to his reading of all sixty-five works by that author, and it is interesting to note that Karl Erp, the librarian hero of *Buridans Esel*, considers taking May's *Winnetou* with him as part of his survival kit when, at the age of forty, he thinks of leaving home.

After Karl May, the main influences would seem to have been the German Romantics, Jean Paul of course, Hölderlin and Hauff. One of the most interesting chapters of de Bruyn's biography of Jean Paul depicts the latter's visit to Weimar in 1796 and how disillusioned he was at finding his idols, Goethe, Wieland and

6. *Preisverleihung*, p. 113.
7. *Buridans Esel*, p. 193.
8. Ibid., p. 189.

Herder split into two warring factions, with Herder fiercely resisting the attempt by Goethe and Schiller to impose a classical façade on German literature. Needless to say, Jean Paul aligns himself with the Herder group and this obviously has the author's approval. Of the modern writers, Thomas Mann and Arnold Zweig have both been the subjects of essays by him, but only once, in *Buridans Esel*, is there a reference to a GDR work, namely Hermann Kant's *Die Aula*.[9]

II

Neue Herrlichkeit, de Bruyn's fifth novel, was published in 1984. It breaks new ground in two respects. First, his characters are not from the intelligentsia but from the lower orders, bordering on the criminal underworld, and the hero, Viktor Kösling, although he comes from the top-drawer of GDR society, has nothing of an intellectual about him and occupies the privileged position he enjoys merely because his father is a high official in the Party.

The second new development is the terse, lean style involving the use throughout of the present tense. This confers a certain immediacy upon the work, enhancing its dramatic impact, which de Bruyn is able to use to good effect on several occasions. On the other hand, the lengthy, sensitive analysis of character which we have come to associate with realist novels, and in particular with de Bruyn, is very much curtailed, an aspect of development with which some admirers of his work have found it difficult to come to terms.

The plot is quite straightforward: Viktor Kösling, a young man in his mid- to late twenties, is sent by his mother to a house in the country for ten weeks to complete his doctoral thesis prior to entering the diplomatic service of the GDR. As it is the depth of winter and the house, 'Neue Herrlichkeit', is cut off by snow from the rest of the world for much of the time, the opportunity would seem to be ideal, but Viktor, who completely lacks the drive of his pushy, powerful parents, is distracted by the presence of the other residents, particularly the young girl, Thilde, and his sojourn there becomes devoted simply to winning her affection. There are three main obstacles, the presence of a rival, the problem of Thilde's grandmother in residence, for whom Thilde feels responsible, and the objections of his parents. Viktor is able to overcome the first

9. Ibid., p. 55.

two but is no match for the third and he abandons his beloved to start the new, glittering career which has been marked out for him, though without the hoped-for doctorate.

De Bruyn's use of the present tense is entirely appropriate, in that virtually everything is enacted within the confines of the house, the cast is supplied by the permanent staff and it would be a simple matter to turn the work into a play. The house itself, which provides the setting and the symbolic title of the work, is a pretentious structure built in 1895 by grandmother Tita's father and has been taken over by the state to provide accommodation for weekend courses and the like.

The staff are a very mixed bunch. Easily the oldest is Tita, now in her mid-eighties, who has, like many of her age-group in Germany, led a hard life – her brothers having been killed in the First World War and her sons in the Second. Her husband died in the harsh conditions prevailing after the Second World War and the house was taken over, but she stayed on as manager under the new regime. Still a person of some presence and physically strong, senility has reduced her to a state of dependence on her granddaughter, Thilde.

Thilde fulfils this role uncomplainingly, as she does all the others which are thrust upon her. Trained as a nurse, she has to function also as a housemaid, an onerous task in such a large establishment, and to keep her eye on her grandmother, who has taken to wandering off at random into the countryside – on one occasion even being picked up by the frontier guards at Frankfurt-an-der-Oder while attempting to get back to an area she once knew as a girl but which is now in Poland.

Into this arduous life comes Viktor, not demanding or exploitative as are the other men she knows, but gentle and understanding. It seems for a time as if he might be the one to rescue her and he promises marriage, but she has two great disadvantages as a consort for him: her mother, who abandoned her as a baby, ran off to the West and is now a West German citizen; secondly, she lacks the sophistication necessary for a member of the ruling élite, her grammar is uncertain and her dress sense inadequate.

The other members of the staff are represented mainly by Max, who has taken over from Tita, and Olga, his common-law wife. Max is simply on the make; apart from running the house, he has a side-line in automobile parts of doubtful legality, for which he is eventually arrested, and he loses no opportunity to push drinks onto the various participants on the courses, on which there is a nice little profit to be made. Olga has no time for him, nor indeed for her four children, three of whom are the result of previous liaisons; she seeks consolation in drinking and smoking – forty to sixty cigarettes a day – proudly displaying her brown fingers and yellow teeth like battle honours. Nevertheless, one feels some sympathy for her. Although not a particularly attractive character she too is one of life's victims.

What is striking about this family group is their alienation. The four children are portrayed as monsters without any redeeming features, and the adults display not the slightest affection for each other; indeed they can and do betray their partners to the authorities, but not from any sense of social responsibility. As far as society is concerned, they might just as well be living on the moon; they are aware of the power of the state (Max ends up in prison, having been denounced by Olga for his illegal activities), but there is not the slightest feeling of involvement. They are simply objects, there to be manipulated by Viktor's father and his kind.

Kösling senior is, of course, the power in the land; his influence makes itself felt, even though he is not for the most part physically present, for it provides a cloak of protection and privilege, of which the weak-willed Viktor is only too happy to avail himself. When the book opens Kösling is out of action, suffering from prostate trouble, something which afflicts him all the more because, he feels, it threatens his masculinity and makes of him a laughing stock. He has no illusions about Viktor, whom he despises as a weakling, but he is concerned about the family name and, when he is alerted by his ex-wife that their son is making a fool of himself over a girl, he descends upon Neue Herrlichkeit like a *deus ex machina*, presenting Viktor with the choice: either Thilde or a career. The Gogol-like scene in which he drives up to the snow-bound house in his sledge, accompanied by his flunkeys and is then danced attendance upon by Max and company can be seen as a microcosm of the political situation in the GDR.

No less a monster is Agnola Kösling, Viktor's mother. She still feels keenly the blow of having been divorced by her husband for a younger, more attractive woman. She maintains contact with him, however, and she has one powerful weapon in her armoury, her son, whom she is happy to exploit in her attempt to make her ex-husband feel how much he has lost. It is her idea that Viktor should go to Neue Herrlichkeit to complete his doctorate, for this is one of the few things his father has not achieved in his career.

Agnola is busy. She runs a state organization for family planning which has contacts worldwide and she is constantly receiving important visitors from abroad. She is no less adept at the other kind of family planning which involves keeping her rather shiftless son up to the mark and, when she learns of his intention to marry a girl of whose background she knows nothing, she goes into action, subjecting Thilde to a grilling, like a duchess in a Victorian melodrama.

Agnola is one of the few totally unsympathetic female characters to be found anywhere in de Bruyn's work. Her son, Viktor, on the other hand, is very much in the tradition of his male leads, only he is more of an anti-hero than ever. His predecessors are all solid family men with careers who have achieved something and who are involved in what they do. Viktor, admittedly much younger than they, resembles nothing so much as the son of a wealthy family in a capitalist society, seeking, not too hard, a prestigious occupation which will not be too demanding.

Thus Viktor goes along with his mother's idea that he should spend ten weeks working on his dissertation, not because he has the slightest desire to do this himself but simply because he is anxious to please. He has not the faintest interest in the subject: 'Die Außenpolitik der preußischen Regierung während der Französischen Revolution – unter besonderer Berücksichtigung des Einflusses der Handwerker- und Bauernunruhen in den Provinzen.' Nor does the thought of all the books he must read appeal, for he does not enjoy a happy relationship with the printed word.

> Die unlebendigen, gleichmäßig bedruckten Seiten töten seinen Elan, machen ihn mutlos. Eine Seite sieht aus wie die andere, verzweifelt sucht er nach Bildern, begrüßt dankbar jeden Kursiv- oder Fettdruck, blättert vor in der Hoffnung, die Abwechslung eines Kapiteleinschnitts bald zu erreichen. Er wünscht sich Bücher so, wie manche Lehrbücher sind, das Wichtige eingerahmt, das Unwichtige durch Kleindruck als überflüssig entlarvt.[10]

It hardly comes as a surprise, therefore, that he makes no progress whatever on his dissertation, being distracted initially by the discomfort of his room, then by the weather and, finally, by Thilde. It is in this relationship that he encounters something which fully engages him. He has, of course, had relationships with women before but in keeping with his passive nature he has always left it to them to take the initiative: 'Sein Gefühl für Frauen gleicht einem Reflektor, der soviel Wärme und Licht zurückstrahlt, wie er empfängt. Nie wird er untreu, er wird nur untreu gemacht.'[11]

10. *Neue Herrlichkeit*, p. 31.
11. Ibid., p. 38.

Now, because Thilde herself is so timid as to be virtually invisible, he has to go into action himself for the first time and encounters the obstacles which traditionally stand in the way of true love. The first of these is a rival, Sebastian, the gardener who has some pretensions to being a philosopher, but who behaves in a markedly unphilosophic manner when he feels Viktor is trespassing on his territory. True to his principles, Viktor collapses even before the blow has landed, but he emerges victorious from the contest since he has a weapon Sebastian cannot match – he can offer Thilde marriage.

Before this can take place, however, there is one further local difficulty to be resolved, namely that of Tita, Thilde's grandmother. The main problem is that Thilde is extremely reluctant to let her grandmother go, and this reluctance is increased when, with Viktor, she commits Tita to a state-run old-people's village and receives an impression akin to that of Dante's Hell: 'Dann sind ringsum Gesichter zu sehen, deren Anblick schwerer zu ertragen ist als der Gestank: nicht, weil sie häßlich und krank aussehen, sondern weil ihnen jeglicher Ausdruck fehlt, weil sie stumpf und bewegungslos bleiben und die Augen, die dem Auto mechanisch folgen, vollkommen leer sind.'[12] The reason for this zombie-like behaviour is that the old people are drugged to keep them quiescent. When they return a few days later, Thilde is appalled to discover that Tita, too, has become a living corpse and is unable to recognize her. She tries to remonstrate with the doctor on duty, who agrees that this is an unworthy procedure, but who claims that, given their limited resources, the home cannot hope to provide proper treatment. 'Wer aber keine Zeit für seinen Nächsten hat, der soll doch die Frage nach der Schuld auf sich beruhen lassen. Der soll doch ehrlich sein und sagen: in unsere Welt der Nützlichkeit paßt eine kranke Alte nicht hinein.'[13] The doctor goes on chillingly to chart the inexorable stages by which the tiresome memory of the ancient relative is gradually eliminated from younger people's minds, so that when the news of the relative's decease arrives, it is felt resentfully as an annoying distraction to their own lives.

This at least is not true for the remaining residents of Neue Herrlichkeit. When the news of Tita's demise reaches them they arrange for her body to be delivered so that she can have a proper burial in the graveyard behind the house. A closed car draws up and they wait expectantly for Viktor to appear; but the figure that

12. Ibid., p. 182.
13. Ibid., p. 198.

emerges is not his but that of Thilde's mother, the dead woman's daughter, the ne'er do well who had gone to the West. Viktor has been reclaimed by his own exclusive world and is even at this moment high above the clouds, winging his way to a first appointment abroad and a career in diplomacy. 'Die neue Herrlichkeit' of the new order has asserted its supremacy over that of the old.

III

In conclusion, how far can we say that *Neue Herrlichkeit* marks a departure from de Bruyn's established pattern of fiction writing? Certainly it comes initially as something of a shock, the urbane, literate tone giving way to an unaccustomed brutalism. In retrospect it can be seen that the work is rather an indication of a continuing trend, for none of his previous works had ended on a note of optimism and the plight of his heroes, culminating in that of Ernst Pötsch in *Märkische Forschungen*, had grown steadily more desperate.

Many of the features noted are preserved: the realism of the setting, the acute analysis of character, the insight into and sympathy for the female characters, with the notable exception of Viktor's mother. There is also a good deal of humour present: in the description of Viktor's half-hearted attempts to get down to work on his thesis, in his roundabout courtship of Thilde by suffering for hours under the tyranny of her grandmother's photo album or her passion for cards, not to mention the antics he gets up to simply to be near his beloved.

Where *Neue Herrlichkeit* breaks new ground is in the intensity of its moral concerns, particularly the abuse of power. This is indicated in the title and it is presented starkly, as a fact of life, in the contrast between the situation of those on top and those underneath. Whereas in de Bruyn's previous works power is disseminated through various institutions, the library, the university, the research institute, here there is nothing intermediate between the brutal Kösling senior and his manipulative ex-wife, on the one hand, and the hapless helots at the house, on the other. Even Viktor, for all his anxious desire to please, emerges as just as much an exploiter as his parents – indeed, his impact is still more destructive.

The social criticism here is also much more prominent. The description of the scene in the old-people's settlement is a nightmare and a further revelation of what life is like for ordinary people; while those in prominent positions in the Party and their dependants enjoy such an exalted life-style – though it should perhaps in fairness be pointed out that the problems of an aging population are by no means confined to the socialist countries.

What is peculiar to the GDR is that coming to terms with the German and particularly the Prussian heritage is not presented in a positive light; there is no sense here of a proud, if misunderstood, tradition. The house from which the work takes its title is a harsh, ugly structure displaying the brash assertiveness of the period in German history when it was built. Tita, the former proprietor, who is herself nearly as old as the building, though not without a certain dignity, is senile and a mere relic of what she was. Nor is the surrounding countryside, which in de Bruyn's earlier works had been a source of comfort and inspiration, presented in a positive way; Brandenburg in mid-winter is a harsh, inhospitable place, and only occasionally are we given a hint of nature in its gentler moments. Contact with the local inhabitants is minimal and only the vast, ever-spreading rubbish dump behind the house provides evidence of human habitation. Here, as elsewhere, society has been atomized and early promise unfulfilled.

On its appearance, the book was hailed in the West as de Bruyn's most outspoken work to date and providing a valuable picture of life 'drüben'. Criticism of the book in the GDR has, of course, been fierce and has been on two main levels: on the one hand, attempting to refute the notion that East Germany has itself become a land of two nations and, on the other, condemning the portrayal of what is perceived as an unrepresentative group of characters on the staff of Neue Herrlichkeit as a boozy, feckless lot, owing allegiance to nothing but their own short-term interests. A number of admirers of de Bruyn have also regretted the new brutalism of his style, which strikes a jarring note for those accustomed to the elegant control he displays particularly in *Buridans Esel* and *Preisverleihung*. Karin Hirdina, writing in 1985, has vigorously defended him, pointing out that it is even accepted officially (before *glasnost* and *perestroika*) that there are societal discrepancies which the new order has still not rectified. She defends the harsh, bare style as entirely appropriate to the subject: 'Die Worte jagen einander nicht, sie überschreien einander nicht, sie fordern Aufmerksamkeit, ruhiges Lesen.'[14]

14. Karin Hirdina, 'Grund zum Ärgern. Günter de Bruyns Roman *Neue Herrlichkeit*', in Siegfried Rönisch (ed.), *DDR Literatur im Gespräch 1985*, Berlin (GDR), 1986, pp. 109–15, here p. 110. Hirdina has also written a study of de

She goes on to point out that, for all the shock that this novel has caused, there is an essential continuity in his oeuvre: that sympathy for the underdog which we see in the portrayal of the long-suffering Berlin tenement dwellers in *Buridans Esel*, the conscientious university lecturer Teo of *Preisverleihung* so taken for granted by his colleagues, the dogged schoolmaster Pötsch in *Märkische Forschungen*, dourly determined to get at the truth in his dispute with the flamboyant Professor Menzel and, not least, the plebeian Jean Paul, disillusioned in his encounter with the patrician Goethe.

From our own vantage point it is possible to see that such a concern must inevitably lead to de Bruyn bumping up against the ceiling of what is permitted by the state of which he is a citizen. It is to be hoped that more liberal attitudes may yet prevail in the age of *glasnost* and *perestroika*, since de Bruyn is a worthy representative of a distinguished German tradition.

Bruyn in the series 'Schriftsteller der Gegenwart': *Günter de Bruyn. Leben und Werke*, Berlin (GDR), 1983.

– 6 –

Christoph Hein: The Novelist as Dramatist Manqué

GISELA SHAW

I

For the past fifteen years or so, literary scholars in the German Democratic Republic have been reconsidering their own roles and functions in the context of new and ever-growing demands placed on them by the leading writers of their country. Not infrequently they have found themselves baffled and irritated, even genuinely lost, when faced with the need to assess the merits or otherwise of literary works that fail to fit into the well-established mould of socialist principles, yet are not sufficiently lightweight to be ignored and relegated to oblivion. Even a cursory survey of debates conducted amongst East German literary critics reveals that the more open-minded and internationally aware among them have been painfully conscious of their own shortcomings for some time and that their sense of unease is growing. One East German writer whose name rarely escapes mention in such debates as evidence of a need to rectify perceived shortcomings of literary criticism is Christoph Hein.[1]

Hein's heart is in drama and stage work, since it is first and foremost the theatre that requires and facilitates the immediate dialogue with the public which he considers essential to his work: 'Theater hat sich durch die Jahrtausende als einigermaßen stabil erwiesen. Auch zeitweises Desinteresse seines Publikums hat es

---

1. Hein's published works to date include: *Cromwell und andere Stücke*, Berlin (GDR), 1981; *Die wahre Geschichte des Ah Q. Stücke und Essays*, Darmstadt, 1984; *Schlötel oder Was solls. Stücke und Essays*, Darmstadt, 1986; *Einladung zum Lever Bourgeois. Prosa*, Berlin (GDR), 1980 (West German edition: *Nachtfahrt und früher Morgen*, Hamburg, 1982); *Öffentlich arbeiten. Essais und Gespräche*, Berlin (GDR), 1987 (I am grateful to Margret Liebezeit from Humboldt University for drawing my attention to this edition); *Der fremde Freund. Novelle*, Berlin (GDR), 1982; *Horns Ende*, Berlin (GDR), 1985. Page references in the text refer to these editions.

überstanden. Tödlich war ihm nur fehlende Öffentlichkeit.'[2]

If being a 'public matter' is an essential precondition for the theatre and its activities, this ultimately goes for literature generally. 'Dichtung' requires 'Öffentlichkeit' if it is not to dry up and wither into insignificance: 'Öffentlichkeit ist nicht allein ihr Adressat, sie ist ihre Vorbedingung. Fehlende Öffentlichkeit trocknet die Poesie zum Stammbuchblatt aus, degradiert die poetische Metapher zur Sklavensprache . . . Ihr Gebrauchswert reduziert sich auf Lebenshilfe, ein Freiraum für eine tatenlos dahindämmernde Fantasie, ein Merkzeichen für vergessene Menschlichkeit.'[3]

Hein's insistence on 'Öffentlichkeit' as an imperative for literature of all genres was reiterated most poignantly in his speech at the Tenth Writers' Congress in November–December 1987. Once again, he singled out the theatre as the area most urgently in need of change.[4]

Given Hein's distinct preference for dramatic and stage work, it seems ironic that his national and international fame should rest largely on his achievements as a writer of fiction, especially as the author of *Der fremde Freund*. Hein himself acknowledged as early as 1978, 'Das gegenwärtige Theater ist Schreibanlaß für Prosa.'[5] He began writing fiction with short pieces; his first attempt at a novel came in the early 1980s, but proved to be problematical. Hein's difficulties with the structure of his novel *Horns Ende* led him to interrupt his work on it to write a *Novelle* (*Der fremde Freund*)[6] which, as it turned out, was then to steal the limelight on the larger and more ambitious work.

In what follows I shall argue that the success of the *Novelle* is connected with the fact that it allowed Hein to remain broadly within the confines of dramatic structure and to apply the principle of severity and economy of form that governs both genres.[7] The

2. 'Hamlet oder der Parteisekretär' in *Schlötel oder Was solls*, p. 181. Originally in *Theater der Zeit*, no. 7, 1978; now also included in *Öffentlich arbeiten* under the title 'Ein Interview'.
3. 'Waldbruder Lenz', in *Die wahre Geschichte des Ah Q*, p. 140. Originally in *Connaissance de la RDA*, no. 13, 1981; now also included in *Öffentlich arbeiten*.
4. *Die Zeit*, 4 December 1987, p. 57.
5. 'Hamlet oder der Parteisekretär', p. 181.
6. See Françoise Barthélemy-Toraille, 'Entretien avec Christoph Hein autour de son roman *Horns Ende*', *Connaissance de la RDA*, no. 25, 1987, p. 18.
7. See his observation in 'Brief an M. F., Regisseur der westdeutschen Erstaufführung von *Schlötel oder Was solls*': 'Stückeschreiber sind angehalten, knapp und dicht zu formulieren, Opulenz und barocke Beredsamkeit können in der Prosa vorzüglich sein, in der Dramatik nie. Die überlieferten Stücke aus einem Zeitraum von 2 500 Jahren verbindet eine Gemeinsamkeit: sie sind schlank' (*Öffentlich arbeiten*, pp. 130f).

novel *Horns Ende*, on the other hand, represents an experiment in a genre not totally suited to Hein's strengths. In the attempt to break down the novel into what he himself described as a series of short stories,[8] the author never quite got the upper hand over his material. The book's ideas and formal structure fail to complement and reinforce each other in the way they do in the *Novelle* and the reader is deprived of the cathartic experience which is a necessary prerequisite for the success of a work so clearly informed by the desire to enlighten and clarify.

II

Der fremde Freund, conceived and written, so we can assume, in a fairly short time-span, is a very personal and a very private book. It clearly reflects Hein's view regarding the essentially subjective nature of any work of literature: 'Literaten sind Exhibitionisten: Es ist nicht möglich zu schreiben und sich bedeckt zu halten.'[9] All literature, so Hein insists, is bound to be primarily autobiographical. This does not, however, relegate it to the status of a purely personal and private utterance. For it is also part and parcel of an objective context.[10] The subjective and the objective are inextricably intertwined in terms of the text's origins and character as well as its reception: 'Die Literatur erregt die Wirkungen, doch diese bezeugen vor allem die Verfassung des Lesers, des Gemeinwesens.'[11] *Der fremde Freund* is the work of an author who allows the world to get under his skin – and who is unlikely to be unfamiliar with the temptation to which the central character in the book succumbs: to eschew the pain caused by close contact with the world she 'bathes in dragon's blood', thereby making herself invulnerable.

Claudia – the very name signals a process of retreat from the world – is an intelligent, professionally successful woman of forty (which was roughly Hein's age at the time of writing as well as the age of Thomas in *Horns Ende* at the point when he is attempting to recollect the past). Her life and behaviour are conditioned by fear

8. See Barthélemy-Toraille, 'Entretien avec Christoph Hein', p. 18.
9. See *Die Zeit*, 4 December 1987, p. 57.
10. 'Meinen Stoff habe ich in meinen Augen und Ohren, er sitzt unter meiner Haut, da er mir tief unter die Haut ging. Wie immer ist es der Balken im eigenen Auge, der Pfahl im eigenen Fleisch. Auch die künftige Literatur wird von dem reden, was Individuen betraf, betroffen machte. Sie wird Autobiografie sein, keine private, aber doch persönliche, keine repräsentative, aber doch gesellschaftliche Autobiografie . . . Der Stoff ist der Autor selbst' ('Öffentlich arbeiten', in *Öffentlich arbeiten*, p. 34).
11. See *Die Zeit*, 4 December 1987, p. 57.

and her helpless attempts to come to terms with it. Her fear is traced back to a number of key experiences, some of which date back to her youth, for example, the loss of a girlhood friendship, the loss of a father figure, a disastrous attempt on the part of her mother to enlighten her daughter on the facts of life and direct evidence of the suppression of truth for reasons of political expediency in June 1953. But there have also been experiences in her adult life that have contributed to her determination to remain aloof from all human contact, in particular an unhappy and humiliating marriage that ended in divorce. Claudia persuades herself that the only way she can go on living with dignity is by severing all links with other people, by surrounding her soul with a protective, impenetrable layer that will shield her. The fact that this entails the loss of not merely interpersonal relationships but also her own sense of identity occasionally causes a flicker in her mind, but this is instantly extinguished.

An account of a nightmare acts as a prologue to the central text: Claudia experiences a state of mental rigidity and total helplessness on finding herself on the edge of a deep gulf. Her one companion desperately clings to her for help. She is determined to shake him off – 'Jeder für sich' (p. 5)[12] – but he refuses to let go. She screams, but not even she can hear herself screaming. She has lost her sense of self ('Ich oder die Person, die vielleicht ich bin') and of other people (her companion appears to her 'traumverschwommen'). On awakening she unsuccessfully attempts to reconstruct the nightmare she has just been through. The visions of her dream are rapidly overlaid by 'alltägliche Abziehbilder' and she finds it impossible to reconcile her subconscious and her conscious experiences. The gulf remains and with it her inability to come to terms with herself and the world. Clarity about her own situation is never achieved. What prevails is a sense of utter helplessness.

The story that follows is an enactment of the dream scene. Claudia, utterly insecure and emotionally lost, constructs for herself a way of life and a sense of identity that promise to exclude pain and humiliation. She manages to secure her friend Henry's consent to an affair without emotional commitment. She comments: 'Unsere Distanz gab unserem Verhältnis eine spröde und mir angenehme Vertraulichkeit. Ich hatte kein Bedürfnis, mich nochmals einem Menschen völlig zu offenbaren, mich einem Menschen völlig auszuliefern. Mir gefiel es, die andere Haut zu streicheln

12. All page references in the text are to the West German edition of *Der fremde Freund* published under the title *Drachenblut*, Darmstadt, 1985.

ohne den Wunsch zu haben, in sie hineinzukriechen' (p. 29).

At the start of the book we hear of the friend's death, a seemingly senseless and even ridiculous occurrence, yet a logical consequence of his existential boredom and fear of never really having lived. The book is an attempt on Claudia's part to reconstruct the events preceding his death and, above all, to record with clinical accuracy and a grotesque sense of triumph the process of her own emotional impoverishment. Just as she consistently suppressed any desire to get to know Henry while he was still alive, so she manages to remain unmoved by his death and funeral – a mere 'Zeremonie des Todes' (p. 15). Only once had she given in to what she diagnoses as her 'stete Bereitschaft, mich aufzugeben, Sehnsucht nach der Infantilität. Der schwere, süßliche Wunsch, geborgen zu sein' (p.51). But this had left her deeply ashamed and lonely, rigid with terror that she might have forfeited her carefully cultivated 'Fremdheit' (p. 54). She subsequently works even harder at restoring it.

During the early phase of East German critical responses to Hein's *Novelle* he was not infrequently accused of having implicitly encouraged the reader to identify with the book's protagonist by giving the narration over to her and not even attempting to balance the picture by introducing other perspectives, whether those of other fictitious characters or his own. How, his critics wondered, could any reader avoid accepting Claudia's view of society at face value, regarding it as the only one possible for a sensitive individual exposed to a seemingly hostile and threatening social environment?[13] However, it was not long before other, dissenting voices argued that careful attention to Hein's use of aesthetic form excluded an interpretation along the lines indicated.[14] This issue, it seems to me, is crucial to any assessment of *Der fremde Freund*. It also helps to clarify what may have gone wrong in the novel *Horns Ende*. What, then, are the formal safeguards in the *Novelle* to prevent readers from naively identifying with Claudia and to get across Hein's 'real' message?

First, the very fact that the story is preceded by the account of a nightmare arising from a deep sense of anxiety and loneliness precludes a possible interpretation of Claudia's behaviour as a

---

13. For example, Rüdiger Bernhardt, [Review] in *Weimarer Beiträge*, vol. 29, no. 9, 1983, pp. 1635–8; also Ursula Heukenkamp, 'Umschau und Kritik', *Sinn und Form*, vol. 35, no. 3, 1983, pp. 625–32; here pp. 630–2.
14. For example, Bernd Leistner, [Review] in *Weimarer Beiträge*, vol. 29, no. 9, 1983, pp. 1642–5; Hans Kaufmann, 'Christoph Hein in der Debatte', in Kaufmann (ed.), *Über DDR-Literatur. Beiträge aus fünfundzwanzig Jahren*, Berlin (GDR), 1986, pp. 231–40.

model to be emulated. The confrontation of nightmare and reality defines the latter as marked by progressive inner impoverishment and isolation. Hein's book then appears not as a glorification of alienation but as an account of an individual's and a society's illness. Secondly, the very fact that Claudia is reduced to delivering a monologue which is really a cry for help, confirms our impression of her as a victim or patient rather than a heroine. Perhaps the most persuasive argument in this context can, thirdly, be derived from an analysis of Claudia's language: as this is in itself contradictory, it allows the author to dispense with the need to introduce contrasting narrative perspectives. The reader is repeatedly called upon to be detached from Claudia's point of view and to provide his or her own interpretation of events and people. To mention just one example: Claudia portrays her fellow men without exception as the victims of civilization, but mistakenly and blindly exempts herself, when, for any observer, she is a prime example of precisely this process:

> Offenbar erfordert das Zusammenleben von Individuen einige Gitterstäbe in eben diesen Individuen. Die dunklen Kerker unserer Seelen, in die wir einschließen, was die dünne Schale unseres Menschseins bedroht. Ich verdränge täglich eine Flut von Ereignissen und Gefühlen, die mich demütigen und verletzen. Ohne diese Verdrängungen wäre ich nicht fähig, morgens aus dem Bett aufzustehen. Gitter, die uns vom Chaos trennen. (p. 86)

Here Claudia begins by stating a hypothesis as if it were a proven principle: in order to survive, individuals need to erect iron bars for their protection. Yet her choice of words, such as 'Gitterstäbe', 'Kerker', 'Verdrängung', 'Chaos', draws our attention to the fact that Claudia is far from coping with her problems. By simply suppressing them she reinforces her state of neurosis. Claudia's monologue is littered with instances of such contradictions which cannot but alert the reader to her desperate inner confusion.[15]

With this in mind, we can hardly read Claudia's own résumé –

---

15. In an interview from 1984, Hein himself described his technique as follows: 'Die Defizite werden fast bis ins einzelne, zumindest bei dieser Person, benannt. Es ist so, daß da die Person etwas behauptet, und daß der Leser etwas anderes auch liest, also das, was Tschechow einmal als den Untertext bezeichnete. Wenn die Person sagt, sie sei zufrieden und ihr gehe es gut, wird eigentlich immer etwas anderes, nicht das Gegenteil, aber etwas anderes noch erzählt. Das war für mich die Spannung dabei, diesen ganzen Untertext eben nicht zu schreiben, sondern in dieser Rollenprosa einen anderen Text darüberzulegen. Und es hat offenbar funktioniert' (*Öffentlich arbeiten*, p. 158).

Christoph Hein: Novelist as Dramatist Manqué

'Ich bin unverletzlich geworden. Ich habe in Drachenblut gebadet, und kein Lindenblatt ließ mich irgendwo schutzlos' (p. 154) – as an instigation to follow her example, but rather, to use Hein's words, as a signal 'daß sie aus all dem, was sie für sich als notwendig behauptet und richtig, dieses dicke Fell und so weiter, im Grunde nur herauskommen will, daß sie eigentlich immerfort nach etwas schreit, was man als wirkliches Leben bezeichnen könnte, das, so wie sie sich eingekapselt hat, natürlich kaum noch vorhanden ist.'[16]

Nor can we take her view of her social environment to be an unbiased one. What Hein is presenting to us is the profile of an illness whose causes are only partially diagnosed. The question whether this illness is primarily to be associated with his own (i.e. East German) society or whether it is inevitable in the context of any modern civilization does not have an easy answer. Given Hein's undeniable and perfectly natural preoccupation with the society most familiar to him, it is not surprising that he himself should, in conversation, have emphasized the story's relevance to the GDR and the socialist world in general.

> Il y a un écart entre cet environnement matériel satisfaisant et cette insatisfaction, qui est spécifique à mon pays et aux pays socialistes. Nos acquis sociaux sont très nombreux, à la différence de ce qui se passe dans une foule de pays capitalistes; chez nous on se sent considérablement sécurisé mais cette sécurité a engendré un certain ennui . . . Et puis, on prend conscience d'une perte, d'un manqué.[17]

Yet, two months previously, he had made it equally clear that the interest aroused by his book outside his own country might well have had to do with the fact that its main topic was modern civilization as such.

> Das Hauptthema ist, daß über unseren Stand der Zivilisation gesprochen wird . . . Daß über Kosten gesprochen wird, die dieses durch die Produktionsweise notwendige Leben uns erbracht hat . . . über diesen Preis rede ich in dem Buch. Insofern sind Fremdheit und Gewalt nur das Abgeleitete aus dem, was wir da aufgegeben haben. Wir haben eine Vertrautheit aufgegeben, aus guten Gründen: Heilige Kuh Fortschritt, und wir zahlen dafür.[18]

If boredom is a central theme in *Der fremde Freund*, it is interesting

16. Ibid.
17. *Révolution*, 13 December 1984, p. 42.
18. *Öffentlich arbeiten*, pp. 155f.

to note that Claudia's experience of it seems very different in kind from Henry's. Claudia's boredom is created by herself to counteract her feeling of being threatened and vulnerable, while Henry's is the genuine product of a life that appears utterly predictable and unexciting: 'Ich fürchte mich nicht davor zu sterben. Schlimmer ist es für mich, nicht zu leben. Nicht wirklich zu leben' (p. 29). A comparison with Albert Camus's Meursault in *L'Étranger* – and it is difficult to avoid such comparisons – might indeed lead one to conclude that Meursault's true heir is Henry, the outsider in an atheist socialist society rather than in a Christian bourgeois one, whose death appears similarly senseless as Meursault's and yet, like Meursault's, makes sense within his own philosophy of life.

By selecting not Henry but Claudia as his main protagonist, Christoph Hein invites an interpretation from a socio-political rather than philosophical perspective and, at least implicitly, calls for social change. This ties up with a number of statements he has made about the contrasting roles of literature and the sciences in society. In his reflexions 'Zu einem Satz von Anna Seghers' he defines literature as 'machtlos . . . aber nicht ohnmächtig'.[19] Poetry, Hein explains, is capable of quietly touching the nerves of our understanding and emotions, thus preventing us from retreating into social isolation. For man is 'das Tier mit dem dicksten Fell', 'einem Fell des Schutzes, des Desinteresses, des Hinnehmens, des Duldens',[20] a skin that enables him to survive but also endangers his life in its full sense, as he can simply decide to close his eyes to undesirable truths. One of the essential tasks of literature is to counteract this ostrich strategy by making accessible to our understanding areas of experience not (yet) accessible to scientific investigation.

> Das ungelöste Rätsel ist, so schlußfolgern wir daher, Sache der Kunst; das gelöste oder doch lösbar gewordene Rätsel ein wissenschaftlicher Forschungsbereich. Worüber man nicht sprechen kann, darüber muß man schweigen, weiß die Wissenschaft bekanntlich seit Jahrtausenden von ihrer eigenen Arbeit. Meine Erfahrung mit Literatur sagt: Worüber man (noch) nicht reden kann, davon kann die Kunst ein Lied singen.[21]

---

19. Originally published in *Connaissance de la RDA*, no. 22, 1986, pp. 61–70; here p. 65. Included in *Schlötel oder Was solls* and in *Öffentlich arbeiten* under the title of 'Worüber man nicht reden kann, davon kann die Kunst ein Lied singen. Zu einem Satz von Anna Seghers'.
20. Ibid., p. 67.
21. Ibid., p. 69.

Der fremde Freund can thus be interpreted as an attempt to articulate human experience not yet accessible to scientific scrutiny, especially the phenomenon of a socially isolated and self-alienating existence in a threatening modern civilization. Literature offers the means to encapsulate such an existence with a stringency and density which no other medium can offer. It sets up a model that invites the thinking through of alternatives and sparks off a process of clarification – the first requirement for the introduction of social change.

Christoph Hein conceded in an interview: 'Für mich ist eine strenge Struktur eine der Bedingungen eines Kunstwerkes . . . Alle Freiheiten sind mir im Grunde nur über eine strenge Struktur möglich.'[22] The *Novelle* offered him the severity and economy of form he needed: unity of space and time, auctorial detachment from fictional characters and strict concentration on the 'unerhörte Begebenheit' – these are the criteria Hein has himself referred to as those of the 'Novelle im klassischen Sinn' which his story seems to meet: 'die ganze Novelle hat etwas Nötigendes, Zwingendes, und ich wollte tatsächlich dieses Nötigende, Zwingende, das im Text der Novelle da ist, auch in der Form haben'.[23] We thus have a perfect match between aesthetic form, story and the author's artistic strengths: 'Vorteil von Dramatikern, wenn sie Prosa schreiben.'[24]

III

If *Der fremde Freund* uncovers contradictions in the fabric of individual and social behaviour, the same applies to Hein's second, larger work of fiction, *Horns Ende*. Within this overall context, the theme of the relationship between present and past acquires central significance. Individuals as well as society as a whole are depicted as the products of their histories. This tallies with Christoph Hein's view that it is one of the functions of art and literature to keep alive an awareness of history: 'Macht erlaubt sich keine Historie, läßt den Sinn für Geschichtlichkeit verkümmern, da sie allein besorgt ist, Anspruch und Erhalt ihrer Herrschaft zu sichern.'[25]

Literature and art are more 'comprehensive'. They aim to place the present into the wider context of past and future, thus depriving

---

22. Interview with Gregor Edelmann, 'Ansonsten würde man ja aufhören zu schreiben . . .', *Theater der Zeit*, no. 10, 1983, p. 55.
23. *Öffentlich arbeiten*, p. 160.
24. Ibid., p. 158.
25. 'Waldbruder Lenz', p. 142.

it of any claim to absolute significance. Knowledge of one's forefathers is a prerequisite of self-awareness.[26] This is precisely the message of *Horns Ende*. The call 'remember' ('Erinnere dich') runs through the book, linking the various episodes and characters. It is the call of one already dead (Horn) to one who has just reached his fortieth year (Thomas) and is therefore old enough to have witnessed history, but also young enough to be involved in shaping the future.

The book is set in a German provincial town by the name of 'Guldenberg' (clearly signifying its bourgeois capitalist origins). The period under discussion is twentieth-century German history, especially East German history of the 1950s. To those subjecting themselves to a process of recollection this period seems dark, confused and disturbing, ruled by intrigues, greed for power, hatred, an inability to love, sadness and desperation. The present (the early 1980s) is still overshadowed, almost numbed, by what happened thirty years earlier; the novel's protagonists have been left emotionally crippled, driven to seek refuge in religion, madness, isolation or even suicide. Hein's concept of 'Vergewaltigung' springs to mind, applied by him in conversation with respect to *Der fremde Freund* and his drama *Ah Q* written shortly afterwards: 'Da ist der Gegenspieler eine für die Figuren nicht mehr faßbare Zeit. Sie haben dann, weil sie mit einer für sie unfaßbaren Wirklichkeit nicht mehr hinkommen, einfach die ganz normale Erwartung an die andere Wirklichkeit.'[27] In *Horns Ende*, five characters, all victims of such individual or social 'Vergewaltigung', embark on an attempt to recapture and thereby defuse the past. In each instance, the process is sparked off by two catalytic events, unconnected in themselves and yet closely associated in everybody's mind: Horn's suicide and the final disappearance of the gypsies from Guldenberg Common.

The concepts of recollection and history themselves become objects of reflexion. However, not only does a consensus fail to emerge, each individual character also utters views that are in themselves inconsistent. Thus, Kruschkatz, the solitary and embittered mayor of Guldenberg, declares all history to be 'eine Fiktion', dreamt up 'um dem Verlust der Zeit einen Sinn zu geben', 'ein Korsett, das uns den aufrechten Gang erlaubt' (p. 24). Yet he also attributes to history an irrefutable logic of its own, which lends

---

26. See 'Anmerkungen zu *Cromwell*', *Schlötel oder Was solls*, p. 173; originally published as part for the programme of the play's première in Cottbus (1980).
27. 'Ansonsten würde man ja aufhören zu schreiben . . .', p. 56.

historical necessity to, for instance, the injustice done to Horn (p. 69) and which frees history's agent from any guilt.

Dr Spodeck, Kruschkatz's opponent, works on a history of the town, projected (in almost Thomas Bernhardian language) as 'eine Geschichte der menschlichen Gemeinheit' (p. 133). Although history seems to him nothing more than a collection of distorted subjective impressions, 'Spiegelungen von Spiegelungen' (p. 231), whose claim to truth needs to be regarded with considerable suspicion, he is quite prepared to exempt his own memories from such provisos.

Horn, having been exiled to Guldenberg in 1952, took on a post on the fringe of society as the director of the town's museum. Having learnt from bitter experience not to trust anyone, he values old objects as they are 'zu alt um noch zu lügen' (p. 66). They offer invaluable assistance in the vital process of reconstructing the past: 'Welch ein entsetzlicher Gedanke, ohne Gedächtnis leben zu wollen. Wir würden ohne Erfahrungen leben müssen, ohne Wissen und Werte. Löschen Sie das Gedächtnis eines Menschen, und Sie löschen die Menschheit' (p. 232). Yet he, too, has to concede that people's memories are subjective and hence deceptive.

In comparing the formal features of this book with those of the *Novelle* that preceded it, we are struck by a number of points of contact as well as by distinctive differences between them. Neither text introduces an omniscient or objective narrator, thus reflecting a requirement of the dramatic genre. But while *Der fremde Freund* represents the subjective account of only one character, *Horns Ende* comprises five different narrative perspectives. The result is an ensemble of subjective views never quite adding up to an objective picture of reality, a mosaic that is never quite complete. Hein's own poetic metaphor intended to capture this structural feature is that of the broken mirror: each of the mirror's pieces reflects one fragment of reality from one particular angle. Any attempt to make them come together in a coherent whole is bound to be futile. Yet it is vital for us to compare and try to match up the various individual world views as they contain the only truth we shall have at our disposal. The world of things as they really are is not our domain. Our world is the world of phenomena, and each subject experiences this world in a distinctive way and from a distinctive perspective. Hein himself had this to say about the narrative perspective in *Horns Ende*:

> Es war bei diesem Roman eine Besonderheit, daß ich versucht habe, ohne Eigenerzähler, ohne den Autor als Erzähler zuzulassen, sondern

mit fünf verschiedenen Erzählern zu arbeiten, die alle das gleiche Recht hatten . . . im Grunde war es der Versuch, einen Roman zu schreiben, wie man ein Puzzle bildet, aus lauter kleinen Teilen, einen Roman, der im Grunde aus Kurzgeschichten besteht . . . Was ich mir davon erhoffte, war, . . . daß sich ein sehr widersprüchliches Bild der kleinen Stadt ergibt, und daß wie bei einem Puzzle, wie bei einem Mosaik, ganz kleine freie Stellen leerstehen, in die der Leser seine Erfahrung einzubringen hat, um das Bild vollständig zu machen.[28]

Contradictions present a challenge, as they set free energies and the will to change the status quo – this is the ethos that informs Hein's work. In the case of *Horns Ende*, what matters is not the ultimate achievement of an accurate reconstruction of events, a definite answer to questions such as who committed an injustice against whom and why. What matters is the process of recollection, the laying bare of what has been busily buried over the years in terms of individual and social experience. The gains are greater openness and clarity of vision concerning past, present and future, and thus ultimately the creation of room for change as well as the incentive to bring it about.

If this is a correct view of the author's underlying intention in structuring his material, there is, I would argue, a significant difference between the two works of fiction in terms of the degree to which this intention is actually achieved. In the *Novelle*, Claudia embarks on a process of remembering, only to get so far and then break off and retreat into self-deception. The reader, however, is provided with the tools to see through this process and its shortcomings and is thus granted enlightenment and catharsis (which Claudia herself is denied). In *Horns Ende* a liberating experience is withheld – as it is in *Der fremde Freund* – from the characters themselves. However, this happens in spite of the fact that their efforts to remember are much more conscious and purposeful than Claudia's; indeed, in the case of Thomas, they are the result of Horn's urgent appeals from beyond the grave. But, more seriously still, even the reader fails to emerge with an enhanced sense of clarity and hope for change, since the contradictions do not add up to one final message to us who look at the scene with some detachment.

In other words, going through the painful process of recollection is not actually seen to be rewarding for anyone, not even the reader. Kruschkatz is left feeling nothing but nausea at his own words,

---

28. Barthélémy-Toraille, 'Entretien avec Christoph Hein', p. 18.

which, he fears, may 'wie Erbrochenes aus dem Munde fallen' (p. 260). Spodeck bids farewell to his dreams of a better and more honest existence and prepares himself to accept the remainder of his life unquestioningly and with indifference (p. 265): an attitude resembling Claudia's 'dickes Fell' as well as the resigned stance of Maske, the policeman in Hein's drama *Ah Q*. Horn's concluding words addressed to the doctor are, 'Das ist zum Kotzen' (p. 233). And Thomas sums up his own state of mind as follows: 'Alles ist widersprüchlich. Verschwommen und unfaßbar. Wie hinter einem Nebel' (p. 215). The girl Marlene never does break through the haze of confusion that serves to protect her mind from direct contact with reality. And Frau Fischlinger, the only one of the five characters to emerge strengthened from the process of remembering, does not so develop as a demonstrable result of the labour of recollection but rather owing to her innate strength of character and a gradual easing of outer constraints.

All this, I would maintain, adds up to an inherent contradiction between the Socratic-sounding appeal 'Erinnere dich' (after all, coming from Beyond) and the total absence of inner clarity on the part of those who followed it or, indeed, the reader. It is for this reason that for me *Horns Ende* ultimately remains a rather unsatisfactory work – a view with which, I suspect, the author himself might not disagree, given his own admission of structural difficulties in writing the book which led him to interrupt his work on it in order to work on *Der fremde Freund*.[29] There are other indications of a certain unease on the part of Hein regarding the structure of his novel: first, the sequence of narrative perspectives (short-story fashion) appears arbitrary; secondly, there is no evidence to indicate that Hein attempted to provide any of the narrators with a linguistic identity; thirdly, it is difficult to see, when the appeal 'Erinnere dich' is only addressed to Thomas, why the process of recalling past events should involve no fewer than five characters; finally, however aged Thomas may feel, it does seem confusing to hear him refer to himself as an 'old man' when his actual age is forty. Obviously, each of these queries can be explained away in a variety of ways. Yet, taken together, they do seem to point to an overall

---

29. Klaus Hammer ('Christoph Hein: *Horns Ende*', *Weimarer Beiträge*, vol. 33, no. 8, 1987, pp. 1358–69) offers a very thorough and (largely) persuasive analysis of the structural weaknesses of *Horns Ende*. This is, to my knowledge, the only focused attempt by an East German critic to come to terms with this work. Nor do West German critics seem to have moved beyond a discussion of main themes.

picture of an author lacking control over his material and the artistic process.[30]

IV

Although Christoph Hein is less concerned with educating his audience than Brecht and rather keener to enter into a dialogue with them, he accepts without hesitation his moral and social responsibilities as a writer – not in order to provide recipes for how to live and think, but rather to instigate reflexion which may ultimately contribute to social change: 'in einem bestimmten Sinn bin ich Moralist: nicht unbedingt auf Veränderungen gehend, aber vielleicht doch Überlegungen so stark provozierend, daß man nicht ohne weiteres an ihnen vorbeikommt'.[31] Hence his repeated call for 'Öffentlichkeit', but also his apparent ability to cope with the frustration of being denied this by retaining what he calls 'diese Gelassenheit' (a feature he much admired in Kleist and Hebel).[32] An example of his inimitable tongue-in-cheek responses when asked for his view on the state of the theatre in the GDR reveals something of this quality:

> Ich bin nicht hoffnungslos. Unsere Theater haben ein prächtiges, ungebrochenes Verhältnis zum Erbe. Wenn wir nur etwas Geduld und Seelenstärke aufbringen, so können wir zu meinem 25., 50. et cetera Todestag Inszenierungen der Stücke erleben . . . Das Verdienst der deutschen Schauspielhäuser an einer guten Prosa ist wiederholt gerühmt worden, und unsere Theater achten da auf Tradition . . . Tatsächlich bin ich recht zuversichtlich: Nach den großen Theaterphasen Anfang bis Mitte der 50er Jahre gab es einen Einbruch. Derzeit ist das Deutsche Theater wegen Baumaßnahmen geschlossen, die übrigen Berliner Sprechbühnen machen einen gleichfalls sehr geschlossenen Eindruck. So viel Stille und Trägheit kündigt erfahrungsgemäß einen neuen Aufschwung, eine Blütezeit des Theaters an.[33]

Similarly, while the incidence of suicide or at least of 'ein ver-

---

30. It is worth noting that Albert Camus, himself originally an actor and dramatist, encountered similar difficulties when working on a longer novel (whose title was to be *La Mort heureuse*), while feeling perfectly at ease with the structure of the shorter work *L'Étranger*. See Germaine Brée, *Albert Camus. Gestalt und Werk*, trans. into German by Guido G. Meister, Hamburg, 1960, pp. 64–7.
31. *Öffentlich arbeiten*, pp. 122f.
32. Ibid., p. 126.
33. Ibid., p. 127.

schleierter Selbstmord'[34] amongst Hein's protagonists is high, the author himself appears to be able to sustain an attitude of hope – hope that each defeat will be followed by a new beginning and that step by step reason will gain ground. He has little time for the 'unaufgeklärten Leser, der es sich in seiner selbstverschuldeten Unmündigkeit behaglich einrichtet und den Autor benötigt als Chorführer und Mentor, als Unterschlupf und Obdach'[35] and regards his writing as one way of combating this self-inflicted state of inner darkness and confusion, yet harbours no illusions as to the degree to which this might be possible: 'Das ist Hölderlins bleierne Zeit, die da auf uns lastet, aber das ist nur die eine Seite, und spannend wird es halt erst dort, wo wir den einigermaßen vorgefundenen Verhältnissen unser gleichfalls einigermaßen anderes Ich entgegensetzen und behaupten . . . Leben, obgleich es absurd ist, um Pascal zu paraphrasieren.'[36]

The very existence of *Der fremde Freund* and *Horns Ende* provides ample evidence of Hein's determination not to accept defeat and to continue to 'öffentlich arbeiten', even if this means writing fiction rather than drama. Artistically, as I have tried to show, the *Novelle* is the more successful work. In terms of moral appeal, both works demonstrate Hein's unconditional commitment to the cause of a more enlightened, a more humane, a more open society.

34. Ibid., p. 128.
35. *Die Zeit*, 4 December 1987, p. 59.
36. *Öffentlich arbeiten*, p. 124.

–7–

'Was da ist, das ist [nicht] mein': The Case of Peter Schneider

GORDON BURGESS

I Introduction

Emblazoned on the front cover of Peter Schneider's *Atempause* is the proud claim: 'Allerdings! ich reiße Zitate aus ihrem Zusammenhang', together with the rider: 'Aber das hindert mich nicht daran, recht zu haben'.[1] The subtitle of *Atempause* is 'Versuch, meine Gedanken über Literatur und Kunst zu ordnen', and the volume is just that, a collection of review articles and other essays on cultural or politico-cultural topics first published between 1965 and 1976. The quotation above in fact opens a piece from 1966 entitled 'Zerhackte Klaviere und andere Sachen. Eine Abrechnung mit Happening, Fluxus, Pop Art', in which Schneider expresses his irritation with the aesthetic shortcomings of much pop art: 'Von Anfang an war der revolutionäre Gestus eindrucksvoller als der revolutionäre Vollzug. Von Anfang an bestand ein Mißverhältnis zwischen dem, was diese Künste theoretisch kritisierten und forderten und dem, was sie selber anzubieten hatten' (p. 89).

In what follows, I shall suggest that Schneider's own literary practice has been akin to that of the pop artists he maligns, taking elements straight out of the 'real' world and inserting them into what purports to be a work of fiction. In this, he has been successful in every case except *Vati*, and I shall suggest, tentatively, reasons for his earlier success and latest failure.

II Schneider's Pre-1980 Work

Schneider's defiantly provocative remark about using quotations

---

1. Peter Schneider, *Atempause*, Reinbek, 1977. Page references in the text are to this edition.

out of context for his own purposes here refers, of course, to his essayistic work, as contained in this collection and in a further collection published in 1981 under the intriguing title *Die Botschaft des Pferdekopfs und andere Essais aus einem friedlichen Jahrzehnt*. The size of these two volumes, incidentally – the former is 235 pages long and the latter 252 – contrasts with the slimness of even his more substantial literary works (*Lenz*, 90 pages, *Der Mauerspringer*, 118 pages in the paperback edition, and *Vati*, just 82 pages of generously large print), and is an indication of Schneider's prolificness and interest in the journalistic and essayistic field. In looking at *Der Mauerspringer* and *Vati*, we will do well to bear in mind Schneider's work as a pamphleteer and journalist. It was on this that he cut his publishing teeth and it is an activity which he continues into the present. Schneider the feuilletonist and Schneider the literary creator are not two separate entities. On the contrary, his work as a creative writer has suffered, it would seem, detrimentally from his activities as pamphleteer and journalist, in that in *Vati* he has failed to distinguish between the two fields of activity and the different types of text which they produce (or should produce). This is blatantly highlighted in his use of material 'borrowed' ('plagiarized' would be a more accurate if more emotive term) for this work, with its pretensions to being 'literature', from the journalism of *Bunte*.

Writers, of course, borrow from the world around them and from each other, in the widest sense, all the time, ranging from the *mot juste*, clichéd or choice turn of phrase, to reworking the themes and topics of whole works. Peter O. Chotjewitz puts this succinctly in an article entitled 'Geistiger Diebstahl oder schöpferischer Dialog?':

> Für den Autor ist die Welt eine Art Steinbruch, dem er nicht nur seine Stoffe, Situationen, Episoden und Figuren entnimmt, sondern eben auch Schlagworte, Idiome, Redeweisen, verbale Stereotypen, bekannte Textstellen und typische Wortfolgen. Schreiben ist immer auch Aneignung von Welt und fremdem Gut. Der Dichter ist sozusagen eine Art Raubfisch und Aasfresser im Tümpel der sozialen Wirklichkeit, zu der halt auch Texturen aller Art gehören.[2]

But Schneider, it seems, has made it a particular virtue (or vice!) of his own. Increasingly, he has been content to take other people's material of a literary and, especially, a non-literary nature and

---

2. Peter O. Chotjewitz, 'Geistiger Diebstahl oder schöpferischer Dialog?', *feder*, no. 9, 1987, pp. 29–32; here p. 32.

refashion this into a text that purports to be creative and imaginative (as opposed to journalistic or factual) in nature. An early sustained example of this was . . . *schon bist du ein Verfassungsfeind* (1975), which portrays what happens to Kleff, a teacher, being investigated under the terms of the *Radikalenerlaß* of 1972. Apart from the last paragraph, the work is written in the first-person singular, from the point of view of Kleff himself, as a series of letters to his solicitor, detailing his (Kleff's) reactions to the proceedings to which he is being subjected and other related events. The apparent subjectivity of Kleff's account, however, is tempered by the insertion, throughout the text, of authentic material (distinguished as such by being printed in italics) and a preliminary statement indicating Schneider's technique in writing the account: 'Die Geschichte, die hier erzählt wird, setzt sich aus mehreren authentischen Fällen zusammen. Ort, Zeit und Personen der Geschichte stimmen insofern mit ihren wirklichen Vorbildern überein.'[3] The 'insofern' in that statement is indicative: . . . *schon bist du ein Verfassungsfeind* is both authentic and exemplary, both documentary and imagined. Schneider's success in transforming authentic material into a work that can stand judgement on aesthetic grounds is clearly seen if Kleff's 'Gedächtnisprotokoll' of his interview with the authorities (pp. 40–2) is compared with Schneider's own, authentic 'Gedächtnisprotokoll' of his interview with the authorities on 19 November 1973.[4] Kleff edits his account, giving his solicitor only what he considers to be the decisive passages – 'die entscheidenden Passagen'. The account runs together as one coherent text, presenting a question and answer session which progresses with smooth logic from one point to the next. An authorial force is clearly at work here, selecting and shaping the material. In Schneider's 'authentic' account, on the other hand, the questioner pursues a number of paths. It is not always clear where the questioning is leading, and there are abrupt and apparently arbitrary changes of topic instigated by the questioner, as in the following exchange:

FRAGE: Sind Ihre Erfahrungen in Ihre theoretische Arbeit eingeflossen?
ANTWORT: Ich habe einen Artikel über Erfahrungen geschrieben . . .
FRAGE: Können Sie uns erklären, was ein Kader ist? Welche Aufgabe hat ein Kader gegenüber den Massen? (p. 153)

3. Peter Schneider, . . . *schon bist du ein Verfassungsfeind*, Berlin, 1975, p. 4.
4. Peter Schneider, 'Das Ohr des Staates', in Peter Schneider, *Die Botschaft des Pferdekopfs und andere Essais aus einem friedlichen Jahrzehnt*, Darmstadt, 1981, pp. 146–57.

If, in . . . *schon bist du ein Verfassungsfeind*, Schneider is successfully reworking authentic material into a literary artefact, two years earlier he had reworked material of both a non-literary and a literary nature, in the form of Georg Büchner's *Lenz*, into his own enormously successful work of the same title, based in part on his own and others' experiences in the student movement of the late 1960s. These publishing successes were to lead (or mislead) Schneider into employing similar techniques in the case of *Der Mauerspringer* (1982) and *Vati* (1987). Each of these works of the 1980s represents an attempt to come to terms, through the medium of literature, with an enduring aspect of modern, specifically German, society: that of a divided Germany (and particularly a divided Berlin) in *Der Mauerspringer*, and that of a continuing guilt for the war crimes of the Nazi past in *Vati*. I shall argue that *Der Mauerspringer* succeeds as literature for the very reason that *Vati* fails, and that this reason is to be found in the way Schneider has used his borrowings from the authentic, journalistic and other sources at his disposal.

III *Der Mauerspringer*

Let us consider *Der Mauerspringer* first. This 'vielbeachtetes Konglomerat aus Fiktionen und Fakten' as *Der Spiegel* called it,[5] told in the first-person by an unnamed narrator (but widely believed in the reviews to be Schneider himself),[6] is concerned to highlight the contrasts between the two societies on either side of the Berlin Wall, and the ways in which each of these social systems has shaped the outlook of its members. The narrator, who grew up in West Germany and has been living in West Berlin for twenty years, repeatedly comes into contact with others who have grown up in East Germany and either are still living there or have moved to West Berlin. There is much in the *Erzählung* that roots it firmly in the real world. References dotted throughout the text, most obviously to the thirtieth-anniversary celebrations in both East and West, date the action as set in 1979–80. There are allusions to Wolf

---

5. Hans-Joachim Noak, '"Hallo, mal wieder drüben gewesen?"', *Der Spiegel*, 11 August 1986, pp. 47–55; here p. 50.
6. See, for example, Günter Gaus, 'Die Mauer nicht als Brett vorm Kopf', *Konkret*, March 1982; Ulrich Greiner, 'Berlin, der übliche Wahnwitz', *Die Zeit*, 30 April 1982; Salman Rushdie, 'Tales of Two Berlins', *New York Times Book Review*, 22 January 1984 ('It purports to be an account by a West Berlin writer, an anonymous "I" whom it is impossible not to identify with Peter Schneider').

Biermann, Rudolf Bahro, Thomas Brasch and others; and a series of news broadcasts and other television programmes augments this backdrop of reality – the Soviet intervention in Afghanistan, *Solidarity* in Poland, for example – as well as gives the narrator and his acquaintances the opportunity to interpret the events, and the media coverage of them, each in his own way. And a number of passages, encyclopaedic in style and tone, give detailed information about the Wall itself: length, fortifications, number of watchtowers, and so on. Given the subject-matter of the work, none of this is, perhaps, remarkable in itself. What does distinguish *Der Mauerspringer*, it seems to me, is the overridingly imaginative use which Schneider has made of his material.

There is (despite the title) no single 'Wall jumper' (as the Anglo-American version translates it) in the work. At the onset of the narrative, the narrator tells us that he would like to find someone who can 'jump' the barrier of the Wall, someone who has become a 'Grenzgänger zwischen beiden deutschen Staaten'.[7] In so doing, this someone will lose the identity imposed upon him by one or other of the two German states and ultimately be at home in neither: 'Mißtrauisch geworden gegen die hastig ergriffene Identität, die ihm die beiden deutschen Staaten anbieten, findet er seinen Ort nur noch auf der Grenze' (p. 21). We never encounter this 'Grenzgänger'. Instead, the narrator is told on four separate occasions of four instances of people crossing the Wall by unorthodox methods and unorthodox routes. They are presented in the form of interpolated stories, 'Geschichten', and it is left to the narrator, and the reader, to decide what degree of credence to accord to each. Certainly, it is suggested in each case that the reported, so-called facts of the matter are unreliable or may have been subjected to post-hoc embellishment:

Andere Berichte wissen von einem VW-Transporter, dessen Dach Kabe als Sprungbrett benutzt haben soll. Wahrscheinlicher ist, daß . . . (p. 28)

Wie Lutz und die beiden Willy tatsächlich ihren Hin- und Rückweg sicherten, ist im Gestrüpp der mündlichen Überlieferung untergegangen . . . (p. 46)

An diesem Punkt beginnt sich die Geschichte im Nebel beschränkter Aussage-Genehmigungen, widersprüchlicher Angaben der Freunde, vor allem aber in Bolles Erinnerung zu verwirren . . . (p. 71)

7. Peter Schneider, *Der Mauerspringer*, Darmstadt, 1982, p. 21. Page references in the text are to this edition.

Wieviel Mühe Gartenschlägers Begleiter tatsächlich darauf verwandten, ihn vom Gang zum Zaun zurückzuhalten, bleibt allerdings fraglich . . . (p. 97)

The seeming reality in each case is firmly fictionalized, an ironic doubt is cast on the exploits of the various figures. The rug is pulled even more decisively from under the claim of each of these figures to be the definitive Wall jumper when, after the last one has been recounted to the narrator, it is suggested that such a figure does not exist except, perhaps, in the narrator's imagination. It is an ideal to which the imperfect reality of a world governed by political rift and division cannot attain: 'In jeder Geschichte fehlt etwas, das eine andere hat, an der ich wieder etwas aus der vorangegangenen vermisse. Vielleicht gibt es die Geschichte gar nicht, die ich suche' (p. 93).

Narrative within narrative, related by one figure to another as unreliable hearsay about a figure who perhaps does not even exist: such is the stuff of fiction rather than documentary; thus it may come as all the more of a surprise that at the heart of Schneider's tale lies authenticity. He is reported as having stated that the book is based on 'authentische Fälle, die [Schneider] als Zeitungsschnipsel gesammelt hat, und meist längst vergessen sind'.[8] One of these 'authentic cases' is documented in *Der Spiegel* of 11 August 1986, that of Rainer-Sturmo Wulf. In *Der Mauerspringer*, this real-life figure is atomized into several characters within the narrative fiction. He shares the characteristics of Bolle, who is said to have wanted 'auf eigene Faust Krieg gegen die DDR führen' (p. 70); of Kabe, who is considered to be mentally ill and is treated in a psychiatric clinic; and of 'die drei Kinogänger', who jump in both directions over the Wall.

For the 'Wall story' of 'die drei Kinogänger', however, Schneider had another literary precedent, apart from any newspaper clippings he may have utilized: Stefan Heym's short story entitled 'Mein Richard'.[9] Whilst there is no direct evidence that Schneider borrowed from 'Mein Richard', circumstantial evidence in the form of his use of Büchner's *Lenz* earlier, as well as marked parallels between the two texts, would strongly suggest that he did, even though it should be pointed out that Heym's tale is itself based on a

---

8. Wolfgang Nagel, 'Der Mauerschreiber', *Stern*, 1 April 1982.
9. Stefan Heym, *Die richtige Einstellung und andere Erzählungen*, Frankfurt/Main, 1976, pp. 121–36. I am grateful to Dr Malcolm Pender for bibliographical information on 'Mein Richard'.

true set of events.[10] In the light of Schneider's authorial procedure in *Vati*, it is instructive to examine the parallels between 'Mein Richard' and *Der Mauerspringer* in some detail. 'Mein Richard' concerns the investigation and trial of two adolescents, both called Richard, in East Berlin for having crossed the Wall illegally in order to watch films in the West. Having no 'Westgeld', they are allowed into the cinema free of charge. They are convicted 'wegen wiederholter Verletzung des Paßgesetzes' (p. 130). The episode in *Der Mauerspringer* concerns three adolescents living in East Berlin who make repeated trips illegally across the Wall in order to watch Westerns (!). Having no 'Westgeld', they are allowed into the cinema free. One finally stays in the West, but the two called 'Willy' are tried and convicted in East Berlin 'wegen Verletzung des Paßgesetzes' (p. 47). Both Richards and both Willys are arrested in school, but only after the attention of the East German authorities has been alerted by a report in a West Berlin newspaper about the boys' activities. The two Richards pass over the Wall fourteen times, the two Willys cross it twelve times. In both cases, the defending counsel suggests that the young offenders have, above all, proved their loyalty to the GDR by returning there so often, but both convictions lead to the same sentence:

... und daß die Erfahrung unsern Söhnen nur nützen könne, ob in Armee oder Jugendwerkhof. ('Mein Richard', p. 136)

Der ältere Willy wurde ... in die Armee gesteckt, der jüngere in einen Jugendwerkhof geschickt. (*Der Mauerspringer*, p. 47)

Several other parallels exist between the two accounts: the position of the house in which the youths grow up, just on the border, and the sharp angle drawn by the Wall as it passes the house; both houses are now deserted and due to be pulled down; both sets of parents are in both cases at least outwardly committed Party members and supporters of the state; and neither the two Richards nor the two Willys have had any intention of remaining in the West.

Despite the apparently close modelling of the episode in *Der Mauerspringer* on its earlier literary counterpart as regards details of 'fact', there are important differences in the way the two stories are told. Schneider's narration is more taut than Heym's: Schneider cuts out all detail extraneous to the central theme of the interpolated

---

10. See Günter Zehm, 'Vom Leiden betroffen', *Die Welt*, 29 May 1982.

story of crossing the Wall illegally in both directions. This episode is in tune with the other interpolated stories in the book. It is introduced with the same phrase as are all the others: 'Kennst du die Geschichte von . . .?' And it is linked to them not only by virtue of its content but also through an overall homogeneity of tone and style. Whilst we may find the extent of the parallels between this episode and Heym's story interesting, perhaps even disturbing, the result, within the confines of *Der Mauerspringer*, is not jarring. This is not the case, on the other hand, with *Vati*.

IV *Vati*

The publication of *Vati* in March–April 1987 was greeted with widespread interest in the West German press, not least because a pre-publication review in *Der Spiegel* had revealed the extent of Schneider's borrowings in the work from a series of *Bunte* articles from 1985 on the subject of Josef Mengele, the 'Angel of Death' who performed experiments on twins and other concentration camp inmates, as told by his son, Rolf, to Inge Byhan. Indeed, as a result of the *Spiegel* article, the *Bunte* took out a temporary injunction prohibiting the distribution of the book, causing its publication to be delayed for some three weeks. The article begins by asking, 'Ist Peter Schneiders Erzählung "Vati" ein schlichtes Illustrierten-Plagiat?'[11] and then suggests that the answer is 'Yes', citing a number of the lengthier and more blatant examples of Schneider's borrowings. Various critics took up the cudgels for or against Schneider. He also defended himself in a public discussion in Berlin on 9 April and elsewhere.[12] The main thrust of the argument caused by the *Spiegel* article is whether Schneider was justified in borrowing to the extent he did without acknowledging his source(s). The name Mengele, for example, never appears in *Vati*: there is only a coquettish allusion to the effect its three syllables have on those who speak or hear it: 'dieses Zögern, dieses Senken der Stimme vor den drei Silben, ganz so, als sei der gut schwäbische Name ganz unaussprechbar'.[13] Schneider himself stated that he had suggested acknowledging the *Bunte* articles in a

---

11. Gerda-Marie Schönfeld, 'So eine Nachbarschaft', *Der Spiegel*, 9 March 1987, pp. 216–19; here p. 216. I am grateful to Frau Schönfeld for supplying me with copies of newspaper material referring to Schneider's works.
12. See for example, *Frankfurter Rundschau*, 18 March 1987.
13. Peter Schneider, *Vati*, Darmstadt, 1987, p. 13. See *Bunte*, no. 28, 1985, p. 29: 'den Namen, bei dessen Nennung jeder zusammenzuckt'.

prefatory note to the book, but that Luchterhand, the publishers, had considered this unnecessary. It may just have been Schneider's bad luck, of course, to have been found out with *Vati* so soon (even before publication!) by a sharp-eyed journalist, but such is the extent of his extractions from the *Bunte* articles that he cannot seriously have expected not to be found out before long. A detailed comparison suggests that almost one tenth of *Vati* is either directly lifted from, or closely modelled on, the *Bunte* articles.

The extent of Schneider's borrowing from his source(s) may have been the concern of the lawyers; it is the quality of what he produces that is the concern of the literary critic. And what remained uncontended among the critics is that *Vati* is a very bad book. 'Gründlicher konnte die Erzählung kaum mißraten', wrote Uwe Wittstock in the *Frankfurter Allgemeine Zeitung*; Gabriele Kreis, in *Konkret*, characterized *Vati* as 'ein heillos schlechtes Buch. Schlecht recherchiert, schlecht konzipiert, schlecht geschrieben';[14] and Wolfgang Nagel wrote in *Die Zeit*: 'Interessant allein ist die Frage, was die Erzählung über die bekannten Fakten hinaus leistet. Die Antwort ist enttäuschend: nichts.'[15] As Goethe is reported to have said to Eckermann on the subject of Byron's alleged plagiarisms: 'Was da ist, das ist mein! hätte er sagen sollen, und ob ich es aus dem Leben oder aus dem Buche genommen, das ist gleichviel, es kam bloß darauf an, daß ich es recht gebrauchte!'[16] In the case of his *Lenz*, of . . . *schon bist du ein Verfassungsfeind*, and of *Der Mauerspringer*, Schneider did succeed in transforming his source material and in making it something of his own.[17] Why not then with *Vati*? Is it simply that his source material here was not as good as before, as one critic scurrilously put it, 'Und daß *Lenz* besser geschrieben ist als *Vati*, liegt daran, daß Georg Büchner einfach besser geschrieben hat als die *Bunte*'?[18]

The question is not as condescending as may at first appear, although it is not so much a question of relative quality as of differing aims. The point is not whether the *Bunte* articles were better or worse written than Büchner's *Lenz*, but that they were written for a different purpose: they seek to sensationalize but also

14. Gabriele Kreis, 'Ach Vati, deine Substantive', *Konkret*, no. 6, 1987, pp. 66f.
15. Wolfgang Nagel, 'Zu Besuch bei einem Ungeheuer', *Die Zeit*, 17 April 1987.
16. J. P. Eckermann, *Gespräche mit Goethe in den letzten Jahren seines Lebens*, Tempel Klassiker, n.d., p. 144 (18 January 1825).
17. For an opposing view, that *Der Mauerspringer* is not successful as a literary text, see Peter Buchka, 'Unser gemiedenes Thema', *Süddeutsche Zeitung*, 1 April 1982.
18. Gerda-Marie Schönfeld, 'Schneiders bunte Anleihen', *Deutsches Allgemeines Sonntagsblatt*, 22 March 1987.

to inform; indeed, it lies at the heart of their very nature that they inform through sensationalizing. The first article in the series, for example, occupies a total of approximately seven columns of actual text, but runs to twenty pages of the magazine. It is heralded by the title 'So entkam mein Vater' in two-inch high letters over a double spread, and is preceded and accompanied by photographs not only of Mengele himself both as an SS officer and later in exile, but also, among others, of naked concentration camp inmates, naked corpses being dragged along the ground and piled high, and crippled survivors of Auschwitz. The sub-title, next to a logo reading '*Bunte* Exclusiv', and occupying half a page, runs:

> Josef Mengele. Auf seinen Kopf waren Millionen ausgesetzt. Tausende haben ihn gejagt. Und doch wurde er nie gefunden. 40 Jahre lang. Wie war das möglich? Wo hielt er sich verborgen? Wer hat ihm geholfen? Es gibt einen Mann, der sagt, daß er alles weiß: Rolf Mengele, der einzige Sohn. Er berichtet.[19]

The series is skilfully packaged: it arrests the eye and assaults the senses; as such, it is good journalism. But what Schneider totally fails to realize in his reworking of this source material is that what makes for good journalism may also make for bad literature. Interestingly enough, some of the weakest passages in *Vati* are precisely those which make most impact on the reader of the *Bunte* articles. The father's reaction to meeting his son in South America is a case in point. The *Bunte* passage reads: 'Rolf Mengele sucht nach Worten. Er spricht von Überraschung, Erschrecken, verbessert sich dann und sagt: "Das erste, was ich empfand, war ein Gefühl der Fremdheit. Aber dann sah ich, wie mein Vater vor Aufregung zitterte. Ich sah, daß er Tränen in den Augen hatte"'.[20] This passage is placed next to a photograph of twin survivors of Auschwitz in wheelchairs, 'Zwei Opfer von Josef Mengele', and above a text entitled 'So entstanden die Vernichtungslager'. Thus we understand who Mengele is and what he was, and we are aware of the terrible crimes he committed: we have two of his victims in front of us. All this serves to heighten the stark contrast between his former brutality and his present sensitivity, indeed oversensitivity, at the sight of his son. Schneider's presentation of the same incident in *Vati*, on the other hand, is much vaguer, woollier, flaccid in tone and style. At this point (it is only one-and-a-half

---

19. *Bunte*, no. 26, 1985, p. 17.
20. Ibid., p. 33.

pages into the story), the reader does not know who the narrator is or who his father is or what he has been in the past; indeed, the narrator is unsure whether the man standing before him is even, in fact, his father: 'Ich identifizierte ihn als den Mann, von dem man gesagt hatte, daß er mein Vater sei, ich erkannte ihn nicht. Die Fotos ähnelten meinem Vater mehr als der Unbekannte, der vor mir stand. Dann sah ich, daß der Mann in der Windjacke plötzlich zu zittern begann, es waren Tränen in seinen Augen' (p. 6). In the *Bunte* article, the pathos of the father's tears made a telling point, contrasting with his earlier inhumanity; in *Vati*, this point has been lost. There has been no preparation of the reader for such a reaction from this as yet only vaguely identified figure, and the reaction itself seems as pathetic and ridiculous as the 'lächerliches Detail' of the untarred road to which the narrator then immediately draws the reader's attention.

Elsewhere, too, Schneider destroys or weakens the point of what he has culled from *Bunte*. Two examples out of many, each very different in its own way, may suffice to illustrate the point. The last article in the *Bunte* series quotes from a number of Josef Mengele's letters, including the following: 'Über staatliche Beihilfen soll der "Erbwert" entscheiden. Unter Punkt 11 heißt es: "Abkehr von frauenrechtlerischen Ideologien hinsichtlich der unbiologischen Forderung von der Gleichberechtigung der Frau." Punkt 12: "Einschränkung der Frauenarbeit in den gehobenen Berufen bzw. Abhängigmachen von der Erfüllung des biolog. Solls."'[21] The style is sparse, the contents make all the more impact on the reader. It is a written style, in which nominalization is predominant and it has the concentrated quality of distilled thought. The content, moreover, is clearly intended to be a commentary on contemporary society in general and to have universal applicability (i.e. also to *Bunte* readers), and the context makes it clear that it was originally written to an intended recipient of like philosophical–political persuasion. All this is undermined by Schneider's presentation. In *Vati*, we are asked to believe that this forms part of a late-night conversation between father and son. The words are shouted out in an angry and emotional outburst – 'einen Wutausbruch' – in which the speaker may or may not have been 100 per cent accountable for what he is saying. The concentrated quality of the source is diffused and weakened by a disconnected and arbitrary reference to a defective water pump. And the universal applicability of the source material is reduced to a commentary on a single divorce case:

21. Ibid., no. 30, p. 114.

> Er wollte staatliche Beihilfen für Studierende an einen jeweils zu ermittelnden 'Erbwert' gebunden sehen, sprach dann ganz unvermittelt von der Wasserpumpe hinter dem Haus, die repariert werden müsse. Ich antwortete, daß ich von Wasserpumpen nichts verstehe. Mein Bericht über eine Scheidungsklage, bei der ich diese Frau vertrat, löste einen Wutausbruch aus. Er wetterte gegen 'frauenrechtliche Ideologien', verurteilte die 'unbiologische Forderung nach der Gleichstellung der Frau': 'Einschränkung der Frauenarbeit in den gehobenen Berufen und Abhängigmachung von der Erfüllung des biologischen Solls.' (pp. 52f)

In its new context, the utterance loses all credibility, and any force it may still have is further reduced by the bathos of the inadequacy of the narrator's reaction: '"Ach Vati, deine Substantive!" – mehr ist mir in meiner Erschöpfung nicht eingefallen' (p. 53).

The second example concerns Mengele's grave, visited by Rolf Mengele in December 1979. The *Bunte* article presents the visit in a matter-of-fact manner, quite straightforwardly:

> Es lag ein gelber Strauß auf dem verwelkten Grab, und der Sohn versuchte zu ergründen, was er empfand. Trauer? 'Nein', sagt er, 'ich hab ihn ja kaum erkannt. Ich bin eine halbe Stunde dagestanden und hab' über ihn nachgedacht. Aber alles, was mir eingefallen ist, war: Da liegt der Mann, der immer mit großen, blonden, blauäugigen Menschen zusammen sein wollte, neben einem Japaner. Und ich dachte, ob ihm das gefallen würde . . .' Dann sind sie zurückgefahren in die Wohnung der Bosserts.[22]

The position and presentation of this episode in *Bunte* is such that it does not draw the reader's attention: it comes after an account of Rolf Mengele's second journey to São Paulo and is followed by excerpts from Josef Mengele's diaries. As such, it is to be accorded no particular significance by the reader. In *Vati*, by contrast, it gains the import of a symbolic statement. The words themselves are very nearly the same as in *Bunte*:

> Ein welker Blumenstrauß lag auf dem verwilderten Grab, ein falscher Name war in den Grabstein gemeißelt. Lange habe ich dort gestanden und über meinen Vater nachgedacht. Aber das einzige, was mir eingefallen ist, war: da liegt nun der Mann, der immer mit großen, blonden, blauäugigen Menschen zusammensein wollte, neben einem Japaner. Und ich habe mich gefragt, ob dem Mann so eine Nachbarschaft gefallen würde. (p. 82)

22. Ibid., no. 28, p. 29.

But they are the last words of the book: the reader's attention is not diverted by what the narrator did subsequently, as in *Bunte*. Instead, we are left to ponder on the discrepancy between the 'ideals' held by this ex-Nazi in life and the reality of his grave. But what works on a restrained, factual level in the journalistic account does not work on the literary, symbolic level in *Vati*: the point is too crass, too trivial, too blatant. The image has not been prepared for in any way (there has been no earlier reference to a Japanese, for example): it jars, is out of place. Journalism works through an appropriate presentation of facts, true or alleged. Literature, on the other hand, works through patterns, parallels and contrasts, structures and symbols. It is a distinction which, here as elsewhere in *Vati*, Schneider has failed to observe. There is only the feeblest of attempts at aesthetic transmutation. The result is, again, that good journalism has become bad literature.

If, in the words of one recent introduction to literary theory, 'literature transforms and intensifies ordinary language, deviates systematically from everyday speech',[23] then *Vati*, which tries and fails to do this, also fails to be literature. But, in a parallel process, ordinary events and individuals are transformed in literature, by the process of creative writing, into something out of the ordinary. *Vati* does the opposite: it takes an extra-ordinary real-life person and diminishes him into a fairly colourless, almost innocuous figure. The imagination of the author has capitulated in the face of the horrendous subject-matter. This is evident, for example, in the narrator's reaction to his father's 'Wutausbruch' quoted earlier, or in the lame statement: 'Dies muß hier genügen: ich habe in jener Nacht . . . meinem Vater Fragen gestellt, die niemals zuvor ein Sohn seinem Vater zu stellen gezwungen war' (pp. 34f). What these questions are, we never learn.

V Conclusion

A more detailed comparison than we have room for here between the *Bunte* texts and *Vati* would show just how much Schneider 'borrowed' from his undisputed source and why these borrowings do not work as literature. Indeed, some of the lapses of style and taste in the work, it may be argued, are explicable only by reference to the source material. The figures, the narrative, the language of the work all remain unconvincing because Schneider has been

---

23. Terry Eagleton, *Literary Theory. An Introduction*, Oxford, 1983, p. 2.

unable to transmute crass reality into a work of art. At one point, the book seems to comment on itself: 'jedes Detail war schon immer falsch, jedes Bild ein Klischee: . . . eine Kinospekulation von Anfang an, die zuallererst ihren Erfinder denunziert' (p. 65). Yet in all his substantial literary works, Schneider has employed fundamentally the same compositional technique: using authentic material in the creation of an imaginative work of art. It is a technique which he, consciously or unconsciously, assimilated from the heady days of pop art in the 1960s, and one which served him well before *Vati*. Why, then, should it have failed him in this case? Why should *Vati* be as aesthetically wanting as the works of pop art with which Schneider took issue in 1966? There are two main reasons, I would suggest, both of which are to be sought outside the text itself. The first lies in the very nature of literature, which is essentially a product of the imagination and claims to be a fictional retelling of reality. *Vati* endeavours to deal imaginatively with the unimaginable, and fictionalizes dreadful fact. In so doing, it is not equal to the subject-matter and as a result trivializes it. As Wolfgang Nagel suggests in *Die Zeit*: 'Vielleicht liegt es auch an der Monströsität des Themas: daß einem Autor die Phantasie und die Mittel versagen.'[24] The second, allied to the first, concerns Schneider himself. *Lenz, . . . schon bist du ein Verfassungsfeind*, and *Der Mauerspringer* all deal with themes which Schneider had himself experienced; indeed, they all represent to a greater or lesser degree his coming to terms with problems of his own life: the failure of the student movement, the consequences of the *Radikalenerlaß* and the problem of being a writer in a divided Berlin, a divided Germany. It is, perhaps, after all in this unfashionable approach of interpreting literature through the biography of the author that the key to Schneider's success and failure as a writer in the 1980s is to be found.

VI Postscript to a Scandal

After the above essay had been completed, I received a copy of Peter Schneider's latest essay collection, *Deutsche Ängste*.[25] With one exception, all the pieces included have appeared before: the one exception is the last, and the longest, entitled 'Vom richtigen

---

24. Nagel, 'Zu Besuch bei einem Ungeheuer'.
25. Peter Schneider, *Deutsche Ängste. Sieben Essays*, Darmstadt, 1988. Page references are given in the text.

Umgang mit dem Bösen', in which, as the book's blurb claims, Schneider '[sich] zum ersten Mal äußert . . . schwarz auf weiß zu dem Skandal, den seine Erzählung *Vati* ausgelöst hat'.[26] It is not my purpose here to review this essay, far less the collection as a whole, but rather to comment on certain aspects which touch on points raised above.

The essay is primarily an attempt by Schneider to defend his practice of literary montage in general and in *Vati* in particular. His defence has two main arguments: first, he has always done this and no-one has objected before; second, other writers before him have set a respectable precedent in this area of creative borrowing. In addition, however, he seeks to discredit the *Spiegel* article and its author (by referring to other articles and the possible 'politische Leidenschaften' of its 'freie Mitarbeiter', p. 113) and to suggest that his book had been attacked on political rather than purely aesthetic grounds.

Schneider admits to being 'erstaunt, daß mein Gewohnheitsverbrechen erst jetzt und bei dieser Gelegenheit aufgedeckt wurde' (p. 99): he had copied 'satzweise' from Büchner's *Lenz*, had utilized 'Senatsbehörden, Richterurteile, Fallsammlungen als Ghostwriter' in . . . *schon bist du ein Verfassungsfeind*, and: 'Im "Mauerspringer" gibt es kaum eine Seite, die nicht auf ein gestörtes Verhältnis zum Urheberrecht verweist' (ibid.). And, accusing the 'Literatur-Detektivin des *Spiegel*' of having 'nur halbe Arbeit geleistet',[27] he promptly adduces two further sources from which he borrowed material for *Vati* apart from *Bunte*. In the case of *Bunte*, he states, a total of no more than fifty lines were 'in wörtlicher oder abgewandelter Form der *Bunten Illustrierten* entnommen' (p. 102). (This figure is at variance with my own findings of approximately 175 lines which displayed a close resemblance to their *Bunte* source.) In any case, Schneider maintains, he is only following in the footsteps of other, respectable and respected, writers: Shakespeare, Lessing, Molière, Goethe, Heine, Thomas Mann (pp. 107f). And he (mis-)quotes Goethe's statement to Eckermann cited earlier, adding to it assertions by Molière and Heine in similar vein: '"Je prends mon bien, où je le trouve"'; 'der Dichter darf überall zugreifen, wo er Material zu seinen Werken findet, . . . wenn nur der Tempel herrlich ist, den er damit stützt' (pp. 107f).

---

26. 'Vom richtigen Umgang mit dem Bösen', *Deutsche Ängste*, pp. 82–121.
27. Ibid. Schneider avoids mentioning Gerda-Marie Schönfeld by name in this essay: she is always the '*Spiegel-Detektivin*' (pp. 100, 109), 'Literatur-Detektivin' (p. 101), or, most neutrally, 'die Rezensentin' (p. 99).

It is this last point, that it is the *quality* of what the writer creates out of his borrowings, which Schneider largely overlooks in the course of his argument in the essay, and which is the stumbling-block with *Vati*, since, as even he is forced to admit towards the end: 'Das literarische Urteil fiel meist verheerend aus' (p. 114) – possibly (although Schneider himself does not make this connection) because of the impossible task he set himself with the narrator of the work: 'Zu erzählen blieb die Geschichte eines Sohnes, der seiner Geschichte nicht gewachsen war' (p. 98). Instead, he attacks the 'Ramboismus des *Spiegel-Feuilletons*' (p. 113), which, in his view, replaces 'Literaturkritik' with 'die Literaturstory': 'sie muß Klatsch anregen . . . sie muß grell sein, aggressiv, Streit anregen. Sie kennt nur den satten Superlativ oder den satten Verriß' (pp. 111f). And this is allied to a shift of focus from the literary artefact to the person of the writer, a 'Jagdtrend' (p. 111) which 'das Interesse am Produkt durch das am Autor ersetzt' (p. 112). It is this of which Schneider feels he has been a victim, since, as he has already noted in another context: 'Mit einer Erwiderung zeigt er nur, daß er sich getroffen fühlt' (p. 83). This sense of injustice on a personal level runs throughout the essay, and colours both the tone and the substance of what he has to say, with such phrases as 'so mancher Ritter der Kritik' (p. 83), 'die unheilbare Eifersucht des Journalisten auf den Schriftsteller' (pp. 109f), 'Bedürfnis nach Schadenfreude' (p. 112). If anything, the personal involvement which comes to the fore in Schneider's remarks undermines the force of his arguments.

Towards the beginning of 'Vom richtigen Umgang mit dem Bösen', Schneider refers to the widespread view, 'der Schriftsteller dürfe sich mit seinen Kritikern nicht durch Erwiderung gemein machen' (p. 82); it might perhaps have been in his interest to have taken his own advice. Excellent as an exercise in rhetoric though it may be, Schneider's essay serves only to underpin the points made in the above paper, and does nothing to put him, his literary practice, or *Vati* in a better light.

–8–

Peter Handke's *Der Chinese des Schmerzes*: The Threshold as a Place of Waiting

PETER PÜTZ

In his *Der Chinese des Schmerzes*,[1] Handke is seeking to make a new beginning in his narrative work by bringing elements of epic irony more clearly into play than in his previous writing – as, for example, in the characterization of a young politician or in the exotic tourists who, having arrived at the outskirts of the town, hold their cameras in their hands, no longer sure what to do with them. In contradistinction to *Die Angst des Tormanns beim Elfmeter* and *Die Stunde der wahren Empfindung*, where the decisive action-dream occurs at the beginning, so that everything that follows is a reaction to what has already happened, and unlike the three prose sections of *Langsame Heimkehr*, whose altogether leisurely pace traverses vast areas and relatively long periods of time, here the tempi change in rapid succession and the key events stand not at the beginning, but at the centre of the action. The first half of the text functions as an approach whose path is marked by a wealth of anticipatory hints which come with increasing frequency. One of the nouns most used is 'Schwelle'. The many threshold situations described or introduced in the dialogue have their counterpart in what might be termed a subliminal narration which never trumpets its presence but instead seeks out and sets up signs in a broad, empty field of possibilities, opening the way for things to come.

In the introductory passage of the narrative, quoted in full below, the way sensory impressions are expressed is characteristic of Handke, particularly in respect of what is perceived visually, when objects, in their never-changing uniformity, are experienced as *déjà vu*. Yet their effect differs from that in earlier works by the

Translation by Arthur Williams.
1. Published by Suhrkamp, Frankfurt/Main, 1983. All references in the text are to this edition.

author, for example, in *Die Angst des Tormanns beim Elfmeter*; they are obtrusive and repellent, but they have an unexpected new lustre as well; as in the line by Eichendorff: 'Schläft ein Lied in allen Dingen.'[2]

> Schließ die Augen, und aus dem Schwarz der Lettern bilden sich die Stadtlichter. Es sind nicht die Lichter der Innenstadt, sondern die gerade aufglimmenden Laternen einer der vielen Neubausiedlungen an der südlichen Peripherie. Die Siedlung besteht aus stockwerkhohen Einfamilienhäusern und liegt in der großen Ebene am Fuß des Untersbergmassivs, die einmal ein natürlicher Stausee war, später zur Moorfläche verlandete – es gibt immer noch Sumpf- und Teichstellen – und jetzt 'Moos' genannt wird: das Leopoldskroner Moos. Die Laternen glosen zunächst nur, und strahlen dann erst auf, in einem reinweißen Licht. Einen rotgelben Schein geben dagegen die an Betonmasten befestigten Bogenlampen am Ostrand der Siedlung, wo, in Form einer Kehre, die Endstation der Obuslinie angelegt ist. Zwischen der Obuskehre und der Siedlung fließt der aus dem Hochmittelalter stammende Kanal, der von der Königsee-Ache und einem Bach des Untersbergs gespeist wird: der Almkanal oder 'die Alm'. Die Siedlung befindet sich gerade schon jenseits der Stadtgrenze (knapp vor der Zufahrt ist auf dem Straßenschild das Wort 'Salzburg' diagonal durchgestrichen) und heißt 'Eichensiedlung'. Alle Straßen da haben ihre Namen von Bäumen: die Erlenstraße, die Weidenstraße, die Birkenstraße, die Föhrenstraße. Nur der aus dem westlichen, fast unbesiedelten Torfmoor kommende Weg ist der 'Mostpressenweg' geblieben. Ihm entsprechen innerhalb der Siedlung die paar früheren, jetzt entweder verfallenen oder anders genutzten Torfbauernhütten.
>
> Ein Oberleitungsbus biegt ein in die Endstation-Schleife, ein langer Wagen, durch einen Gelenkabschnitt zweigeteilt. Mehrere Leute steigen aus, Schulkinder, Einheimische, Ausländer (diese wohnen in den paar Holzhäusern); alle in Eile; nur die Kinder trödeln. Man bewegt sich in einem Schock über die kleine Kanalbrücke, gefolgt von einigen Jugendlichen auf ihren tagsüber an der Station abgestellten Fahrrädern, und betritt gemeinsam die Siedlung, die, gerade noch fast ohne Menschen, auf einmal bevölkert erscheint. Hunde kommen bellend an die Gartentüren gerannt. Die Telefonzelle an der Schwelle zur Siedlung, vor einem Augenblick trübhell und leer, wird jetzt verdunkelt von Benutzern und draußen Wartenden. (pp. 7–9)

The first, apparently paradoxical, sentence of the book comes as a surprise: 'Schließ die Augen, und aus dem Schwarz der Lettern

---

2. Joseph Freiherr von Eichendorff, *Neue Gesamtausgabe der Werke und Schriften in vier Bänden*, ed. Gerhart Baumann in collaboration with Siegfried Grosse, vol.1, Stuttgart, 1958, p. 80.

bilden sich die Stadtlichter.' As the narrator thus directly addresses the reader he seems to prohibit him from reading; for how can the reader perceive the black letters, that is, the printed word, if he closes his eyes. In fact, the narrator is demanding a more intensive reading in which the lines are not simply received optically but in which they are translated, by aid of the imagination, into the world of real things, thus, by the act of reading, creating a (new) world with the power of the imagination. There is in this something of the ancient myth of poetry, which, disregarding outward appearances, creates its own world and becomes fictionally master over real things. Typically, Homer is said to have been blind, and the indomitable power of poetry is related in the myth of the minstrel Arion who gained great riches in foreign parts. On his journey homewards the avaricious sailors plot to rob him and throw him into the sea. At his last request – to be allowed before his death to sing just once more – the sailors plug their ears in order not to be bewitched by his art. But Arion's singing instead vanquishes the apparently raw forces of Nature, and when he is thrown to the sea, he is carried unharmed to the shore by a dolphin. The rapacious seamen are later captured and punished and the music-loving dolphin immortalized as a constellation. The Romantic poet Novalis drew on the legend of the minstrel Arion in his novel *Heinrich von Ofterdingen*. If, in the religious sphere, faith can move mountains, so, in the secular, art takes up the lofty claim that poetic imagination can move and level them. Scaliger, the theorist of Renaissance poetry, gave this early formulation: *sed velut alter deus condere* (to create like a second god).[3]

The paradox of the first sentence in *Der Chinese des Schmerzes* is heightened by the striking contrast between the black of the letters, signifying all that is ossified and lifeless, and the power of the poet who awakens the reader's imagination and makes the lights come alive. This 'Schließ die Augen' might also acquire particular significance in another context: Homer has already been mentioned; Virgil, too, plays a dominant role in Handke's text. The great epics of Antiquity were recited by a performer, they were thus listened to rather than read; consequently the preference for the ears over the eyes suggests a connection with the European epic tradition. The reader can then also close his eyes because a rhapsodist transports him from the text to the creation of the world.

Every mention of objects and states in the course of the book seems, on first impressions, to fall short of the high artistic claim to

---

3. Julius Caesar Scaliger, *Poetices libri septem*, Lyon, 1561, p. 3.

create a world; for what is presented are the apparently exceedingly banal things of our everyday world: the new estate with its two-storey houses and the streets, all of them named after trees and resembling so many thousand others, even where birds or poets provide the names for them. This everyday arsenal even includes the road-sign with its diagonal line through the name Salzburg. By the second sentence the reader has already learnt that the narrator is not in the centre of the town, but on the 'südliche Peripherie', and this 'life-at-the-edge' is the spatial expression for the fringe existence of the protagonist, to whom I shall return; passers-by and friends compare him with a 'Red Indian' or a 'Chinese'. The place where the trolleybus turns round, which marks its terminus, is also part of this peripheral zone. Here the people get out of the trolleybus as it stops and behave in their usual manner: the adults hurry away, the children dawdle and a few young people swing themselves onto the bicycles they have left parked at the terminus all day. Dogs, which here run barking to garden fences, have always been a subject of interest and detestation for Handke; his *Die Lehre der Sainte-Victoire* has a few pages of the most brilliant prose on precisely this subject.[4]

What the narrator offers us are almost without exception sights and sounds which recur countless times every day and in every place, and whose constant repetition comes as a torment or a comfort, depending on whether one views habit primarily as a depressing or a cheering phenomenon. What, however, removes the text from a pure stringing together of the commonplace and gives it a special tone is to be found inter alia in the function of the lights which are to be formed out of the 'Schwarz der Lettern' in the first sentence. Here we should note that, almost throughout, the passage quoted above talks about change, that is, emergent light. Let us emphasize the relevant phrases again: 'die gerade aufglimmenden Laternen' or 'Die Laternen glosen zunächst nur, und strahlen dann erst auf, in einem reinweißen Licht' ('glosen' is a dialect word for 'glimmen' or 'glühen'). The large arc-lamps give off a 'rotgelben Schein'. A different light effect is produced by the telephone box which just a few minutes ago was still 'trübhell und leer' and is now darkened by the people using it and waiting to use it. All these phenomena point in the same direction: the situation, all in all, is one of transition from day to night, from the light of day to evening lighting, with an almost emphatic recounting of 'Es werde Licht'. It is the end of the day: people are returning to their

---

4. See Peter Handke, *Die Lehre der Sainte-Victoire*, Frankfurt/Main, 1980, pp. 45–7.

homes from work, from school; the trolleybus arrives at its terminus; in the telephone booth people are making arrangements for the evening ahead, for the night to come or the next few days. Everything is aglow in an attitude of, so to speak, Adventistic expectancy, in readiness for what is to come – and in this resides the underlying tension in the opening narration of this prose work. In the final sentence of the passage quoted, there are two substantives which, as images and ideas, are leitmotifs for the whole book. The telephone box stands 'an der Schwelle' of the housing estate, and the paragraph closes with the 'draußen Wartenden'. The bridge over the canal which is mentioned, the threshold, and the expectant pause: these are typical of the action as a whole and above all of the gently circumspect preparation for it. In the next section of the text there are references to the advancing night and the 'orangefarbene Streifen' visible in the western sky (p. 9). The lights, the people's movements and their tasks – everything is in a state of anticipation. Towards what event, towards what deed is everything working?

The first-person narrator, Andreas Loser, father of a family and teacher of classical languages, after knocking down a passer-by, has requested temporary leave of absence from school ostensibly in order to complete his report on the excavation of a Roman villa. He lives in two rooms above a supermarket close to the trolleybus terminus on the outskirts of Salzburg and from time to time visits his wife and children. In his second occupation as an archaeologist the focus of his interest is less what is already to hand than what has disappeared, which has to be totally reconstructed from the faintest of traces. In his excavations he looks for impressions of the thresholds of doors, from which he infers the former layout and construction. When he calls himself a 'Schwellenkundler' and 'Schwellensucher' (p. 24), he is indicating dimensions of meaning which are much more far-reaching: the idea of having time, of asking questions, of waiting and, above all, of listening. He makes the connection between his own name 'Loser' and 'losen', the local word for 'lauschen' and 'horchen' (p. 32). When, during a round of tarok, he asks a priest whether thresholds exist in religious tradition, all of those present (their host, a young politician, a painter and a priest) immediately start to give their views on thresholds and in doing so characterize themselves and, to some extent, their occupation by their respective attitudes to this topic. The priest's contribution, which is particularly detailed and instructive, emphasizes the functions of thresholds as sites not only of shelter and strength ('Das Schwellenbewußtsein sei die Naturreligion' (p. 128)), but also of trial, challenge and decision – thus of crisis in its several senses of a time of severe difficulties, a time of criticism, a time of impending transition. There is in this restrained and yet determined focusing of the will on the act of crossing-over an affinity to Nietzsche who, with his superman, with his diverse images of boats and bridges (which also play an important role in Handke's text) and, not least, with his concept of the 'großer Mittag',[5] seeks to evoke a state of transition and victory.

To these various levels – construction engineering, history of art and of culture, religion (from the Bible to superstition) and anthropology – there is finally added that of poetics and the narrative: no other word, according to the text (p. 133), will more effectively and more quickly inspire people to tell stories than 'Schwelle'; indeed, storytelling itself becomes a threshold event as it delivers the isolated individuals – at least temporarily – from their solipsism and facilitates a state of intersubjectivity, as is the case with the circle of players who are initially tense and strained. As an image of the epic, the threshold takes precedence over the staircase (to be specific: the staircase of the Salzburg Festival, see pp. 145–7). Similarly both staircase and streets are ranked below squares, open countryside and empty plateaux as areas of potential more appropriate to human beings. This also reflects the general precedence given to the epic over the dramatic that we can observe in the 1980s. Prose, in which the narrator moves as in great squares, where he can stroll about as suits him best, has primacy over the staircase, which draws the author forcibly upwards to the dramatic climax. Handke had already renounced many of the traditional techniques of drama in the fourth play of his tetralogy *Über die Dörfer*.

In keeping with the fundamental awareness of the threshold are the state of suspense, the lack of a definite focus and the open void which, in their various forms, predominate throughout, and which in the journal *Phantasien der Wiederholung* were even declared to be an aesthetic principle: 'Die Leere offenhalten: das wäre die höchste Kunst.'[6] In many respects Loser exists in an interim state: in his professional life between leave of absence and dismissal and in his family-life between separation and divorce – he does not know for sure whether he has been sent away or whether he has gone of his own accord. His name suggests a state of waiting and listening, and for all his painful attachment to his country he remains a stranger. A girl calls him an 'Indianer' (p. 48), a bus driver says to him: 'Gute Nacht, Herr Chinese!' (p. 155) and even the woman with whom he

---

5. Friedrich Nietzsche, *Also sprach Zarathustra*, in *Werke. Kritische Gesamtausgabe*, eds. Giogio Colli and Mazzino Montinari, vol. VI, Berlin, 1968, p. 98.
6. Peter Handke, *Phantasien der Wiederholung*, Frankfurt/Main, 1983, p. 41.

is to be united at the Easter Festival compares him to someone who is seriously ill and who, when he takes his leave of his friend, gives a strained smile which makes his eyes look like slits, so that his friend calls him a 'Chinese des Schmerzes' (p. 218). This designation then becomes the title of the book. Later, Loser's mother characterizes him as a 'Sägemenschen' (p. 220), who, in a state of eternal restlessness, constantly moves back and forth between places.

The first of the book's three parts is called: 'Der Betrachter wird abgelenkt' (pp. 5–77) and begins, reflecting Loser's state, in periods of transition: from winter to spring, from day to night and, in addition, in an area between mountains and lowlands, plateau and marsh. The narrator fills this time with apparently irrelevant descriptions of lights, colours and sounds, of the town, the environs and nature, of thoughts and feelings, and as he does, even the most casual of details acquires significance for the future, signs which come so thick and fast that the anticipation of what is to come almost has the force of compulsion: the early mention of the rock-faces where any slip means death (see p. 15), knocking a man off his feet (see p. 19), reflections on the desire to kill and on violence, the tearing down and destroying of election placards and the faces on them, of waymarkings for long-distance footpaths, and of all kinds of posters and texts (see pp. 65–8). His future action and also the event at Easter are hinted at during the visit to an inn where a man and a woman at a table appear as the living image of 'leibliche Vereinigung' (p. 62). The repeated references to the airport, the aeroplanes taking-off and landing, anticipate the site of subsequent events. The first part ends with a child's cry of terror in the night. The web of references encircles the thematic centres of gravity: Eros and Thanatos.

The second part is headed 'Der Betrachter greift ein' (pp. 79–166) and again begins on an eve, this time of Maundy Thursday. The days of Holy Week are upon us, and they will be followed by a resurrection of the flesh. Loser, on his way to play tarok, is too early and takes the path over the hill, where he is veritably beset by signals to 'intervene'. Coffins which have been carried into a home for the elderly and infirm, a raven as a flying 'schwarzes Tuch' (p. 88), the shooting of crossbows with the corresponding noises, a hare on the alert, an elder-tree with eyes, helicopter and ambulance, hospital and cries for help: everything is 'auf dem Sprung' (p. 95). It is here that Loser spots the freshly painted swastika, grabs a lump of rock, begins to run, past a hedgehog and gigantic owl (the sounds of the trolleybus fall like whiplashes), and then he comes face to face with the malefactor, his aerosol can is a 'bomb' (p. 101). With no hesitation Loser throws the stone at his forehead, striking him dead; he drops the body down the rock-face. A few moments of triumph at his annihilation of the incarnation of evil follow; thereafter his condition fluctuates between satisfaction and discontent.

In the third part of the book, 'Der Betrachter sucht einen Zeugen' (pp. 167–242), he experiences no sense of guilt, but he is aware of living 'in der Verdammnis' (p. 174). He spends the next few days in bed and is tortured by the false and distorted things that grin out at him from objects, animals and church towers. After days of dizziness he raises himself up on the afternoon of Easter Saturday, eats a little light food and begins to get his breath back. His will to self-determination commands him not to let any threshold pass him by, not to regard them as obstacles but always to take them as an opportunity to act. His walk on Easter morning takes him to the airport, where erotic signals multiply: posters and inscriptions on walls, a woman at the wheel with unambiguous accoutrements, a remark to a woman hurrying along on foot, booking a room for himself and the woman he expects and then, finally, her arrival. At first she is visible only as an outline of neck and hips, then as a 'nachdenkliche Schönheit' (p. 211). The night together allows him to get to know both her and himself.

After their parting, which in the words of the woman permits questions but not wishes, Loser takes a trip to Italy, above all to places associated with Virgil, and subsequently goes back to his teaching. Having noticed in a glance at the mirror his resemblance with his son, he would like to gain him as a witness. He announces to him that he will tell him a threshold story but in a dream recognizes the storyteller himself as a threshold, so that he has to pause. Handke's text is the expression of a universal state of waiting which does not exclude individual actions but which holds out no prospect of any definitive result from them.

This state of sceptical, yet not completely despairing, anticipation seems to me characteristic of the novel in the 1980s, even when the prophecies of doom (*Rufe Kassandras*) are coming true and the end of the world which we fear is, in fictional terms, already behind us. However, such apocalyptic visions as these are, in the final analysis, the result of the defiant hope that catastrophes are not inevitable (cf. Christa Wolf's *Kassandra* and *Die Rättin* by Günter Grass).

Criticism of Peter Handke's *Der Chinese des Schmerzes* articulates reservations primarily in two respects: first in the aesthetic sense and secondly in the moral and legal sense. The aesthetic objections are concentrated almost without exception on what is seen as the overloaded narrative manner, too pregnant with meaning, which pretends to recognize in even the most mundane and trivial items something akin to such fundamental ingredients of myth as 'the deed', just punishment and expiation. This criticism contains the essence of much that the author has been accused of since the beginning of his tetralogy *Langsame Heimkehr*. These reservations stretch from the reproach that he has surrendered to a rotten positivism, to the gibe that he is part of the cheap change in direction in the Federal Republic. If these objections are justified, then they are weighty ones. And yet I do not think that the author of *Langsame Heimkehr* and *Der Chinese des Schmerzes* is seeking to come to terms with the existing state of affairs; he is not giving his blessing to factuality. Instead, in his continuing and constantly broadening attacks on the system, he is ultimately countering the systematization of pure negativity – not in order to confront this naively with the positive, but to reveal the rotten positivity in the negative that all have agreed to admire.[7] Thomas Bernhard, who demonstrates in every one of his books – indeed makes us aware with the most compelling evidence – that the world in its present state is the worst of all possible worlds, is completely vindicated by existing conditions and even surpassed by their demonstrable truth. Yet where is it set down, except perhaps in the dull programme of a banal theory of art as reflection, that poetry has the task of reproducing given reality? Without understatement – and Handke is a million miles from this as his tirades full of hate and horror prove – we can ask the question, which is not simply a literary question, how do ideas about alternatives, that is, counter-proposals, become possible and aesthetically acceptable? Handke's problem is how to resist the uncomplaining acceptance of negativity without himself slipping into a smirking acceptance of the existing state of affairs. I see the challenge facing Handke to lie in how he makes a distinction between himself and those with whom he is in danger of being confused. It is for this reason, because he contains so many tensions within himself, that I regard him as one of the most interesting German-speaking authors of the 1970s and 1980s.

The second major objection of Handke's critics to *Der Chinese des Schmerzes* is aimed at its implications and consequences in the moral and legal spheres. Here we must proceed with extreme caution because what is involved is a single individual who, entirely on his

7. See Peter Pütz, *Peter Handke*, Frankfurt/Main, 1982, pp. 108ff.

own responsibility, kills a man who, it is true, is guilty of nothing less than a neofascist outrage, but who, notwithstanding, had a right to a proper legal trial and not to become an immediate victim of lynch law. It is risky, not to say pointless, to argue against moral maxims, since anyone who does so, on the one hand, questions a moral postulate, while, on the other hand, they hold fast to the general principle of morality, unless, like Nietzsche, they investigate its provenance and in so doing uncovers its dark prehistory, concluding that morality grows out of resentment. And yet there is a world of difference between the bold venture of recognizing this fact and the pragmatic workings of human co-existence, which cannot permit one individual to execute another at a single blow, even if the latter is spraying swastikas.

I share these reservations and make the following comment, not as justification but at best to explain Loser's dubious action: critics, even the most competent of the brotherhood, often relate literature all too directly and immediately to real-life situations. Here Handke has his protagonist slay a neo-Nazi who is daubing swastikas and immediately people say that the author is setting up a moral maxim that neo-Nazis who spray swastikas may, or even should, be killed on the spot. The fact that Handke does not himself carry out the act, but lets it be carried out, demands that account be taken of the situation and personal conditions pertaining to the deed. At no point is the killing glorified, appearing rather as an individual's breaking loose, in a way that cannot be legitimized but that can be explained, from the narrow bounds of his almost autistic fringe existence – without, however, the killing of the other person resulting in a liberation of his own self. How much Loser's ego stands at the fore when he commits the deed is clear from his feelings when he catches sight of the swastika:

Dieses Zeichen ist das Urbild der Ursache all meiner Schwermut – all der Schwermut – und des Unmuts hierzuland. Und das verfluchte Mal, war eben nicht aus Laune oder Leichtsinn schnell so hingewischt, vielmehr mit böswilliger Genauigkeit und schwarzer Entschlossenheit gezeichnet, dick aufgetragen und gründlich ausgemalt worden: die auf die Spitze getriebenen Haken sollten als Unheilandrohung ins Gesicht springen; und sie sprangen mir auch ins Gesicht. Mir? Ich? Ein einziges großes Aufwallen. (pp. 97f).

The problems of the self, which are constantly in the foreground in Handke's work, acquire here an existential dimension over and above their epistemological significance; much more clearly than in

Peter Handke's Der Chinese des Schmerzes

his early works we are concerned with questions of existence and not with questions of perception. The killing of a neofascist who provokes justified resistance becomes the problematical case, altogether open to criticism, of the step from the state of waiting to that of taking action. The fact that the transition from reflection to action remains highly dubious is corroborated in no uncertain way by the title of the third part, which speaks of Loser's effort to win over his son, who might possibly exonerate him: 'Der Betrachter sucht einen Zeugen.'

−9−

The German Academic Novel of the 1980s, or a Tale of Four Hetero-Academic Novels

BRIAN KEITH-SMITH

Siegfried Mew's article, with its title 'Martin Walsers *Brandung*: Ein deutscher Campus-Roman?', makes the essential point that whereas the English 'university-novel' and the American 'college-novel' reached a high plateau in terms of formal development in the 1950s and 1970s and have recently undergone major changes the so-called 'campus-novel' in German literature is almost unheard of.[1] The different social structures of German universities have meant traditionally more emphasis on the *Professorenroman* which has latterly been focused on the figure of the teacher and occasionally on (usually rebellious) students. My intention is not to enquire further into different national traditions and their effect on the form of the 'university', 'college', 'campus' and *Professoren-* or *Lehrer-*novels, but to give an account of four recent examples written in German that share certain themes and suggest at least some evolutionary aspects corresponding to social concerns.[2]

Martin Walser wrote *Brandung* (1985) to express his reactions to

---

1. In *The German Quarterly*, vol. 60, no. 2, spring 1987, pp. 220–36. The sub-title of the present article is an allusion to David Lodge's novel *Changing Places: A Tale of Two Campuses*.
2. An informal, not exhaustive, checklist of novels and related texts: Kingsley Amis, *Lucky Jim*, 1954; Randall Jarrell, *Pictures from an Institution*, 1954; Hermann Kant, *Die Aula*, 1965; Hans Egon Holthusen, *Indiana Campus. Ein amerikanisches Tagebuch*, 1969; Walter Höllerer, *Die Elephantenuhr*, 1973; Tom Sharpe, *Porterhouse Blue*, 1974; Malcolm Bradbury, *The History Man*, 1975; David Lodge, *Changing Places*, 1975; Urs Jaeggi, *Brandeis*, 1978; Martin Walser, *Ein fliehendes Pferd (Novelle)*, 1978; Günter Grass, *Kopfgeburten*, 1980; Amanda Cross, *Death in a Tenured Position*, 1981; Robertson Davies, *The Rebel Angels*, 1982; David Lodge, *Small World*, 1984; Don Delillo, *White Noise*, 1984; Frank Parkin, *Kippendorf's Tribe*, 1984; Martin Walser, *Brandung*, 1985 (edition referred to: Frankfurt/Main, 1987); Alois Brandstetter, *Die Burg*, 1986 (edition referred to: Salzburg, 1986); Renate Feyl, *Idylle mit Professor*, 1986 (edition

an almost four-month stay as a guest professor at the University of California at Los Angeles, Berkeley, in the autumn of 1983, thereby becoming one of an ever-increasing club of German writers to make guest appearances on the other side of the 'pond'.[3] In many ways *Brandung* illustrates a comment made in Hans Egon Holthusen's *Indiana Campus. Ein amerikanisches Tagebuch* (1969), where we find him quoting Paul Valéry: 'Die wichtigste Lehre, die man aus der Geschichte ziehen könne, sei "daß wir rückwärts in die Zukunft schreiten, mit dem Hinterkopf voran"' and, Holthusen continues: 'Die Frage wäre dann: Wie verstehe ich meine Erfahrungen?' (pp. 16f). Precisely this need to interpret one's experiences bugs the re-emergence of *Studienrat* Helmut Halm, the immature teacher of *Ein fliehendes Pferd* in his new guise as a fully-fledged aging Stuttgart senior teacher invited as Visiting Professor to the University of Washington in Oakland, California. He is doomed, it would seem, to be bewitched by Fran Webb, a rich undergraduate whose representative role as the *Ewig-Weibliche* only heightens the ridicule that he suffers and fears. The sexual hang-ups in *Ein fliehendes Pferd* are to a certain extent redeemed by Halm being only one of a constellation of four central characters. In *Brandung* his role is central, and his attitudes and needs appear all the more out of keeping with his new surroundings. The comfortable holiday retreat and the authority-role Halm could fill as a teacher in the *Novelle* allowed for a relatively relaxed and reflective response to his problems. In *Brandung*, the campus atmosphere is more demanding, the spotlights of social interest pick out the slightest character-weakness or flaw. Even his command of English, as a highly-gifted foreign specialist, is vulnerable to the slang and in-talk of student and collegial life. The current local issue of 'sexual harassment' is one which should cause Halm no concern, yet it drives on his responses to Fran's charms into ritualized shared readings of suggestive texts (Shakespeare's Sonnet number 129, for example) and towards a hide-and-seek enquiry into his own motivations and sense of identity.

The opening and final chapters in Stuttgart show Halm as a fifty-five-year-old with a wife and two grown-up daughters, who feels he has no energy left for the one-upmanship struggles that

---

referred to: Berlin (GDR), 1986); Michael Zeller, *Follens Erbe. Eine deutsche Geschichte*, 1986 (edition referred to: Bad Homburg, 1986). (Page references to these works are given in the text.)

3. For example, Alfred Andersch (Providence), Max Frisch (East Coast), Hans Egon Holthusen (Indiana), Uwe Johnson (New York), Peter Handke (all over the States), Wim Wenders (Paris, Texas).

feature in his daily professional life. Nor can he cope with a family situation whose immediate disintegration threatens the total disorientation, even collapse, of his own existence. His mother-in-law is dying, his father-in-law is threatened with cancer, one daughter has left for good with a married man twice her age, the other has strayed into the isolation of a meditation-cult, and the mother-in-law's funeral provides a scenario for family dispute and final reckoning. It is not surprising that he flees to America, to the land of fullness of opportunity and intensity of life.

The most frequent themes in *Brandung* point to the bitter-sweet tone of its writing: continual references to death, often violent and unexpected, and the predominance of marriages or affairs between couples with large age-differences. Wherever the reader looks there is a clash between brash insistence on a full life of the senses and nagging reminders of disease and death. Despite Halm's new confidence while on the flight to San Francisco with his wife Sabine and daughter Lena: 'Beide wollten fort aus dieser verwirkten deutschen Gegend . . . "Lena, Sabine, wir sind entronnen! Schaut nicht zurück!"' (p. 27), Halm cannot quite avoid looking back, cannot quite break out completely into a new way of life. This is presented on many levels: as an internal struggle with his conscience as 'ICH-Halm' and 'ER-Halm' where he can never finally bring himself to make the first real pass at Fran but protracts his own agony by feeding off his fantasy world; as a macho performance throwing himself into the 'anstürmenden Glaswände' (p. 91) of the Pacific breakers in order to break free and swim out into the open sea; and in an escapist reading to his wife and daughter from the book *Inspiration Inn* by Kirk Elroyd, the husband of his new secretary, since Elroyd could become his only escape: 'Ihm fehlte die Höhle, der Zuhörer, die Erzählung, in der er sich verbergen konnte' (p. 125).

A leitmotif of 'Der Tod und das Mädchen' runs through the book often linking together the world of metaphor with that of reality. Already during the family quarrel in Stuttgart Halm reflects: 'Alles hat jetzt eine Tendenz, unheilbar zu werden' (p. 25), and so it turns out: the American Head of Department commits suicide probably out of shame that he had not prepared his manuscript for a conference, Halm's father-in-law for whom Sabine returned only one month after their arrival in America is a victim of cancer, even the dog Otto dies after Halm's return and – most alarmingly – Fran Webb perishes in a car that plunges over a cliff, unable to escape because of injuries received when she and Halm collapse over an ornamental fender when dancing at her farewell party. Halm, symbolically, avoids death if not injury on many occasions: he is battered by the breakers, collapses just before the delivery of his public lecture and suffers bad bruising in the dancing accident with Fran.[4]

Halm flirts with danger as he flirts in his imagination with Fran. He finds a fitting poem to lecture on in Heinrich Heine's 'Der Asra' with its haunting couplet: 'und mein Stamm sind jene Asra / Welche sterben, wenn sie lieben'. He gives it a new name: 'Laura and Asra' to express his envy of youth, which he had never fully enjoyed, since: 'Er wollte im Heineton seine Sache betreiben. Nichts war ihm lieber als diese Art, mit sogenanntem Schmerz umzugehen . . . Ein Asra kann nur sprechen, wenn er gefragt wird . . . Eben das mußte er sagen. Daß nichts sein kann – , das ist sein Thema.'[5] When he realizes that Fran is describing a parallel situation between Benedick and Beatrice in *Much Ado About Nothing*, he is jubilant, for mutual self-destruction in undeclared love now becomes the driving force in his life.

Halm nearly, but not quite, breaks loose, because he does not analyse in a self-controlled manner but constructs a fantasy world that prevents him from more than temporary commitment and leads him to the brink of disgrace. The potential humiliation that Sabine might find his returned, unacceptable typescript for a book on Nietzsche may well be one of the items in the confession that he starts at the end of the book (similar to the one made in *Ein fliehendes Pferd*); however, the function of hiding the fact from her has been to provide an opening towards discovery of his own self. Halm has had all the discipline and control of a Gustav von Aschenbach and now wishes to escape, at least (perhaps only) in his imagination, in his four-month confrontation with a new world. Fran becomes the incarnation of this possible voyage of self-discovery on a course already plotted out in lines of Shakespeare and Heine after a preliminary encounter made while translating *the* poem of imprisonment: Rilke's 'Der Panther'. To bring the worlds of Fran and Halm fully together would need considerable credulity on the part of the reader, and Walser clearly wants to keep them

---

4. Halm is luckier than a character in Don Delillo's *White Noise*: Cotsakis, the rival of Jack Gladney (Chairman of the Department of Hitler Studies at Blacksmith College), who was 'lost in the surf off Malibu. During the term break' (p. 168).
5. Also quoted are lines from Heine's *Buch der Lieder*: 'Sie liebten sich beide, doch keiner / Wollt' es dem anderen gestehn; / Sie sahen sich an so feindlich / Und wollten vor Liebe vergehn' (p. 230). Halm also takes refuge in writing out Heine's poem 'Die Unbekannte' with its ironic final lines: 'Laura heißt sie! Wie Petrarka / Kann ich jetzt platonisch schwelgen / In dem Wohllaut dieses Namens – / Weiter hat er's nie gebracht' (p. 201).

apart. Halm, after all, has never really spoken to any woman, unless he has been quite certain first that he would not be rejected. His only premarital encounter was with the Stuttgart millionaire's daughter Nicole Klingele who made it abundantly clear to him she was too expensive to be sacrificed to a mere teacher of German. In keeping with this, he runs no real risks with Fran, yet what remains platonic comes close to genuine dialogue, or at least this is what Halm would like to think. For he remains almost a tragic, at least a pathetic, caricature of a man whose rectitude has been reinforced by his established status, and whose experiences of other people are almost solely interpreted through literary models. His 'love' is genuine but unexpressed, necessary for him but also a convenient commodity to be found on any campus. Unfortunately (or is it fortunately?) for him, Fran makes no real attempt to shake him from his apparent pedagogic supremacy – perhaps she realizes that his 'expense of spirit in a waste of shame / Is lust in action', that he suffers from a sickness of heart and culture which she and nobody else can cure. The departmental secretary, forty-year-old Carol, whose husband, Kirk Elroyd, is thirty years older, is, however, sensitive to every step in Halm's progress and arouses in Halm awe and a fleeting sense of gratitude and mutual understanding not devoid of lust. Clearly the age-gap in itself is no real problem with examples of apparently successful liaisons with differences of twenty, twenty-one, thirty, thirty-three and even forty-one years. Halm, however, lives on the brink of self-destruction, deliberately courting danger within the bounds of his own imagination. He has been caught up in the swirl of campus life but is already victim of an academic disease summed up with reference to some Austrian novels of the 1970s by Hubert Lengauer: 'Hier erscheinen Fähigkeit zur Abstraktion (also Sprachkritik) und Unfähigkeit zum Handeln aneinandergekettet. Diejenigen, die den Blick auf das Allgemeine (der Sprache und der Gesellschaft) hinlenken sollen, sind so spezialisiert auf den Bau und Gebrauch ihrer Optik, daß sie selber zur gesellschaftlichen Besonderheit werden.'[6]

Threatened by many examples of death close to him, set loose in a society where age-gaps apparently prove no obstacle, yet internally drifting between his albeit selective knowledge of certain personally significant texts and an inhibited desire for self-expression, Halm understands all too well in the final chapter that there is nothing for him to look forward to in going back to school.

6. Hubert Lengauer, 'Zerstörte Hoffnung. Zur Kritik bürgerlicher Bildung im realistischen Gegenwartsroman', in Alois Brandstetter (ed.), *Gegenwartsliteratur als Bildungswert*, Vienna, 1982, pp. 83–95.

What he will thus achieve, either literally or metaphorically, is an 'Entblößung durch Gedanken' (p. 318), a confession to Sabine and a resolution of the 'unauflösbare Mischung aus Mißgunst und Genuß' that his mirror reflected to him in fact on the opening page and in memory on the final page of the novel.

Renate Feyl's *Idylle mit Professor* (1986) seems at first to have little to do with an academic novel and far more to do with a feminist marriage-novel. It tells the historically half-familiar story of Luise Adelgunde Victoria Gottsched's marriage with the infamous eighteenth-century theorist and academic. Whatever contemporary allusions might lurk behind the safe 250 years' distance in this novel from the German Democratic Republic, and however commonplace Victoria's fate may seem to be, we are forcibly reminded here of Juvenal's comment: 'Nulla fere causa est, in qua non femina litem moverit' (*Sat.* 6, 242–3), that is, 'there is hardly a cause which has not been the result of some woman's action'. Victoria married an already famous man when she was twenty-two in circumstances which seemed to offer her a Utopian future. In the early days, she is content to accept Gottsched's prescription of the ideal wife as a continuous provider for her husband's needs, as he puts it in the stagecoach after their marriage: 'Wo *er* sein Vergnügen sieht, hat *sie* ihre Existenz' (p. 9). She hopes to reflect his glory, to live in his comfortable home and follow the precept of thrift spelt out in the housekeeping book he formally presents to her. But it is not long before she sees through the false provincialism of a luxurious and exclusive literary salon in Leipzig.

The book develops with a description of Gottsched's self-appointed roles including that of educating his young wife, who as a woman and potential disturbing influence is not allowed to appear at his lectures, but can listen from the next room through a slightly open door. Recognizing undeveloped talents, he makes use of her as a copyist, using flattery to retain her admiration. Feyl links Victoria's development as a wife and eventually as a writer by referring to advice on the woman's role given to her before marriage: first to be reticent and passive, then suggestive and arousing expectation, then through playful artistry and shamelessness to develop from 'einer Künstlerin der Verwandlung zum Genie der Verstellung' (p. 45). This marriage-novel becomes a 'Hohe Schule der Weiblichkeit' (p. 45) not so much in descriptions of sexual encounters as in Victoria's gradual emancipation from her husband's control over her mind and creative talents. Thus, her natural desires to continue with her own writing and translations (as a 'Künstlerin der Verwandlung') and to mother a child are at first tempered by her pride in Gottsched's achievements fuelled by his excessive industry. Her first great joy comes when he takes to the printer her significantly entitled comedy, *Pietisterei im Fischbeinrocke oder die doktormäßige Frau*.[7] It is the first expression of her 'Spottlust' and reveals her as a 'Genie der Verstellung'.

This success gives her the confidence not to accept membership on her own account of the 'Deutsche Gesellschaft' because of its élitist self-adulatory character, and this infuriates Gottsched. On his return from a visit to Dresden, however, he presents her with a garden, which becomes her 'Idylle' of peace; but, whereas he wants to develop it as a formal work of art to express his cultural sensitivity: 'Victoria will nur eins: ein dichtes Ineinander von Blumen, Sträuchern und Bäumen und mittendrin ein Häuschen, wo sie sitzen, lesen und schreiben kann' (p. 70).

From now on the idyll of marriage with the Professor turns sour, and she soon realizes that the lot of an academic wife is to have no claims of her own. The eighteenth-century debates on literary theory are played out in their marriage, for where he sees the poet's task as one of education and improvement, leading the reader to the light of reason, for her poetry is 'ein Himmelshauch, unsichtbar, unmeßbar und nur in den Tiefen der Empfindung spürbar' (p. 91). From now on she realizes that a 'reasonable, philosophical love' as he terms it is not enough, and that his self-justification will only increase with age. Despite the outward appearance of her home as the literary centre of Leipzig, the relationship within her marriage becomes stifling, and when she finds herself described as 'seine Gehilfin' without her name in the list of Bayle's Dictionary she experiences pain and humiliation. Gottsched claims her name is 'in seinem aufgehoben' (p. 110), but she feels she has been extinguished, and a few days later refuses to write a satire against Bodmer and Breitinger.

Gottsched soon becomes the focus of all the injustice she sees in the world, and she decides to translate a ten-volume history of the Paris Academy alone, using this as a sheet-anchor against the increasing uncertainties of her marriage. His response to her purchase of a large new writing-desk on which she hoped to assemble the works of Haller, Milton and Young, is to line up ten of his own volumes, and in two sentences that underline both the marriage and scholarship features of the novel we read: 'Gottsched will in ihrer Welt an erster Stelle stehen. Er will nicht nur ihr Ehemann, sondern auch noch ihr Lieblingsschriftsteller sein' (p. 126).

7. A recent edition is edited by Wolfgang Martens, Stuttgart (1986).

The carefully controlled balancing of the two characters, their personal and literary lives, visits and excursions, successes and failures, that also emerges as a stylistic principle in short sentence groups, is continued with Victoria's run of publishing successes that follow the virtual collapse of her marriage. At a time when she believes all she wants is to die with her pen in hand, the growing spate of invitations leads her to make a triumphal tour with Gottsched in tow. But Gottsched can only put down her success to being a woman, since 'Der Erfolg einer Frau beruht auf ihrem Geschlecht und ist zufällig. Der Erfolg eines Mannes beruht auf seinem Geist und ist gesetzmäßig' (p. 198).

The final sections of the novel introduce the invasion of the Prussian army and the visit of the king. Victoria's inner separation from Gottsched becomes complete, and his dotage awakens in her deep contempt. She now finds the way to herself by writing the first history of the lyric in German, discovering in the poets' lives what she could never experience herself: 'ein verwegenes, ungestümes und wildes Draufzugehen, das die Phantasie aufwühlt und dem Dasein Glanz verleiht' (p. 229).

The war prevents publication of her three-volume work, yet even at this stage Gottsched claims she is nothing without him. In her final weeks before the fever and stroke she suffers after twenty-eight years' continuous work she seeks inner harmony mainly alone in her garden. After her death Gottsched spends a year writing his 'Nachruf' to go with a collection of her poems, but the final sentence in this novel, whose underlying tone throughout is one of sharply expressed irony, is the most ironic of all: 'Die Trauer vergeht, der Kummer weicht, und er heiratet die neunzehnjährige Susanne Katharina Neueneß' (p. 245).[8]

It may seem a long way from the narrow-mindedness of an eighteenth-century Leipzig professor to the restricted accommodation of a contemporary Austrian lecturer in medieval German. Alois Brandstetter, however, uses a combination of modern academic conditions and a backward-looking cast of mind in his novel *Die Burg* (1986) to equate the world of medieval scholarly research with a huge plastic toy-castle kit. As there is no other room in the lecturer's flat, his two sons' toy is proudly constructed on their father's writing-desk, thus preventing progress with his *Habilitationsschrift* and providing the nightmare that he will have to present his examiners with the final construction in lieu of the

---

8. The 'Nachruf' is to be found in Johann Christoph Gottsched, *Ausgewählte Werke*, ed. P. M. Mitchells, vol. 10, pt 2, Berlin, 1980, pp. 507–83; 'Kommentar', pp. 703–22.

finished typescript. The super-kit symbolizes the dominance of the Middle Ages in his family life, but it also reveals a contrast between the fruitless long researches of Art(h)ur and the efficient constructivism of his sons Georg and Michael. On one level, then, there is a playful conflict between the generations, offering scope for much pedagogic paternal introduction to his spiritual world. On another level, we see Arthur's critical resistance to the social graces and graft he needs to make progress in the academic world. His long-suffering wife Ginover's critical remarks describe her own academic background, for she sees through the exactness and growing pedantry of her knight in shining armour.

Die Burg is written from Arthur's point of view with tongue in cheek. He applies the in-jokes of his trade, its references and its puns, as a form of self-defence and resigned acceptance that nothing modern is worth bothering about. Despite this, he has a sneaking admiration for the 'Playmobile' castle, for: 'Die Burg steht definitiv auf ihrem Platz, eine feste Burg, durchaus eine Veste' (p. 7). Indeed, the model becomes an analogy for his own beleaguered position, its finer architectural details paralleling the intricacies of his mental world constructed over layers of puns and half-hidden linguistic allusions. The choice of object to represent his mental world, by extension the whole world of medieval German studies, and still further the academic world in general, is highly apposite. For the castle is made up of individual bricks and sections that can be arranged, put together, unmounted and rearranged at will – in other words, academic life is shown up as a form of construction and deconstruction limited only by the number of parts available to play with, the time allowed and the range of the players' imaginations. The kit is, of course, the luxury model (number 839) with 509 elements as opposed to the standard (number 838) with a mere 264, a kit to encourage 'Gigantomanie' (empire-building) (p. 10). German studies, like all other disciplines, can have links with other subjects, so we find the kit comes with extra sets of pieces for a fort with a post-office waggon, a saloon, drug-store etc. (which allow for cross-cultural fertilization), and a circus set. The analogy is taken further when the social life of the 'Mittelbau' of the university is taken into account, and when Arthur describes with painful precision the detailed implications of his link with the medieval past in the ritual of promotion to professorial status.

The book develops as an almost cruel revelation of the working of an academic mind, drifting into areas of interest that show links back to the medieval world. In general, Arthur makes use of German Classical and Romantic writers as a 'Zwischenstation auf dem Weg zum Mittelalter' (p. 35) – they become part of the endless quest in which he thrives.[9] Texts such as the *Hildebrandslied* are reinterpreted against the experience of playful family struggles and are linked by analogy in Arthur's mind forward to Kafka's *Das Urteil* so that the worlds of Old High German and twentieth-century German associate to provide a new construction; it is as if artefacts from an archaeological site were being brought together to provide a new interpretation, a new construct of reality. Just as the archaeological discovery depends on both previous scholarship and luck, so was the medieval castle often an ad hoc combination of craftsmanship and availability of suitable materials in the area, as opposed to the factory-made unchanging regularity of the plastic model. The analogy, then, of plastic model and academic life is an ideal; but the novel *Die Burg* has the roughness of texture of an original medieval castle in keeping with the individuality and imperfections of Arthur himself. He can revel in an analysis of what an actual ruined castle reveals to him about its construction; he can lament the reduction in the plastic kit of human figures to precast three-dimensional logos; but what he most fears is that his son Georg will become so totally absorbed in the incomplete analogy offered by the plastic castle, that the 'feste Burg' will become a 'fixe Idee' (p. 63) and he will also become a medieval specialist, but one who has an imperfect appreciation of the issues involved, for: 'Nicht das Mittelalter ist "finster", sondern unser Wissen über das Mittelalter' (p. 78).

One of the most remarkable features of *Die Burg* is the highly developed critical sense of awareness Arthur has of the imperfections of his own position, which he invariably expresses with reference to the academic in general. We read for instance: 'Wer viel "schreibt", das heißt studiert und geistig arbeitet, der wird dadurch auch lebensfremd, und gerade der Burgen- und Ritterforscher wird dem Athletischen und Militärischen, mit dem er sich letztendlich beschäftigt, mehr und mehr entfremdet' (p. 87). The ivory-tower mentality of the scholar is ridiculed through the anecdote of a professor who fell off his horse trying out some of the stunts described in the medieval texts on which he was working, still further by the in-jokes at the expense of his colleagues at a conference shortly afterwards. Yet, as so often in this book, this whole

---

9. For example, he recites Schiller's ballad 'Der Handschuh' twice daily to his son Georg, cutting it short before the glove is thrown into Dame Kunigunde's face, for he finds this educationally problematical and difficult to explain. He even changes the word 'Weiber' to 'Frauen' to avoid 'ein häßlich gewordenes altes Wort' (p. 29), and bowdlerizes the text to fit the reader's abilities and taste.

section becomes only a pretext for the expression of personal anxieties about Arthur's own future *Habilitation* and the purpose in general of medieval German studies, and by extension academic work as a whole. This transference technique from personal problem to specific discipline to overall significance and back becomes the key stylistic device of the work. As in the construction of a castle, the original plan undergoes many variants which, in turn, redetermine the direction and character of the first idea, or, as Arthur puts it: 'Die alten Literaturen, ja alle Literatur ist für die Wissenschaft eine Art *perpetuum playmobile*' (p. 99). Furthermore, the scenario of the aptly named 'Spielarbeitwohneßzimmer' (p. 101) is merely the external, physical stage on which are played out the interlinkings of different levels of awareness in Arthur's mind. With tongue-in-cheek, Arthur admires the way in which his son Georg makes use of the model:

> Erkennen beginnt mit dem Vergleichen . . . Er vergleicht die Figuren, wie die Forscher ihre Belege vergleichen. Auch seine Methode ist in gewisser Weise strukturalistisch. Georgs Burg ist ein Kinderspielzeug, die mittelalterliche Literatur ist für die Literaturwissenschaftler und Literarhistoriker ein Riesenspielzeug, wenn man ein wenig übertreibend und übertrieben von den Altgermanisten als einem Geschlecht von Giganten sprechen will, wie es in Chamissos Ballade vorkommt. (p. 103)

The past, with its simplicity and openness, becomes for Arthur a magic well, a 'Jungbrunnen' from which one can draw as when dealing with young children.

After the acts of comparison comes the quest, or as Hartmann von Aue has his Erec put it: 'Ich wußte wohl, daß der Weg zum Höheren irgendwo in der Welt liegen mußte, aber ich wußte nicht genau wo, und so bin ich auf die Suche geritten, ohne zu wissen wohin' (p. 125). Precisely such an open-ended, naive approach to life marks out Arthur's personal and academic life, and it is not surprising to find that his wife, Ginover, once a librarian, is 'keine von jenen sattsam bekannten Assistenten- und Dozentengattinnen, die ihre Männer täglich mit dem Kriegsruf: "Auf, auf, Karriere machen!" wecken' (p. 137). Indeed, it is on his search for a possible topic for his *Habilitationsschrift* that he finds his wife. Again, the apparent main aim of a new section of the book – which is in fact one long discourse with no divisions into chapters – is left in abeyance as an alternative comes into view. The *Habilitationsschrift* is lost sight of in pages of description of Arthur's courtship and early married life. The castle-novel becomes a novel about philology, becomes a novel of education, becomes a marriage-novel and in its later stages a satire on an unsuccessful but delightfully errant academic. In keeping with the general theme of discovery and quest, its form becomes a series of 'Verlängerungen', that phenomenon of 'extra-time', the prospect of which can quicken the pulse of the eager *Assistenten* not yet ready to present his *Habilitationsschrift*, but quite prepared to live out the full sixteen years allowed in this process.

Unfortunately (or is it fortunately?) for Arthur, his supervisor is primarily interested in university politics and a step up into the higher echelons of university administration, whereas Arthur's interests are confined to the library and to his department. The motif of the new vice-chancellor spending hours having his portrait painted instead of attending to the needs of his senior students appears here, just as it does in *Idylle mit Professor*, only here the opportunity is taken not only to ridicule the vanity of the individual, but also to criticize harshly the conservative, even philistine, character of the official portrait. Arthur mars any chance he had of developing a good relationship with his supervisor when he insists on replacing prints of the supervisor's favoured artist in his office with one of his own choice. Then, invited to a dinner at his supervisor's house, he makes it clear he is not a potential suitor for the elder and aging daughter. Finally, he dares to break with hallowed traditions in editing the 'Festschrift' for his supervisor, by writing an introduction that links him with the great teachers of German literature from Notker Balbulus (the stammerer) onwards. The resulting volume is received, with its other abnormalities, perhaps not surprisingly, as a 'Schmähschrift'.

The final pages of the novel (in keeping with the overall model of the castle) offer a series of comments on various aspects of university life: student fashion, relationships between staff and students and the intrusion of national politics into university government. The totally subjective character of Arthur's comments is at its clearest in his description of a moto-cross rally seen from – where else? – the terrace of a castle. For Arthur the slang of such a sport is summed up in the word 'Signifikation', where neologisms such as 'Schlammspezialist' or 'Weltmeister', and his wife's vision of the contestants as modern knights jousting, arouse his contempt. The interlinking of contemporary episode with historical event is cemented by the inclusion of Arthur's chauvinistic views on discovering that women, too, are now adept at this re-enactment of the tournament in Freisach in the first half of the thirteenth century, playing their traditional roles of nursing the wounded and spurring on the combatants. With delight, he discovers that a bystander with binoculars when swearing at the distant motorcyclists is quoting more or less unconsciously from the chronicle of Götz von Berlichingen. The proofs of interrelationship lie then for Arthur in the, for him, traditionally fixed roles for women, in repetitive analogous situations seen from afar, and in the only slow evolution of semantic forms – a clear case of misogyny, teichopsia and etymology combined.

The humour of this novel is peculiarly Germanic in its serious intent, for instance, in the following passage:

> Einer vergleicht sein Motorrad mit einer Gemse und fährt fort und sagt im selben Atemzug auch noch, daß sie 'bockt'. Ein wirklich klassisches Beispiel von Bildermischung. Ginover sagte, das schlage dem Faß den Boden ins Gesicht. Wahrhaftig, sagte ich, da wiehern wirklich die Hühner. Da gackern die Pferde, sagte Ginover. Eine solche Redefigur nenne die Poetik eine 'Katachrese', sagte ich, die Situation didaktisch nützend, zu Georg. Ginover aber lachte mich aus, obwohl ich meinen Unterricht auch selbst nicht ganz ernst gemeint hatte. (p. 268)[10]

The humour can also display a childish delight in the noises and expletives of modern comic strips on medieval legends; or it can be lavatorial–satirical in a passing reference to Peter Handke when describing a water-closet as 'eine der wichtigsten Verbindungen zur Außenwelt, der Innenwelt der Außenwelt gewissermaßen' (p. 126); or after a loving account of medieval descriptions of their loved-ones' breasts we read the somewhat crude phrasing of: 'keine *übertriebene* Brust, kein mit Plastik aufgeschäumter sogenannter Atombusen, keine "Schaumburg" vor dem Brustkasten' (p. 150).

It is such details that prove, as Arthur well knows, that he is a 'Gestriger', bound to tradition but not affected by the sickness, as the word itself implies, of so-called nostalgia. He is painfully aware of the ritualization process that has grown up in the use of certain pictorial and verbal images, of 'Sprachmagie und Sprachfetischismus' (p. 285). To become aware of the relativity of all images destroys Arthur's faith in academic life and demands of him either retreat into his own family, where his role as *paterfamilias* commands respect, or some *Tarnung* by which to outwit his examiners.

---

10. This is a form of 'Gallettianismus' derived from the Gotha Professor of Geography and History, Johann Georg August Galletti (1750–1828). See Dieter Arendt, 'Der Gelehrte im Spiegel der Literatur. Oder: Der zerstreute Professor in der Freiheit der Wissenschaft', *Stimmen der Zeit*, vol. 187, no. 104, 1979, pp. 677–88; esp. pp. 681–5.

His confidence is reduced to a state akin to that of the 'Sängerin' in Kafka's tale 'Josefine, die Sängerin oder das Volk der Mäuse', and he begins to dream of sessions before his examiners in Kafkaesque style. In the end, he gives up going into the university, and three weeks later we leave him signing for a recorded delivery communication from his vice-chancellor.

If *Brandung* records an all-too naive encounter of a German teacher with the American college way of life, Michael Zeller's *Follens Erbe. Eine deutsche Geschichte* (1986) reminds us of the conflicting traditions in German academic life. Both the main character of the title, Karl Follen, and the lecturer in German literature, Hellmut Buchwald, who sets out to rewrite the nineteenth-century revolutionary's biography as his *Habilitationsschrift*, eventually find their new world in America.[11] Buchwald was attracted by Follen's belief in a state educational dictatorship and by the writer E. T. A. Hoffmann's eventual comments as a jurist on the dangers of student unrest in Jena in which Follen undoubtedly played a formative role. Buchwald, who gives up his work on Follen, experienced the pressures of university politics in the late 1960s, both from his colleagues and his students. In a Utopian search for more lasting values, he teaches a seminar on Goethe's autobiography. When he realizes that his four-year relationship with Judith, a student of German literature, has finished for ever, he sums up the wisdom he has learnt in the long *Lernprozeß* during the four seasons of a year in which the book is structured: 'Du mußt lernen dich zu vernachlässigen. Life is Xerox. You're just a copy. Wozu dann noch Tagebuch?' (p. 351), and more succinctly, a few lines later he learns from Goethe's *Lehrjahre*: 'Hier und nirgends ist Amerika.'

By an arrangement of alternating paragraphs that describe Follen's life in Germany and eventually in America, Buchwald's more or less casual sexual encounters and his involvement with student politics, Zeller encourages the reader to interpret Buchwald as Buchwald does Follen, namely with the eye of historical distance and with much kindly scepticism. In the same way that Buchwald sees Follen's struggle with the Grand Duke of Hessen-Darmstadt in

---

11. Follen arrived in Jena in 1818, aged twenty-two, to lecture on natural law, having been suspended as a student from Gießen and searched for by the Hessen-Darmstadt authorities. Exiled to Switzerland and France, he became the first teacher, later Professor, of German Literature at Harvard. He became an American citizen, a Unitarian minister in 1829, a vice-president of the anti-slavery society in 1834 and was drowned after a fire on the ship taking him to a new parish in East Lexington.

terms of an old black-and-white film (he even imagines casting Charles Laughton as the Grand Duke), Buchwald's attempts to stop an increase in control by the Ministry of Education (choosing the issue of a new set of regulations for the *Zwischenprüfung*) are played out in staff-meeting and lecture room, at the student barbecue and at dinner with his head of department. These are scenarios that with their accuracy of linguistic jargon bring back forcibly the chaotic interchanges of 1967 and 1968. However, where Follen continuously sought political involvement with society, Buchwald realizes he and his generation could live up neither to Follen's radical verbal expressions nor to Karl Ludwig Sand's fanatical action in coolly planning the playwright Kotzebue's murder eleven months in advance. Inspired by these two exponents of word and action, forgotten in recent German history as *un-Personen*, Buchwald hopes to develop a poetics of violence powerful enough to force respect from his examiners.

Perhaps the most memorable section of the work is a scathing and at times funny section entitled 'Vor Saison: Der Classische Cuddel' describing the life and behaviour of the bird of paradise of literary scholarship: Professor Curd Schäfel. This academic life-story is full of comment on one possible product of the German university system, extreme in its personal and professional aspects, yet told with an obvious sneaking sense of loss that such an eccentric has become as rare as a bird of paradise. Schäfel is an obvious counter-figure to Brandstetter's Arthur, each one successful where the other is not. Both, however, are clearly grotesque extensions of possible figures. For a truly convincing portrait of a successful German professor, we have to turn to the current head of department, the medievalist Karl-Joseph Feineis, a close friend of Schäfel, who has a direct telephone line to the education minister. Despite the apparent way-out nature of his major two-volume history of medieval German literature entitled 'Minne und Arbeit' based on Adorno's aesthetic theory discrediting the unresolvable hostility of writer and society, and despite his learning his book by heart and using nothing else in his teaching for more than ten years, he is immediately credible. Even his hope of revising Christian dogma since Augustine, as a result of interpreting numerous illustrations of Mary and Christ on the model of a Freudian Oedipal relationship, is within the bounds of recognizable research aspirations. The description of Buchwald's dinner at the lavish home Feineis shares with his wife, who still hopes one day to continue her research on Rilke, is close to the extravagant details of some of David Lodge's scenes, sharing with them that mixture of the provincial and the exotic which characterizes the more affluent aspects of academic life. Buchwald has invited a contemporary woman poet to read her works in the department; her distant connection with and alleged support of a terrorist group have brought the university and the department into the public spotlight. He is thus summoned to dine and to be told unofficially whether or not his refusal to disassociate himself from a student strike constitutes a breach of contract, and what, if any, disciplinary action the minister has decided to take. Buchwald says all the right things, ducking Frau Feineis's half-veiled attack on his teaching the contemporary lyric, mentioning he is now going to teach Goethe's early works, as viewed through the eyes of the maturer Goethe. Feineis is pleased, for this will bring him closer to Schäfel, Buchwald's former arch-enemy in the department. In this episode, as in Buchwald's involvement with student politics, an atmosphere of hurried necessity and of keeping a foothold on ever-shifting political ground is effectively conjured up.

Buchwald, like Gottsched, like Halm and Arthur, is in many ways an incomplete person. Too honest intellectually to make rapid progress with his research, he is perceptively called a paper tiger by one of his students. His wish to teach lyrics from the *Vormärz*, thus filling in the background to his nineteenth-century historical research, is hardly relevant to them: 'Über den Herwegh jetzt zu germanitisieren, so mit Sekundär-Gedöns und Pipapo – nee, du, echt, das kekst uns an' (p. 114). So he allows himself to be persuaded to teach the contemporary lyric, explaining this away to Judith as 'Angst vor der Geschichte' (p. 117). Buchwald has to steer a course between the student group 'LUST' (= 'Liga undogmatischer Schnaps-Trinker') and the political ambitions of Rudi, whom he appoints as a temporary assistant, also the Liberals represented by the cool, rich and beautiful Johanne von Drohna-Zettelfeld, or Jo for short. She charms him into practising 'Konstruktive Neutralität' (p. 174) towards the student strike which is ostensibly against new examination regulations. His own involvement is focused on his interpretation of a poem called 'Tusculum' by Norma Holbe and subsequent writing of an article on her works. However, the least satisfactory aspect in his life is his incapacity to sustain a meaningful relationship with any woman, exemplified in his short-lived affair with a Russian girl, Hilma. His coldness emerges after his journey to Amsterdam with Judith, where she has an abortion, and on their return she goes off to her own flat rather than come to his: 'Er beneidete Judith um ihre Tränen. Das Weinen hatte er verlernt' (p. 209). When she leaves him for another lover, after four years of a partially successful relationship, he releases his loneliness in a series of notes in his 'Stundenbuch', and, as in *Brandung*, we find the theme of language: 'Die Sprache als Ursprung aller Trennung . . . Nur beim Arbeiten dreht sich der Zeiger nach vorn. Die Hoffnung, darüber zu ermüden bis zum Ende des Tags, kampfloses Aufgehen im Schlaf' (p. 291). Significantly, after he is dragged off by Imme, whom he meets at a student commune party and who totally overwhelms him, he is only too pleased the next morning to return to a reality he knows: 'Das Aroma des Steh-Cafés, am altvertrauten Platz von früher, genoß Buchwald beinahe schon wieder als das reine Glück' (p. 232).

When we look back on these four novels, one overall mood emerges: they are all studies of frustration, even of despair. Their central characters, whether by force of circumstance, personal feeling or sexist prejudice, struggle against certain demands made by life in general and academic life in particular. In two of them, *Die Burg* and *Idylle mit Professor*, the demands of scholarship practically overwhelm the sanity of Arthur and Victoria. In *Die Burg* these demands are those of an élitist system requiring total dedication to research; in *Idylle mit Professor* they are those of an increasingly crabbed academic celebrity and husband. In the other two, *Brandung* and *Follens Erbe*, the escape of research and teaching provides at least a temporary spur to lives that have become meaningless on a personal level. Formally, one is tempted to pair *Die Burg* with *Brandung*, both making considerable use of interior monologue and inner dialogue techniques, whereas the other two are structured mainly on a series of alternating episodes with differing perspectives. The effect of the 'Verlängerungen' in *Die Burg* is, however, akin to the sequential diversions of Kafka's *Das Schloß* with which there are many other less important similarities. The use of literary quotation and interpretation together with an actual recitation of an independent narrative in *Brandung* and the additional opening and closing chapters in Stuttgart as a framework, give the central part of that text a technical sophistication and variety of psychological portrayal not achieved in the other novels. The obsessive quality of Arthur's scholarship is paralleled by Halm's fascination with the prospect of 'real' experience. Perhaps ironically, there is for both Victoria and Buchwald more potential for development than for Arthur and Halm. Victoria, in protesting her independence from her husband through her own works never learns the secrets of the 'Hohe Schule der Weiblichkeit' for her own person, but applies the arts of 'Verwandlung' and 'Verstellung' in her comedies. Buchwald achieves reintegration into his academic career, achieves recognition by staff, students and administration, but has to turn his back on history and ends as a lonely bachelor intellectually enjoying at the very end of the book the pathetic fallacy of the winter to come: 'Es war, als wäre über Nacht die nächste Eiszeit ausgebrochen. "So ist es recht!" lachte Buchwald in sich hinein. "Dieses meteorologische Wunder hat seine vollkommene Richtigkeit"' (p. 352).

Yet, both Victoria and Buchwald achieve that mecca of all aspiring academics: publication, whereas Arthur, despite his doctorate and associated articles, at the end virtually commits academic suicide, and Halm – in fact a schoolteacher – was only invited to taste of the Californian golden idyll because his old friend had become head of a university German department. All four novels have in-built idylls, featuring ironically in the implications of their titles, yet in none of them is the opportunity taken to enjoy them to full advantage except as a means of escape.

In my account of these novels certain themes have emerged: the need for self-realization as a particularly acute problem for the academic; a sense of powerlessness of the individual before the demands of academic and/or personal expectations; a belief in an alternative (idyllic) setting which by reason of its distance in either place or time might provide a scenario for inspiration and individuation; a half-hidden fear of the implications of historical change; serious flaws in personal relationships; finally, a mistrust in language together with a fascination for its flexibility and power to control others. Some of these themes point to familiar concerns in both life and literature, and, technically, there is little that is innovative in these novels. However, taken together as four texts appearing in under eighteen months they show a remarkable renaissance of interest by the German literary world in a form of life whose ivory-tower qualities belong to the past, and whose characters are shown, ideally, to return to Paul Valéry, stepping into the future 'mit dem Hinterkopf voran'.

−10−

Themes in the German–Swiss Novel of the 1980s: Beat Sterchi's *Blösch* and Gertrud Leutenegger's *Kontinent*

MALCOLM PENDER

The 1980s in Switzerland have been characterized economically by the continuing prosperity which is the continuing envy of the Western world. However, a dichotomy of attitude exists in Switzerland itself in relation to this wealth: on the one hand, the Swiss are driven by the 'Ehrgeiz, auf dem Weltmarkt zu den Ersten und Besten zu gehören', and, on the other hand, Swiss politics has to do with the preservation of the 'Idyll einer von allen historischen Unwettern verschonten Heimat'.[1] In 1991 Switzerland's historical independence and neutrality will doubtless feature prominently in the celebration of the 700th anniversary of its foundation. Yet the following year will see the complete integration of the internal market of the EEC, the economic power of which has, as a Swiss leader-writer recently conceded, 'sowohl Neutralität wie Souveranität [der Schweiz] . . . schon längst in wesentlichen Punkten in Frage gestellt'.[2] It is interesting to speculate on how the Swiss will respond in the 1990s to matters of image and reality, since the 1980s began with a clash between the two. The riots which started in Zurich in the summer of 1980 were, unlike the disturbances of 1968, confined to Switzerland, and represented a rejection by some of its youth of Switzerland's self-image. Other realities of the late twentieth century became especially apparent in Switzerland. The consequences of unchecked development of facilities for the motor vehicle manifested themselves devastatingly in the restricted terrain of the country; the pollution created in Switzerland and in neighbouring

---

1. Rolf Niederhauser and Martin Zingg (eds.), 'Vorwort' to *Geschichten aus der Geschichte der Schweiz nach 1945*, Darmstadt, 1983, pp. 7–14; here p. 10.
2. Rudolf Bächtold, 'Die Schweizer Narrenfreiheit geht zu Ende', *Die Weltwoche*, 18 February 1988; see also Oscar Reck, 'Wird Europa den Bundesstaat sprengen?', *Die Weltwoche*, 28 April 1988.

countries by the accidents in the powerful chemical industry in Basle in 1986 highlighted the environmental cost of unrestrained economic expansion, a point further underscored by the discovery at the end of 1987 that over half the country's stock of trees was diseased. The combined effect of all these factors on a traditional perception of the country was considerable. Extolled for long, both internally and externally, as a model of linguistic co-existence and rational statehood, the benefits of which were apparent in its burgeoning economy, Switzerland now seemed, in matters affecting the environment at least, to be becoming a negative model for the rest of Europe.

Switzerland as a negative model, not simply in matters of the environment, is a theme which emerges in German–Swiss literature in the 1970s and which receives its most concentrated expression in E. Y. Meyer's *Die Rückfahrt* (1977). Here, one of the three mentor figures who guide the hero towards the adoption of attitudes which can sustain him in the face of the debilitating pressures on the individual in modern Switzerland says: 'Falls man die Schweiz als ein Experiment betrachten würde, eine zukünftige, für die ganze Welt gültige Lebensform auszuprobieren . . . dann könnte die Schweiz und die schweizerische Lebensart nur als abschreckendes Beispiel dafür angesehen werden.'[3] It is not, however, that *Die Rückfahrt* seeks to dissociate itself from the past. A large part of the critique of the novel is directed against a misuse of the past which, because it was not capable of today's technological achievements, is not regarded as a valid repository of human experience. Instead, perceptions of the past serve to justify attitudes and practices in today's world. The Swiss perception of the Tell legend, for example, becomes, as Max Frisch claimed, the 'Legitimation heutiger Vögte'.[4] Frisch, who gave such impetus to the questioning of Swiss society with *Stiller* (1954), had published at the beginning of the 1970s *Wilhelm Tell für die Schule* (1971), an ironic demythologization of the Swiss past. But Meyer, in a manner which was to have its importance in the 1980s, seeks to re-create in *Die Rückfahrt* a meaningful link to the past, not in a narrow patriotic sense, but as a necessary factor in the emotional and spiritual stability of the individual and of society as a whole. It is difficult to imagine that Meyer could have adopted this wide view in his novel without the prior, more specific work of Frisch.

The generation of German–Swiss writers born immediately be-

---

3. E. Y. Meyer, *Die Rückfahrt*, Frankfurt/Main, 1977, pp. 213f.
4. Max Frisch, 'Schillerpreis-Rede', in *Gesammelte Werke in zeitlicher Folge*, ed. Hans Mayer, vol. 5, Frankfurt/Main, 1976, pp. 362–9; here p. 363.

fore, during and immediately after the Second World War, of whom Meyer is one of the principal representatives, began, broadly speaking, to publish in the 1970s, and in their texts and in those by others at the same time, Swiss society is depicted in an increasingly differentiated fashion. The workplace becomes the setting for examinations of the manner in which the factory or office make crippling demands on the individual. Disease and death, both related to socially incurred stresses, were given resonance far beyond Switzerland with the publication in 1977 of Fritz Zorn's *Mars*. Other works on this theme were published, some of them, significantly perhaps in the context of Swiss society, by women writers, who began in the 1970s to become less isolated figures in the Swiss literary landscape. In addition, both the influence of the two living 'classics', Frisch and Dürrenmatt, and the perception of parallels to rediscovered writers from before 1945, helped to create a growing awareness of a German–Swiss literary tradition which is not characterized by justification and affirmation of the social and political structures of the country. Externally, the status of German–Swiss literature has benefited from political changes in German-speaking Europe and from the increased acceptance of cultural variety in Europe as a whole. And so, Adolf Muschg, speaking in 1980, was of the opinion that traditional views of German–Swiss literature, always dubious because they had been incapable of accommodating so many German–Swiss writers, were now redundant: 'Die Gemeinplätze stimmen alle nicht, oder nicht mehr.'[5]

It is perhaps worth reflecting, however, that the status and reception of literature in Switzerland might not have changed at quite the same tempo. Might not the plethora of publicly and privately funded literary prizes and awards bear witness to self-satisfied indifference to a literature which increasingly questions the premises of Swiss society? Does Dieter Bachmann's assessment in the 1970s of the activities of writers in Switzerland still hold good in the 1980s: 'Sie stören den Frieden nicht, sie beleben nur ein wenig die Ruhe'?[6] In Hermann Burger's short story 'Die Leser auf der Stör' (*Bork. Prosastücke*, Zurich, 1970), well-off people continue to buy books, but not to read them. Instead, individual readers, or

---

5. Adolf Muschg, 'Gibt es eine schweizerische Nationalliteratur?', in *Deutsche Akademie für Sprache und Dichtung. Jahrbuch 1980*, Heidelberg, 1980, pp. 59–68; here p. 63.
6. Dieter Bachmann, 'Schreiben in der Schutzzone', in Dieter Bachmann (ed.), *Fortschreiben. 98 Autoren der deutschen Schweiz*, Zurich, 1977, pp. 505–13; here p. 507.

even teams of readers, can be hired to read books and to provide thumbnail sketches of the contents; for the appropriate fee, books can be made to look well-used, and exclamation marks or even notes can be entered in the margins. Burger satirizes the manner in which the merchandising of literature nullifies its possible impact, and points, by implication, to some of the difficulties of writing in prosperous and conservatively orientated Switzerland.

Three additional points relating to the prose-writing of the 1980s help to complete an outline framework for the two texts which I wish to discuss. First, it is possible to gauge altering attitudes in writers by comparing a debate of the early 1980s with one of the mid-1960s. In 1966, the discussion, initiated by Frisch, turned on the absence in contemporary German–Swiss writing of a traditional depiction of Switzerland. In 1983, on the other hand, in the so-called 'Realismus-Debatte', the focus was wider and the discussion called in question the validity of former definitions of realism in a highly developed capitalist society in the late twentieth century.[7] This latter debate also defines the tone of attitudes in the 1980s in another way. The confidence of the 1960s, engendered by the awareness of change, has gone, and the resignation of the 1970s as reflected in, for example, O. F. Walter's *Die ersten Unruhen* (1972) or in Adolf Muschg's *Albissers Grund* (1974) has given way in the 1980s to what has been called 'die Haltung der Verweigerung',[8] which might in one way be defined as a refusal to accept as the only solution a system which proclaims itself as the only solution.

A second point relates to differing perceptions of Switzerland. Peter von Matt claims that the 'emotionaler Patriotismus' which sustained Switzerland during the period of encirclement in the late 1930s and early 1940s was increasingly challenged after 1945 by what he calls 'kritischer Patriotismus', of which Frisch was the foremost proponent.[9] These two positions characterized public debate in the 1960s and 1970s until they were challenged by Gertrud Leutenegger in her essay 'Das verlorene Monument'

---

7. For the first debate, see *Die Weltwoche*, 11 March, 25 March, 1 April and 22 April 1966; for the second debate, see Fredi Lerchi (ed.), *Vorschlag zur Unversöhnlichkeit*, Zurich, 1984.
8. Elsbeth Pulver, 'Als es noch Grenzen gab. Zur Literatur der deutschen Schweiz seit 1970', in Robert Acker and Marianne Burkhard (eds.), *Blick auf die Schweiz. Zur Frage der Eigenständigkeit der Schweizer Literatur seit 1970*, Amsterdam, 1987, pp. 1–42; here p. 29.
9. See Peter von Matt, 'Kritischer Patriotismus. Formen und Zielrichtungen der Auseinandersetzung mit der Schweiz bei den Schriftstellern der sechziger und siebziger Jahre', in Klaus Pezold (ed.), *Entwicklungstendenzen der deutschsprachigen Literatur der Schweiz in den sechziger und siebziger Jahren*, Leipzig, 1984, pp. 41–9.

(1979). Here Leutenegger sees the demolition of the *art nouveau* main station in Luzern, with the rich associations it had for her, as a parallel in the physical world to the process of demythologization being conducted in the intellectual world by 'kritischer Patriotismus' which, while historically necessary for the removal of impediments to a proper perception of the past, had also removed a necessary emotional element. Leutenegger seeks to redress a balance, to revive powers of emotional reaction, of revolt, which were originally associated with the legend of Wilhelm Tell. Von Matt calls this view, reflected in the work of Leutenegger and some of her contemporaries such as E. Y. Meyer and Franz Böni, 'kritische Irrationalität', a term which he admits to be inadequate.[10] What seems to me to be useful is the attempt by von Matt to define a less restrictive view held by the younger generation which they can attain because of their historical position.

A third point might be formulated in the question: What is specifically Swiss about German–Swiss prose-writing of the 1980s? Literary movements and trends increasingly ignore frontiers so that there are no 'Schweizer Autoren' but rather 'Autoren aus der Schweiz'.[11] Yet it is reasonable to suppose that a common history can create an ethos which promotes certain literary themes rather than others. The Nazi past, for example, which by no means leaves Switzerland untouched, simply does not have the dominating position in German–Swiss literature which it has in West German literature. On the other hand, the 'Haus-Motiv' provides an example of a theme which is both more specific to German–Swiss literature and which reflects changes in attitude there.[12]

Traditionally, the house was the literary emblem of the solidity and cohesive variety of the Swiss state, a classic example being provided by Meinrad Inglin's *Schweizerspiegel* (1938). A postwar development of the theme is seen in Stiller's counterfeit *ferme vaudoise*, the symbol of his own and of Switzerland's inauthentic images of themselves, and later, Muschg's *Gegenzauber* (1967) and Burger's *Schilten* (1976) provide other examples. Towards the end

10. 'Das verlorene Monument', first published in the *Frankfurter Allgemeine Zeitung* in 1979, has been republished in the essay collection *Das verlorene Monument*, Frankfurt/Main, 1985, pp. 39–52; Klaus Pezold, 'Die deutschsprachige Literatur in den 70er und frühen 80er Jahren', *Zeitschrift für Germanistik*, vol. 8, 1987, pp. 404–14, draws attention (p. 412) to E. Y. Meyer's warning in *Die Rückfahrt*, p. 386, against dethroning reason in this adjustment.
11. Muschg, 'Gibt es eine schweizerische Nationalliteratur?', p. 63.
12. See Martin Kraft, '*Schweizerhaus*'. *Das Haus-Motiv im Deutschschweizer Roman des 20. Jahrhunderts*, Berne, 1971, for a discussion of six novels incorporating the theme.

of the 1970s and at the beginning of the 1980s, the theme of the inadequate or inappropriate house continues in the work of Christoph Geiser, where the enervating tensions and debilitating restrictions of the apparently solid 'großbürgerliches Haus' are portrayed; in the Bindschädler and Baur trilogy of Gerhard Meier, where the many descriptions of alterations past and present to the buildings which the two men encounter in their walks underline the impermanence of human habitation; in the novel *Lieber Leo* (1980) by Hansjörg Schneider, where the hero has, symbolically, no wish to inherit the house for which his father has worked all his life; and in the work of Franz Böni, where dwelling houses, if they occur at all, are places of discord and unremitting noise. Additionally, Marianne Burkhard has identified, in recent novels by German–Swiss women writers, 'a common pre-occupation with the house as the space of human existence'.[13] She attributes this to two historical factors peculiar to Switzerland: there was, after 1945, a much greater consistency in attitude towards, for example, the role of women in society, and secondly, this role had in any case been determined in a way different from other German-speaking countries by the greater public role of the Swiss man which reinforced the perception of the home as the sphere of the woman.

The two texts which I have selected for more detailed comment relate to this 'Haus-Motiv' as well as to other contemporary themes, but they also seem to me to be representative in another way. They are both by writers born in the late 1940s (Leutenegger in 1948, Sterchi in 1949), and this means that these writers are beneficiaries of the widening of horizons which has occurred, and that their own work is contributing to the process of evolution.

Blösch (1983) opens with the Spanish *Fremdarbeiter* Ambrosio clocking off for the last time at an abattoir on the edge of a city which is obviously Berne, and simultaneously recalling his arrival some seven years previously as a dairyman 'im wohlhabenden Land' (p. 7),[14] his designation for Switzerland. Very precise descriptions of the work in the abattoir on his last working day in March 1969 alternate with Ambrosio's recollections of the few months he spent on his arrival working on a smallholding in the

13. Marianne Burkhard, 'Gauging Existential Space: The Emergence of Women Writers in Switzerland', *World Literature Today*, vol. 55, 1981, pp. 607–12 (here p. 608); see also, by the same author, 'Diskurs in der Enge. Ein Beitrag zur Phänomenologie der Schweizer Literatur', in Albrecht Schöne (ed.), *Akten des VII. Internationalen Germanistik-Kongresses. Göttingen 1985*, Tübingen, 1986, pp. 52–62.

14. Beat Sterchi, *Blösch*, Zurich, 1983. All page references in the text are to this edition.

Themes in the German–Swiss Novel of the 1980s

Canton of Berne. His employer there, Hans Knuchel, had held out against the installation of milking-machines and had hired Ambrosio to help milk his cows, amongst which Blösch, a magnificent animal, took pride of place. But Ambrosio was not accepted in the village, and Knuchel, finally driven by a combination of pressures to install milking-machines, had found work for Ambrosio in the city abattoir. Here the Spaniard performs menial and repetitive tasks in what has been called the 'disassembly line'[15] which transforms living animals into various forms of meat and other products. Ambrosio's revolt against the entire system of which the abattoir forms a part is sparked in 1969 by the delivery for slaughter of Blösch, now ruined by the milking-machine. Ambrosio, the *Fremdarbeiter* and unskilled factory-hand, recognizes in Blösch his own exploited condition and immediately terminates his employment.

The scenes set in the smallholding are portrayed mainly from the perspective of Ambrosio. Sterchi takes to its logical conclusion a distancing technique in the German–Swiss novel which goes back to Keller's *Martin Salander*, namely the return of the hero to Switzerland after an absence. But whereas in all the novels employing this device to view Switzerland critically some bond of emotion exists between the returning native and Switzerland, this is not the case with the foreigner Ambrosio. Painfully aware for the first time of his own small stature, he experiences everything 'im wohlhabenden Land' as being on a needlessly gigantic scale, a reversal of a traditional perception of Switzerland. The menace for the small Spaniard in the large scale is heightened by his observation of the widespread possession of firearms and of their frequent use at shooting competitions which offer him 'ein Bild von Wut und Schmerz' (p. 97) as the marksmen compete for good scores. An important Swiss social ritual is presented as having links in the eyes of Ambrosio with the organized killing and destruction of the abattoir.

Ironically, Ambrosio has been engaged to help with the milking because no Swiss is available to do a traditionally Swiss job. Moreover, whereas he, with his acquired skills and genuine liking for farm work, is regarded with suspicion and finally forced to leave, the farming community is shown to be in thrall to two forces of modern life deeply inimical to its husbandry. In the first place, the industrialization of farming, a product of the belief that all

---

15. Michael Hofmann, 'Beat Sterchi: *Blösch*', *Times Literary Supplement*, 5 October 1984.

progress is created by machinery, reduces everything to the simplicities of technological exploitation. Knuchel is assured by the local mayor, for example, that the days of the 'Mehrzweckkuh' (p. 47) have long since passed, a fact ironically underlined when the carcase of Blösch, the milk-producer, is later designated unfit for human consumption as meat. Secondly, the remorseless logic of production economics dominates agriculture. The demands of the market are controlled by the multinationals, the price for failing to comply with their demands is high – a smallholder obliged to sell to pay his debts is shown to be about to join the urban proletariat. Symbolically, the cattle-dealer of the old school, who had maintained personal relations with the farmers who supply him, suffers a stroke as a result of pressures created by the large firms which, for all their impersonality, can outbid him. Thus the alternating scenes between smallholding and abattoir do not form a contrast between idyll and brutality, since Sterchi shows them to be related parts of the same picture. Moreover, Knuchel is not shown holding out heroically against destructive forces; he is sufficiently of his age to share many of its attitudes: he has already to a large extent mechanized his farm, and he knows that he can continue to resist the milking-machine only as long as his cows, especially Blösch, continue to produce spectacular quantities of milk. The farmhouse itself – in a development of the 'Haus-Motiv' – reflects insecurity and disharmony: the unexplained, wellnigh continuous thumping noise which plagues Ambrosio in his room turns out to be caused by Knuchel's three younger children banging their heads against the wall of the living-room.

The novel uses Ambrosio's departure from the smallholding after a few months to take stock of his experiences. Obviously, he has been made aware of the xenophobia in the village, and he has seen the force of social sanctions in the suicide of one local who befriended him and another *Fremdarbeiter*. Of course, these are attitudes and mechanisms which are not peculiar to Switzerland, but another conclusion reached by Ambrosio is. For, overwhelmed as he had been at the outset by the gigantic scale of everything, he now asks himself, as he leaves the village: 'War das wirklich alles echt?' (p. 313). He now sees the villagers comporting themselves 'als wären sie von der Wichtigkeit ihrer Gesten überzeugte Schauspieler', and he reflects on this strange environment: 'Wenn alles, was da herumstand ... lediglich zu den Kulissen einer gigantischen Theateraufführung gehören sollte, die eigens, um ihn irrezuführen, inszeniert worden war, so war das Unternehmen gescheitert. Ihn, Ambrosio, hatte man nicht getäuscht' (p. 314). On one level, Ambrosio is seeking to maintain his dignity in face of the treatment he has received; on another level, the outsider perspective has maintained its distance, the inauthenticity which Ambrosio is portrayed as sensing is a measure of the inner insecurity behind the apparently solid façade. In 1972, E. Y. Meyer, in his novel *In Trubschachen*, had presented, through the eyes of a Swiss town-dweller on a short stay, a deeply ambiguous picture of the realities of life in the Swiss countryside. The novel was a modern *Heimatroman* which inverted the values of the traditional genre. Exactly a decade later, Sterchi adapts some of the same themes in writing what has been called the last *Bauernroman*,[16] a genre with a long Swiss tradition.

The scenes in the abattoir, on the other hand, to the extent that they present a most precise depiction of a work process, would not be out of place in an *Arbeiterroman*, a genre which began to make its appearance in German–Swiss literature in the 1970s. And here the novel *Blösch* pinpoints an important similarity between smallholding and abattoir which demonstrates why the traditional *Bauernroman* is no longer a viable literary form. As the notion of a craft based on knowledge and experience is shown on the smallholding to be vanishing with the increasing industrialization of farming, so a similar process is depicted at a more advanced stage in the abattoir. Most of the workers there have one simple task to perform in the dismemberment of the animals, and this facilitates the employment of a large percentage of untrained *Fremdarbeiter*. Those workers with some kind of skill derived from experience are shown to be under pressure to relinquish it in favour of simple machine-assisted methods which accelerate the throughput. Thus the work in the abattoir does not present a difference of kind to that on the smallholding, but rather one of degree, since the same ethos holds sway in both places, an ethos dominated by lack of respect for anything but the profit-motive.

The main perspective from which the abattoir scenes are viewed is not that of Ambrosio but of an eighteen-year-old Swiss apprentice. Through his eyes are seen the hectic repetitiveness of the work, the minimal human contact between workers as they struggle to execute their part in the slaughter process and the unremitting pressure to accept and tolerate the unacceptable and

---

16. Elsbeth Pulver, 'Bauernroman – Arbeiterroman – Zeitroman. Der Roman *Blösch* von Beat Sterchi als Beispiel der Gegenwartsliteratur der deutschen Schweiz', in Gürsel Ayac, Viktoria Rehberg and Sara Sayin (eds.), *Izmirer Colloquien. Die Schweizer Literatur der Gegenwart*, Izmir, 1987, pp. 17–26; here p. 17.

intolerable. 'Durchstehen ist ihr Lieblingswort' (p. 218), reflects the young man on the adult world. Yet he marvels constantly at his own inability to protest, to rebel. One impediment to this in the Swiss context is the no-strike agreement, the so-called 'Friedensabkommen' concluded in 1937 between unions and owners and still in force today, which has created what the novel calls 'verinnerlichte Selbstdisziplin' known as 'Arbeitsethos' (p. 384). Just as there are parallels between the smallholding and the abattoir, so there are parallels between the *Fremdarbeiter* and the apprentice. For if the former are characterized by the apathy of those who do not belong, the latter is alienated from the work and from the attitudes of those in charge to the extent that he feels like a 'Fremdarbeiter im eigenen Lande' (p. 230). It is interesting in this respect to compare *Blösch* to the *Erzählung: Im Zementgarten*, published by Raffael Ganz in 1971, the first depiction in contemporary German–Swiss literature, as far as I am aware, of a *Fremdarbeiter* in a central role. In Ganz's story the *Fremdarbeiter* does not recover from his rejection by the Swiss community, whereas in *Blösch* the departure of the *Fremdarbeiter* is presented as a rejection by him of an intolerable and unworthy bondage. That he can leave is precisely his advantage over the Swiss apprentice who, on the same day, escapes to the cinema. The young man's revolt will continue to be internalized, and the limits of the rebellion by some of the workers on Ambrosio's last day are indicated by the arrival of a police-car at the abattoir.

Blösch, the catalyst for Ambrosio's gesture of liberation, is shown finally to defeat the system, first, in the failure of the foreman completely to dismember her carcase, and secondly, in the fact that the meat obtained from her is stamped 'Ungenießbar' (p. 433), unfit for the world of consumption upon which the entire undertaking is based and which is indicated by fitful glimpses of the passengers in the trains passing the abattoir as they enter and leave 'die schöne Stadt'. The unfitness of the meat relates also to the theme of sickness in contemporary German–Swiss literature. The smallholder Knuchel's skin complaint is linked to the pressures on him, those who work in the abattoir are subject to intense forms of mental, emotional and physical stress with no opportunity for release or respite, and the physical mutilations which many of them, including Ambrosio, suffer are an external manifestation of the cost to them. The experience of Ambrosio 'im wohlhabenden Land' paints a sombre picture of the price exacted for prosperity. If Sterchi sets the action of his novel in the 1960s, it might be in part to suggest to the reader that, by the time of its publication in 1983, the inexorable pressures depicted had advanced further.

Themes in the German–Swiss Novel of the 1980s

Blösch is formally a novel in a realist tradition from which Gertrud Leutenegger, the author of *Kontinent* (1985), has sought to distance herself: 'Ich habe mich immer ein wenig gegen die Sachlichkeit und Realitätsbezogenheit eines Großteils der deutschschweizer Literatur gesträubt,' she is quoted as saying in 1975 when her acclaimed first novel was published.[17] Her associative style of writing, which provokes mixed reactions,[18] has a certain affinity with the complex naivety of Robert Walser. With her contemporaries she shares a concern for a relationship to the past which gives meaning to the present and the future. On the one hand, as already indicated, she seeks a resuscitation of the vital force of legend within a Swiss context; on the other hand, in a wider context of myth, she examines the historical development which has led to the emotional and spiritual impoverishment of the patriarchal society in, for example, the dramatic poem *Leb wohl, Gute Reise* (1984), a modern setting of the Sumerian legend of Gilgamesh.

Kontinent takes place principally in a village identifiable as being in the Canton of Valais.[19] The first-person narrator has come there to prepare cassettes for a 'Jubiläumsplatte' (p. 21)[20] for the approaching seventy-fifth anniversary of the powerful aluminium factory. Her predecessor, who had left six months beforehand, occupied the red-painted house known as the 'Observatorium', but the narrator is assigned to the nearby house of the 'Bewässerungsinspektor', whose funeral is taking place as she arrives. A first narrative strand relates to the recent past of the village: it emerges that the narrator's predecessor had regarded the 'Bewässerungsinspektor' as a father-figure, who also appeared to embody the main opposition to the economic might of the factory and its destructive effect on the local ecology. However, he had betrayed the trust placed in him, appearing at the 'Musikfest' of the village the previous year in the robes of 'der chinesische Kaiser'

17. Quoted in Peter Rüedi, 'Fluchtpunkte. Die Schweizer Autorin Gertrud Leutenegger und ihr Erstling: *Vorabend*', *Die Weltwoche*, 30 April 1975.
18. Whereas Silvio Blatter claims of Leutenegger's novel *Gouverneur* (1981): 'Es ist ein vergeblicher Versuch, diesem Buch eine nacherzählbare Geschichte abgewinnen zu wollen', 'Das Buch ist der Berg. Gertrud Leuteneggers *Gouverneur*', *Die Zeit*, 23 October 1981, Manfred Jurgensen feels that the same novel 'seems destined to become the most outstanding work of German women writers since the war', *Women, Writers, Women Writers – An Alternative History of German Literature*, Queensland, 1984, p. 19.
19. There are clear parallels to the essay 'Die dankbaren Toten von Chippis', first published in the *Tages-Anzeiger Magazin* (Zurich) in 1982, republished in *Das verlorene Monument*, pp. 67–77.
20. Gertrud Leutenegger, *Kontinent*, Frankfurt/Main, 1985. All page references in the text are to this edition.

(p. 42), and his authoritarian and domineering behaviour in this costume had revealed this to be 'seine wahre Rolle' (p. 150), a fact confirmed by his subsequent affirmation of the factory and its activities. The development of this strand is intertwined with memories of the narrator's recent visit to China, now governed in a fashion different from the historical imperial rule evoked by the costume of the 'Bewässerungsinspektor'. In China, the narrator perceives a role, however imperfectly realized, for the people, and she also achieves a clearer definition of herself as a result of a relationship with a young man. A third narrative strand is provided by the narrator's observation of, and involvement in, the life of the village from her arrival in the spring until the grape harvest in the autumn. As the three strands interweave, a relationship begins to establish itself between the narrator and the behaviour of her predecessor until the narrator is in a position to accept that behaviour as her own past. Her work, discarded by the factory, is rescued by the workers for the benefit of the villagers, who invite the narrator to re-install herself in the 'Observatorium'.

In the novel *Vorabend*, the narrator pondered on a subject for her writing: 'Soll ich erzählen vom Dorf. Aber das ist nicht repräsentativ. Schon gar keine Aktualität . . . Aber will uns jemand weismachen, nur in der Verstädterung fließen die Widerspiegelungen der Zeit zusammen.'[21] *Kontinent* depicts how far 'die Widerspiegelungen der Zeit' clash with a traditional perception of village life. The factory, as well as being the only employer in the area, is also the largest landowner, and applies industrial methods to cultivation so that, as in *Blösch*, a process of specialization has been set in train, the formerly varied husbandry having been gradually replaced solely with vines. These are regularly sprayed with chemicals so powerful that even miniscule amounts can cause violent illness in humans. But, as in the factory itself where safety and environmental regulations are flouted, those who might seek to have recourse to law for damage or injury from the spray are bought off against a promise of silence. The village cemetery, where the plastic flowers are 'schwarz von den Abgasen', is, symbolically, 'ohne Übergang in das Werkareal hineingebaut' (p. 41), a situation reminiscent of Burger's *Schilten*, where the cemetery forms part of the school. The villagers' sense of continuity with the processes of Nature has been ruptured, and the harsh jarring yellows and blacks of the plastic chemical sacks scattered throughout the landscape act as visual reminders of damage at other levels.

21. Gertrud Leutenegger, *Vorabend*, Frankfurt/Main, 1980, p. 95.

A disregard of the former careful cultivation of the hilly terrain brings about a serious landslide, the results of which are removed 'unauffällig wie eine Schande' (p. 58). At some distance from the village stand baleful 'Hochhäuser', 'durch nichts mit dem Dorf verbunden' (p. 138), which harbour visitors for a few days each year and which represent other economic forces. Walther Kauer, in his novel *Spätholz* (1976), portrays the exploitation by outside money of the countryside in southern Switzerland for industrial and leisure purposes, which results in the alienation of the local population and the dislocation of ecological balances. But whereas Kauer presents a traditional model of a confrontation between an individual hero and evil forces, Leutenegger, like Sterchi in *Blösch*, depicts a more sophisticated awareness of limitations, the villagers confining themselves to sporadic acts of peripheral defiance and subversion. Thus, if *Kontinent* is at one level a *Dorfgeschichte*, it possesses, in terms of its portrayal of the pressures of modern society, an 'Aktualität' which vindicates the ironic implication of the comment made in *Vorabend*.

The designation *Dorfgeschichte* contrasts with the title *Kontinent*, which relates in part to the narrator's stay in China. Other recent German–Swiss novels have featured China, Muschg's *Baiyun oder die Freundschaftsgesellschaft* (1980) and, less centrally, Erica Pedretti's *Valerie oder Das unerzogene Auge* (1986). In all cases, such faraway settings no longer reinforce and highlight by their exotic distance the qualities of a Switzerland which today offers, as Rolf Kieser points out, 'kein Refugium, kein Herd mehr, an dessen Wärme sich der Heimkehrer von den Strapazen seines Abenteuers erzählend erholt'.[22] And whereas, in the literary tradition which I have mentioned, the return was the point at issue, now the country from which the return is made may serve, not simply as a yardstick of comparison with Swiss conditions, but as an example to be emulated. In *Kontinent*, as in *Stiller*, this return is a double one, to Switzerland and to an individual past. But, unlike Stiller, the difficulties encountered by the narrator in *Kontinent* with both of these contrast with positive experiences in China which have no counterpart in Switzerland and which have rendered the distant continent closer to her than the village in the Valais.

On a personal level, she has attained, in her relationship with the young Chinese, a self-awareness which contrasts with her suppression of the experience of betrayal in her relationship with the

---

22. Rolf Kieser, 'Schweizer Literatur nach 1945. Versuch eines Portraits', in 'Deutschsprachige Literatur der Schweiz nach 1945', *Text und Kontext*, vol. 11, no. 2, 1982, pp. 217–40; here p. 236.

'Bewässerungsinspektor'. In a variant of the 'Haus-Motiv', her past is symbolized by the red-painted 'Observatorium' where she once lived: 'Das Rot des Observatoriums schreckt mich wie ein verborgener Teil meiner selbst. Ich will, daß dieses Verborgene keine Herrschaft mehr errichte, jeder Traum gehört dieser Welt' (p. 106). Her suggestion, warmly welcomed by the tactful and sympathetic villagers, that the house be repainted the blue colour which formerly offered 'dem Wegsuchenden ein ungeduldig erwartetes Zeichen' (p. 121), indicates her rehabilitation, both as an individual and as a member of the community. The indissolubility of the link between the two had been emphasized in China: the narrator, impressed by the covered Chinese teacups and seeking to buy one, had been gently rebuked by her companion – 'bei uns trinkt man den Tee immer zu zweit' – causing her to feel that she had unmasked 'meine ganze eigene Zivilisation' (p. 90).

On a public level, she has sensed a coherent purpose in Chinese life which contrasts with the fragmented nature of life in the village. It is not, however, that the narrator sees China and its millions in a romantic light. If, in the throng, she is invigorated by 'dieses durchaus freundliche doch zielbewußte Vorwärtsgestoßenwerden' (p. 88), she is also aware of the necessity of 'das geliebte Gesicht, durch das hindurch ich allein alles erkenne, ohne das die Menschenmengen unterwegs Ströme von Unermeßlichkeit und Trauer sind, und die Freundschaft der Völker ein totes Wort' (p. 68). Within the framework of this dialectic, the narrator experiences, in a 'Wohnhof' in Peking, the potential of human community. That she perceives such community, not as an apolitical idyll, but as an intensely political driving force is emphasized when she calls the exemplary 'Wohnhof' 'meine Verbotene Stadt': for here the 'kaiserliche Rat' used to meet each morning and to decide 'über das Schicksal des Reiches'; but these former structures of power have been replaced – 'mein kaiserlicher Rat sind die Menschengruppen' – and as she leaves the 'Wohnhof', she knows 'daß mein Leben nie mehr so sein wird wie zuvor' (p. 119). Thus the narrator's vision is closer to realization in China than in the Valais, where accepted economic practices have brought about a repressive situation in which existing power structures are inimical to the development of human potential. In manifesting a belief in the sustaining power of community which, it has been claimed, is rare in contemporary writing in German,[23] *Kontinent* resembles aspects

---

23. Manfred Jurgensen, 'Gertrud Leutenegger', in *Deutsche Frauenautoren der Gegenwart*, Berne, 1983, pp. 233–72; here p. 255.

of Gertrud Leutenegger's other works and, in a further parallel reinforcing this, the action of the novel occurs almost exclusively in public places.[24] Certainly, the emotional significance of the continent of China within the structure of the novel advances the concept of the negative model of Switzerland a stage further, since the positive example of China, it is implied, will, through the future behaviour of the narrator, work towards a strengthening of human links within the hostile framework of the Swiss village.

Blösch and *Kontinent* relate in a variety of ways to trends in contemporary German–Swiss writing: to developments in a regenerated concept of *Dorfliteratur*; to what has been labelled 'universellen Regionalismus',[25] portrayals of locality which have wider application and significance; to depictions of the stresses and depredations which the *Leistungsgesellschaft* inflicts on those within its ambit; and to searches, within the framework of contemporary Swiss conditions, for a modus vivendi for the individual which takes full cognizance of the political dimension of life. The two novels show relentless economic forces which appear to be beyond political regulation, indeed, the depicted power structures lend all strength to these forces, buying off opposition, as in *Kontinent*, or employing disenfranchised labour, as in *Blösch*. It seems worth insisting, in the Swiss context, on this more generally valid point, since the Swiss tradition of direct democracy figures prominently in the image of the country. Yet these novels show a reality in which a sense of individual helplessness is quite at odds with any notion of meaningful control. *Blösch* and *Kontinent* describe responses to a perceived lack of protection for the individual in the political framework, and in this they relate to a major theme in recent German–Swiss literature already mentioned, that of 'Verweigerung', which is associated with the work of E. Y. Meyer, Gerhard Meier, Christoph Geiser, Gerold Späth and others. This theme might be defined generally as consisting of the identification and articulation of those aspects of the individual which are steadfastly resistant to political and social manipulation. In *Blösch*, it is the innate dignity of the animal in its stoically borne degradation which strikes the deepest chord in Ambrosio, making him aware of his own abused humanity and motivating his departure from the

---

24. Dorothee Schuscheng, *Arbeit am Mythos Frau. Wirklichkeit und Autonomie in der literarischen Mythenrezeption Ingeborg Bachmanns, Christa Wolfs und Gertrud Leuteneggers*, Frankfurt/Main, 1987, draws attention to the prevalence of public places in Leutenegger's work (pp. 187, 328).
25. Pulver, 'Als es noch Grenzen gab', p. 9.

abattoir. In *Kontinent*, the power of human solidarity within a repressive system is likened to dams withstanding and deflecting flood-waters. These irreducible human factors set themselves against the seeming omnipotence of the system: Blösch's carcase disrupts the process of demolition, the workers in the aluminium factory subvert the prohibition on the dissemination of the narrator's tapes.

The demonstrations of 1980 in Zurich and elsewhere were directed against an image of life in modern Switzerland, and represented, at least in part, the protests 'einer Generation von Verweigerern . . . denen in einer normierten Gesellschaft die unerläßlichen Freiräume fehlen'.[26] Interestingly, the same concept 'unerläßlich' was employed by Gertrud Leutenegger in 1985 to describe the role of literature: 'Unerläßlich ist Literatur, weil sie ein Instrument ist für die Erforschung unserer Wirklichkeit.'[27] When we reflect that, for many in Switzerland, the disturbances of 1980 are almost as if they had never been, since the memory of them could disrupt an image of the country which has no place for 'die unerläßlichen Freiräume', then the force of Leutenegger's claim becomes apparent. In 1946, Max Frisch justified the position of Swiss writers in a European context during the recent war by claiming that they were portraying 'das Vorhandensein einer anderen Welt'.[28] It seems to me that, almost fifty years later, the novels *Blösch* and *Kontinent*, and the themes in contemporary German–Swiss writing to which they relate, are fulfilling a similar function, not so much in a European as in a Swiss context.

---

26. Ibid., p. 29.
27. Quoted in Elsbeth Pulver (ed.), *Zwischenzeilen. Schriftstellerinnen der deutschen Schweiz*, Zurich, 1985, p. 23.
28. 'Dritter Entwurf (eines Briefes)', in *Gesammelte Werke*, vol. 2, p. 474.

−11−

Beyond Reality: Theory and Practice of Austrian Prose in the 1980s

HUBERT LENGAUER

I Fairy-tales are Coming True

Peter Handke has called one of his recent books, *Die Abwesenheit* (1987), a fairy-tale (*Märchen*), while maintaining at the same time that the genre and this example of it were 'realist'. We should do well to heed this signal: Handke, so it would appear if we look back at literature since the mid-1960s, has always set trends, given concise expression to the latest 'mood in the West'. And he has done this, no matter how paradoxical it may sound, always from the position and with the pathos of the lone wolf, the unique figure − and, one paradox dissolving into the next, in so doing he confirms the way his profession habitually sees itself.

At the beginning of the 1970s, Handke's *Wunschloses Unglück* provided a text of fundamental importance for the decade that followed, one to which the upsurge of (auto-)biography in that period can be related. That this text fully warrants its key position becomes abundantly clear when it is understood as a definition of the writer's status: his return to his 'self', to the 'Ich' (which in Handke's case was jerked out of its shell of professionalism by his mother's suicide) that now promises immediacy and authenticity.

For a good part of the literature of the 1970s the criterion by which it qualifies is the avoidance of status − writing below the state of the art. And this, it appears, is what is to be revised and explicitly so. As if to confirm the self-depiction both present in latent form (in works) and made manifest in public, the little book *Nachmittag eines Schriftstellers* (also 1987) decrees this reversal of priorities: 'Also nicht: "Ich als Schriftsteller", vielmehr: "Der Schriftsteller als ich"';[1] the person whose afternoon is depicted not only takes the

---

Translation by Arthur Williams.
1. Peter Handke, *Nachmittag eines Schriftstellers*, Salzburg, 1987, p. 6.

serious step of addressing himself with the title 'Schriftsteller' in order to give himself an anchor for the 'Tag für Tag ungesicherten Neuanfang', he takes one further important step and makes the activity itself sacred: 'Er hob beide Arme und verbeugte sich vor dem Blatt, das in der Maschine steckte.'[2] For the whole of the afternoon in question the writer goes through the world almost as if pronouncing his benediction upon it, observing things and by taking note of them, making them meaningful – that is, *real* in the emphatic sense; the activity culminates at the most elevated point, which is also the point of self-dissolution: the book ends logically with the quotation from *Torquato Tasso*: 'es ist alles da und ich bin nichts' (Act 5, Scene 5).

The revision in the status of writing as an activity and the creation of an aura around it are accompanied by changes which become apparent in the works themselves and which could be described – hypothetically and crudely – as the 'return of the metaphor'. As examples, Handke's landscape metaphors in the novel *Die Wiederholung* can be quoted, first and foremost that Utopian idyll, the dolina in the karst:

> So freundlich war der Raum, in den ich hinabblickte, und eine solche Kraft stieg aus der Tiefe empor, daß ich mir vorstellen konnte, selbst der Große Atomblitz würde dieser Doline nichts anhaben; der Explosionsstoß würde über sie hinweggehen, ebenso wie die Strahlung. Und in der Vorwegnahme sah ich dann die zu meinen Füßen, in der fruchtbaren Erdschüssel, Tätigen als Rest-Menschheit, nach der Katastrophe, wie sie da wiederanfing zu wirtschaften.[3]

These are clear counter-images to reality as it is generally experienced; in this case they are images of 'warmth' – just as there are elsewhere, in the coincidence of opposites, synonymous metaphors of cold: in Christoph Ransmayer's *Die Schrecken des Eises und der Finsternis* (Vienna, 1984) and Michael Köhlmeier's *Spielplatz für Helden* (Munich, 1988); as its subject (or pretext) the first has a nineteenth-century expedition to the North Pole, the second a journey across Greenland. These metaphors of the universal are fractured by actions in the present, which project into them in order to guarantee the transfer of meaning.

The problematical relationship of metaphor to reality is perceived nowhere with greater clarity – aesthetic clarity, not concep-

---

2. Ibid., p. 7.
3. Peter Handke, *Die Wiederholung*, Frankfurt/Main, 1986, p. 289.

tual lack of ambiguity – than in a passage from Josef Winkler's latest novel, *Der Leibeigene*:

> Auf der Suche nach einer Metapher habe ich einem neugeborenen Fohlen das Maul aufgerissen, als es geburtsfeucht im Stroh lag, und habe mit meiner Hand den Schleim entfernt, damit es nicht daran erstickte, aber ob das Tier weiterlebt oder krepiert, war mir vollkommen egal, die Metapher war mir wichtig . . . Bin ich nicht mit meinem Filmkamerakopf in mein Elternhaus zurückgekehrt, um im letzten Winkel meiner Kindheitskammer eine Metapher zu finden? . . . Habe ich nicht zwei Meter unter dem Wasserspiegel der Drau im Sand gewühlt, um den Krebs wiederzufinden, der einst dorfgroß über den Häusern meines Heimatdorfes schwebte und dessen Fühler beim Schrei eines Dorfkindes zitterten? Um eine Metapher zu finden, plünderte ich die Dornenkrone am Haupte Jesu Christi, in der sich junge Schwalben eingenistet hatten. Mit dem Zwiebelmesser meiner Mutter sezierte ich eine Ratte, um in ihrem Innern eine Metapher zu finden. . . . Am Zoll bin ich gestanden und habe mitansehen müssen, wie der Beamte in meiner Reisetasche nach Metaphern suchte . . . Ich schreibe knieend, falte in sätzeleeren Zeiten meine Hände und bete um Metaphern. Den Kriegsgott kenne ich, den Gott der schwangeren Katzen ebenfalls, aber jetzt bin ich auf der Suche nach dem Gott des Bleistifts. Du bist der Metaphernhund, sagen die Bluthunde. Ich werde solange Metaphern suchen, bis ich selbst eine Metapher bin.[4]

The self-irony of the 'Metaphernhund', which, to use a mixed metaphor, rummages through all the realms of reality like a pig hunting for truffles, reinvests reality with the quality of being real; in face of the irrefutable claims of reality, it diminishes the subject pursuing this activity: but it is precisely the subjectivity within the writing which rescues this reality, its strangeness and individuality (of the foal, of the rat, to a certain extent of the goods to declare) from the avaricious power of the metaphor-hound and places it at the disposal of other powers. It is the recognition of this paradox which engenders the aesthetic precision characteristic of this passage and raises Winkler's writing, as intensive work with language, above descriptive realism.

II Where have all the 'Realists' Gone?

Yet, what has happened to all the reproductions of reality provided

---

4. Josef Winkler, *Der Leibeigene*, Frankfurt/Main, 1987, pp. 212–14.

by the 1970s? We must also describe (to a certain extent *ex negativo*) the route to the counter-images, to the metaphors and their creators, and this is what is to be attempted below in terms of the difficulties and problems of that 'realism' which had, in the 1970s, become characteristic of 'Austrian literature'.

It did, in fact, seem relatively easy about ten years ago to schematize the most recent literature in Austria under the heading 'realism', and it did seem possible, without recourse to analysis, to reach agreement that this was a fairly homogeneous phenomenon – especially with reference to the success on the book-market of authors like Michael Scharang, Franz Innerhofer, Helmut Zenker and Gernot Wolfgruber, to the 'Arbeitskreis der Literaturproduzenten', and to the *Wespennest* group and their journal.

The output of these authors is clearly less prolific now than it was before, it is less homogeneous, and – with the exceptions of Josef Haslinger and Gustav Ernst – there are hardly any authors who, in terms of their themes and techniques, could be included in the present context. This is surprising if one considers that 'realist' literature in the above sense is particularly concerned with social and political conditions and that these, given the levels of unemployment, have become increasingly problematical. The deficit in 'realist' literature, that is – so people believe – in literature which is politically effective, is indeed bemoaned, and well-meaning critics demand that it be made good.[5]

However, according to a report from the ranks of the writers themselves, the branch of literature which would have carried this responsibility, 'diese, eine bestimmte Art des (österreichischen) Realismus, [ist], kaum 6 Jahre nach ihrem Auftauchen aus dem Untergrund, 1978/79 zugrunde [gegangen]'. The level of unemployment was immaterial – the reasons were 'intra-literary', so *Wespennest* author Thomas Redl claims: namely the unresolved or insoluble 'bipolarity' between the generality of concepts (from the realm of politics or social theory) and the peculiarities of actual cases (from the life to be depicted).[6]

Thus it becomes patently clear that literary and social developments cannot be synchronized. The reasons are to be found equally in the processes of development and aging inherent in literature,

---

5. Evelyne Polt-Heinzl, 'Literatur und Arbeitslosigkeit', unpublished lecture at a meeting of the Walter Buchebner-Gesellschaft (1987); the author also edited a volume of the journal *Wespennest* in spring 1988 (no. 70) on the special theme of unemployment and literature.
6. Thomas Redl, '"Unglaublich präzise". Auf Besuch beim Realismus', *Wespennest*, no. 55, 1984, pp. 53f.

and in the difficulties of predicting and describing changes in society. In this situation one can find both the old sentimentality and the brash flight into the future. Urs Jaeggi writes:

> Unsere Geschichten, unsere Gedichte liegen, prallvoll oder blutleer, unterhalb der Ebene, auf der sich die gesellschaftlichen Entscheidungen anbahnen und abspielen. Kein Zufall, daß wir schreibend, eher verstört, unsere eigene enge Alltagswelt ausbreiten, uns selbst, auch im Fiktiven. Am Bodensee, in Hamburg, Berlin, Solothurn oder Wien erfinden wir Figuren, die in ihrer Hilflosigkeit Ebenbilder sind. Wenn wir Glück haben, beschreiben und umschreiben wir das, was unsere Generation, unsere gesellschaftliche und geographische Herkunft berührt . . . Dagegen anschreiben, anreden und wissen, unsere Rhetorik nutzt sich, weil wir Pathos und Ethik einsetzen, weil dies unsere Mittel sind, immer wieder ab.[7]

This, then, let us make the claim, is where the realists have gone. The emotional appeal of their resistance is directed, getting older but apparently unchanging, at the impertinent assumption that they have slipped out of fashion.

Peter Glaser, who was born in Graz but emigrated from Austria to Germany – and from literature to music – expresses the opposite standpoint, from where 'social conditions can be made to dance' (after Karl Marx): no longer is it resistance, particularly literary resistance, that 'losgeht, fetzt, reinhaut':

> Der offene Protest hat sich in den letzten Jahren viel zu oft als unerfülltes Kindergeschrei nach Spielzeug von Papa Staat erwiesen oder sich selbst erstickt durch die Wiederholungen seiner Forderungen und Widersetzlichkeiten bis zum Überdruß und ist zum Sandsack geworden, an dem die konservativen Systeme ihr Sparring abschlagen . . . Es ist nun schockierender und wirkungsreicher geworden, *einverstanden* zu sein . . . Die Gegenwartsliteratur ist langweilig, kriege ich rundherum zu hören. Wenn ich im Ratinger Hof, der Düsseldorfer Wellen-Brutstätte, schreie: 'Literatur', rennen mehr Leute weg als wenn ich schreie 'Polizei'. Vielen Jungen erscheint das Erlebnis Literatur heute als 'falsche Bewegung', und die zum Lesen erforderliche Beruhigung und monologische Gefaßtheit haben den Beigeschmack freiwillig angenommener Lahmarschigkeit.[8]

7. Urs Jaeggi, 'Aufrichtigkeit – Schreiben als Widerstand', in Jochen Hörisch and Hubert Winkels (eds.), *Das schnelle Altern der neuesten Literatur*, Düsseldorf, 1985, pp. 121–30; here pp. 129f.
8. Peter Glaser, 'Die neue Deutsche Wanderdüne', in Hörisch and Winkels (eds.), *Das schnelle Altern*, pp. 231–47; here p. 234.

It is difficult to deny that there is a certain logic about this latter judgement, although the theory that conformity is the sharpest form of resistance has still to be proved, and it is an open question whether more has been achieved, after all the noise and bourgeoisie-bashing, after the long march through the discos and media, than by 'the long march through the institutions' once envisaged.

Underlying the rejection of literature cited above is a comprehensive shift in relationships between the media which, on the one hand, reduces the 'utilization coefficients' of literature as compared with television, radio and other sound media, and, at the same time, as a result of this, makes authors of books very sensitive to the 'Verwertungsmöglichkeiten ihres vergleichsweise kärglichen Produkts. Daß Literatur immer trendempfänglicher wird, hängt mit diesem ihrem Sitz im Leben zusammen.'[9]

The question of the whereabouts of the realists is thus also a question of current general trends and their effects on literature. Given the development of the political situation since the Kreisky era, we can safely assume that the tricks of realism – one of which was once highlighted as permitting authors 'einen Bankdirektor nun Arsch zu heißen' – are now no longer opportune.[10] When social democracy calls in bank directors to help it manage the unemployment crisis, what use are poets, not to mention 'realists', then?

However, it was precisely the literature of the 1970s which termed itself 'realist' that was trying to escape such ascriptions of function and in so doing found itself increasingly bereft of theory. This lack of theory, which leads to the unthinking assumption that realist literature is the representation of reality just as it is, encouraged all manner of expectoration on childhood, youth, work and domestic hardship. Thus Reinhard Baumgart calls the 1970s, whose beginning saw the débuts of most of the 'realist' authors mentioned in the early part of this paper, the most unclear and diffuse of the postwar decades and attributes to this era 'ein[en] kaum bewußte[n] Eskapismus in Fragen der Ästhetik'. He goes on to say:

> Ob politisch oder apolitisch motiviert, ob im Faktenroman oder autobiographischen Erguß: eine neue Unschuld begann draufloszuschreiben, als hätte es das kritische Produktionsbewußtsein der Moderne nie gege-

9. Alexander von Bormann, 'Literatur als Wetterfahne', in Hörisch and Winkels (eds.), *Das schnelle Altern*, pp. 105–20; here p. 107.
10. Redl, '"Unglaublich präzise"', p. 54.

ben. Deren Distanz zum Publikum, ihre Arroganz und ihr Leiden in der splendid isolation, das alles wird nun kassiert, bis hin zur Nullösung von Verständigungstexten, in denen jeder Sender oder Empfänger spielen kann.[11]

The transaction in which the author could purvey authenticity while the reader paid to be affected seemed to require no further explanation; the immediate cause, the cruelty rife in the world both on the large and the small (domestic) scale, seemed to guarantee substance. The loss of professionalism which went hand in hand with this was often attributed to 'realism' or the 'realists' – for example, by Antonio Fian in a lengthy polemic in the *Wespennest*, a journal he criticized:

> Ich rede also, wenn ich von Realisten rede, nicht von Realisten, ich rede überhaupt nicht von Schriftstellern, sondern von einer Sorte Menschen, wie man sie leider allzuhäufig, auch und gerade in der Zeitschrift *Wespennest* antreffen kann, Menschen, die nicht den Ehrgeiz haben, Literatur herzustellen, sondern es für ihre Aufgabe halten, Inhalte zu transportieren; ich rede von Transportarbeitern, von – was das Schlimme daran ist – Transport-Kopfarbeitern, ich rede von Transportarbeitern, die den Begriff 'Realismus' usurpiert haben: ich rede von Realisten.[12]

This lack of respect and discretion towards both art and reality creates a relationship which is altogether too close and which consists in the simple duplication and replication of the reality which it pretends to criticize.

> Der Realist ist alle Festwochen wieder mit einem Projekt zur Stelle. Im Jahr der Behinderten schreibt er über Behinderte, im Jahr der Frau zieht er den Schwanz ein, im Jahr des Kindes macht er ein Kind. Schreibt er gerade nicht, so fährt er seine Gesinnung spazieren; täglich muß er sie in die verschiedenen Redaktionen bringen . . . Den Satz 'Es lebe der antifaschistische Kampf des chilenischen Volkes' beispielsweise kann er so schnell sagen, daß ihm der Kellner zehn Minuten später ein Schaschlik bringt.[13]

---

11. Reinhard Baumgart, 'Postmoderne – fröhliche Wissenschaft', *Die Zeit*, 16 October 1987, pp. 67f.
12. Antonio Fian, 'Versuch, im Stillen Ozean zu schwimmen', *Wespennest*, no. 55, 1984, pp. 46–51; here p. 49.
13. Ibid.

III Experience and Perspective

The state (or behavioural topos of the author) described here in polemical terms arises out of specific, determinable circumstances. Josef Haslinger, 'auf der Suche nach der österreichischen Literatur des letzten Jahrzehnts', identified and depicted them – not without self-irony – as the 'sozialen' and the 'ökonomischen Zugang' of the authors to literature.

'Über den Schatten der Herkunft', so Haslinger reports in his sketch of a model author, 'kommt er . . . nicht einfach hinweg. Er kennt die Welt nur von unten', 'dort oben, wo der Druck entsteht, den der Autor unten so schön registriert' in the 'deformierten Spiegel einer kleinen Angestelltenseele', up there 'wird ihm die Luft zu dünn, da versagt ihm das Vorstellungsvermögen'. The claims which Haslinger makes for his model author, however, remain lofty: 'Der Autor will . . . nicht irgendetwas erfinden. Seine Geschichte soll stimmig sein und soll, wie man so schön sagt, ein Stück Welt enthalten, und zwar mehr, als in den Tiefen der Seele eines kleinen Angestellten zu finden ist.'[14] Given the origins and public status of our present literature, this is neither conceivable nor possible.

What Haslinger here (ironically) loads onto the narrow shoulders of the typical Austrian author of today is something that, as a result of applying universal standards, had long ago been thrown open to doubt as a principle: Hegel had predicted the end of art on the grounds that the complexity of the modern world had increased to such an extent that the means available to art were no longer adequate; art was no longer in a position to reduce and represent reality meaningfully.[15]

What Realism in the literature of the nineteenth century had nonetheless attempted was the 'Reduktion komplexer Strukturen und Prozesse auf individuelle Handlungen und individuelle Konflikte', in order to wrest a 'lebensweltlich nachvollziehbaren "Sinn"' from a reality which was felt to be alien. However, the world could not successfully be reconstructed proceeding from the individual and so the 'Handlungstyp des "Scheiterns", der die

---

14. Josef Haslinger, 'Auf der Suche nach der österreichischen Literatur des letzten Jahrzehnts', in Friedbert Aspetsberger and Hubert Lengauer (eds.), *Zeit ohne Manifeste. Zur Literatur der siebziger Jahre in Österreich*, Vienna, 1987, pp. 7–15; here p. 7.
15. See Gerhard Plumpe, 'Systemtheorie und Literaturgeschichte', in Hans Ulrich Gumbrecht and Ursula Link-Heer (eds.), *Epochenschwellen und Epochenstrukturen im Diskurs der Literatur- und Sprachhistorie*, Frankfurt/Main, 1984, pp. 251–64; esp. p. 262.

Nichtverfügbarkeit komplexen Geschehens registrieren mußte',[16] became dominant in the nineteenth century.

Remnants of this Realist practice are still in evidence today, even if the perspective has changed somewhat: one after the other Gernot Wolfgruber's novels recount, in a sequence rising socially from the novel about the apprentice to the novel about the architect (*Die Nähe der Sonne*), the *failure* of the protagonists and the intransigence of reality; Innerhofer's prose works (through to *Der Emporkömmling*, 1982) have similar traits. Admittedly, the humour for which the Realists of the nineteenth century were noted (where it served as an element of harmony within persistent contradictions) has been lost. What has been discarded most emphatically is the transfiguration of middle-class work which Gustav Freytag, for example, had attempted to preserve as a subject of poetry.

If one holds to the principle – and the 'realist' prose of today seems to have laid claim to this part of the heritage of the nineteenth century too – that nothing can be viewed except by way of subjective experience, that is, experience that has been transmitted through the self, then the question of perspective becomes crucially significant. The autobiographical approach, which is often taken to establish perspective, appears to make this problem immediately soluble, with a naive absence of reflection. It is, however, no accident that, above a certain artistic and intellectual level, this naivety is found to be unsatisfactory and begins anew to be problematical. Proof of this in contemporary literature is the alternation of figures in Franz Innerhofer: from 'Holl' (*Schöne Tage*, 1974) to 'Ich' (*Schattseite*, 1975), to 'Holl' (*Die großen Wörter*, 1977), and finally to 'Ich, Hans Peter Lambrecht' in *Der Emporkömmling*. Nonetheless, depiction of the worlds of childhood also has its attraction nowadays: because these contain father and mother, heaven and earth, death and the devil (admittedly with distorted – but authentically distorted – perspectives), they seem to relate to the whole of life. A large section of contemporary literature can be categorized along these lines, that is, as the 'Re-Etablierung des Einfachen aus dem Geist der Authentizität'.[17] In stark contrast to this we have Josef Winkler's prose works with their constant, excessive, linguistic liquidation of the world of childhood and its (de)formative powers (father, religion).

These latter motifs would require separate discussion. The protagonists' fathers cast their (smaller or larger) shadows everywhere

16. Ibid., p. 263.
17. Karl Wagner, 'Über die literarischen Dörfer. Zur Ästhetik des Einfachen', in Aspetsberger and Lengauer, *Zeit ohne Manifeste*, pp. 166–80; here p. 168.

across the biographies of their sons: from Peter Henisch and Jutta Schutting to Innerhofer's *Der Emporkömmling*, Wolfgruber's *Die Nähe der Sonne*, to Scharang's *Harry* (1984) (whose father is well known from one of the author's other novels, *Charly Traktor*, 1973), to Josef Haslinger's *Der Tod des Kleinhäuslers Ignaz Hajek* (1985). And mothers, too, of course: in Wolfgruber's *Verlauf eines Sommers* (1981), for example, or in Anna Mitgutsch's *Züchtigung* (1985). Expressed somewhat crudely, this offers a possibility for 'history' to put in an appearance in the reality of postwar everyday life, which is otherwise largely bereft of history or, more precisely, is presented in an ahistorical perspective.

In order to gain a larger slice of reality, which Haslinger suggests is the objective of the contemporary Austrian author, a *single* perspective is insufficient. This is true also of the author who has always been credited with mastery of the particular art of developing reality strictly out of just *one* perspective: Gernot Wolfgruber. The reason for this is not, as was thought, that his characters, as 'Menschen' in the emphatic sense, are 'durch ihren Sozialstatus nicht erschöpfend definiert',[18] rather is it that the characters which lend his work perspective are *in themselves* synthetic, not individual (in the sense of indivisible) concepts, and it is precisely this that reflects their and 'our' social state. They are in themselves veritable ensembles of social relationships which can be taken apart and synthesized in keeping with prevalent patterns of thought and emotion, and according to social roles. And in the process of reading, as can be shown by reference to a representative selection of reviews, the in part parallel, in part contrasting patterns of experience are recombined to make the experience of reading a pleasant or an unpleasant one. This gives rise in literary criticism to very divergent views. I quote two prime contradictory examples: 'Erfahrungen, die jeder erlebt hat oder leicht nachvollziehen kann. Gerade das ist die Stärke und das Neue an Wolfgrubers Darstellungsweise';[19] and: 'Der Leser kennt das alles schon, erfährt nichts Neues, hat vermutlich ähnliche Erlebnisse schon gehabt, ähnliche Gedanken gehegt, ähnliche Impressionen empfangen – wozu dann Wolfgruber?'[20]

18. Ulrich Greiner, 'Ein Liebesroman, also ein Kriegsroman', *Die Zeit*, 4 December 1981 (on the novel *Verlauf eines Sommers*).
19. Roland Innerhofer, 'Fluchtbewegungen oder der Verlauf eines Befreiungsversuches', *Wiener Tagebuch*, no. 2, February 1983 (on *Verlauf eines Sommers*).
20. Ditta Rudle, 'Höhensonne', *Wochenpresse*, 7 January 1986 (on *Die Nähe der Sonne*).

IV At the Very Top – At the Very Bottom

In his latest novel, *Die Nähe der Sonne*, Wolfgruber, who has always concerned himself with unhappy social climbers, risks a view from the very top, from the 'Nähe der Sonne', in the terms of the titular metaphor. From here absolutely everything is possible, the world is again available, admittedly in the paranoia of the architect Stefan Zell, who is troubled with psychotic phases and, by means of lithium salts, is temporarily 'eingestellt' on the 'Normalachse. Die gerade Linie der Normalen'.[21] Hardly perceptible shifts in language take us from the quite normal lunacy of the architects' and interior designers' clique to the insane belief that it is possible to have an overall view of reality and to control it. Such fantasies of omnipotence and totality are a recurring theme in the book. Zell believes that he has been turned into James Dean and, with his foot on the accelerator, fits the fragmented world together again. This cannot go on for long; reality proves him wrong: when Zell wants to change the traffic lights at which he has stopped and they refuse to obey his will, he has an accident:

> Als sie grün wurde, ist er nicht weitergefahren. Es war ihm klar, daß es jetzt seine Pflicht war, die Ampel zu schalten. Alles hing davon ab. Er hat sie angesehen und mit dem Kopf exakt schalten können. Das Hupen, die auf der Kreuzung sich verkeilenden Wagen und die gestikulierenden Menschen draußen um sein Auto haben ihn nicht im geringsten gestört. Auch das Blaulicht nicht, das sich zuckend auf dem Pflaster und in den Fenstern der Häuser brach, dazwischen hin und her sprang wie in einer Galerie von Spiegeln. (p. 97)

The reverse of this pathological experience of omnipotence is that other experience, built up towards the end of the book, of total control imposed via the conscious mind: the command network of lithium, metal, wires and guide-rails in which the protagonist is trapped; the world as a cage:

> das Netz!, das ist das Netz! . . . Befehlsnetz!, alles aus Metall!, Fernsteuerung!, Lithium!, er merkt nicht einmal, daß sein Fuß hart auf die Bremse tritt . . . krampfhaft hält er sich am Lenkrad fest, um in der Spur zu bleiben, Abstand zu halten, dieses Netz aus Metall!: damit steuern sie alles, hat man ihn gesteuert, Lithium ist ja ein Metall, sein

---

21. Gernot Wolfgruber, *Die Nähe der Sonne*, Salzburg, 1985, p. 188. Page references in the text are to this edition.

ganzer Körper voll damit, sie hatten ihn unter Kontrolle, und da draußen überall Drähte, *Leitungen*, neben ihm *Leit*schienen. (p. 334)

However, these quotations indicate only the pathological peaks in the novel's progress; between them a whole variety of objects and situations appear in the mirror of the main figure's conscious mind: from the burial of his parents to Christmas Eve with the bereaved family up to the memory of the Preludynamo Company, a (fictional) group of architects to which Zell belonged and which is reminiscent of (real) experimental groupings of the 1960s.[22]

Thus, all in all, the impression of a richly unfolding reality is communicated through a consciousness which has itself been set into violent motion, from the 'normal state' into a pathological state, swinging to extremes of depression or euphoria and then returning. However, for long stretches of the novel the possibility of identifying with reality exists, through the consciousness of the main figure, because the extent of the alienation, the feelings of isolation, do not go beyond the experience of everyday awareness. The raising of awareness above the 'Normalachse' – in both the sense of the pathological experience and that of artistic awareness (Wolfgruber narrates the convergence of these two conditions, the imperceptible transition) – is an essential shaping force because in this way hypotheses about reality can be formulated without the need for verification.

It has, of course, always been one of the tricks of Realism to prop itself up with art (or to use art as a springboard) in order to reveal the character of the reality of actual real life. Think for example of Grüner Heinrich, who betakes himself to Munich, the artists' town, in order to become a painter, and paints flagpoles.

A similar contrast is used by Gustav Ernst, himself once the holder of an award from the Austrian Cultural Institute for study in Rome, when, in his (short) novel *Frühling in der Via Condotti*, he sends his married couple, the Guschelbauers, in search not of art, but of their lost love. The previous happiness of the honeymoon and also the aura and genii loci of Rome play an essential role: they are the backcloth in front of which reality makes its entrance: 'Die Ewige Stadt, sagte er. Heiß ist es, sagte sie.'[23]

This pattern of contrasts determines the shape of the novel from the start. But it is not always embodied in the words of the figures; often it is also apparent that somebody knows more than the

22. See Kristian Sotriffer (ed.), *Der Kunst ihre Freiheit. Wege der österreichischen Moderne von 1880 bis zur Gegenwart*, Vienna, 1987, p. 191.
23. Gustav Ernst, *Frühling in der Via Condotti*, Vienna, 1987, p. 73.

characters do – the author who is arranging the contrasts. Thus we read in the first sentence:

> Genau an jener Stelle, wo rechter Hand, bevor die Aurelianische Mauer beginnt und der Zug in den Bahnhof Termini einfährt, sich unter einer Reihe von Häusern, die mit ihren Fronten bis knapp an die Geleise reichen, jene Ruine befindet, in der immer, sooft man[!] vorbeikommt, Wäsche zum Trocknen aufgehängt ist, begann Marianne Guschelbauer ihren Mann dazu zu überreden, die Extrawurst aufzuessen. . . . Ich habe jetzt keine Wurst im Kopf, sagte Walter Guschelbauer, sondern das Gepäck. (p. 7)

Of course, everything goes wrong and only towards the end does the narrator lead the protagonists to the place where once they were happy – as onto a stage with a false floor, indeed with two false floors:

> Er hob den Kopf und sah durch Tränen auf Rom, das noch immer vor ihm lag wie das Leben.
> Er onanierte. Er schaute auf das Tor, durch das Goethe 1887 [*sic!* – 1787 is correct] die Stadt betreten hatte. Er schmierte den Samen mit der Schuhspitze so lang im Staub herum, bis nichts mehr zu sehen war. (p. 111)

By this time, if not sooner, the book has become recognizable as the inverse of the work which is prefaced by the motto, 'Wie wir einst so glücklich waren! / Müssens jetzt durch euch erfahren': the *Römische Elegien*, the first section of which depicts the poet's entry into the town and how the stones, palaces and streets come alive:

> Noch betracht ich Kirch und Palast, Ruinen und Säulen,
> Wie ein bedächtiger Mann schicklich die Reise benutzt.
> Doch bald ist es vorbei; dann wird ein einziger Tempel,
> Amors Tempel, nur sein, der den Geweihten empfängt.
> Eine Welt zwar bist du, o Rom; doch ohne die Liebe
> Wäre die Welt nicht die Welt, wäre denn Rom auch nicht Rom.[24]

It would be altogether possible to relate the harsh contrast which Gustav Ernst creates to a late dictum of Bertolt Brecht, namely: 'Wir müssen einen großen Ballast von erhabenen Gefühlen abwerfen, welche nur die Gefühle der Erhabenen waren, und uns den

---

24. Johann Wolfgang von Goethe, *Poetische Werke*, vol. 1, Berlin, 1976, p. 167.

niedrigen Beweggründen zuwenden, welche die Beweggründe der Niedrigen waren.'[25]

Michael Scharang also makes use of this principle – at least in his theoretical reflections on recent Austrian literature – to criticize the inventory of middle-class modernity. The new literature, in contrast with both that at the turn of the century and that of the interwar years, is a 'Literatur, die klein daherkommt'.

> Wie sonst hätte sich die Literatur nach dem Krieg verhalten sollen? Ein Blick auf die Literatur der Zwischenkriegszeit mußte ihr nahelegen, vorsichtig zu sein, den Mund nicht zu voll zu nehmen . . . sie hatte sich mit großen Werken eingemischt in große gesellschaftliche Auseinandersetzungen . . . Doch der Triumph des Nationalsozialismus relativierte das aufs Bösartigste . . . Wozu der große literarische Aufwand, wenn er nicht einmal das Schlimmste verhindern konnte.[26]

The other explanation for the 'klein daherkommende Literatur' is, as in the case of Haslinger, social in a direct sense: writers are no longer recruited from the middle class (which occupies posts in the culture industry and culture administration), but – the obvious conclusion – from the lower middle class and the proletariat; in any case, so Scharang believes, the conditions created by the culture administration turn literature into a 'proletarian' literature. Here, of course, he is making a virtue of necessity: the presentation of working conditions which are acknowledged as bad gives rise to the emotional tone of the writer as underdog. The situation allows two possible conclusions – and here one cannot disagree with Scharang: the author is predestined to be an 'ideale[s] Medium der Medienindustrie. Anderseits derjenige, der ihr schärfster Gegner werden kann'.[27] Given the principles of the media industry, and this can be linked also to Antonio Fian's criticism quoted above, both positions are possible at the same time.

No attempt will be made here to deny that Scharang, the author, displays the same proletarianization that is the basis for his condemnation of the new literature and which he uses to explain its emotional appeal. One can, however, in my view, detect in his

---

25. Bertolt Brecht, 'Realismus als kämpferische Methode. Notizen für die Rede auf dem Schriftstellerkongreß 1956', in *Über Realismus*, Frankfurt/Main, 1971, pp. 171–3, here p. 172.
26. Michael Scharang, 'Die proletarisierte Literatur', *Wespennest*, no. 55, 1984, pp. 2–6; here pp. 2f.
27. Ibid., p. 5.

book *Harry. Eine Abrechnung*[28] all the difficulty involved in gaining a viewpoint 'ganz unten', an air of 'klein Daherkommen'.

The technique of using a perspective from the very bottom seems to me to have been applied much more successfully in the *Novelle* by Josef Haslinger, *Der Tod des Kleinhäuslers Ignaz Hajek*, where, because only sparing use is made of supporting constructions, it disappears from view beneath the surface of the narration and yet, on closer analysis, allows the contours of the story to emerge to greater effect. This is a sort of 'chronicle of a death foretold'. Set in the backwaters of Lower Austria and narrated in traditional manner, it is the extremely confined story of the suicide of a small farmer; at the same time it hints at the history of three generations, war, denunciation and National Socialism, and yet the author never allows his power (within the story) over men and materials to impose itself on a single line as the know-all voice of the moral or political preacher. The graphic nature of the text arranges the details of this rustic 'culture of survival' (John Berger) in such a way that the unheard-of event, the suicide, appears at once paradoxical and logically consistent:

> Mit der Rückseite des Beils schlug er dem Schafbock so kräftig auf die Stirn, daß der augenblicklich umfiel. Während er das Tier auf die Leiter legte, begann es zu zittern und mit den Füßen zu zappeln. Er hielt es fest und stieß ihm am Hals das Messer durch das Fell, schob es ein paarmal hinein und drehte es in der Wunde, aus der warmes Blut über seine Hand herausschoß. Als der Bock nur mehr leise zuckte, wusch er an der Wasserleitung das Messer und seine Hand, warf noch einen Blick auf das ruhig daliegende Tier und ging heim. Eben wollte er die Haustür schließen, da stand der Schafbock mit großen, glasigen Augen hinter ihm. Aus seinem Hals rann noch ein Faden Blut . . . Gebannt starrte Ignaz Hajek in die Augen des Tieres. Es konnte sich kaum auf den gespreizten Beinen halten, neigte langsam den Kopf zu Boden und sank in sich zusammen.[29]

The memory of this event is the prelude to the suicide.

As his last service to those who will survive him, the old man, who on this particular day has hardly the strength to stand, drags home a sack of acorns for the sow and watches her eat; he goes to his neighbour's where a sow has just been stuck. His gaze wanders once more over the objects which fence in his world: gate, kitchen

---

28. Darmstadt, 1984.
29. Josef Haslinger, *Der Tod des Kleinhäuslers Ignaz Hajek*, Darmstadt, 1986, pp. 76f.

window, bedroom window, dung heap at the side of the sty. Then Hajek goes home and hangs himself. His wife 'molk zu dieser Zeit gerade die Geiß. Sie hörte, als die Schubkarre umfiel, ein Geräusch, aber sie wußte nicht, woher es gekommen war und fuhr, da es still blieb, mit ihrer Arbeit fort' (p. 89).

The story is not exhaustively characterized by these few pointers. In particular, there is the additional dimension of the historical and social awareness it displays: this is always developed within the horizons of the characters in the story, but in the combination of these individual horizons it goes far beyond them.

V Does Reality Unmask Itself?

Josef Haslinger's ambition as a writer, however, goes far beyond the world of acorns, sows, rams, rural suicides, etc. In the certainly somewhat self-ironizing portrait of the Austrian writer to which we have made reference (see p. 176, n. 14), he discusses a hypothetical scheme for a novel about a senior politician, a powerful entrepreneur and, at least in a secondary role, a cardinal. Because of a lack of direct experience and in the light of this, given his assessment of the chances of a true-to-life portrayal, he lets the politician drop, demotes the cardinal to abbot and the entrepreneur to chief clerk of a similarly scaled-down firm.

We must ask whether this 'realist' reduction is in any way still meaningful when we compare it with what Austrian reality (for practical reasons I cite the latter as a collective protagonist) has produced on the very field that Haslinger was struggling to till: ministers prosecuted for tax evasion, an abbot in gaol for collusion with an insurance manager, a public prosecutor burying bribes in his garden, etc. No realist writer, not even one with the lowest claims of probability for what he has invented, would have dared present this in a novel. Taking all of this into consideration, are there not good grounds for doubting the power of literary 'realism' to unmask? To formulate this scepticism, which I share, I again quote Antonio Fian:

> Die literarische Technik des Realisten ist eine journalistische: die der Entlarvung. Wozu aber ein Börsenmakler in einem Fernsehinterview zwei Minuten benötigt, dazu braucht der Realist einen Roman, und all die grausamen Wahrheiten, die fünfzig Realisten nach jahrelangen Recherchen in fünfzig Büchern zutage fördern, sagt Strauß in einer einzigen Wahlkampfrede. Der grundlegende Irrtum, dem der Realist aufsitzt,

ist der, daß er glaubt, die Ausbeuter, die Menschenverachter hätten es notwendig, etwas zu verschweigen. Das Gegenteil ist der Fall: Je mehr einer *zugibt*, desto mehr hat er zu reden.[30]

Given recent developments, even this last conclusion is not implausible. By way of illustration, Fian quotes the debate during the winter of 1982–3 about the appointment of the Third President of the Austrian Parliament; as he himself admits, he formulated the following with a fair degree of exaggeration:

> Man hätte bloß einen zu finden brauchen, der öffentlich bekennt, er habe einige tausend Juden eigenhändig ermordet: es tue ihm leid, aber er sei eben jung gewesen und werde es auch nicht wieder tun: Er wäre nicht nur dritter Nationalratspräsident geworden, sondern auch aussichtsreicher Kandidat gewesen für das Amt des nächsten Bundespräsidenten.[31]

Haslinger, the realist, has also treated – perhaps journalistically – the matter referred to in the final *exaggeration* above (the Austrian presidential election, which resulted in a victory for Kurt Waldheim). The essay in question, *Politik der Gefühle*, sold out of two print runs in no time at all.[32] This is a success without parallel, at least in Austria, although Haslinger is probably right when he suggests it is limited to those who read political essays: 'Ich merk' nur eines, daß ich die falschen Leser habe. Solche, die im Grunde aus dem Buch gar nicht viel Erkenntniswert, oder viel Widerstandskraft beziehen können, weil sie alles ohnedies in einer ähnlichen Form gesehen oder empfunden haben.'[33]

Thus he must continue to search longingly for a form which is effective above and beyond the circle of those who have already appointed themselves custodians of the true view:

> Ich hätte lieber einen Roman geschrieben, in dem jene politischen Machtstrukturen, die ich in meinem Essay darzustellen versuche, vielleicht dann doch exakter rauskommen, und zwar detaillierter und weniger auf eine handgreifliche These reduziert, sondern auch in ihrer Widersprüchlichkeit deutlicher, lebendiger. Aber die literarische Tradition, in der ich arbeite, schien mir dieser Aufgabe nicht mehr gewachsen zu sein: Der literarische Realismus hat sich sehr beschränkt auf die

---

30. Fian, 'Versuch, im Stillen Ozean zu schwimmen', p. 50.
31. Ibid.
32. Josef Haslinger, *Politik der Gefühle. Ein Essay über Österreich*, Darmstadt, 1987.
33. Interview with Franz Schuh, *Falter*, no. 43, 1987, pp. 1–4; here p. 3.

detaillierte Darstellung der geknechteten Subjektivität und auf die sehr undetaillierte Darstellung eines gesellschaftlichen Apparats, dem die Schuld an diesem Geknechtet-Sein zukommt und der den Grund abgibt für die ständige, zu ihrer Rettung nötig gewordene Fluchtbewegung der Subjekte.[34]

In spite of the provisional nature of any statement made, as this is, in an interview, this does have programmatic implications. And it envisages a repertoire of forms that would take us beyond the subject of the present analysis.

Reality lays itself bare, openly and without inhibition. This has been known, in principle, at least since Karl Kraus. And yet, paradoxically, we do need those who make us aware of when and how this happens: they drill holes (of perspective) in our mental blocks, through which we, readers and voyeurs of reality, can share its (often indecent) self-exposure.

---

34. Ibid.

–12–

Thomas Bernhard's 'Musical Prose'

ANDREA REITER

I

> Das war bei mir daheim schon so, wenns mich gsehn habn sinds immer schon hinausgestürzt, wanns irgendwas Unangenehmes erwartet haben, obwohl ich das liebste war, das man sich als Kind überhaupt vorstellen kann, wirklich, ich war reizend, mit großen langen Locken, lieb zum Anschaun, angenehme Stimme hab ich ghabt. Mit siebzehn hab ich schon die großen Wagnerrollen gesungen, mit achtzehn bin ich auf Mozart übergegangen, mit zwanzig hab ich mich schon bescheiden mit Bach begnügt, in der Kirche hab ich dann aus dem Liederbuch der Anna Magdalena gesungen, sehr schön, wirklich, ich war so gerührt, daß ich selber . . . Tränen sind mir heruntergelaufen, wie ich das gesungen hab. Und der Höhepunkt für mich war das Ave Maria von Bruckner in der Kirche in St. Veit im Pongau, also so was Schönes (unverständliches Wort) hab ich wirklich mein Leben nie wieder gehört.[1]

If it were not for music this essay could not have been written, since Thomas Bernhard, whose death at the age of fifty-eight has just been announced (12 February 1989), would have died an unknown eighteen-year-old in a Salzburg hospital. This, at least, is how he viewed his miraculous survival of a normally fatal lung disease. Indeed, Bernhard's five-part autobiography demonstrates that, since early childhood, music has been part of his life. In his recollections he talks about music in terms of its sociopsychological and psycho-physical influence on his life. He admits that his practising of the violin in the windowless shoe-cupboard of a Salzburg boarding school was quite unsuccessful. The exercise, however, had brought him to his own self. This is, at least, how Bernhard views the matter retrospectively. He thus establishes a

---

1. *Die Ursache bin ich selbst. Thomas Bernhard. Ein Widerspruch.* A film by Krista Fleischmann, Madrid, June 1986, transmitted by ORF and ZDF (my transcription).

pattern characteristic of his self-analysis. The child, as indeed the adult, could find his self only by experiencing and overcoming utter despair and even self-surrender (Ur 12ff).[2] And it is in this sense that the unsuccessful violin practice becomes a metaphor of his intention to live as an outsider. In the following period of his life, too, Bernhard views music as decisive in the shaping of his personality, considering it as the ideal counter-balance to his vocational training: 'Diese drei, Gesang, Musikwissenschaft und kaufmännische Lehre, hatten aus mir plötzlich einen ununterbrochen in größter Anspannung existierenden, tatsächlich völlig ausgelasteten Menschen gemacht und mir einen Idealzustand in Kopf und Körper ermöglicht' (Ke 100).

Bernhard's interpretation, in the third part of his autobiography, of his illness as a necessary termination of this ideal balance shows how important this psychological equilibrium was to him in his adolescence. Music, however, did not just help develop his personality, it also helped him establish social contact in the form of a teacher–student relationship. In earliest childhood, Bernhard's grandfather supported and furthered his artistic development. Later, other teachers – 'Lebensmenschen', as Bernhard calls one of them elsewhere[3] – replaced his grandfather. In spite of his practical attitude towards life, Podlaha, Bernhard's employer in *Der Keller*, was a 'musikalischer Mensch': 'In Podlaha, von dessen Biographie mir nicht mehr bekannt geworden war, als daß er aus Wien stammte und daß er Musiker hatte werden wollen und ein kleiner Krämer geworden . . . ist, hatte ich aufeinmal und unvorhergesehen wieder einen Lehrer, der von mir akzeptiert werden konnte' (Ke 74f).

It is hardly surprising that Bernhard attributes his renewed involvement in music to Podlaha's influence (Ke 94). Subsequently Bernhard found also in his singing and composition teachers, Maria Kehldorfer and her husband Theodor Werner, the conductor in Grafenhof and the organist of St Veit, friends who were to influence his view of life. This is important for the second function

2. The following editions of Thomas Bernhard's works are quoted extensively in this article. The five autobiographical novels: *Ein Kind* (Ki), Salzburg, 1982; *Die Ursache. Eine Andeutung* (Ur), Salzburg, 1975; *Der Keller. Eine Entziehung* (Ke), Salzburg, 1976; *Der Atem. Eine Entscheidung* (At), Salzburg, 1981; *Die Kälte. Eine Isolation* (Kä), Salzburg, 1982. Novels and plays: *Watten. Ein Nachlaß* (W), Frankfurt/Main, 1969; *Beton* (B), Frankfurt/Main, 1982; *Wittgensteins Neffe. Eine Freundschaft* (WN), Frankfurt/Main, 1982; *Der Untergeher. Roman* (U), Frankfurt/Main, 1983; *Holzfällen. Eine Erregung* (H), Frankfurt/Main, 1984; *Alte Meister. Eine Komödie* (AM), Frankfurt/Main, 1985.
3. See WN.

which Bernhard attributes to music in his autobiography, the psycho-physical one. When Bernhard, lying in the bathroom of the Salzburg Landeskrankenhaus, defied death and decided to live (At 16f), he made music 'zu einem, wenn nicht zu *dem* wichtigsten Mittel meines Heilungsprozesses' (At 38). His lungs, too, healed 'auf . . . musikalischem Wege' and 'die praktische Ausübung der Musik war aufeinmal mein Lebenstraining' (Kä 145).[4] In his fictional works Bernhard generalizes the link between music and existence. Wertheimer, for example, in Der Untergeher categorically claims: 'Kein *Musiktalent*! . . . Kein *Existenztalent*!' by which he wittingly – or unwittingly – pushes himself into committing suicide (U 70). In *Alte Meister* Reger, the narrator's partner in the dialogue, makes the following remark: 'Solange ich noch Lust habe, über die *Sturmsonate* zu sprechen oder über die Kunst der Fuge, so lange gebe ich ja nicht auf, sagte Reger. Die Musik rettet mich ja immer wieder . . . das ist es, durch die Musik jeden Tag in der Frühe, doch wieder zu einem denkenden und fühlenden Menschen gemacht, verstehen Sie!' (AM 243).

II

'Die Musik war meine Bestimmung' (Kä 145). This conviction supplied the critically ill Thomas Bernhard with the necessary will to live on. His novels and plays, too, draw on this experience, not only on the practice of music, as in *Der Ignorant und der Wahnsinnige*,[5] but also on music research, such as in *Beton* and in *Der Untergeher*.[6] This, too, is rooted in Bernhard's personal experience: 'Ich hatte das Glück, nicht nur von einer der zweifellos gebildetsten, gleichzeitig subtilsten Gesanglehrerinnen . . . in Gesang . . . ausgebildet zu werden, der größte Vorzug war die

---

4. What Bernhard describes here in his autobiography and fictionalizes in his novels, is a phenomenon that interests psychologists working with concentration-camp survivors. Viktor Frankl, for example, attributes survival in the camps to the fact that the inmates clung to a meaning of life beyond and after the camp. Thus artistic activity in general, and literary activity in particular, was performed as a strategy for survival by many inmates; see Viktor Frankl, *. . . trotzdem Ja zum Leben sagen. Ein Psychologe erlebt das Konzentrationslager*, Munich, 1985.
5. In *Salzburger Stücke*, Frankfurt/Main, 1975, pp. 7–93.
6. As recurrent words and sentence patterns transcend the individual work so, as Hans Höller notices, the theme of music dominates Bernhard's prose and plays; see '"Es darf nichts Ganzes geben" und "In meinen Büchern ist alles künstlich". Eine Rekonstruktion des Gesellschaftsbildes von Thomas Bernhard aus der Form seiner Sprache', in Manfred Jurgensen (ed.), *Bernhard. Annäherungen*, Berne, 1981, p. 45.

gleichzeitige musikwissenschaftliche Disziplinierung gewesen' (Ke 99).

What fascinates Bernhard about music theory is what could be called its formal, logical aspect: 'Ich entwickelte die Musik als wäre sie nichts als eine höhere Mathematik' (Ke 98). Contemplating Beethoven's *Eroica* puts Reger into a 'philosophisch–mathematischen Zustand' (AM 125). Rudolf, the narrator in *Beton* who is desperately trying to write a book on Mendelssohn, realizes that 'gerade Mozart' was for his work 'der wichtigste, aus Mozart erklärt sich mir alles, denke ich; ich muß von Mozart ausgehen' (B 147f). Bernhard's narrator in *Der Untergeher* appreciates the mathematical element not only in classical but also in modern music, especially in Schoenberg (U 59f).

Apart from mathematics, Bernhard stresses the link between music, philosophy and literature: 'Es ist ja klar, daß Literatur ohne Philosophie und umgekehrt und Philosophie ohne Musik und Literatur ohne Musik und umgekehrt nicht denkbar sind' (AM 257). Bernhard's self-characterization as a 'philosophischer Schriftsteller' (AM 178) is based on his interest in the philosophers Arthur Schopenhauer, Blaise Pascal and Ludwig Wittgenstein. His friendship with the latter's nephew is recorded in the novel *Wittgensteins Neffe*, where the protagonist Paul Wittgenstein illustrates another of Bernhard's fundamental ideas: that genius and insanity are just two sides of the same coin. He believes in the dialectics of intellect and madness, without, however, making clear whether madness is to be seen as a subjective or an objective condition. (Even the person concerned cannot be sure.) It is significant that Bernhard should express this view in a musical image: 'Bald denke ich, ich bin verrückt, bald, ich bin nicht verrückt. Es ist eine völlig durchinstrumentierte Partitur Wahnsinn' (W 86). This sentence, taken from one of the early novels, is often referred to as a clue to Bernhard's 'musical style'[7] but, in fact, says more about his controversial understanding of the nature of madness than about the character of his prose style. Bernhard considers insanity largely to be a linguistic phenomenon, a view which relates him closely to Wittgenstein's early philosophy.[8] The narrator in *Watten* realizes that he writes 'urplötzlich . . . in einer Sprache . . die ich selber

---

7. See Manfred Jurgensen: 'Die Sprachpartituren des Thomas Bernhard', in Jurgensen, *Bernhard*, pp. 99–122, and Otto Lederer, 'Syntaktische Form des Landschaftszeichens in der Prosa Thomas Bernhards', in Anneliese Botond (ed.), *Über Thomas Bernhard*, Frankfurt/Main, 1970, pp. 42–67; esp. p. 53.
8. See Wolfgang Stegmüller, *Hauptströmungen der Gegenwartsphilosophie*, vol. 1, Stuttgart, 1978, pp. 526–63.

überhaupt nicht mehr verstehe' (W 64); and subsequently generalizes this experience to: 'Wir sprechen aber alle doch immer nur die Sprache, die keiner versteht' (W 78). In his autobiography, Bernhard identifies with this verdict (Ke 112).

The link between music and madness is not new. Thomas Mann also explored this theme, as is well known, in his first novel *Buddenbrooks*, and was obsessed with it for the rest of his literary career. In Bernhard's works the sudden shift from (musical) excellence to psycho-physical collapse figures in numerous variations. The 'Koloraturmaschine' in *Der Ignorant und der Wahnsinnige* cancels all further engagements after a good two hundred performances as the Queen of the Night; at the end of the play she breaks down from exhaustion. Wertheimer dies from the knowledge that he will never reach Glenn Gould's genius: 'Es ist Tatsache . . . daß nichts anderes als die von Glenn interpretierten *Goldbergvariationen*, wie auch sein *Wohltemperiertes Klavier* an seinem [Wertheimers] Selbstmord schuld seien, wie überhaupt an seiner Lebenskatastrophe' (U 218). What Bernhard wants to bring across here is that, no matter whether one is oneself a genius or suffers from inferiority to somebody else's genius, catastrophe is the inevitable consequence.

III

What is the source, then, of Bernhard's fascination with music? We have already mentioned the influence of his grandfather, Johannes Freumbichler, himself a writer.[9] Bernhard, whose mother was unmarried when he was born, spent the decisive years of his childhood in the care of his grandparents. His much-loved grandfather introduced him to art and, in spite of financial hardship, supported the boy's musical education. He foresaw a career for Bernhard as a violin virtuoso or a celebrated singer. While Bernhard had gladly abandoned his unloved violin lessons in 1944, by which time the Second World War had reached Salzburg, he started to take voice lessons in the late 1940s of his own initiative. His career as a singer was terminated abruptly by his contracting pleurisy. From 1952 to 1954 Bernhard studied music and representational art at the *Mozarteum* in Salzburg, and in Vienna. But he never made a living from music.

Bernhard considers that his first encounter with Mozart's *Die*

---

9. For a biography of Johannes Freumbichler see the recently published book by Caroline Markolin, *Die Großväter sind die Lehrer. Johannes Freumbichler und sein Enkel Thomas Bernhard*, Salzburg, 1988.

Zauberflöte was his musical 'initiation', when he first heard it from the roof of the *Felsenreitschule* in Salzburg. He enthusiastically asserts that the opera fulfilled 'alle musikalischen Wünsche auf die vollkommenste Weise' (Ke 106). The impression that modern music made on Bernhard is also important. In an early attempt to talk about the shaping of his personality, he characterizes his childhood metaphorically as 'Musikstücke, allerdings keine klassischen' and subsequently more precisely as 'Zwölftonstücke'.[10]

How relevant is Bernhard's interpretation of his life for his work? In other words how 'musical' is his work, and does this musical quality have anything to do with Schoenberg, the inventor of dodecaphony and the term 'musical prose'?[11]

IV

Arnold Schoenberg does not simply imply a connection between music and literature, he sees in it the future of musical composition as such. The development of 'musical prose', according to Schoenberg, began with the Viennese classicists, Mozart and Haydn, and constituted the progressive element in Brahms's music. What Schoenberg means by this term is the increasing courage of composers to free themselves from traditional forms and regulations and to move towards asymmetrical structures. 'Musical prose should be,' he writes, 'a direct and straightforward presentation of ideas, without any patchwork, without mere padding and empty repetitions.'[12] Schoenberg contrasts 'musical prose' with verse and advocates renouncing metre and rhyme-scheme and a regular rhythm. 'All the units,' he says of the last movement of Mahler's *Das Lied von der Erde*, 'vary greatly in shape, size and content, as if they were not motival parts of a melodic unit, but words, each of which has a purpose of its own in the sentence.'[13]

How, then, are we to define the term 'musical prose' from the point of view of literature and to apply it to the writings of Thomas Bernhard? Only a few critical works have so far appreciated the musical character of Bernhard's prose style. Even where this is recognized, the authors either remain entangled in musical

---

10. Thomas Bernhard, 'Drei Tage', in *Der Italiener*, Salzburg, 1971, pp. 144–203; here p. 144.
11. See Arnold Schoenberg, *Style and Idea. Selected Writings*, ed. Leonard Stein, London, 1975, p. 339.
12. Ibid., p. 415.
13. Ibid., p. 426.

metaphor[14] or content themselves with stressing the need for a musical interpretation of Bernhard's prose.[15] Is it really the lack of an 'anerkannte Metasprache'[16] that has so far prevented detailed discussion along these lines? Problems arise, of course, whenever technical terminology is transferred from one discipline to another. It is not just a matter of terms making equal sense in both disciplines: it is more important that the two systems of meaning are compatible. Music and literature have, as we know, enjoyed a long relationship. In the Middle Ages composer and poet more often than not were one and the same person; even in the Renaissance, most music was sung and therefore dependent on language. Only gradually did it emancipate itself by developing its own grammar. Even so, poetry and especially song have preserved a close connection between words and music to this day. The two systems of meaning thus are compatible to the extent that they share a common tradition.

As for Bernhard's prose, we have just seen that he himself suggests an analysis in music–theoretical terms. This does not mean, however, that his work is sufficiently characterized as musical by virtue of an interpretation which applies musical metaphors: this would merely be a mannerism of the interpreter. In order to avoid this pitfall we should first discuss musical strategies in juxtaposition with examples of Bernhard's prose. My hypothesis is that Thomas Bernhard's prose works can be broken down into individual motifs, which are developed in a musical sense, logically put together and 'quoted' later in the work.

To test this hypothesis we have to look more closely at the musical theory of motivic development. In music a motif is the smallest meaningful and recognizable unit of a composition, a definition which literary theory would also accept.[17] Contrary to literature, however, comprehension of a musical composition is closely dependent on repetition. Arnold Schoenberg attributes this to the role which memory plays in the constitution of musical meaning.[18] Simplified motivic development typically looks like this: a musical idea (the theme) is consolidated through repetition,

14. See Jurgensen, 'Sprachpartituren'.
15. See Helmut Gross, 'Strukturphilosophischer Versuch über Thomas Bernhards "Gehen"', in *Text + Kritik 43: Thomas Bernhard*, Munich, 1974, pp. 29–35.
16. Karlheinz Rossbacher, 'Thomas Bernhard *Das Kalkwerk*', in Paul M. Lützeler (ed.), *Deutsche Romane des 20. Jahrhunderts. Neue Interpretationen*, Königstein, 1983, p. 382.
17. See Gero von Wilpert, *Sachwörterbuch der Literatur*, Stuttgart, 1969, p. 497.
18. 'The more easily graspable a piece of music is to be, the more often all its sections, small or large, will have to be repeated. Conversely, the fewer

possibly at various pitch levels or by inversion, and subsequently individual parts of it (the motifs) are independently repeated and extended. A different idea then undergoes the same or a similar process. (See Music Example 1, p. 195 below.)[19]

The motifs which make up a theme can be extended or shortened; or their order can be changed; or they can be repeated at a higher or lower pitch level, a technique known as sequence. (See Music Example 2, p. 196 below.)

There are at least two different kinds of 'sequence' in Thomas Bernhard's prose: in the following example he uses the adjective and its comparative form to achieve this effect:

> Unter den Verwandten einen berühmten Dichter zu haben, ist schon etwas Besonderes, dazu aber auch noch einen berühmten Philosophen unter den Verwandten zu haben, ist naturgemäß noch ungeheuerlicher, sagte Reger, aber dazu auch noch mit Anton Bruckner verwandt zu sein, ist das Höchste. (AM 98)

Here it is the main clauses which express an opinion or a judgement, which Bernhard advances sequentially, while the subject clauses express a variety of ideas. Compared with the musical sequence, Bernhard's is employed more freely. In the other instance where Bernhard draws on this compositional means, he digresses even further from his model, yet preserves enough of its character to make its relationship recognizable.

> Sie haben zwei Verbrechen an mir begangen, zwei Schwerstverbrechen, sagte er, sie haben mich erzeugt und sie haben mich unterdrückt, sie haben mich, ohne mich zu fragen, erzeugt und sie haben mich, wie sie mich erzeugt und in die Welt gestürzt hatten, unterdrückt, sie haben das Erzeugungsverbrechen an mir begangen und das Unterdrückungsverbrechen. (AM 111)

The emphatic augmentation in this example consists of, on the one hand, a hypotactic extension, on the other, the contraction of the original parataxis into a simple main clause. Thus the sequences do not progress in the same direction but, figuratively speaking, they move 'upwards' and 'downwards'.

---

sections are repeated, and the less often the harder the piece of music is to understand.' Schoenberg, *Style and Idea*, p. 103.

19. For the compilation of the music examples and assistance with the formulation of the music-theoretical arguments, I am indebted to William Drabkin of the Music Department at the University of Southampton.

Thomas Bernhard's 'Musical Prose'

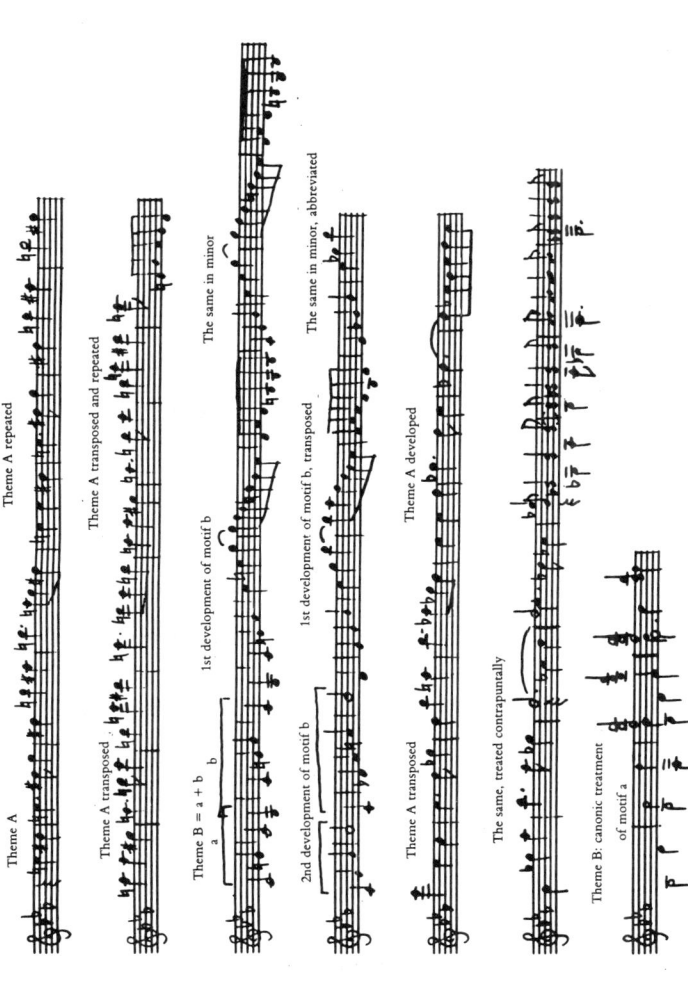

Music Example 1 Beethoven: *Eroica* Symphony, 1st movement, bars 284–341

Andrea Reiter

Music Example 2 Beethoven: *Eroica Symphony*, 1st movement, bars 15–23

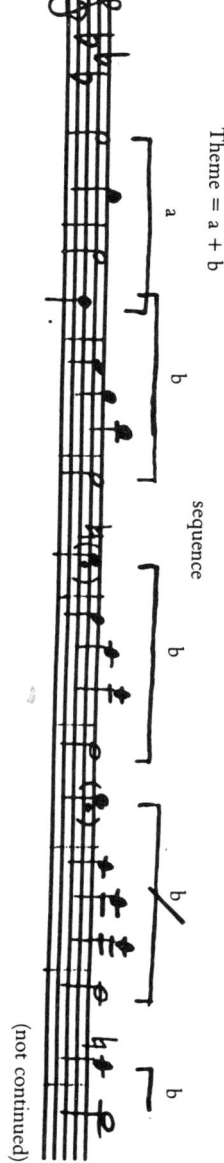

Theme = a + b

Music Example 3

Eroica Symphony, 1st movement, (a) principal theme = a + b

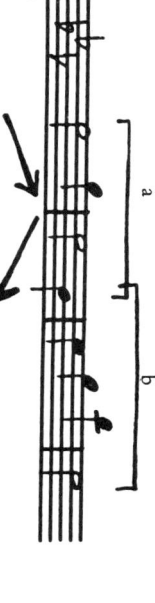

(b) new theme, derived from the inversion of motif a (bars 109–12)

The quoted extracts also show another musical figure. The variation in the first two subject clauses of the first example is achieved by mirroring groups of words.[20] This interconnectedness of musical figures shows how compact Bernhard's prose actually is. Symmetry, however, is not confined to the sentence-level but also governs greater units of the text. In *Beton* (p. 41) Bernhard organizes a motif symmetrically around the term 'Freundin'.[21] The narrator there reflects on his inability to have friends. He can only bear the company of deceased philosophers and composers. The symmetrical arrangement of the 'Reizwörter'[22] TOTE – FREUND – FREUNDIN – FREUND – TOTE is reminiscent of Schoenberg's mirror principle in serialism.[23]

A further musical technique is inversion, defined as the repetition of a motif with the direction of its intervals reversed. (See Music Example 3, p. 196 above.)

Bernhard is not the only writer to use this figure. Others, too, rely on it, without, however, exploiting its musical connotation. Any pair of adjectives, nouns or even verbs that express opposition allows an imitation of musical syntax. Bernhard once again makes use of the potential of the comparative: 'die Polizei bezahle allerdings mehr, das kunsthistorische Museum weniger' (AM 11).

Neither in classical nor in modern music do the described techniques merely facilitate the development of a musical idea: they also supply the framework in which the development takes place. If we progress from the musical nucleus – the theme – to larger units of a work, we arrive at a different set of structural principles. The most striking and best known in the musical tradition of the eighteenth and nineteenth centuries is modulation, the transition between keys, usually by the reinterpretation of one or more pivotal chords. (See Music Example 4, p. 198 below.)

In 'Monologe auf Mallorca' (1981) we find a convincing example of 'prose modulation'. Towards the end of the interview the author employs a masterly change from the term 'Ernst' to 'Tod': 'Ich

---

20. Mirror forms are quite frequent in ancient rhetoric, as is proved by the terms 'oxymoron' and 'chiasm'. Today they are regarded as formalistic strategies. Bernhard, however, uses them because they lend themselves well to his 'musical' style (see AM 58 for chiasm, 215 for oxymoron).
21. This symmetrical section of the text is interesting because it suggests Bernhard's indebtedness to Franz Kafka, especially when he has Rudolf claim: 'An Freundin *und* Geistesambitionen ist nicht zu denken!' (B 41).
22. See Rossbacher, *'Das Kalkwerk'*, p. 374. These key-words also have an existential meaning in Bernhard's work, as the expression 'Lebenswörter' (H 304) suggests.
23. See Schoenberg, *Style and Idea*, p. 224, 'Example 4'.

Music Example 4

Eroica Symphony, 1st movement, (a) bars 440–8: no modulation

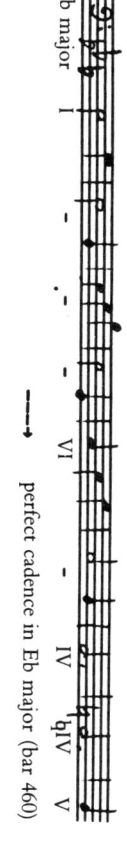

(b) bars 37–45: modulation by reinterpretation of the subdominant (IV)

liebe den Ernst. Nicht den Ernst Meister, aber den Ernst als Meister, den Meister aus Österreich, nicht den Meister aus Deutschland – das ist wieder der Tod.'[24] This image, which is constructed by way of a chain of associations, testifies to its creator's intellectual alertness, linguistic playfulness and a sense of (black) humour in its reference to Paul Celan's famous poem 'Todesfuge'. Bernhard's 'modulation' relies on ambiguous terms which change their meaning constantly in accordance with their environment. First, Bernhard contrasts 'Ernst' and 'Unernst'. Eventually, however, 'Ernst' is juxtaposed with 'Tod' and thus is given a new meaning: 'Der Schatten des Todes, der begleitet mich natürlich immer, und den lieb ich dadurch, weil er mir den Ernst garantiert.'[25] In a manner typical of Bernhard this sentence modulates by way of juxtaposition and negation.[26] His fiction extends modulation to longer sections of the text. In *Alte Meister*, a sarcastic exaggeration characterizes Reger's reflection about Martin Heidegger. Here philosophy is connected with the animal world via the vegetative body functions. According to Reger, Heidegger is 'gerade recht für den deutschen Philosopheneintopf . . . mit Heißhunger ausgelöffelt . . . ein urdeutscher Philosophiewiederkäuer, eine unablässig trächtige Philosophenkuh . . . auf der deutschen Philosophie geweidet . . . [hat sie] . . . darauf . . . ihre koketten Fladen fallen gelassen' (AM 88). Bernhard draws on diverse fields and situations for his metaphors. Their collation yields an image which, in its own particular way, sneers at the Germans as well as at Heidegger. As with the previous example, the function of this modulation in the literary text diverges from its musical model. Bernhard does not primarily want to achieve a thematic change via keywords; his objective is to vary the terminology and structure of Reger's revulsion.

Bernhard also repeats key sentences with only slight variation. Unlike modulation, this technique structures the narrator's fits of rage and torrents of words, allowing both narrator and reader to regain their bearings and to summon new strength before the next onslaught. In his reflexion on the relationship between teachers and

24. 'Monologe auf Mallorca. Thomas Bernhard – eine Herausforderung', interview by Krista Fleischmann and Wolfgang Koch, ORF, 11 February 1981, in *ORF-Nachlese*, no. 4, 1981, p. 8.
25. Ibid.
26. This example demonstrates how much Bernhard's prose and spoken discourse resemble each other. The influence of the vernacular on Bernhard's work has already been demonstrated (see Rossbacher, '*Das Kalkwerk*', p. 381); however, an investigation in particular of the structural interrelationship is still to be done.

art, Bernhard – through Reger – runs through a series of reproaches against the teaching profession which he loathes. This strategy has a structural effect beyond its mere content function. He uses it as a tool to organize what would otherwise be a totally erratic section of the text (AM 51–3). The constellation: 'Die Lehrer' + verb (or: 'sind') supplies the basic structural pattern. Variation is confined to the verb and its object and to the subordinate clauses respectively. In some cases this structuring by 'key sentences' can even be interpreted as a rondo-like form, especially where a longer key sentence is repeated periodically in a section of the text. A kind of refrain embraces shorter sections of the text, which in their turn elaborate on the refrain by way of association. In *Alte Meister*, Bernhard puts Reger's unbridled fits of anger into a frame and at the same time supplies them with a certain amount of emphasis. The refrain consists of either a paradoxical statement: 'Die Kunsthistoriker sind die eigentlichen Kunstvernichter' (AM 34f) or a far-fetched claim, which at first sight does not make much sense: 'Die Stadt Wien und der Staat Österreich und die katholische Kirche sind am Tod meiner Frau schuld' (AM 247). In both cases the text between the refrains tries to make the assertion plausible. Apart from the refrain, the frequent repetition of the narrator's comment, 'so/ sagte Reger im Ambassador', aids in structuring the passage.[27] This strategy also permits the narrator to emphasize Reger's stubbornness from a higher level, and, at the same time to ascertain his own detachment from the narrative.

Repetition assumes a decisive function in Bernhard's prose. Although this has been mentioned repeatedly in research, its significance for the musical quality of Bernhard's prose has so far, to my knowledge, escaped attention. It is this very repetition of single words or phrases which characterizes a motif. The 'motivic development' then relies on changes and variations within the repetition. Bernhard's motifs are typically developed via contrasting pairs of keywords.[28]

V

In the following section I shall exemplify what I have discussed so

---

27. Rossbacher compares this kind of insistent repetition in Bernhard's prose with the liturgical form of 'litany', a 'säkularisierte Form der bannenden Beschwörung von Dingen und Sachverhalten', ibid.
28. Jurgensen calls this element of Bernhard's style 'korrelative Tautologie', 'Sprachpartituren', pp. 102f.

far with two extracts from *Alte Meister*. This novel lends itself well to my purpose as it deals with Bernhard's view of art and its reception. In the course of the novel he liquidates his subject in a series of diatribes against art, its production and reception. The question we have to answer is: does he support or even reinforce this on the stylistic level?

A 'motif' and its development characteristically stretch over one to three pages in this text. The development is sparked off by a keyword, which Bernhard has elsewhere referred to as the 'Empfindlichkeitswort'.[29] This is paralleled or contrasted with one or more other words. The core of the motif thus consists of a group of words or a sentence and falls into the pattern of keyword plus assertion. Grammatically speaking, it comprises a noun phrase plus a verb phrase.[30] In our first example (pp. 84–6) this is 'Die Natur ist hoch in Kurs'. (See Example 1, p. 202 below.)

The following main clause substitutes 'Stifter' for 'Natur' and thus suggests paradigmatic interchangeability. The subsequent main clauses repeat this mechanism with a change in the verb phrase. 'Ist hoch in Kurs' is now replaced by 'ist höchste Mode'. The four statements form the nucleus of this motivic development, setting both the linguistic material and the simplest strategies of variation. In the main clauses which appear at a later stage of the development the verb phrase remains the same except for one single isolated (and thus emphasized) 'allerhöchste Mode'. The noun phrase, on the other hand, introduces a new group of terms ('Sentimentalität'/'Kitsch'), which at first sight does not bear any relation to 'Stifter'. Even grammar seems to exclude any possible connection, since both terms are placed in the same paradigm: a possible connection can only come about by way of association. In any case, this unexpected change in the noun phrase heightens the reader's expectation. Subsequently, the noun phrase progresses according to the already known pattern: the two terms are introduced separately, used as a pair, and emphasized by repetition of the verb. This clearly marks an incision in the development. The following section of the development contains the most radical changes. Passive constructions containing the impersonal 'es' as a subject push all information into the verb phrase. The pair 'Sentimentalität'/'Kitsch' is varied by combining different parts of speech: adjective pair ('kitschig und sentimental'), attributive

29. See Thomas Bernhard, *Verstörung*, Frankfurt/Main, 1979, p. 85; quoted in Rossbacher, '*Das Kalkwerk*', p. 374.
30. For the terminology see *Funk-Kolleg Sprache. Eine Einführung in die moderne Linguistik*, Frankfurt/Main, 1973, p. 226.

Example 1

NP	VP		
Natur		hoch in Kurs	
Stifter	ist	hoch in Kurs	
Natur		höchste/allerhöchste Mode	
Stifter		höchste Mode	
Wald		höchste Mode	
Gebirgsbäche		höchste Mode	
Stifter		höchste Mode	
Stifter		höchste Mode	
Sentimentalität		höchste Mode	
Kitsch		höchste Mode	
Sentimentalität/Kitsch		höchste Mode	
	wird geschrieben		in Lit/Malerei/Musik (place)
	wird gemalt		
	Komponisten	übertreffen sich	sentimentaler Kitsch (sC)
	wird geboten		kitschig und sentimental (manner)
	ist		in Kitsch und Sentimentalität (pO)
	wird gezeigt		Theater (place)
	hören		Ausstellungen (place)
Bücher			Konzertsäle (place)
			Kitsch/Sentimentalität (dO)
			mit Kitsch/Sentimentalität (pO)
	gebracht	in Mode	Stifter (dO)
Kitsch		Kitschmeister	
Bruckner		sentimental und kitschig	auf einer Seite Stifter (place)
Schriftsteller			
Stifter	eingeführt	in Mode	Kitsch/Sentimentalität (dO)
Stifter	endet		
Wald/Waldsterben		in Mode	geistlosen und kopflosen Kitsch (dO)
Begriff Wald			kitschigem Selbstmord (pO)
'Hochwald'		viel gekauft	der gebrauchte/mißbrauchte

Key:
NP – noun phrase
VP – verb phrase
place – adverbial phrase of place
manner – adverbial phrase of manner
pO – prepositional object
sC – subject complement
dO – direct object

adjective and noun ('kitschige Sentimentalität' or 'sentimentaler Kitsch'). What Bernhard does here can also be found in other works of his. Hans Höller refers to it as 'morphologische Verschränkung'.[31] In a treble onslaught, Bernhard applies 'Kitsch' and 'Sentimentalität' to individual kinds of art. He divides the general statement 'höchste Mode in der Literatur, in der Malerei, auch in der Musik', into three individual ones. The intertwining of statements here takes place on the semantic level. The verbs associated with the various kinds of art ('geschrieben'/'gemalt') are followed by their respective locations ('Theater'/ 'Ausstellung'/ 'Konzertsäle'). This section of the development ends with the assertion about the 'book' and eventually comes full circle back to 'Stifter'. The extension of the verb phrase follows rules typical of Bernhard's writings in general:[32] like complex events, he breaks down complex statements into small steps and sections evoking the impression of an improved penetrability of his subject. What he achieves, however, is a sense of urgency and inescapability. By moving 'Kitsch'/'Sentimentalität' into the verb phrase and thus into a different paradigm, it is now possible to draw a connection between 'Stifter' and 'Kitsch'. Likewise the way is free for the noun phrase to be varied by the introduction of 'Bruckner' and to be generalized from 'Stifter' to 'Schriftsteller'. The development of the motif ends with the repetition of its beginning. In the noun phrase, however, Bernhard now associates 'Wald' with 'Waldsterben' and 'Begriff Wald' with 'Hochwald'. In the verb phrase he returns to the statement 'ist in Mode'.

The overall structure of the motif follows the pattern *ABA*, which it shares with the well-known ternary or three-part song form in music. Together with the micro-structure of the motif, it is quite obvious that Bernhard had the musical 'grammar' in mind while writing this passage. In the literary example the 'development' is based on the dialectic between unchanged and changed elements. Every radical alteration of a statement is preceded by a consolidation through repetition of identical statements. The motivic development follows a symmetrical structure so that beginning and end are the same.

The second example consists of biographical material. The juxtaposition of school and private education had been found in *Ein Kind* (p. 125). Bernhard took over his grandfather's contempt of education organized by the state or a religious body, and described in

---

31. See Höller, '"Es darf nichts Ganzes geben"', p. 48.
32. See Rossbacher, *'Das Kalkwerk'*, p. 379.

Die Ursache (p. 92) his own aversion to grammar school, which he left prematurely of his own accord. In *Alte Meister* (pp. 57–8), finally, he disguises this same autobiographical idea by presenting it in 'musical' form. In Example 2 (p. 205 below) contrasting statements which share a common syntactic order are juxtaposed.

The strong resemblance to a rigidly constructed contrapuntal composition – for example, a double fugue, where a theme is assigned a counter-subject – can hardly be overlooked. This example represents one of the purest and most striking transferrals of musical principles of composition in Bernhard's novel. Due to the identical syntax of theme and counter-subject, the paradigms – time, precise time, location, precise location, evaluated location, assertion, emotional assertion – are arranged in a parallel pattern. Not every single paradigm is occupied all the time. The changes within them account for what can here be called motivic development. In the counter-subject the paradigm 'emotional assertion' shows the greatest variation where a shift from 'staatlich' to 'unnatürlich' takes place. This allows Bernhard to achieve an even closer connection between theme and counter-subject.

The most striking element of this extremely economical motivic development is its parallel structure, which emphasizes the juxtaposition of theme and counter-subject. 'Ging ich in die Kleinstadt hinunter, ging ich ins Unglück (des Staates!), ging ich auf den Berg zu den Großeltern nach Hause, ging ich in das Glück' (p. 58).

In a variation of this scheme Bernhard mirrors the arrangement of these parallel statements: 'Bei den Großeltern . . . der natürliche, glückliche, in der Schule . . . der unnatürliche unglückliche Mensch // Kleinstadt . . . Unglück . . . Berg . . . Glück // Großeltern . . . Glück . . . Kleinstadt . . . Unglück' (p. 58). This symmetrical structure which temporarily replaces parallelism is reminiscent of symmetrical forms both in music (inversion and retrograde) and in literature (chiasm). As already mentioned, the actual development of the motif in question does not take place in the paradigms but on the syntactic level. The paradigms 'precise location' ('Großeltern'/'Schule') and 'assertion' ('natürlich'/ 'staatlich') are substituted by 'precise time' ('am Nachmittag'/'in der Früh') and 'emotional assertion' ('Glück'/'Unglück'). The motivic development in the autobiographical example thus suggests a progression of the argument from the presentation of the objective situation to the perception of the subjective condition.

Example 2

Theme

Time	Precise time	Location	Precise location	Evaluated location	Assertion	Emotional assertion
			Großeltern		natürlich	
halber Tag	nachm.	zu Hause	Großeltern		natürlich	
halber Tag	nachm.				natürlich	glücklich
	nachm.				natürlich	der glückliche Mensch
						der allerglücklichste Mensch
(Mirroring)		zu Hause	Großeltern		natürlich	glücklich
(Mirroring)		zu Hause	Großeltern	Berg	Natur	Glück
			Großeltern	Berg	Natur	Glück
	Mittag					Glück

Counter-subject

Time	Precise time	Location	Precise location	Evaluated location	Assertion	Emotional assertion
			Schule		staatlich	
halber Tag	vorm.		Schule		staatlich	
halber Tag	vorm.				staatlich	unglücklich
	vorm.				staatlich	der unglückliche Mensch
						der allerunglücklichste Mensch
(Mirroring)			Schule	unten	unnatürlich	unglücklich
				hinunter		Unglück
			Schule	hinunter		Unglück
	in der Früh					Unglück

VI

What, then, does the term 'musical prose' mean for literature in the light of what we have learned about Bernhard's style? As I have attempted to show, Bernhard's 'musical style' results largely from his adaptation of classical composition techniques. It has been pointed out that Bernhard's prose bears some similarity to serialism. This is, however, not because of its structural characteristics, as Helmut Gross suggests.[33] Although Bernhard is highly impressed by the modernists (Schoenberg, Webern), as we learn in *Der Untergeher* (p. 49), the compositional principles of twelve-tone music would not lend themselves readily to a one-to-one transposition to literature. Serialism is too rigid, too specifically musical a system, in which the idea of development is not restricted to the parameter of duration: it is pitch itself that reigns supreme in Schoenberg's motivic development. And for this there is no equivalent in a prose text. In Schoenberg's twelve-tone system, the potential forty-eight forms of the basic set of twelve tones result from its statement, inversion, retrograde, and retrograde inversion at each of twelve levels of transposition. While inversion in literature, as we have seen, can be realized as a comparison or a negation and the retrograde corresponds with literary mirror forms, the concept of interval (which is the basis of transposition) has no parallel in literature and so defies meaningful translation. It is thus rather the specific function which structure assumes in Bernhard's prose that makes this comparable with atonal music. Like atonality, which revolutionized traditional compositional techniques with the so-called 'emancipation of the dissonance',[34] the musical style in Bernhard's prose, too, expresses opposition. His objective, however, is not the revolutionary political statement, but the presentation of 'das radikal andere'. 'Ich liebte den Gegensatz, wie ich auch heute vor allem den Gegensatz liebe' (Ke 100), Bernhard claims categorically in his autobiography. The opposition which marks his work, and which is also responsible for the contrapuntal character of his motivic development, is occasionally turned against his environment.[35] Bernhard's oppositional intentions thus are

---

33. See Gross, 'Strukturphilosophischer Versuch', p. 35.
34. 'The term *emancipation of the dissonance* refers to its comprehensibility, which is considered equivalent to the consonance's comprehensibility. A style based on this premise treats dissonances like consonances and renounces a tonal centre.' Schoenberg, *Style and Idea*, p. 217.
35. Ingrid Seibert conceives Bernhard's literary career as a series of scandals: Ingrid Seibert and Sepp Dreissinger, *Die Schwierigen. Portraits zur österreichischen Gegenwartskunst*, Vienna, 1986, pp. 6–31.

expressed threefold in and by his work: thematically, linguistically and pragmatically. What his prose style also shares with dodecaphonic composition is its function. In both cases the technique serves the integration of the disparate.[36] By using a more rigid structure, however, Bernhard commits himself also to a more rigorous formal force. Contrary to its significance in music, 'musical prose' in literature denotes approximation to verse, to poetry. Thus Bernhard's *Alte Meister*, while it celebrates the destruction of art at the level of literal reading of the text,[37] at the same time sublimates it by virtue of its manipulation of musical techniques on the grammatical level.

36. See Schoenberg, *Style and Idea*, p. 244. Rossbacher asserts, 'Im Musikalischen enthält Bernhards Werk eine ästhetische Einheit stiftende Qualität', Rossbacher, 'Das Kalkwerk', p. 382.
37. Pointedly Wedelin Schmidt-Dengler calls Reger's (Bernhard's) attacks 'Kunstvernichtungskunst': *Der Übertreibungskünstler. Zu Thomas Bernhard*, Vienna, 1986, p. 91.

–13–

Power, Politics and Pornography: Elfriede Jelinek's Satirical Exposés

JULIET WIGMORE

Although Elfriede Jelinek has been publishing fiction since the early 1970s, her major successes have occurred since 1980, particularly with *Die Klavierspielerin* (1983) and its successor *Oh Wildnis, oh Schutz vor ihr* (1985).[1] While the generic aspect is not really an issue here, one difference between these two works is that *Die Klavierspielerin* is a 'novel' in the more conventional sense of the word, whereas the extended prose fiction of *Oh Wildnis* can only be called a novel in a looser sense, for it marks a return to what the author herself has referred to as 'experimentelle Prosa'[2] – though it is of a different kind from her early prose works which were largely experiments in montage techniques.[3] Both of these works of fiction are satirical in different ways, in so far as they target certain issues, shedding a witty and critical light upon them by means of a number of specific techniques. These include the familiar devices of parody, irony of various sorts and particularly the reversal or distortion of familiar situations, as well as other forms of language manipulation. Rather than go into detail about the way in which Elfriede Jelinek creates these effects, I intend to outline her main targets and to suggest how she makes use of satirical effects as a critical tool to attack in a number of different directions.

The political and ideological context which informs Elfriede Jelinek's satirical writing is, on the one hand, feminist and, on the other, Marxist, a combination which has provoked some controversy, not least in feminist critical circles, which is where her work first received serious attention. Seen in this context too, her

---

1. *Die Klavierspielerin*, Reinbek, 1983; *Oh Wildnis, oh Schutz vor ihr*, Reinbek, 1985. Page references in the text refer to these editions.
2. Georg Biron, 'Wahrscheinlich wäre ich ein Lustmörder. Ein Gespräch mit der Schriftstellerin Elfriede Jelinek', *Die Zeit*, 28 September 1984, p. 40.
3. For example, *Wir sind lockvögel, baby!*, Reinbek, 1970.

writing, which includes highly successful plays as well as fiction, may be regarded as symptomatic of one direction taken by feminist writing since the late 1970s: in the 1980s particularly, feminist writing has departed from its earlier, overtly confessional character and has become generally more problematic and at the same time more diversified. Correspondingly, feminist criticism has extended its scope, developed different methodologies, and become more controversial. Elfriede Jelinek herself is sometimes guarded about her position as a woman writer and has stated, for instance, that she prefers to see herself in the context of satirical writing: 'Ich sehe mich nicht unbedingt in einer weiblichen Tradition, sondern in der Tradition der ironischen Literatur, der satirischen Literatur, in der es kaum Frauen gibt, wenn ich eben von der Fleißer absehe.'[4] Nevertheless, a feminist perspective does indeed inform much of her writing as well as much of the critical discussion it has received.

Two contrasting critical approaches to women writers as satirists, which refer extensively to Elfriede Jelinek's writing, discuss the relationship of her feminism to her use of satire and come to different conclusions. Thus, the American critic Dagmar Lorenz, analysing humour in women's writing, finds satire inherently patriarchal: satire relies on the satirist's subordination of some inferior party, who is often already a member of a disadvantaged group, including, for instance, women and ethnic minorities, in the German tradition particularly Jews. She concludes that both Elfriede Jelinek and the largely non-feminist writer, Gisela Elsner, whose work she also considers, merely reverse patriarchal discourse in favour of women but do not break out of the framework it imposes.[5] That is to say, the satire is at men's expense but is presented in essentially the manner in which men have satirized women and shown them to be inferior. Sigrid Weigel, on the other hand, argues that, because women's reality is constructed differently, women's satirical writing is different in the way it perceives reality, and is thus different in its nature and implications; this she exemplifies with reference to *Die Klavierspielerin*.[6] Both arguments centre on the narrative position adopted, Lorenz concentrating more on the technical aspects of the narrative, while Weigel takes a broader view of the context of the satire: both need to be borne in

4. Jacqueline Vansant, 'Gespräch mit Elfriede Jelinek', *Deutsche Bücher*, no. 15, 1985, pp. 1–9.
5. Dagmar Lorenz, 'Humor bei zeitgenössischen Autorinnen', *The Germanic Review*, vol. 62, no. 1, winter 1987, pp. 28–36; here pp. 30f.
6. Sigrid Weigel, *Die Stimme der Medusa. Schreibweisen in der Gegenwartsliteratur von Frauen*, Dülmen-Hiddingsel, 1987, pp. 193–5.

mind if one is to do justice to satirical writing, which inevitably has a 'political' end of some sort in sight. Insofar as the two positions mentioned are indeed mutually exclusive, they have implications for the way one assesses Elfriede Jelinek's writing, particularly whether she is to be regarded as furthering an innovative feminist aesthetic approach or whether she merely reproduces patriarchal processes. In Lorenz's view, humour itself is generally characterized by the fact that it makes reference to the status quo, and although she associates satire mainly with realism, in the historical context, she maintains that it is still the case that 'Humor und Aktion sind eine contradictio in adiecto'.[7] In view of the political contexts to which Elfriede Jelinek states her allegiance, the static aspect which this statement implies is clearly problematic.

While *Die Klavierspielerin* has a realistic framework, which is, however, not rigidly adhered to throughout, *Oh Wildnis, oh Schutz vor ihr* departs from traditional narrative structure to a much greater extent. Thus, in terms of the conflicting views of satire outlined above, *Die Klavierspielerin* presents greater problems with regard to the issue of whether the author actually subverts the patriarchal order associated with satire. However, it is not only in this respect that Jelinek's two novels differ, but also with regard to the targets at which the satire is directed, as well as in their range and scope.

In *Die Klavierspielerin* the satirical element is directed at the issue of power in society, a theme which is shown in its various ramifications. The central situation is a grotesque parody of a family relationship, in which the main figure, Erika Kohout, a music teacher in her late thirties, lives with her mother in what amounts to a state of bondage. This exaggerated imagery already suggests a departure from realistic writing into metaphor, and indeed an incursion into the realm of pornographic representation with which the imagery of bondage which occurs throughout the novel is closely associated. Thus, the person of Erika Kohout is subject to strict rules and regulations, scarcely appropriate even to a teenager, while she and her mother are referred to by the narrator as 'das Kind' and 'die Mutter', emphasizing Erika's infantile role, as well as suggesting that the two women may have paradigmatic status. The bondage motif is borne out further by the fact that Erika and her mother live together in an oppressively confined space, partly, however, of their own volition, for they sleep together in the same room, in what is ironically called the 'Ehebett', despite the fact that such proximity is not entirely necessitated by the dimensions of

---

7. Lorenz, 'Humor bei zeitgenössischen Autorinnen', p. 29.

their living quarters. Thus this concrete situation gives rise to a grotesquely exaggerated image of confinement, and the domestic situation of the family structure itself is presented as oppressive. Because the mother and daughter are represented as being to some extent 'model' figures, their claustrophobic relationship may be seen as a metaphor for the narrow and oppressive social structure at large, which is reflected in the family.

The satirical element arises to a great extent from the narrative perspective, which frequently echoes the thought patterns of different characters, particularly Erika, while at the same time parodying them. For example, the territorial divisions in the flat are described at first as if from Erika's point of view and then from her mother's: Erika's room is 'nur ein provisorisches Reich, denn die Mutter hat jederzeit freien Zutritt. Die Tür von Erikas Zimmer hat kein Schloß, und kein Kind hat Geheimnisse' (p. 9). While the narrative often resembles *erlebte Rede*, presenting situations and events from a point of view close to one or other of the characters themselves, the narrator nevertheless introduces incongruous vocabulary, such as 'ein provisorisches Reich', which parodies the characters' own values and thereby introduces a satirical and political dimension to their situation. Yet the effect is not merely to diminish the characters, to laugh at them, but rather to present them in a political context, to suggest, for example, that the personal is indeed political, a technique which Elfriede Jelinek developed particularly in an earlier novel, *Die Liebhaberinnen* (1975). The negative perspective on the characters in their domestic situation ultimately implicates society at large.

The shifting narrative position illustrated above as a feature of Elfriede Jelinek's political style has sometimes been criticized, but the author herself defends it, with a suggestion that it allows both insight and the maintenance of distance simultaneously: 'Es geht jetzt nicht um meinen Standpunkt, den Standpunkt des Autors, sondern um die Beleuchtung einer Situation von möglichst vielen Seiten. Wie mit einem Vexierspiegel, wie in einem Spiegelkabinett, wo man auch nicht recht weiß, wo man eigentlich ist, weil das Bild so oft zurückgeworfen wird.'[8] Like the distorting mirrors, the technique is used to exaggerate or enlarge a particular feature, so that both that aspect itself and the whole surrounding context appear in a different light, usually with the effect that they look absurd. Jelinek's shifting imagery also contributes to this effect, moving, for example, between metaphorical and concrete levels of

---

8. Vansant, 'Gespräch mit Elfriede Jelinek', pp. 8f.

description: 'Die Mutter schleicht unhörbar tiptoe auf das Zimmer des Kindes los, um herauszukriegen, was für ein Instrument dort gespielt werden soll. Klavier nicht, denn das Klavier prunkt im Salon herum' (*Klavierspielerin*, p. 261). The shifting back and forth between different levels in this way creates a sense that connections do indeed exist between individual behaviour and social values. Thus, this style to some extent undermines the notion of a controlling and superior narrator, which Lorenz associates with satire, since it is frequently difficult to determine whose perspective is being reflected at any given moment.

The image of bondage which emerges forcefully in the dire family circumstances depicted pervades *Die Klavierspielerin*, and it is extended to society more generally through the subject matter of music, which is the predominant medium through which Erika relates to the outside world. For, in what amounts to a negative version of a *Künstlerroman*, Erika's profession as a music teacher brings her social status, yet it is also a vehicle for criticizing Viennese bourgeois society, in which musical ability is especially esteemed. In this novel, music and the culture that surrounds it are treated satirically since, far from the art of music being valid as an end in itself, music is shown to acquire value in this society purely because it presents a means of satisfying some less than admirable aspirations, notably the pursuit of prestige and the acquisition of material assets. The same principle applies in Erika's own life, while its undesirable aspect is actually intensified by the fact that through her activity as a music teacher she helps to perpetuate this type of society. Erika herself has suffered for the sake of her art, but always with a negative outcome: for music has been the means whereby her mother has subjected her to severe discipline since childhood, using it as an excuse to keep her daughter apart from the riff-raff, particularly men, and thus of increasing her possession of her daughter and, correspondingly, Erika's own dependence. The bondage motif, which is extended to the point where it becomes grotesque, is attributed not merely to human attitudes and the society in which music occupies a special status, but to the nature of musical structure and notation itself: 'In dieses Notationssystem ist Erika seit frühester Kindheit eingespannt . . . Dieses Rastersystem hat sie, im Verein mit ihrer Mutter, in ein unzerreißbares Netz von Vorschriften, Verordnungen, von präzisen Geboten geschnürt' (p. 237). Success or failure in music is a means of attaining power, or at least of denying it to others, and since Erika, who once aspired to become 'eine überregionale Pianistin' has only become a teacher of music, her mother insists that it is in her interest to deter others who might otherwise outshine her: 'Du hast es nicht geschafft, warum sollen es jetzt andere an deiner Stelle und auch noch aus deinem pianististischen Stall erreichen?' (p. 15). The mean attitude reflected here, and underlined by the animal imagery of 'Stall', is a parody of the individualist, bourgeois principle 'I've made it; so can anyone if they try hard enough' (a sure manifestation of false consciousness!) By introducing a negative ('*nicht* geschafft'), the ideological significance of the cliché is exposed, a significance which was, of course, present all the time, but whose impact has been lost by overfamiliarity.

In many instances music, this sacred cow of bourgeois society, is cast in a dubious light because it is shown to offer occasion for social gatherings, including particularly competitions, which tend to call forth people's most unpleasant characteristics. During one such competition at her school, Erika tracks down one of her male students, cornering him in the junior-school toilets. There ensues a sordid sex scene, in the sense that it is devoid of any actual passion or even physical contact. Instead, Erika's position is that of an alienated voyeur, one of a number of such episodes in which she indulges. In parallel to the music competition taking place downstairs, this scene is also about a pupil exposing and humiliating himself at the hands of the music teacher who is his social superior and who enjoys exploiting what little power she has over those who are vulnerable. This concrete image suggesting exposure, alienation and humiliation contributes to the way Erika's attitudes, and simultaneously the values of society, are satirized. The pornographic representation which is implied here contributes to the satirical effect partly through the shock impact of reversing the male and female roles, since Erika is here the dominant party. Yet in the context of the novel as a whole, the effect of the scene is not purely pornographic, as it probably would be if seen from the perspective of a male narrator or male protagonist, but instead it serves the cause of satirizing the bondage motif, which is both a comment on bourgeois society and a metaphor representing it.

Erika's sexual exploits and deviations are indeed one of the main pivots of the satire in the novel. While this aspect reflects the power relations in society in general, it does so specifically in relation to women in this society. Erika, who has been deliberately and systematically separated from other people in the cause of her musical training, experiences alienation of a psychological and of a political kind. It is manifested particularly in her attitude towards her own body, emerging in the form of self-mutilation, a type of extreme self-degradation to which women are especially susceptible. She also undertakes acts of public self-humiliation and is prone to sado-masochistic fantasies, which are taken to their grotesque conclusion when she even attempts to put them into practice. These behaviour patterns, which are not so much psychologically as socially motivated, give the impression of being grotesque, yet they are the essentially logical consequences of conforming to the demands of this society. While these behaviour patterns are embodied in the person of Erika herself, she is never allowed to become a caricature.

Two episodes are particularly revealing specifically in relation to the sexual politics of Erika's oppression. Near the beginning of the novel, she escapes from her mother's ever-watchful eye and goes to a seedy suburb, where she visits a peepshow. She apparently does this on a regular basis, for it is here, rather than in her art, that she obtains a form of gratification which is unavailable to her in other contexts. Thus it helps to undermine the value of music and all that it represents. In the peepshow two sets of values come into conflict: the oppressive and repressive bondage of bourgeois society, as against the escape into pornography, which is where the image of bondage is normally more at home. There is thus an ironic reversal of values which implicates bourgeois society, not least since it bears the responsibility for creating in Erika a need for ever greater self-humiliation, which reveals her alienated state. Erika becomes a voyeur, like the other visitors to the peepshow, who are, of course, all men, many of them *Gastarbeiter*, and as such aliens, an appropriate concrete image for the alienation to which Erika is subject in all aspects of her life. According to Dagmar Lorenz's argument, which specifically cites this episode, the scene in which a woman acts the part of voyeur/voyeuse is satirical purely in the sense that it reverses the usual patriarchal perspective, including the fact that Erika turns her attention more to the other voyeurs than to the show itself. Her enjoyment derives from her awareness of how they are humiliating themselves and hence the sense of superiority which she is able to achieve. Yet the satirical aspect is also dependent upon Erika's acute consciousness of the disgusting aspects of the scene and her absence of self-abandonment. In terms of the ethics of satire, this factor appears to be different from the way in which the episode would be narrated if seen from the point of view of male voyeurs, or indeed a male narrator who shared their point of view and assumptions, particularly concerning male sexuality, which is here derided. The starting point for a female narrator is different in kind, because of the way power is distributed in patriarchal society. Hence, while Elfriede Jelinek does indeed reverse the usual situation, with satirical effect, she thereby draws attention to the specific aspect of power in this context and thus produces a qualitatively different form of satire. In the light of the novel as a whole, this episode contributes to exposing the power structures in society. Because Erika is aware of her own degradation, and the episode is narrated from a position close to her own, the narrator cannot be said to assume a position of smug satisfaction or superiority. Any sense of superiority which Erika manages to attain, in fantasy, is revealed to be extremely transitory in the context of the novel as a whole.

The implications of the power structures also emerge forcefully in Erika's relationship with her pupil, Walter Klemmer. They compete for power, she, as his teacher, exploiting her superior position and attempting to humiliate him sexually, while he in turn sees the conquest of his teacher as a step up the ladder of social success. Thus their 'Liebesverhältnis', as it is ironically called, is revealed to be a grotesque distortion of what is in reality a power struggle. That power is an essential component is conveyed by the sado-masochistic terms in which the relationship is structured, as emerges clearly when Erika sets out her fantasies – mainly masochistic – in a letter to Klemmer. As he reads it, his incredulity is conveyed by the narrator's detached tone, echoing the sense of alienation and with it the absence of eroticism already seen in earlier, similarly voyeuristic episodes: 'Stimmt es wirklich, wie es hier steht, daß sie ihm die Zunge in den Hintern stecken muß, wenn er rittlings auf ihr sitzt. Klemmer bezweifelt sehr, was er liest, und schiebt es auf schlechte Beleuchtungsverhältnisse' (p. 283). While the ironically understated tone allows the reader to think that Klemmer is perhaps more worried about the physical possibility of the situation than the morality of it, it soon becomes clear that Erika's fantasies do indeed have a correlate in reality. Moreover, while her self-exposing fantasies at first appear exaggerated and ludicrous, when Klemmer brutally assaults and rapes her, having presumably overcome his initial scruples, she is no longer a laughable figure. Similarly, when she goes in search of him armed with a knife, a certain conventional expectation of revenge is set up, yet this is totally undermined when she turns the knife upon herself, in an act of self-degradation which is pathetic and far from humorous. Thus, one does not ultimately laugh at Erika, in the way one might do with a more traditional form of satire, where the central figure is the main target and the narrator is in a more consistently superior position. Erika's behaviour is at times amusing, but the satirical effect relates mainly to the exposure of the prevailing power relations in society. The humour does not have a cathartic effect, or reinforce the status quo, but instead leaves the reader with a profound sense of discomfort.

While the setting of *Die Klavierspielerin* has a certain concreteness and, in part, realism, which is satirized largely by the presence of Erika as an anarchic element, in the later novel *Oh Wildnis, oh Schutz vor ihr* there is no such realistic setting. The satirical elements are therefore differently constructed, since there are no actual situational reversals. There are, however, still many reflexions of social and political realities in the thought processes of the various characters, who are also the narrators of the novel. But while *Die Klavierspielerin* directly attacks aspects of cultured bourgeois society, in *Oh Wildnis* attention is focused on rural society and attitudes towards Nature, which are presented in a specifically Austrian context, although their significance is more generally applicable.

In each of the three sections of this work, the narrator homes in on a particular character, or group, and presents their perception of reality in the form of a series of associated ideas: first Erich, the woodcutter, representative of the rural worker; then, in the central section, a woman poet, named Frau Aichholzer, formerly the lover of a now-deceased and unnamed philosopher, to whom she always felt inferior; finally, the third section depicts the behaviour and attitudes of a group of wealthy bourgeois who have come to the country to hunt, and who are set off against local elements, such as Erich.

While the figure of Erich is present throughout, it is the woman poet who occupies the central section and also determines the structure of the novel. While each section has a neutral sounding title set by an external narrator – 'Außentag', 'Innen. Tag' and 'Außen. Nacht' – there is, in addition, a sub-title echoing the poet's perspective: 'Gedicht', 'Keine Geschichte zum Erzählen' and 'Herrliche Prosa! Wertvolle Preise!' The juxtaposition of these two levels produces an ironic conflict, which also reflects the conflicting perspectives and interests expressed in the text, often with satirical effect. With its 'poetic' framework, this work is, like *Die Klavierspielerin*, a type of negative *Künstlerroman*, yet it is less concerned with the position of the poet herself than with the attitude towards Nature which is fostered by Romantic poetry and *Heimatdichtung*, since these in turn reflect suspect social and political attitudes.

The way in which the various elements interact may be exemplified by the first section, entitled 'Außentag', with the subtitle 'Gedicht'. It brings together attitudes towards Nature and towards society in a manner which tends to undermine the Romantic view of rural life. Here Erich, the woodcutter, is depicted on his way to visit the poet 'hoch oben' in the forest. His thoughts are expressed using many techniques which are traditionally associated with poetry, such as internal rhyme, metaphor and allusion, yet here they are totally incongruous with Erich's down-to-earth concerns. Thus, for example, he meditates on the nature of work, on the family who have deserted him because of his brutality, and on material possessions: 'Die Forstgesetze sind heftig, die Naturgesetze sanft. Leider eine sehr schwere Pflicht die Verständigung, lustiger die Versündigung. Arbeit macht das Leben süß. Ein süßes Geheimnis teilt die Frau mit dem Vorgesetzten des Waldes, dem Förster . . . Sie sprang aus unserer Ehe wie ein Güterwaggon aus den Schienen. Gütig ist sie nicht mehr. Jetzt ist sie ehrgeizig' (p. 13). The juxtaposition of Erich's various strands of thought, together with the movement between literal and metaphorical levels of meaning, initially appears grotesque and incongruous. Yet the different elements which are alluded to in this way are revealed to be indeed connected: possessiveness and the exploitation of Nature, for example, have a parallel in the patriarchal family and also in the hierarchical organization of society more generally.

The title *Oh Wildnis, oh Schutz vor ihr* is ambivalent and ironically announces conflicting attitudes towards the countryside itself, which are then taken up by the poet in particular. The Romantic idea of a 'Wildnis' is undermined by the fact that it is here peopled by barbarians of a traditional, uncultured type, such as Erich, on the one hand, and on the other hand, by tourists, who in turn make it into a true 'Wildnis' in the metaphorical sense. Conversely, those who pretend to protect rural life do so only to further their economic interests, for example, by promoting tourism, or their destructive interest in hunting. At the same time, the poetic invocation of the 'wilderness' overlooks the real suffering which is in evidence there, such as that of Erich, who resents the hard work that he has to perform in order to survive, while perpetrating brutality on his own family. The unsatisfactory aspect of the situation is revealed satirically through the 'poetic' juxtaposition of disparate elements, and the awareness which this technique produces in the reader conflicts ironically with Erich's own total lack of consciousness about his own behaviour or motivation.

The poet herself, Frau Aichholzer, realizes that poetry is a form of exploitation of Nature: 'Der Künstler zwingt die Natur zur Übereinstimmung mit sich, sie soll gefälligst klingen lernen für den Individualisten (Individualtouristen), der sie recht verstehen könnte' (p. 157). This banal use of anthropomorphism, as well as punning, satirizes Romantic poetry, but above all it satirizes an incongruous attitude towards Nature in the modern age. The poet has seen through the economics of poetry, her perspective being reflected through the narrator's words: 'An der Natur naschen und profitieren zu viele. Zum Beispiel, was ist der Wald im eigentlichen Sinn, den sie jeden Tag sieht? Angenehme Einbildung, köstliche Ungereimtheit, die sie zu reimen vermag' (p. 182). She can certainly 'rhyme' the mysteries of Nature, and the reader is encouraged to do likewise, through the incongruity of this poetic use of language. A thoroughly negative view emerges, as doubts are cast on poetry and ecological *Naturschützer* as much as upon the forces which explicitly exploit Nature for economic reasons, since it is suggested that they can all be attributed to similar motives.

Thus, like *Die Klavierspielerin*, *Oh Wildnis, oh Schutz vor ihr* satirizes an aspect of society whose value is often taken for granted and which is particularly, though not exclusively, relevant to aspects of Austrian society. In terms of the approaches to satire mentioned earlier, *Oh Wildnis* relies to a lesser extent on the mere reversal of familiar situations than *Die Klavierspielerin* does, which, as in other respects, is a more traditional type of novel. By contrast, *Oh Wildnis* departs from recognizable settings to a great extent, and in doing so the author has created a different and more radical type of structure through which to subvert social phenomena which are a part of patriarchal and capitalist society.

Note Since the completion of this article Elfriede Jelinek has continued to explore these themes in *Lust* (Reinbeck 1989), a novel in which she sets out to attempt, as a woman writer, to write pornography.

-14-

Culpabilities of the Imagination: The Novels of Monika Maron

MARTIN KANE

Two sources have given me the cue for this paper. First, the title of Gerd Neumann's *Die Schuld der Worte*, a collection of prose pieces published in 1979.[1] And secondly Monika Maron's opening contribution to the 'Deutsch–deutsche Briefwechsel' with Joseph von Westphalen conducted in the columns of the *ZEITmagazin*. In Maron's contemplation from an East Berlin perspective of the nature of the border separating the two Germanies, one observation in particular makes an impact: 'Die Gesetze sind das Schlimmste, sie kriminalisieren schon die Träume.'[2] What connects, in differing ways, these offerings from two GDR writers who still live[3] in the country which denies them publication are their pointers to the literary imagination as a concocter of nefarious and subversive activity. Neumann's painfully self-reflexive endeavours with the language of his prose texts are a reaction to the cynicism – as he once put it – of socialist realism.[4] His concept of the 'Schuld der Worte' refers explicitly to the failure of language to represent 'Die Würde der Dinge',[5] but also hints at the consequences of attempting to overcome this: to dare to give a view of reality which is unadulterated and undistorted by ideological expediency is, implicitly, to become entangled in further levels of culpability and to be condemned, as one critic has put it, to 'der traurigen Zukunft, daß seine Bücher nicht in der DDR erscheinen werden'.[6]

1. Gert Neumann, *Die Schuld der Worte*, Frankfurt/Main, 1979.
2. Monika Maron, 'Warum zieht es Euch nach Sachsen?', *ZEITmagazin*, 10 July 1987, p. 6.
3. Monika Maron left the GDR in June 1988 (after the completion of this paper) on a three-year visa.
4. See Egmont Hesse, 'Geheimsprache "Klandestinität". Gespräch mit Gert Neumann', *Neue Rundschau*, vol. 98, no. 2, 1987, p. 6.
5. Ibid., p. 8.
6. On the cover of Gert Neumann, *Elf Uhr*, Frankfurt/Main, 1981.

The issues of language raised by Neumann's mode of writing, what has been called his 'Krieg gegen die Sprache',[7] clearly would warrant separate treatment. But the purloining of his title may nevertheless serve its purpose here as an approach to the problems articulated in Monika Maron's two novels, *Flugasche*[8] and *Die Überläuferin*.[9]

One is occasionally confronted with the agreeable problem of recommending to enquiring friends or colleagues who know little of GDR society and less about its literature a book or books which might satisfy their curiosity on both scores. *Flugasche*, hitherto published only in West Germany but which – had it not been for a series of *faux pas* committed by Maron in her *ZEITmagazin* correspondence – would have seen the light of day in 1988 in the GDR (albeit, as Maron herself noted cryptically 'mit zehnjähriger Verspätung'[10]), commends itself admirably to this end, not least because it is also available in a passable English translation.[11] In the dramatization it offers of the gulf between the GDR's official view of itself and the day-to-day realities of life there through a treatment of the world of work – encompassed in the different milieux of journalism and industry – this novel touches on many of those literary and social issues which lend the study of GDR literature its particular fascination: the role of women, the generation gap as it manifests itself in the problems of the offspring of the founding generation and, perhaps above all, the psychological effects of unrelenting exposure to ideological pressures.

The origins of *Flugasche* are to be found in Monika Maron's own experiences as a journalist working, until 1976, on the weekly *Wochenpost*. The novel's heroine, Josefa Nadler, is despatched by her editor to write a feature on B. – clearly Bitterfeld, a town celebrated for marking a particular stage in the development of East German literature, but seen here in its reputation as 'die schmutzigste Stadt Europas' (p. 36), a place where the air is flavoured daily by 180 tonnes of industrial filth, the bronchitis rate is five times higher

---

7. Harald Hartung, 'Der Krieg gegen die Sprache', *Frankfurter Allgemeine Zeitung*, 23 June 1979.
8. Monika Maron, *Flugasche*, Frankfurt/Main, 1981. Page references in the text are to this edition.
9. Monika Maron, *Die Überläuferin*, Frankfurt/Main, 1986. Page references in the text are to this edition.
10. Monika Maron, 'Kein Recht, sondern Gnade', *ZEITmagazin*, 2 October 1987, p. 6.
11. Monika Maron, *Flight of Ashes*, trans. David Newton Marinelli, London, 1986.

than elsewhere, where trees 'über Nàcht ihre Blüte verlieren, als wäre ein böser Zauber über sie hinweggefegt', and which is dominated by a 'Kraftwerk, in dem das Wort Sicherheit nicht erwähnt werden darf' (pp. 58f).

On an initial level the novel deals with Josefa's failure to get her article about B. published and the conflict with colleagues and officials this precipitates, which threatens her membership of the Party. The psychological and cultural prerequisites for this conflict on which she will eventually founder are rapidly established. Her reflexions in the opening chapter of the novel about her grandparents, 'Die Verrücktheit des Großvaters war verlockend, verrückte Menschen erschienen mir freier als normale' (p. 9), in conjunction with her own complex anxieties – 'Die Machtsucht primitiver Gemüter läßt mich zittern . . . Was habe ich zu befürchten? Das Bett, in dem ich sterben werde. Die Leben, die ich nicht lebe. Die Monotonie bis zum Verfall und danach' (p. 12) – outline a personality of incipiently anarchic and restless disposition who will be ill at ease with the task of delivering the identikit portraits of exemplary *Helden der Arbeit* and the bromide vision of the industrial milieu which her editor requires.

And so it proves. Her visit to Bitterfeld is a dramatic eye-opener. Of her ignorance of the appalling circumstances in which the people of the town live and work she asks: 'Und warum habe ich das alles nicht gewußt? Jede Woche steht etwas in der Zeitung über ein neues Produkt, über eine Veranstaltung im Kulturpalast, über vorfristig erfüllte Pläne, über den Orden des Kollegen Soundso. Nichts über das Kraftwerk, kein Wort von den Aschekammern, die das Schlimmste sind' (p. 21).

Particularly telling is the experience at first hand of what she subsequently calls 'die Gewalttätigkeit industrieller Arbeit' (p. 81). A crucial confrontation with the stoker Hodriwitzka – a figure initially reminiscent of the conventional socialist-realist hero, but given here an entirely convincing contour – makes her determined not to follow the example of colleagues who had been similarly 'betroffen und erschüttert' (p. 21) but had gone away to produce whitewashing reports. Of greatest significance in this meeting with Hodriwitzka is Josefa's embarrassed realization – dramatized in her involuntary recoil from his coal-dust handshake – of the gulf between workers and intellectuals. It is a gulf which had allowed her to accept without questioning the newspaper image of B. and to dwell neatly isolated and untroubled in that realm of non-manual work which Thomas Brasch once described as being more instrumental in determining the quality of life than the ideological and political system under which one lives.[12] Illustrating the divide of which she has suddenly been made aware, Josefa notes that 'er sah mich an wie ein höflicher Chinese, mit dem man türkisch sprechen wollte' (p. 50).

This divide between reporter and worker is treated in somewhat more reconciliatory fashion than it is in Gert Neumann's story 'Die Reportagen', where journalists visiting a large building-project are treated with suspicion and barely muted hostility.[13] Nevertheless, here and in a further abrasively humorous encounter with another worker, the red-haired Herrmann, which forces her to acknowledge her 'uneingestandener, sozial verbrämter Standesdünkel' (p. 141), the public ideology of the 'Volksverbundenheit' of the intellectual and of the solidarity forged by socialism between the different classes in the Workers' State is as resoundingly deflated as it is in Neumann's account.

Experiences such as these fortify Josefa's resolve to reject the solution of her friend Christian that she should write 'zwei Varianten. Die erste wie es war, und eine zweite, die gedruckt werden kann' (p. 24). She completes and submits her manuscript, setting in motion a process which begins with acknowledgement from Luise, her older colleague and mentor – 'Das ist eine Reportage so ganz nach meinem Herzen' (p. 70) – but goes on to offer us unusual insights into the relationship between the mechanisms of censorship and journalistic practices in the GDR and the psychological repercussions for those involved in them. One example, the baleful vignette of Josefa's *Illustrierte Woche* colleague Fred Müller, who needs a liberal dose of schnaps daily to keep at bay the feelings of revulsion aroused by his job. Not until the alcohol has taken its numbing effect can he exercise his editorial function and 'gleichmütig, als handele es sich um mathematische Formeln, die Sätze durch sein taubes Gehirn strömen lassen' (p. 64). Recalling his earlier bitter and drunken outburst – 'Ich habe die ganze Scheiße satt. Diese Arschlöcher. Schleimscheißende Kriechtiere. Alles fette Ärsche und hohle Eierköpfe, Hirnaussauger!' (p. 63) – we glimpse, as he goes about his work, a once creative talent stultified by over-exposure to the ideological image and cliché which are the stock-in-trade of his profession: 'Die immer bessere Durchführung komplexer Wettbewerbsmethoden, das immer offene Ohr eines Bürgermeisters, die immer neueren Neuerermethoden befreit er

---

12. See Fritz J. Raddatz, 'Für jeden Autor ist die Welt anders. Ein ZEIT-Gespräch mit dem aus der DDR ausgewanderten Schriftsteller Thomas Brasch über sein neues Buch *Kargo* und seine Erfahrungen im Westen', *Die Zeit*, 22 July 1977.
13. In Neumann, *Die Schuld der Worte*, pp. 16–60.

vom gröbsten grammatikalischen und syntaktischen Unsinn. Die verbleibenden sprachlichen Ungereimtheiten folgen den eigenen Gesetzen einer Formelsprache und lassen sich nicht redigieren' (p. 64).

Or, in Josefa's case, we are witness to the destructive effects, on an individual ill-equipped and unprepared to compromise, of blocks and hindrances to the expression of an authentic view of reality. At an early point in the novel she rehearses in an imaginary conversation with Luise the arguments which will ultimately lead her into fraught confrontation with her colleagues and authority: 'Wem nützen unsere Schwindeleien, Luise' (p. 34), she asks in an uncanny echo of the opening lines of Wolf Biermann's poem 'Frage Antwort und Frage',[14] linking herself to all those critical spirits in the GDR who want to use their commitment to socialism as a springboard to more open discussion of its faults and deficiencies. But it must also be stressed at this point that *Flugasche* is much more than a dramatic disquisition on the obfuscatory ways of GDR journalism in its treatment of the world of work or of environmental problems.

What gives the novel its particular force is its wedding of these issues to questions of identity and self-realization, the search for what Josefa calls 'die ihr gemäße Biografie' (p. 99). Her rejection of 'Schizophrenie als Lebenshilfe' (p. 24) is a refusal to compromise not only in her professional, but also in her private life. The desire for separateness and independence, not wanting to be defined in terms of a relationship with a man – 'die Angst, ein Vierbeiner zu sein' (p. 42) – is as much an attempt to preserve her integrity as are her efforts to resist compromises in her work as a journalist. The two spheres are of course connected in a further sense, in that the possibility of personal fulfilment and private happiness is destroyed by her inability to function and operate as she would like in the public world: not being permitted honestly to record what she sees and experiences in her professional capacity destroys any chance of finding peace in her private life. She is the very opposite of what a character in Dieter Eue's novel *Ketzers Jugend* termed the '16 Millionen Schizophrene' who make up the population of the GDR:[15] not for her the comforting reassurance of Günter Gaus's 'Nischengesellschaft'[16] – the rendering unto Caesar in her

---

14. Wolf Biermann, *Mit Marx- und Engelszungen*, Berlin, 1968, p. 18.
15. Dieter Eue, *Ketzers Jugend*, Hamburg, 1982, p. 325.
16. See Günter Gaus, *Wo Deutschland liegt. Eine Ortsbestimmung*, Munich, 1986, pp. 115–69.

professional life balanced by the compensations of the private sphere. She desires to be all of a piece, but this proves to be an impossible and destructive desire. In a crucial exchange with Luise, she compares herself to a car travelling with the handbrake on: 'ein Auto, das man hundert Kilometer mit angezogener Handbremse fährt, geht kaputt'; she feels cheated of her life: 'Ich werde um mich selbst betrogen . . . Sie betrügen mich um mich, um meine Eigenschaften. Alles, was ich bin, darf ich nicht sein' (p. 78). She sees this, furthermore, not as a problem peculiar to her, but as part of a widespread malaise resulting from the very nature of GDR society. In one of the most highly charged passages in the novel she sketches a nightmare vision of a society emerging which is ruled entirely by cold rationality and in which only in dreams will the individual be able to find freedom of expression:

> Und ein Mensch, glaubst du, der bleibt heil? Der geht auch kaputt. Er bleibt nicht stehen, fällt nicht um, aber er wird immer schwächer, bringt nichts mehr zustande. Seine wichtigste Beschäftigung wird die Kontrolle über sich selbst, das Verleugnen seiner Mentalität, seiner Gefühle. Er reibt sich auf in dem Kampf gegen sich selbst, stutzt seine Gedanken, ehe er sie denkt, verwirft die Worte, bevor er sie gesprochen hat, mißtraut seinen eignen Urteilen, schämt sich seiner Besonderheiten, verbietet sich seine Gefühle; und wenn sie sich nicht verbieten lassen, verschweigt er sie. Schlimmer noch: Allmählich beginnt er unter der künstlichen Armut seiner Persönlichkeit zu leiden und erfindet sich neue Eigenschaften, die ihm Lob und Anerkennung einbringen. Er wird vernünftig, bedächtig, ordentlich, geschäftig. Anfangs zuckt sein mißhandelter Charakter noch unter den Zwängen, aber langsam stirbt er ab, wagt sich nur noch in den Träumen hervor . . . Noch vierzig oder fünfzig solcher Jahre, Luise, und die Menschen langweilen sich an sich selbst zu Tode. Dann sind die letzten Aufsässigen ausgestorben, und niemand wird die Kinder mehr ermutigen, mit der Welt zu spielen. Sie werden vom ersten Tag ihres Lebens an den knöchernen Ernst dieses Lebens kennenlernen. Ihre Lust wird getilgt durch maßvolle Regelung des Essens, des Spiels, des Lernens. Sie lernen Vernunft, ohne je unvernünftig gewesen zu sein. Armselige kretinöse Geschöpfe werden heranwachsen, und die Schöpferischen unter ihnen werden eine unbestimmte Trauer empfinden und eine Sehnsucht nach Lebendigem. Und wehe, sie finden es in sich selbst. Verstoßene und verlachte Außenseiter werden sie sein. Verrückte, Spinner, Unverbesserliche. Du bist zu lebendig, wird man so einem sagen als schlimmsten Vorwurf. Ich denke nur, unsere Natur ist stärker als jedes noch so perfekte System der Nivellierung und bäumt sich auf, wenn sie zu tief gebeugt wird. (pp. 78f)

It is inevitable that Josefa should seek to remedy this malaise, to find outlets for her frustrations and to counter-balance those forces which are robbing her of identity. She does this in part – and here we arrive at the nub of the argument – by excursions into fantasy and dream. Fantasy is escape, dream an expression of protest.

These various excursions take different forms. On the street a gust of wind catches her coat and she suddenly finds herself circling in the sky above the Alexanderplatz. Reality and fantasy merge here quite naturally to convey, in poetically literal fashion, a yearning to spread her wings and a desire to escape the deadening routine of everyday reality:

> Und jetzt zur Sonne, Dädalus, ach ich weiß schon, das darf man nicht. Brüder, zur Sonne, zur Freiheit; Brüder zum Lichte empor. Wir haben keine Zeit zum Fliegen. Wir müssen uns beeilen, immerzu beeilen. Zum Wurstladen, zur Sparkasse, ins Büro, in den Kindergarten, zur S-Bahn. Überall können wir zu spät kommen. Das Geld ist ausverkauft, die Sparkasse abgefahren, der Chef hat geschlossen, das Kind weint. (p. 71)

But the motif of flying also signals Josefa's feelings of elation and relief at having completed the modest reportage about B. entirely according to her own lights: 'Nichts Sensationelles, keine Entdeckung, kein Gedanke, den nicht jeder denken könnte, der einmal durch B. gelaufen ist. Nichts als der zaghafte Versuch, die Verhältnisse zu beschreiben, wie sie vorgefunden wurden. Trotzdem Grund genug zu fliegen' (p. 73).

In the second part of *Flugasche*, as Josefa retreats to her bed to recapitulate and review her deepening personal and professional crises and her increasing alienation from her colleagues, the novel moves further into the sphere of her dreams and imagination. The second section opens directly in this vein – 'Es häuften sich die Träume, die in Josefa aufstiegen, sobald sie einen Fluchtweg fand aus den vielen Reden, die um sie herum geführt wurden und die sie selbst führte' (p. 145) – paving the way for a species of dream cum self-induced dramatization of her inner tensions which anticipates the central preoccupation of her second novel *Die Überläuferin* and what one reviewer termed the 'Theater im Kopf'.[17] This very terminology points to a theatricalization of the psychological processes under scrutiny, to a puppet theatre of the soul:

> Sie mußte nur auf eine spiegelnde Tischoberfläche oder in graue Wolken

---

17. Elsbeth Pulver, 'Theater im Kopf. Monika Maron: *Die Überläuferin*', *Neue Zürcher Zeitung*, 9 January 1987, p. 37.

starren, bis sich der Vorhang vor ihre Augen spannte, hinter den sie ungehindert ihre Geschöpfe zitieren konnte . . . ob sie sich würde wehren können gegen ihre hämischen Gestalten . . . Sie mußte nur die Augen öffnen, dann war sie ihnen entkommen, konnte sie in die Kiste sperren, bis sie Sehnsucht nach ihnen verspürte und ihnen ihre Spiele gestattete. (pp. 145f)

Two dream-scenes follow each other in quick succession. In the first, an aged mother and daughter, in an all-pervasive lilac setting, are locked in a psychological and physical battle. The tyrannical domination by the mother, squashing her daughter's wish to learn and expand – '"Ich will so gerne lesen können," sagte die jüngere, "es ist so langweilig." "Du hast deine Bilderbücher."' (pp. 147f) – clearly has its roots on one level in Josefa's relationship with Luise, as well as being in a broader sense an expression of the ubiquitous *Bevormundung* and prescriptiveness emanating from the political apparatus which have such an oppressive effect on her professional life. In a further scene Josefa sees herself – dramatically attired – striding on stage from a front row seat to deliver a passionate, bitter and, in part, ironical speech on the lamentable plight of women in the GDR and the nature of their sexuality. The all-woman audience respond enthusiastically but have seemingly comprehended and absorbed none of the urgency of her comment. Dramatically illustrated here are Josefa's grievances, despair and, perhaps above all, her sense of growing isolation.

What is common to these various examples of fantasy and dream is that they are essentially solitary activities, and solitary activity, in the society which Josefa Nadler inhabits, can as she is well aware be viewed only with suspicion. In an imaginary dialogue with Party colleagues, Josefa hints at the guilt, the culpability which retreat into an individual viewpoint, the exclusion of oneself from the 'Wir', may incur:

Diese Genossen 'Wir'. Gegen mein klägliches 'Ich habe gesehn' stellen sie ihr unerschütterliches 'Wir', und schon bin ich der Querulant, der Einzelgänger, der gegen den Strom schwimmt, unbelehrbar, arrogant, selbstherrlich. Sie verschanzen sich hinter ihrem 'Wir', machen sich unsichtbar, unangreifbar. Aber wehe, ich gehe auf ihre majestätische Grammatik ein und nenne sie 'ihr' oder 'sie', dann hageln ihre strengen Fragen: Wer sind 'sie'? Wen meinst du konkret? Warum sagst du 'ihr' und nicht 'wir'? Von wem distanzierst du dich? (p. 33)

We leave unresolved the extent to which attitudes such as this result from her paranoia or a brand of abrasiveness which makes her the sort of person who, as Christian notes, would rather go head first through a wall than use the open door next to it. In this context, where to use 'I' rather than 'we' is to arouse distrust, in a society which in stressing collectivity seems to monotonize and level down existence, individual imagination and flights of fantasy become a way of escape, of asserting a sense of self. But they are also – by contravening generally accepted values – a way of incurring guilt. In one sense it could be argued that it is Josefa Nadler's very powers of imagination which make her unable to ignore or gloss over the reality of B. and which lead to her controversial and, by implication, criminal reportage. But on another, more complex level, they are the cause of her greater 'crime'. In the crucial move which leads to her downfall she leapfrogs accepted procedures and refers her reportage and grievances about the obstructiveness of Party colleagues to higher authority, to the 'Höchste Rat'. What is of most relevance to our deliberations here, however, is that the immediate trigger for this reprehensible and culpable move is not her reformer's zeal – the rational, crusading journalist side of her – but her fatal tendency to view a highly prosaic world in poetic terms. One day in Berlin she sees a ministerial car bringing the traffic to a halt. A familiar and everyday sight in the capital perhaps, but one which is transformed by her poetic fantasy into a scene of dramatic eeriness. A strange constellation, perceived only by Josefa, of light, sound, a bird falling dead as it is about to break into song and an official limousine moving as if through a silent vacuum, builds into paradigmatic significance: 'Die Stille war es, dachte Josefa, die Totenstille. Sie schoben die Stille vor sich her; wohin sie auch kamen, die Stille war vor ihnen da. Sie müssen taub sein davon, dachte Josefa. Sie werden nichts wissen über B., sie können es gar nicht wissen. Sie . . . fuhr nach Hause, um den Brief zu schreiben' (p. 176). It is as if the silence which seems in this moment to surround the car and the influential figures it is spiriting along is a symbol of the unreachability of the mighty, a metaphor for the imperviousness of the powerful to the complaints of the insignificant.

The letter which Josefa rushes home to write precipitates disastrous consequences. It alienates colleagues who might have been eventually won over to her reportage, and releases the avalanche of petty accusations and detailing of past misdemeanours which gives the orthodox and opportunistic the chance to debate whether she is worthy of remaining a member of the Party. But of most significance for our present argument is that this 'crime' has resulted from her responding with the intoxicating perception of the poet; it flows from the poet's gift of seeing the everyday in highly charged fashion. Imagination has made her culpable. When, on being confronted with her misdemeanour, she subsequently tries to offer this explanation for her behaviour she is met with blank and hostile incomprehension: 'die schwarze Limousine, der tote Vogel, die Stille, es hätte gespenstisch geklungen, sagte Hans Schütz' (p. 206).

It is at this point, as we begin perhaps to place the novel in a wider context and confront a society in which there seems little place for the vagaries of the poetic imagination, and where the hypersensitivities of the poet are regarded as pathological – 'Beweis für krankhafte Selbstüberschätzung' (p. 206) – that a much wider vista opens up. As one example among many of what might befall the artistic temperament at the hands of a system too insistent on its rational and scientific principles, Günter Kunert and his defence of Kleist comes prominently into view.

The final pages of *Flugasche* find Josefa Nadler in bed, to which she has retreated, and from which perspective in time and place the second part of the novel has been narrated in flashback. Maron's second novel *Die Überläuferin* opens with its heroine, Rosalind Polkowski, likewise or similarly located: 'Seit zwei Tagen lag, saß sie im Bett, auf dem Teppich, im Sessel' (p. 9). Despite the fact that the names and professional circumstances of their respective protagonists have been changed – Rosalind Polkowski works in an institute for historical research – the two novels nevertheless seem to flow one from the other and the second may be seen as a continuation of the problems left unresolved at the end of the first. In *Flugasche* we had seen someone relegating herself to the sidelines, put out of action by her failure to realize goals in both her private and professional life. We were witness to a kind of crippling of individual aspiration which was partly self-inflicted, partly the consequence of collective intransigence and expediency. The first novel was set largely in the real world, it dealt with the efforts of an individual to contribute to the solution of serious social problems – pollution and inhuman working conditions. Fantasy here had a directly social application. The imaginative sensibilities of Josefa Nadler enabled her to be shocked by the disturbing realities of life in B., but were also the cause of those breaches of discipline and of accepted norms of political behaviour which made her culpable and led to her fall from favour. They also had a further important role to play in the articulation of her difficulties and anguish, provoking the dreams, nightmares and escapist fantasies through which these were expressed.

In the second novel – billed on the dust jacket as beginning where *Flugasche* left off – we are presented with a heroine who is literally crippled, who is 'lahmbeinig' (p. 40). We move, furthermore, out of the real world, the world of the industrial milieu, the realm of journalism and the sphere of Party officials. Gone completely in *Die Überläuferin* are the elements of socialist-realist setting and character to be found in *Flugasche* and instead we move wholly into the realm of memory, fantasy and the world of the socially peripheral. But this novel is more than a continuation of aspects of a process begun in *Flugasche*, where Josefa Nadler had taken to her bed and increasingly retreated into her inner self. Rosalind Polkowski's story may also be seen as the attempt to show how the pieces of a shattered life may be gathered up, or at least how a modus vivendi and a way of dealing, however escapist, with one's perceived persecutors might be arrived at. The second novel, if not a complete answer to the problems posed by the first, could be interpreted as offering a kind of therapy for them.

What form does this therapy take? As Rosalind gives in to her 'Bedürfnis nach Verzicht' (p. 13) and is freed from the obligations of daily routine into a state of limbo, time ceases to be a tyrant and becomes instead 'einen bemessenen Raum, in dem sie die Erlebnisse sammeln wollte wie Bücher in einer Bibliothek, ihr jederzeit zugängliche und abrufbare Erinnerungen', a place in which she is presented with 'eine nicht endende Orgie phantastischer Ereignisse, ein wunderbares Chaos ohne Ziel und Zweck' (p. 13). As these fantasies take shape, she becomes – as Josefa Nadler had been – a spectator of her own inner landscape.

After excursions into the past which begin with the catastrophic circumstances of her wartime birth, there develops, through a series of surreal 'Zwischenspiele', a kind of Mad Hatter's Tea Party, a spectacle of endless permutations and possibilities in which Rosalind's ideological and spiritual adversaries, as well as a handful of eccentric women friends, are called up to act out their parts:

> Nach einigen Augenblicken der Unsicherheit traute ich meinen Augen und verfolgte voller Spannung das mir dargebotene Spektakel, in meiner Aufmerksamkeit nur gestört durch eine übermütige Freude, hervorgerufen durch meine wunderbare neue Fähigkeit. Ein nüchternes Delirium, vernünftiger Wahnsinn, Traum ohne Schlaf. Sie spielten und spielten, während ich mir ausmalte, wen ich in Zukunft an mein eben gegründetes Zimmertheater berufen könnte. Jeden, alle, ob ich sie kannte oder nicht, alle könnte ich vor mir tanzen und reden lassen, selbst den Papst, wenn die Lust dazu mich ankäme. (pp. 40f)

The inhabitants of this spectacle think of her as a 'Gastgeberin'. In fact she is a ringmaster who can control them at whim, summon or dismiss them as she wishes. The most dominant and aggressive figure, for instance, the man in red uniform, a symbol of authoritarian ideological inflexibility who later turns out to be a 'Beauftragter der Staatlichen Behörde für Psychokontrolle' (p. 122), can be immediately despatched into oblivion by the 'Strafe des Vergessenwerdens' (p. 41).

What initially appears to be a purely private and escapist process of controlling her fears and anxieties – she has after all had to cut herself off from the outside world in order to enact and exorcize them – is intercut with reflection on past experiences and individuals who have had an important role in her life, to produce a philosophy of much wider significance. This is anchored in the figure of Martha, Rosalind's alter ego and the epitome of the free and anarchic spirit that Rosalind had never been able to be. Martha, at an early point in her life – in a somewhat extravagant episode, typical of the awkward blend of the bizarre and the didactic which occasionally detracts from the effect of *Die Überläuferin* – had taken on board the philosophy of a renegade mathematics professor turned pirate chief:

> du mußt deine nutzloseste Eigenschaft herausfinden. Denn schon ehe du geboren wurdest, hat man dich statistisch aufbereitet und deinen möglichen Nutzen errechnet: die durch dich verursachten Kosten im Kindesalter, die Verwendbarkeit während der Arbeitsphase, die zu erwartenden Nachkommen, die wieder entstehenden Kosten im Alter bis zum statistisch ausgewiesenen Sterbealter, kurz: deine Rentabilität ist veranschlagt und wird erwartet . . . Aber in jedem Menschen gibt es etwas, das sie nicht gebrauchen können, das Besondere, das Unberechenbare, Seele, Poesie, Musik . . . Dieses scheinbar nutzloseste Stück von dir mußt du finden und bewahren, das ist der Anfang deiner Biografie. (pp. 50f)

This subversive, but eminently appealing advice from the pirate professor leads again to what may be seen as the dominant theme of this second of Monika Maron's novels: the culpability which certain kinds of imaginative expression can bring. It has to be said, however, that the dramatization of it in *Die Überläuferin* seems much more crass than had been the case in *Flugasche*. What in the first novel was delicately suggested and left to the reader to deduce, is here made painfully explicit. First Martha is called to account by 'ein führendes Mitglied der Assoziation dichtender Männer' who accuses her of crimes against literary taste – 'Wir haben Romantizismen, Lyrismen, Pathos, Selbstmitleid, Infantilismus und modisches Feministengeplapper nachweisen können' (p. 156) – while Rosalind herself is accused of 'unerlaubte Phantasie in Tateneinheit mit Benutzung derselben im Wiederholungsfall' (p. 170). In other words, there tumbles out before us a bundle of entirely justified feminist, aesthetic grievances about a male-dominated, excessively rational and scientific world which seeks to shackle the imagination, and particularly the female one, in an ideological straitjacket; in the words of the man from 'Psychokontrolle': 'Wer sagt denn, daß ich gegen die Phantasie bin. Ich bin sogar für die Phantasie, für eine konstruktive, positive, saubere Phantasie' (p. 171). Unfortunately, however, not only do we feel bludgeoned by 'message' at points such as these, but expression fails to do justice to the passion of the sentiment. Particularly in its final sections, the novel falls into a series of bizarre but essentially arbitrary images, which aim at the poetic allusiveness of the surreal, but decline into cabaretistic ephemerality.

Although neither of these novels has been published in the GDR, one may reasonably surmise that it is for quite different reasons. For all their more obvious closeness to the publicly unarticulated realities of the GDR and the vigour with which they prod its weak spots – those areas in which real existing socialism is palpably defective – there is at least an answer to be made to the criticisms voiced by Josefa Nadler in *Flugasche*. Through the figure of Luise, a staunch and plausible communist, Maron offers a reasonably persuasive response to them by drawing attention to the social and economic achievements of the GDR and by legitimizing the present system by reference to the iniquities of the past. Josefa herself indeed is briefly stopped in her tracks by Luise's arguments:

> keine Gesellschaft kommt ohne ihre Kritiker aus. Aber dann kämpfe und hör auf zu jammern. Das sind nun mal die vielzitierten Mühen der Ebene, und kein Mensch hat uns versprochen, daß sie ausbleiben. Wenn ich nicht tief überzeugt wäre, daß unsere Mühe sich lohnt, auch wenn es länger dauert, als wir geglaubt haben, wäre ich längst nicht mehr hier. (p. 84)

At the heart of *Die Überläuferin* there lies something potentially far more challenging. If the solution that Rosalind Polkowski has devised to cope with her problems is a pathological one – only by retreating from the world can one deal with it – then the brand of anarchic fantasy it proposes, the advocation by the heroine of the irrational and the mystical and her rejection of the notion that salvation may be found in 'progress' and scientific functionalism, constitute a profound threat – and not just to the ethos of the GDR and other socialist societies. Monika Maron has observed of her heroine Rosalind Polkowski:

> Wenn ich glauben würde, das Problem dieser Figur in meinem Buch läge nur in der DDR, würde ich das Land verlassen. Wenn ich glauben würde, ich wäre frei davon, wenn ich das Land wechselte, würde ich gehen. Ich gehe eher von Grenzen aus, die innerhalb unserer Zivilisation liegen, in der Art der Industriegesellschaft, in der wir leben. Im Westen sind die Mechanismen gewiß anders, aber sie würden mich auf ähnliche Weise belasten.[18]

The need, it would seem, for the liberating effects of fantasy and the poetic imagination is universal. It is, she implies, as potentially subversive to a capitalist as to a socialist way of ordering things.

---

18. 'Literatur, das nicht gelebte Leben. Gespräch mit der Ostberliner Schriftstellerin Monika Maron', *Süddeutsche Zeitung*, 6 March 1987.

–15–

Loyalty and its Limits: Christa Wolf's *Kassandra* as a 'Schlüsselerzählung'

DAVID JENKINSON

I

In her Frankfurt lectures Christa Wolf tells us that the figure of Kassandra evolved as her story grew in the author's mind from a projected 'Lehrstück' to a 'Schlüsselerzählung' (V 119).[1] The more precise nature of this evolution can be seen in certain discrepancies both within *Kassandra* and between the novel and the accompanying lectures, the *Voraussetzungen einer Erzählung*. These discrepancies need to be kept in mind when distinguishing the different layers of meaning in the novel. They suggest that it began in its author's mind as a novel about the experience of women in a male-dominated world facing the threat of extinction, in the form of a retelling of the story of the fall of Troy, which has been told from the point of view of the victors (Homer) and the ultimate beneficiaries (Virgil), but not from either the Trojans' or from a woman's point of view. Later the novel increasingly took on the quality of a *roman à clef*, with the contrast and conflict between Troy and Greece coming to stand as a cipher for the present-day East–West confrontation. This shift in intention accounts, for instance, for the discrepancy between Kassandra's 'Grauen und Scham' (K 20) at the ritual defloration which Herodotus describes as taking place in Cyprus (V 103) and which Wolf transfers to Troy,[2] and her later conviction that no woman could possibly wish to exchange Trojan chivalry towards women for Greek lasciviousness.

1. References in the text are to Christa Wolf, *Kassandra* (K), 4th edn, Darmstadt, 1983, and *Voraussetzungen einer Erzählung: Kassandra* (V), 2nd edn, Darmstadt, 1983.
2. There is nothing in the text of *Kassandra* to suggest that this practice is 'new' to Troy, as is claimed by Jacquie Hope, who sees it as a product of the transition from a matriarchal to a patriarchal society: Jacquie Hope, 'Creating the Past in Memory of the Future: Christa Wolf's *Kassandra*', in Ingrid K. J. Williams (ed.), *GDR: Individual and Society*, Conference Proceedings, Ealing College of HE,

David Jenkinson

The conception of a 'Schlüsselerzählung', it would seem, subsequently evolved further into a fictional strategy for an examination of the strains which Kassandra's experiences put on her loyalty to Troy, a theme of the most painful personal relevance to the author which, not surprisingly, is scarcely touched on in the lectures. This would explain the discrepancy between the two accounts of Kassandra's marriage to Eurypilos: at first it is presented as an outrage, a forced marriage without precedent in Troy, but at its later reappearance it has become a marriage to which Kassandra consents without protest as an indication of her continuing loyalty. Similarly, Polyxena is first promised to Achill in return for revealing Greek military secrets; this exploitation of a woman as a political bargaining counter belongs to the feminist layer of the novel and also marks a stage in the moral decline of the Trojans which makes them increasingly similar to the Greeks in their ruthless pursuit of victory at any price. Some time later, however, Polyxena is used again, this time as bait to lure Achill into an ambush, behaviour so appalling that Kassandra's loyalty finally snaps and she withdraws her support for the Trojan rulers.

I should like in this paper to look more closely at the implications of reading *Kassandra* as a *roman à clef*, in particular at the presentation of Kassandra's crisis of loyalty as an imaginative projection of the author's own position vis-à-vis her society, and at the relationship between the novel and the Frankfurt lectures.[3] The ten-year long war between Greece and Troy provides a precise metaphor for the Cold War, the 'Nicht-Krieg' (V 95) that was revived and intensified in the early 1980s. It is a war to which people become accustomed, which stagnates for long periods during which normal life continues, with a wide variety of personal contacts between the two sides, and considerable 'Ost–West-Handel' (K 56). It would be hard not to equate the annual Trojan autumn fair with the Leipzig Trade Fair: Trojans and Greeks mingle and trade, Agamemnon even buys a 'Halsschmuck' (K 118) for Kassandra.[4] It is a war

---

London, 1987, pp. 124–35; here p. 125. Wolf spoke of the possibility of such a transition in her lectures but also expressed the view that the question was unimportant and the concern with it merely a sign of women's contemporary desperation (V 56f). She did not incorporate the theme into the novel.

3. I shall touch only marginally on the issues raised by the many widely varying feminist readings of *Kassandra*, which are so complex as to require separate investigation. Suffice it to say here that although the gross abuse of women is clearly one of the themes of *Kassandra*, no superior wisdom, insight or capacity for more humane leadership is ascribed to women in the novel.
4. An echo perhaps of the *Agamemnon* of Aeschylus, where Cassandra becomes Agamemnon's booty after the fall of Troy.

between two countries that are fundamentally part of the same culture (see V 89), whose actual causes are purely a matter of economic considerations (Trojan gold and access to the Bosporus).

Behind the Greeks, as perceived by Kassandra – impetuous, foolish and credulous, who 'tun, was sie nicht wollen und betrauern selbstmitleidig ihre Opfer' (K 118), whose civilian population have never experienced war on their own soil, in particular behind the bestial Achill who ravages the Trojan hinterland, murdering, plundering, raping, killing livestock and destroying crops, and who weeps over Penthesilea after he has killed and violated her – behind these clearly stand the Americans as perceived by Christa Wolf, with the Christianity that inspires their leadership and the self-regarding sentimentality that led them to drop toys over Vietnam for the children of the cities which they destroyed in order to save them. Faced with an enemy, in this view, of such monstrous evil, any measure, however immoral and demeaning, is justified, as Kassandra reluctantly but inescapably admits.[5] The corresponding parallel between Troy and the GDR has often been noted, sometimes in somewhat crude terms,[6] but deserves further elaboration: Troy has a Wall, 'jene [die Stadt] schützend, auch beengend' (K 39) whose moral legitimacy has been the subject of recent dispute, and a past history (the intended sacrifice of Paris) whose revelation causes acute embarrassment. When the Trojans become as coarse as the Greeks in their sexual conduct, this deterioration can easily be taken as a disguised comment on the deleterious effect on life in the GDR of that Anglo-American popular culture from which it has proved impossible to shield the country's youth. And, of course, the militarization of Troy as a consequence of the Greek threat is clearly intended to convey the view that the remilitarization of the GDR has been forced on it by the pressures of the Cold War. The parallel breaks down, however, at the point where the Trojans pay their coveted gold to the Greeks to obtain Hektor's corpse for burial: the contemporary 'Freikauf' operates in the opposite direction.

5. In the Achill–Polyxena episode Wolf has articulated a common contemporary moral dilemma. The stony outrage and incredulity with which the Trojan rulers react to Kassandra's refusal to support their plot was exactly paralleled by the reaction of the British government in 1988 to those who raised ethical objections to the shooting by the SAS of suspected IRA terrorists in Gibraltar; Kassandra's agonizingly contradictory feelings reflect a widespread ambiguity in the public response to such events.
6. See as a typical example, Hedwig Rohde, 'Die unbelehrbaren Besiegten. Christa Wolfs analytischer *Kassandra*-Monolog', *Rhein-Neckar-Zeitung*, 28 May 1983. Rohde, among other idiosyncrasies, describes Aineias as a 'Widerstandskämpfer'.

It is tempting to see even more specific equivalences. Can one, for example, resist seeing Hermann Kant behind Helenos the 'Orakelsprecher', Kassandra's twin brother, an 'andersgearteter Gleichaussehender' (K 34), the always cheery, utterly conformist pillar of society, with his 'lahme konventionelle Verlautbarungen' (K 35), who believes unquestioningly that Troy's fundamental superiority to Greece justifies the spurious manipulative ideology which he serves with a commitment wholly untempered by scepticism or irony. And can Christa Wolf possibly not have had her mentor Anna Seghers in mind when she portrayed the aged leather-cheeked priestess Herophile, equally conformist, unwaveringly supporting the war, sternly admonishing Kassandra to perform her duties in the manner expected of her and not to question the wisdom of the rulers? It is, of course, equally important to realize the extent to which Troy *cannot* be equated with the GDR (or Kassandra with Christa Wolf); the novel is not an allegory which invites the reader to seek equivalences for every character and episode. Much of the time we are dealing rather with imaginative reconstruction of alien experience. The Frankfurt lectures vividly reveal the author's fascination with the ancient world *before* the novel became a *roman à clef*. But there is a much more important point to stress. Wolf's intention in *Kassandra* is not simply to provide a disguised equivalent to contemporary East–West tensions. It is also to create a fictional framework within which she can imaginatively project her own tensions, conflicts and fears onto a character who embodies those problems in a far more extreme form. In the figure of the disillusioned prophetess Wolf is experimentally testing, as it were, the strength and limits of her own loyalties. This creative procedure of imaginative self-projection into a distant figure links *Kassandra* with *Kein Ort. Nirgends*; one cannot say that Wolf *is* Kassandra, any more than she *is* Kleist or Günderrode (or Rita Seidel or Christa T. for that matter). But what happens to Kassandra *could* happen to Wolf herself, or to anyone in her position: as she points out, Kassandra's imprisonment is merely 'eine verschärfte Form des Unglücks ihrer Landsleute' (V 110).

Kassandra finds herself in the worst possible position for a loyal supporter of a society of which she is a privileged leading citizen: her beloved country stumbles, despite her warnings, into a war which it cannot win, and for which it is unequivocally to blame. As her country becomes as savage, belligerent and degenerate as the enemy, her loyalty compels her to continue to fulfil her supportive public function as a famous and revered figure, despite having lost her belief in the official ideology. When the limits of her loyalty are reached, when she is required to express public approval of behaviour that finally removes any last residual grounds for believing that her country is in any way morally superior to the enemy, her refusal is harshly punished by the father she adores, but who can now see her only as a self-indulgently recalcitrant egoist. She knows that the war must be won, for to lose it would mean the destruction of her society by an unsurpassably vicious enemy; but she knows also that the war is unjust. In the end her worst fears are realized: not only is Troy annihilated in an orgy of murder, looting and rape, it has by then become the mirror-image of Greece. As Nietzsche put it, he who fights the dragon becomes the dragon.

Of all this the Frankfurt lectures say very little. Wolf has said that the lectures and the novel should be treated as one work and read together,[7] but this does not mean, as it has often implicitly been taken to mean, that the lectures constitute an interpretation of the novel. The lectures are concerned not with the final product but with some aspects of its genesis. It is, of course, not surprising that, faced with so dense and complex a work as *Kassandra*, readers should have looked to these lectures for elucidation. But quite apart from the general scepticism appropriate to an author's statements about his/her own work (trust the tale not the teller!), the nature, purpose and circumstances of the Frankfurt lectures were clearly such as to preclude a discussion of the work's more intimately personal and painful themes.[8] A celebrated East German writer, loyal to her country and with extensive experience as its emissary in the West, takes up an offer to lecture at a West German University in the spring of 1982 some six months before the deployment of medium-range nuclear missiles in West Germany, when that proposed deployment was the subject of intense public debate. At the same time, of course, the GDR is undergoing a similar remilitarization. She has much to say on this highly contentious topic, and does not propose to allow her ostensible subject, poetics, to deflect her from saying it. But she must also woo her audience. So she strenuously cultivates safe areas of common ground, most notably women's problems, culminating in a lengthy discussion of the work of Ingeborg Bachmann which is of little specific relevance to *Kassandra*. (This is not to say that women's experience and problems do

---

7. Jacqueline Grenz, 'Gespräch mit Christa Wolf', *Connaissance de la RDA*, no. 17, 1983, pp. 68–80; here p. 71. The novel and the lectures have been published as a single volume in the GDR.
8. I have made a similar point elsewhere with reference to *Kein Ort. Nirgends*: David E. Jenkinson, 'Artist and Society in Christa Wolf's *Kein Ort. Nirgends*', in Williams (ed.), *GDR: Individual and Society*, pp. 136–42; here p. 137.

not play an important part in *Kassandra*, but it *is* to say that they are presented differently and less tendentiously than many readers have supposed, having read into the novel the more polemical passages of the lectures.) Concerned to establish a relaxed rapport with her young audience, to whom a committed communist woman-writer is as queer a fish as a Trojan princess–priestess is to the Greeks, she first entertains her audience at extraordinary length with banal touristic reminiscences that would appear grossly self-indulgent if one did not recognize them as part of a finely calculated exercise in public relations. She goes on, at various points in the lectures, to admit that the *Iliad* bores her, to dissociate herself from 'eine vulgärmaterialistische Interpretation des Menschen und der Geschichte' (V 118) and unobtrusively, for the knowledgeable, from Lenin ('das mörderische wer–wen', V 151). She shows that she can be critical of Marx (twice pointing out his error in regarding the Greeks as 'childlike'), alludes in passing to Peter Weiss's *Die Ästhetik des Widerstands*, and presents as if it were a brand-new discovery Marx's insight that Christianity provided the ideology of capitalism, a tenet of Marxism so basic that she must surely have been familiar with it for thirty years or more. Playing on the popularity of Greece for modern German tourists, she teases her listeners by including herself in the 'Western' world of high living standards and mass-produced consumer goods, while relegating the impoverished Greek village women to the 'Eastern' world. She also warns her audience at the outset against expecting a full account of what her novel will actually be about: 'Vieles, das meiste vielleicht und Wichtigstes, bleibt ungesagt, auch wohl ungewußt' (V 7). And indeed it does: when Wolf discusses her central character she is concerned – what else could one expect? – not to spell out the crisis of loyalty that is Kassandra's central experience, but rather to assert, not wholly convincingly, a distance of irony and superior insight between herself and her creation (see V 89, 119).

At the heart of the novel is Kassandra's reappraisal of her life, her relationship to Troy and its rulers, and her part in its decline and destruction.[9] This self-reappraisal of an individual's past life not only links *Kassandra* with *Kindheitsmuster*, it is a theme common to much GDR writing, to be seen in works as disparate as Hermann Kant's *Die Aula* and *Der Aufenthalt* and Plenzdorf's *Die neuen Leiden des jungen W*. For Kassandra it is harsh reckoning, both with Troy

---

9. There is no justification for dismissing Kassandra's self-examination as 'narzißhaft': U. Heukenkamp, [review of *Kassandra*], *Weimarer Beiträge*, vol. 30, no. 8, 1984, pp. 1361–6; here p. 1365.

and with herself. She admits that her self-image: 'umgänglich, bescheiden, anspruchslos . . . aufrecht, stolz und wahrheitsliebend' (K 14f), was quite at odds with her actual dominant qualities of 'Unwissenheit . . . Bequemlichkeit . . . Hochmut . . . Feigheit, Faulheit, Scham' (K 26). She admits that she failed to rise to the challenge either of Polyxena, by accepting the insights into sexual psychopathology that her behaviour should have yielded, or of Penthesilea, with all the feminist issues raised by her ethos and actions, embodying as she does that 'Weiblichkeitswahn' (V 115) from which Wolf forcefully dissociates herself in the Frankfurt lectures.[10] Above all, Kassandra admits that she was blind and deaf to the realities of Troy and her own situation there, with an obtuseness which she can, retrospectively, scarcely comprehend; the mechanisms of self-censorship and the screening out of unwelcome perceptions remain a mystery to her to the end: 'War ich denn taub? Ich glaube, ja. Ich glaube, in gewissem Sinne ja. Ich habe es durchgemacht, doch es mir selbst zu erklären ist noch immer schwer' (K 97).

To the recurrent key question: 'Warum wollte ich die Sehergabe unbedingt?' (K 6), Kassandra gives, as her story unfolds, increasingly honest and painful answers. Her first answer is: 'Mit meiner Stimme sprechen, das Äußerste. Mehr, andres hab ich nicht gewollt' (K 6). Only with immense reluctance does she later confess to a less flattering motivation: 'Priesterin werden, um Macht zu gewinnen? Götter. Bis an diesen äußersten Punkt habt ihr mich treiben müssen, um diesen schlichten Satz aus mir herauszupressen' (K 60). She has also to face her own authoritarianism: she condemns Paris as 'übereinstimmungssüchtig' (K 144) for his acquiescence in the plot to ambush Achill; only with the greatest difficulty does she realize that this craving for conformity was in fact her own major failing, part of the 'Eumelos in mir' (K 79). But her most sombre insight is that she bears within herself the capacity for all the extremes of murderous violence to which the war has led. When, after Penthesilea's death, the women – Trojans as well as Amazons – go berserk in an orgiastic frenzy and bludgeon Panthoos to death, Kassandra comes within a hair's breadth of being caught up in the atavistic violence: 'Sollte die Wildnis wieder über uns zusammenschlagen. Sollte . . . der Urgrund uns verschlingen. Tanze, Kassandra, rühr dich! Ja, ich komme. Alles in mir drängte zu ihnen hin' (K 138).

10. I do not share Jacquie Hope's difficulty in seeing the relevance of Penthesilea to the present-day women's movement: Hope, 'Christa Wolf's *Kassandra*', pp. 131f.

An almost equally painful realization is that when Paris's brazen provocation of Menelaus made Kassandra foresee the war and Troy's defeat, her ensuing fit of madness subtly encouraged the palace of Troy in its self-regarding posturing and ascription of lofty tragic significance to demeaning events (see K 63, 68). This is related to her more general guilt, as Wolf put it (see V 110), of being foredoomed not to be believed, so that by predicting disaster she ensures that it will come about. Since Wolf explicitly equates the figure of the prophetess with that of the writer in her own culture (see V 90), the implications of this 'guilt' is that literature, by virtue of operating in a safe institutionalized space, utters its warnings in a context that ensures that they will not be acted on. We are thus invited to see Kassandra as in essence an artist who aspires to the role of a significant social commentator, only to become imprisoned by that role and suffer all the dilemmas of an institutionalized writer in a tightly controlled society. One of the things which it takes Kassandra so long to grasp is that she has to choose between seeking and uttering the truth, and saying what her privileged position requires her to say, and what indeed she genuinely desires to say, between, as Arisbe puts it, 'meinen Hang zur Übereinstimmung mit den Herrschenden' (K 72f) and 'meine Gier nach Erkenntnis' (K 73).

Kassandra's role of 'prophetess' has given her the deep happiness of combining self-fulfilment with social usefulness: 'Das Glück, ich selbst zu werden und dadurch den anderen nützlicher – ich hab es noch erlebt' (K 15). The loss of this fruitful dialectic between individual and society is an essential aspect of her tragedy, reflecting the position of the writer in our own age, utterly powerless to affect those who control our destiny (see V 85). Yet looking back, Kassandra realizes that even in those happy early years she was acting a part, 'spielte die Priesterin' (K 32); never was she more inauthentic than in the first flush of her newly acquired authority: 'Getragen von der Achtung der Troer, lebte ich scheinhaft wie nie' (K 33). Wholly unaware of how unfree and manipulated she is – 'Frei, ach frei . . . in Wirklichkeit: gefesselt' (K 28) – she becomes proud, aloof and remote from ordinary people and turns her back on those relaxed circles where free, ironic criticism of the authorities is the norm: 'Ich verbot es mir selbst, nachdem ich Priesterin war' (K 33). No censorship is necessary where such self-censorship is practised.

Unable to reconcile social commitment with an uncensored perception of reality, Kassandra, along with others, adapts reality to her image of it, rather than vice versa: 'Um die unheimliche

Wirklichkeit hinter der glanzvollen Fassade nicht sehn zu müssen, veränderten wir flugs unsere Fehlurteile' (K 43).[11] Although she immediately realizes that the Greeks' demand for the return of Helena is wholly justified, she wholeheartedly sides with Priamos in his refusal to meet that demand, displaying the most hidebound patriotism of 'my country, right or wrong', and resists with every fibre of her being the realization that Helena is actually not in Troy at all, a crucial fact which she, the seer, is the last to see. But as Troy changes more and more for the worse under the effects first of the threat of war, and then of the war itself, Kassandra is gradually forced to recognize the imperfections behind that self-congratulatory façade. She sees the triumph of propaganda: news becomes truth, what is repeated often enough is believed. She learns that there is cruelty and indifference to individual human welfare in Troy as well as in Greece, reluctantly recognizing that Priamos's intended sacrifice of Paris was morally no more acceptable than Agamemnon's sacrifice of Iphigenie. She discovers a world of intrigue, tension, concealment and dishonesty. But she holds fast to her basic conviction that however much she may disagree with Priamos's bellicose stance towards the Greeks she and he are fundamentally on the same side, and for a long time tries to separate Eumelos, who brings about the militarization of Troy, from the real rulers, to conceal from herself the fact 'daß Priamos und Eumelos ein Paar warn [sic], das einander brauchte' (K 105). Her conception of loyalty obliges her to stand by silently as the war begins. Even after she has lost her faith in the gods – a gradual disenchantment that she likens to recovering from an illness – and when her doubts are approaching panic proportions, Kassandra continues faithfully to play her allotted social role, performing the ceremonies with 'Handreichungen, Gebärden, Worte ohne Sinn' (K 99), and to enjoy public veneration, teaching young priestesses to speak in chorus as with one voice ('das ja nicht einfach ist' (K 112), as she ironically comments). Kassandra justifies this adaptive behaviour to herself by persuading herself that she is inwardly free; she is dismayed to discover that in Aineias's eyes her reservations about public policy, 'der Unterschied, auf den ich mir soviel zugute hielt' (K 99), do not constitute a substantive difference between her and the wholly conformist Herophile. Only when Priamos demands her public support for the plot to ambush Achill

---

11. Kassandra thus falls into that self-deception which Anna Seghers pointed to as the prime danger facing the socialist-realist writer: Anna Seghers, *Über Kunstwerk und Wirklichkeit. Die Tendenz in der reinen Kunst*, Berlin (GDR), 1970, pp. 173–85; esp. p. 178.

does she finally rebel. Only after her consequent imprisonment does her voice become soft and does she lose – 'glücklicherweise' – the 'Ton der Verkündigung' (K 7).

Kassandra's glad renunciation of the role of priestess is not dissidence. It does not lead her either to a withdrawal of loyalty or to any simple conviction that she is right and the others wrong. Earlier, faced with Helenos's pragmatic justification of ideological manipulation in a just cause, Kassandra can find no answer. Later, having failed to convince Eumelos that his repressive measures are harming Troy more than Greece, she agonizes to the point of near-collapse over her fundamental uncertainty: 'War es nicht wichtiger, nach unserer Art, nach unserem Gesetz zu leben, als überhaupt zu leben? Aber wem wollte ich das weismachen? Und stimmte es denn überhaupt? War nicht Überleben wichtiger? . . . So wäre Eumelos der Mann der Stunde?' (K 117). Now, alone in the pain and humiliation of her imprisonment, after the successful assassination of Achill, Kassandra goes over the issues in her mind time and time again, and comes inescapably to the conclusion that, although she has to repudiate what Priamos and Eumelos have done, they were right to do it: 'Sie hatten recht, und mein Teil war, nein zu sagen' (K 148). She finds herself facing the same insoluble dilemma as Christa T: 'Mir steht alles fremd wie eine Mauer entgegen . . . Das alles ändert nichts, unlösbarer Widerspruch, an meiner tiefen Übereinstimmung mit dieser Zeit.'[12]

II

While clinging with the fervour of increasing uncertainty to her priestly office, Kassandra witnesses the decline of Troy to the point where it has taken on all the worst qualities of the enemy, and the Troy of her childhood exists only in her memory. Wolf ended the second of her Frankfurt lectures by saying that the Troy in her mind was 'ein Modell für eine Art von Utopie' (V 83), having explained how she created a consciously idealized image of Troy, projecting onto the fortified (and hence evidently not wholly unwarlike) Troy excavated by Schliemann – which she does not appear to have visited – an image, recognized as the product of wishful-thinking rather than historical research – 'aber ich kann es nicht ändern' (V 63) – of a supposedly peace-loving, happy and relaxed early Minoan civilization. This Utopian conception is at

12. C. Wolf, *Nachdenken über Christa T.*, 4th edn, Darmstadt, 1974, pp. 90f.

odds with Wolf's later formulation of her intention: 'Mein Anliegen bei der Kassandra-Figur: Rückführung aus dem Mythos in die (gedachten) sozialen und historischen Koordinaten' (V 111), and what, of course, she did not discuss in her lectures at all was the use of Troy as a cipher for the GDR. The overlapping of these three conceptions of Troy creates interesting complexities: it is a Utopia, but one that is very vaguely defined; it is corrupted by the effects of war, but it bears within itself from the beginning at least some of the seeds of that corruption.

It is essential to the whole conception of *Kassandra* that this imaginary Troy is superior to Greece, but as regards the nature of this superiority the author is vaguer than one might expect; Kassandra speaks in a phrase very reminiscent of the final sentence of *Der geteilte Himmel* of 'die reiche Fülle unseres Daseins' (K 97), and of 'unsere troische Tradition' (K 97), but without specifying that plenitude and tradition. However, we are given some clues. Kassandra's Troy is not, of course, a proto-socialist society, free of economic exploitation (it is after all a slave society), but it *is* at least not obsessed with class distinctions. One of Kassandra's closest relationships is with the slave-girl Marpessa, and even Eumelos is powerless to enforce strict class segregation, that is, this virtue survives even after Eumelos's militarization has rendered Troy in other respects indistinguishable from Greece. The Trojans also have the virtues of subtlety, sophistication and irony, until Eumelos's military regime reimposes strict conformity to a simplistic ideology. They inhabit a relaxed society where sexual love is benevolently protected, with no need for secrecy and no insistence on marriage. Most importantly, women are respected and have no need to fear sexual harassment from men; the sexual coarseness of the Greeks is the first thing that Kassandra notices about them when she takes Briseis to Greece, and she is dismayed and incredulous that Kalchas should want his daughter to live there. Whereas in Greece women can be married off at the behest of their fathers and brothers, in Troy no free woman has ever been forced to marry against her will, until Priamos demands that Kassandra marry Eurypilos as a price for the latter's military assistance.

Yet even before the threat of war, all is not as perfect as it seems in this Trojan–Minoan Utopia. The Trojans believe in the 'Golden Age' to be ushered in by Priamos and cannot forgive Kassandra's eventual refusal to go on supporting this notion. But among the imperfections which come to light during the novel, and which are not presented as the result of the militarization of Troy, are the rigging of sporting contests (see K 53), the deportation of prisoners, including people who publicize facts embarrassing to the government, sexual humiliation as a punishment for disloyalty, and the existence of a brutalized 'Auswurf' (K 147), the women who guard, feed and humiliate Kassandra during her imprisonment. Well before the ascendancy of Eumelos there has been censorship in Troy and pressure on priests to predict what the rulers wish to be predicted – the pressure that led to the defection of Kalchas, who lacked the strength of character to resist orders to tailor the truth to political requirements. (News of his defection is also censored.) Of all this Kassandra at first knows nothing, and it may even be that Priamos is not fully aware of it either: it is implied that Eumelos's rise to power is only possible because Priamos is out of touch with the true nature of the society which he rules, being prone to live in 'Phantasiewelten' without a clear understanding of the 'Bedingungen . . . die seinen Staat zusammenhielten' (K 16f). Moreover, Trojan culture is at least partly in the hands of people such as the Greek high-priest Panthoos, who has no belief in the religion he serves and no commitment to Trojan values.

The Greek threat has always been present, in a shadowy way, for Troy, just as the GDR has never known a world of genuine peace. But the pernicious influence of the Greeks on Trojan values only begins when that threat is substantially magnified. The two accounts of market-trading between the Greeks and the Trojans illustrate this: the 'Große Markt' (K 60) takes place in an amicable if somewhat tense atmosphere, but the later 'Herbstmarkt' is 'ein Gespenst von einem Markt' (K 118), with Eumelos's spies everywhere disguised as both buyers and sellers, to the dismay and fear of the real traders. Troy comes more and more under Eumelos's control and becomes more and more like Greece, with nobody save Kassandra realizing that they are paving the way to war: 'in aller Unschuld und besten Gewissens bereiteten wir ihn [den Krieg] vor; Sein erstes Zeichen: Wir richteten uns nach dem Feind' (K 74). Troy becomes aggressive, xenophobic and authoritarian; border controls, curfew, stop-and-search procedures and increased powers for the security forces are introduced. All Greeks living in Troy come under automatic suspicion, patriotism poisons intimate personal relationships, notably Troilos's love for Briseis, the daughter of the defector Kalchas (better known to readers of Chaucer and Shakespeare as the fickle Cressida, but here an utterly helpless, pitiable victim of various men). The chivalry that once made it safe for Trojan women to walk out alone disappears, so that they come to fear their own menfolk as much as the enemy.

In war, it has been said, truth is the first casualty. Eumelos, with his 'Sprachregelungen' embraces both the philosophy and vocabulary of Goebbels: 'Was öffentlich geworden ist, ist auch real' (K 97). Any comparison of Troy with Greece becomes treasonable, as does any talk of war or any suggestion that the Trojans are not free. The Trojan rulers deceive the people with talk of peace while preparing for war, and established artists reinforce this manipulation. The Greeks are cast as the enemy before they have committed a single aggressive act against Troy, since national unity requires the channelling of hatred against the 'enemy' of whom an appropriate *Feindbild* has to be constructed; Achill thus becomes, in a sardonic phrase worthy of Brecht, Troy's 'bester Feind' (K 98). Loyalty is then defined as slavish adherence to this image and uncritical support for the government in propagating it. There are precise and valuable insights here for an age in which, on both sides of the Iron Curtain, such images of the enemy are assiduously cultivated, indeed where competing politico-economic systems derive their legitimacy as much from the supposed failings of the opposing system as from their own supposed virtues. In enforcing this conception of patriotism and loyalty, the Trojan rulers become the real enemy of their people; if there is one lesson worth handing down to posterity about how to prevent war, Kassandra reflects, it is this: 'Laßt euch nicht von den Eigenen täuschen' (K 77).

The final degeneration of Troy into the mirror-image of Greece comes in the use of Polyxena to ambush Achill: all ethical values are abandoned in favour of that pragmatic approach to military issues which Wolf discusses at length in the Frankfurt lectures and, as part of a broader scientistic ethos, in *Störfall*. Polyxena is reduced to pure instrument, violating the Kantian ethic, on which Wolf has always insisted, of treating people as ends, never as means.[13] The last trace of the Trojan chivalry that cost Hektor his life in battle with Achill is abandoned, the sanctity of the temple is violated, Paris's heroism in slaying Achill is as spurious and contemptible as that of Agamemnon and Achill, who are driven to ferocity on the battlefield by impotence and sexual ambiguity respectively. Polyxena herself has become more and more like the man-hating Penthesilea, and is avid to use her sexuality as a weapon of destruction: 'Sie ist gierig darauf. Eine wahre Troerin' (K 143), as Paris puts it, in a grim comment on what being a 'true' Trojan has come to mean. Achill is slain, but in all real respects he has defeated the Trojans long before the subterfuge of the Wooden Horse brings

---

13. See C. Wolf, 'Subjektive Authentizität. Gespräch mit Hans Kaufmann', *Weimarer Beiträge*, vol. 20, no. 6, 1974, pp. 90–113; here p. 112.

actual victory: 'Achill das Vieh hielt außer uns und in uns jeden Zoll besetzt' (K 129).

For Achill Kassandra feels undying hatred; she cannot forgive herself for not having killed him with her bare hands (she is not a pacifist, any more than Wolf herself, see V 88). But she feels, to begin with, no generalized hostility towards the Greeks, but rather combines a sense of belonging to a demonstrably superior culture with a cosmopolitan open-mindedness about other cultures. But she too acquires a *Feindbild*, a stereotyped view of the Greeks as naively simple-minded, with a fatal tendency to see the world in black-and-white terms, along with a naive positivism: 'Für die Griechen gibt es nur entweder Wahrheit oder Lüge, richtig oder falsch, Sieg oder Niederlage, Freund oder Feind, Leben oder Tod. Sie denken anders. Was nicht sichtbar, riechbar, hörbar, tastbar ist, ist nicht vorhanden' (K 121). Through the war she acquires a general hatred of the Greeks which is sustained by Achill's horrific actions; by the end she has lost this hatred but she is unsure whether she has transcended her *Feindbild*; her specific hatred for Achill is undiminished and could, if she allowed it to, revive her general hatred.

The portrait of Kassandra exhibits as many Greek as Trojan characteristics, and there is no suggestion that all the Greeks are like Achill. Just as Wolf is well acquainted with West Germany and the United States, so Kassandra knows the Greeks well; she speaks Greek, understands the feelings of Greek women, even though they shrink from her in horror, and feels an almost sisterly kinsmanship with Klytämnestra. She talks at length with Greek prisoners about their homeland, and keeps her open-minded curiosity even during the war, 'da man den Feind schlagen aber nicht kennen sollte' (K 16). She knows that in essence 'sie sind wie wir' (K 16), with the same virtues, vices and limitations as the Trojans. The portrait of Panthoos, Kassandra's high-priest and lover, is Wolf's most detailed, judicious and complex presentation of a sophisticated Greek (i.e. 'Westerner'). Panthoos is cosmopolitan, urbane, undogmatic, shrewd, sophisticated, tolerant and relaxed. He is also enlightened and humane: like Goethe's Iphigenie, he has been instrumental in the abolition of human sacrifice in Troy. But the price of his intellectual freedom is rootlessness: he is committed neither to the land of his birth nor to that of his freely chosen exile. He tells the Trojans what they want to hear, regarding them with generalized contempt as primitive and childish, 'halb Bestien, halb Kinder' (K 76). He is a callow rationalist with no belief in the religion which he serves and, as is most insistently stressed, an arrogant cynic who insists on reducing all human behaviour to calculation and self-interest; he cannot believe in Kassandra's genuine commitment to Troy, which he assumes must be opportunistic (paralleling the not uncommon assumption in the contemporary Western world that any intelligent supporter of a communist state must be a dissimulating opportunist). Beneath his suave sophistication lies crude sexuality, 'das rohe Fleisch unter der Maske' (K 77). Kassandra is fascinated by him, and puzzles over his personality, so much the antipode of her own, to a degree that she herself cannot explain. But despite their long intimacy he remains alien to her; she is never tempted to become like him, though she recognizes in herself some of his worst qualities: arrogance, over-sensitivity, conviction of intellectual superiority. Her contemptuous generalization: 'Alle Männer sind ichbezogene Kinder' (K 11) – provoked by a particularly contemptible man (Agamemnon) and immediately qualified to exclude Aineias, at least – is a momentary descent to Panthoos's level. Wolf treats him harshly: by the end, before he is beaten to death by the women after the killing of Penthesilea, he has become like a polecat, leering, grimacing with fear when threatened, snarling with rage like an animal when impotent.

III

The 'Ringen um Autonomie' that Wolf defines as the essence of Kassandra's 'innere Geschichte' (V 118) is not to be understood undialectically as a shedding of all loyalties. Wolf imagines, in the opening pages of the novel, a more extreme position of disaffection than Kassandra ever subsequently comes to occupy. Thus Kassandra begins her self-appraisal with statements that are not wholly confirmed by what we later see of her actions: that she has wished for Troy's downfall (K 14) and that an inner detachment, a 'negative capability' (Keats), prevented her from the fullest commitment: 'Da von jedem etwas in mir ist, habe ich zu keinem ganz gehört' (K 6). She adds later that her imprisonment has robbed her of her sense of Trojan identity (K 40). But in fact Kassandra's fundamental loyalty to Troy survives both her disenchantment with the behaviour of its rulers and their harsh treatment of her. When the Greeks enter the Trojan citadel she is there, having tried till the very last to avert disaster. Kassandra's loyalty, deep-rooted and indestructible, is not the product of blood-ties but of social experience and insight; she brusquely dismisses the notion of a patriotism based purely on the accident of birth: 'Nicht durch Geburt, ach was, durch die Erzählungen in den Innenhöfen bin ich

Troerin geworden' (K 40). Kassandra could never live in exile, like Panthoos; she never remotely considers defecting to the Greeks, or helping them in any way, indeed her visit to Greece greatly strengthens her (and her companion's) loyalty to Troy and sense of identity as a Trojan: 'Mehr Troerin bin ich, bis auf diesen allerletzten Tag, an keinem Tage meines Lebens je gewesen. Den anderen, ich sah es, ging es ebenso wie mir' (K 96). A similar loyalty to the GDR is evident throughout Wolf's Frankfurt lectures, along with occasional glimpses of similar strains.

Kassandra reaches her tragic conclusion, 'Sie hatten recht, und mein Teil war, nein zu sagen', after the most intense reflection, and it is no mere theoretical insight: Kassandra draws the practical consequences from it when, although she no longer provides public support for the war, she continues to help Troy as best she can. After her total collapse following the deaths of Penthesilea and Panthoos she spends a considerable time with the community presided over by Anchises and Arisbe in the caves of Mount Ida, in an episode in which the possibility of a peaceful, humanly fulfilling apolitical life on the fringe of society is evoked with an intense lyrical sense of conviction. The ethos of the cave community (which is neither socialist nor feminist) is lovingly elaborated. Life within it rescues Kassandra from suicidal despair. Undoubtedly an ideal is adumbrated here which offers at least a glimpse of hope for the future, and heavy weight is given to it towards the end of the novel. But for Kassandra life in the caves cannot wholly replace the sense of belonging to a wider community. She goes back to the Trojan citadel and stoically agrees to the arranged marriage with Eurypilos. (Her later rejection of Agamemnon, where Wolf alters the versions of Homer and Aeschylus, shows that she is not simply a broken woman without the will to reject a man.) She returns again for Paris's funeral and tries to warn the Trojans against letting in the Wooden Horse – in the Homeric version it is Laokoön who does this, as Wolf of course knows (V 86) – and stays in the citadel to share the fate of her fellow Trojans.

The thematic progression from *Kein Ort. Nirgends* to *Kassandra* is from the problems of the outsider to the problems of the insider. In *Kindheitsmuster* one of the narrator's main problems was the problem of saying 'Ich', and in the Frankfurt lectures Wolf seems still concerned with that problem (see V 146). But Kassandra's problem is that of saying 'Wir'. As Ulrich Plenzdorf has put it: 'das Problem des Ich ist das Wir und des Wir das Ich'.[14] For Kassandra

---

14. Ulrich Plenzdorf, interview in *Der Spiegel*, 12 April 1976.

there is no 'Ich' without 'Wir'; as her sense of solidarity falters, so does her sense of individual identity: 'Durchsichtig, schwächlich, immer unansehnlicher wurde mein Wir, an dem ich festhielt, unfühlbarer daher für mich selbst mein Ich' (K 108). By the end she has recovered that 'Wir', not replaced but dialectically complemented by a sense of kinship with the cave community and, the most difficult and problematic 'Wir' of all, with the human race in all its capacity for evil: '"Wir" sag ich, und von allen Wir, zu denen ich gelangte, bleibt dies dasjenige, das mich am meisten anficht. "Achill das Vieh" sagt sich um so vieles leichter als dies Wir' (K 135).

Kassandra's deepest problem is the clash between the 'Wir' in which her loyalty to Troy is grounded, and her commitment to truth, to 'subjective authenticity' in the phrase that Wolf has made her own. She struggles to uphold her conviction that truthfulness cannot ever be harmful: 'was wahr ist, wahr zu nennen, und was unwahr falsch: das mindeste, so dachte ich, und hätte unseren Kampf weit besser unterstützt als jede Lüge oder Halbwahrheit' (K 97). But in another part of her mind she knows that in politics this is not always the case. (Her odd description of Aineias's honesty is perhaps intended to show this: 'Aineias war es, dem ich immer glaubte, weil die Götter es versäumten, ihm die Fähigkeit zu lügen mitzugeben' (K 45).) The tragic essence of that final realization that the Trojan rulers were right is the realization that truth and honesty are *not* the most powerful weapons in the necessary struggle against an evil adversary. Kassandra tries desperately to hold fast to what Max Weber termed 'Gesinnungsethik', an ethic of absolute standards, in a situation which increasingly demands 'Verantwortungsethik', morally responsible action in the face of concrete realities, which may require, indeed almost always does require, that absolute ethical criteria be set aside. Marxism–Leninism deserves no special prominence in the acceptance of this hard fact;[15] Machiavelli spelled it out nearly five hundred years ago,[16] and there is not a government in the world that does not accept it with equanimity as a fact of daily life. The Trojan rulers lead their country first into moral degradation and then into physical destruction, by allowing themselves to take on the ethos of the enemy that is bent on obliterating them. But what else could they do? They might well appeal to the survivors Aineias and Anchises in

15. As Peter Graves is at pains to argue: Peter J. Graves, 'Christa Wolf and the Concept of Morality', in Williams, *GDR: Individual and Society*, pp. 115–23; esp. p. 117.
16. *Il Principe* was first published in 1513.

Brecht's words: 'Ihr, die ihr auftauchen werdet aus der Flut, in der wir untergegangen sind, gedenket unsrer mit Nachsicht.'[17] In holding fast to her memories of Troy as it was before its decline, Kassandra, as she goes to her death, perhaps achieves something of that conciliatory understanding.

---

17. From the poem 'An die Nachgeborenen'.

–16–

Myth in Contemporary Women's Literature

RICARDA SCHMIDT

'Mythos ist ein vielverwendetes und vielmißbrauchtes Wort', Klaus Heinrich wrote at the beginning of *Parmenides und Jona*.[1] Its meaning has become wider and wider, both in everyday use and in critical studies. In this investigation into myth in contemporary women's literature I shall go the opposite way and examine only one of the many possible meanings of myth. I shall not be concerned with myth in Roland Barthes's sense, which comes very close to *falsches Bewußtsein* in capitalism, seen from the point of view of semiology. Nor shall I look at myth as Sigrid Weigel defined it in *Die Stimme der Medusa*, that is, 'als gesellschaftliches Imaginäres'.[2] What I want to analyse is not the myths of everyday life as abstracted structures of thinking and feeling, but the much narrower field of contemporary reworkings of the Western mythic tradition.

The fact that myth has met with such widespread interest in recent years has generally been attributed to the social crisis of postmodern times, a crisis characterized by a loss of belief in progress, rationality, or even revolution, and by a lack of justification for social institutions, a lack of meaning. Myth has an attraction under such historical conditions, since, according to Manfred Frank and Hans Blumenberg, myth has a communicative and normative function; it is about coming to terms with the world, working through something that is disquieting, and making sense of the world.[3]

For women – who for the greatest part of history have been

1. Klaus Heinrich, *Parmenides und Jona. Vier Studien über das Verhältnis von Philosophie und Mythologie*, Basel and Frankfurt/Main, 1982, p. 11.
2. Sigrid Weigel, *Die Stimme der Medusa. Schreibweisen in der Gegenwartsliteratur von Frauen*, Dülmen-Hiddingsel, 1987, p. 269.
3. See Manfred Frank, *Der kommende Gott. Vorlesungen über die Neue Mythologie*, Frankfurt/Main, 1982, p. 11, and Hans Blumenberg, *Arbeit am Mythos*, Frankfurt/Main, 1979, pp. 32f.

excluded from participation in public life and power – myths have the additional attraction that they tell stories of extraordinary women, which may serve as an exploration of women's mythic, historical and potential role in society. In wanting to examine the nature of references to myth in contemporary women's writing, I find there is no substantial corpus of material which concentrates on the same mythic figure. Although there has been a lot of interest in myth both in women's fictional and critical writing since Christa Reinig's pioneering novel *Entmannung* (1976),[4] the absence of a continuous tradition of working through specific mythic themes reflects the status of women's literature as one that has little tradition, or, at least, little consciousness of a tradition. While in literature written by men one encounters a host of variations on, for example, the myth of Prometheus that lend themselves to concise literary analysis, I shall have to look at the mythic material in contemporary women's literature in relation to different mythic themes.

In discussing myth and women's literature of the 1980s I must of course include Christa Wolf's *Kassandra* (1983). But I shall also examine two less-prominent novels, Grete Weil's *Meine Schwester Antigone* (1980) and Christa Reinig's *Die Frau im Brunnen* (1984), as well as touch on Libuše Moníková's *Die Fassade* (1987).[5]

The narrator of Grete Weil's autobiographical novel, *Meine Schwester Antigone*, in working through her own past, juxtaposes the narration of her and other Jews' lack of resistance to Nazi terror by imaginative speculation about the motives and the character of *the* mythic female figure of resistance: Antigone. The rewriting of Antigone's story aims at identifying personal features which enabled Antigone to pursue her act of resistance against the law of an authoritarian ruler. By comparing herself with Antigone, the narrator thus tries to come to an understanding of the absence of resistance in her own life, which still haunts her at the time of writing, the 1970s, which is the third time-level in this novel. In

---

4. Christa Reinig, *Entmannung. Die Geschichte Ottos und seiner vier Weiber erzählt von Christa Reinig*, Düsseldorf, 1976; see also Christa Bürger (ed.), *Zerstörung, Rettung des Mythos durch Licht*, Frankfurt/Main, 1986; Barbara Schaeffer-Hegel and Brigitte Wartmann (eds.), *Mythos Frau. Projektionen und Inszenierungen im Patriarchat*, Berlin, 1984; Renate Schlesier (ed.), *Faszination des Mythos. Studien zu antiken und modernen Interpretationen*, Basel and Frankfurt/Main, 1985; and Dorothee Schuscheng, *Arbeit am Mythos Frau*, Frankfurt/Main, 1987.

5. Christa Wolf, *Kassandra*, Darmstadt, 1983; Grete Weil, *Meine Schwester Antigone*, 3rd edn Frankfurt/Main, 1986; Christa Reinig, *Die Frau im Brunnen*, Munich, 1984; Libuše Moníková: *Die Fassade*, Munich, 1987. Page references in the text are to these editions.

this reflexion upon 'human nature', Antigone is romanticized and idealized. She serves as a screen onto which 'eternal' aspirations of social harmony are projected, as becomes apparent in the fact that the following conceptions of law and order are attributed to her: 'das Recht, das sich Antigone vorstellte, bei dem es um die Belange des Individuums geht; . . . die von ihr erträumte Ordnung, die das Leben zwischen den Menschen hilfreich regelt' (p. 51).

However, oscillating between wishful identification with the mythic model and rejection of one-sided heroism, the narrator – predictably – also discovers negative characteristics in Antigone, such as 'Hang zur Selbstvernichtung', 'Eitelkeit', 'Arroganz der Märtyrer', 'Todessehnsucht' (pp. 10f), an inability to compromise and a tendency to act compulsively against reason and all expectations of effect.

By focusing on the assumed psychic disposition of the mythic character, the historic specificity of subjectivity is discarded. As the narrator cuts away the historic distance between us and Sophocles' Antigone, she is able to recognize a contemporary Antigone in a 'Sympathisantin' of terrorism to whom she briefly gives asylum during the period of anti-terrorist witch-hunts in West Germany in the 1970s. Apart from the acknowledgement which this encounter with contemporary resistance wrings from her – that an Antigone would be hard to bear in real life – the novel's tendency to romanticize the mythic character is also alleviated by one other aspect, namely the introduction of the question of why Antigone did not kill Kreon and assume power. While this question might have led to an interesting investigation into the history of women's relationship to power, to the public sphere of politics, the narrator answers it in a depoliticizing, personalizing, conservative (though 'scandalous') way. An incestuous relationship between Antigone and Polyneikes is imagined as the centre of Antigone's life. His death is thought to leave her without purpose, without aim other than the desire not to become but to be – a sister and nothing else. Thus the limited nature of Antigone's resistance is finally made to tie in with reactionary concepts of women's lives being eternally determined by personal love alone.

The narrator's life-long fantasy of resistance against Nazi terror finds fulfilment in a dream in which Antigone shoots at a Nazi *Hauptsturmführer*. She reverses her famous statement to 'Nicht mitzulieben, mitzuhassen bin ich da' (p. 151). Yet, the narrator runs away from supporting her, thus confirming in the subconscious world of the dream that her choice lies not in heroism but in ordinariness. Finally accepting the ugliness of the ordinary in her waking life means freeing herself from the oppressive weight of the mythic figure which had atrophied into a model of morality. However, in spite of the intersection of time-levels, the 'timeless' normative image of Antigone is paradoxically dismantled by means of an ahistorical psychological humanism.

While Weil's novel in the end achieves a liberation from the myth's claim to moral validity, Christa Wolf's story *Kassandra* aims at showing the continued (or renewed) relevance of myth. Wolf's approach to myth illustrates Hans Blumenberg's insight that the need for myths increases in times of rapid change, because a story has a stabilizing function: 'Die Geschichte sagt, . . . daß es schon immer so oder fast immer so gewesen ist wie gegenwärtig.'[6] In *Voraussetzungen*, Wolf writes about the myth of Kassandra as it was told by Aeschylus:

> Kulturgewinn durch Naturverlust. Fortschritt durch Leid: die Formeln, vierhundert Jahre vor unserer Zeitrechung benannt, die der Kultur des Abendlandes zugrunde liegen.[7]

> Annahme: In Kassandra ist eine der ersten Frauengestalten überliefert, deren Schicksal vorformt, was dann, dreitausend Jahre lang, den Frauen geschehen soll: daß sie zum Objekt gemacht werden.[8]

> In Troia aber, das glaube ich sicher, waren die Leute nicht anders als wir es sind. Ihre Götter sind unsere Götter, die falschen. Nur sind unsere Mittel nicht ihre Mittel gewesen.[9]

In *Kassandra*, Wolf wants to convey insights about contemporary patriarchal society by relating it to its assumed historical origin. Thus Wolf does *not* try to do what Hans Blumenberg has called 'den Mythos zu Ende bringen',[10] that is, aim for a new form of the old myth that could claim to be its last possible form, and would thus show that the myth's validity has come to an end. Wolf, on the contrary, is interested in stripping away layers of historical transformation in order to uncover a historical 'original truth': 'Wer war Kassandra, ehe irgendeiner über sie schrieb?'[11] Whereas in male literature, working on myth can mean working on the tradition of

6. Blumenberg, *Arbeit am Mythos*, p. 41.
7. Christa Wolf, *Voraussetzungen einer Erzählung: Kassandra*, 2nd edn, Darmstadt, 1983, p. 76.
8. Ibid., p. 86.
9. Ibid., p. 95.
10. See Blumenberg, *Arbeit am Mythos*, pp. 295, 305, 312, 319, 684f.
11. Wolf, *Voraussetzungen*, p. 127.

literary transformations of myth, a woman writer, who can draw neither on a tradition of women rewriting myths, nor on a tradition of women as historical agents, will have to develop a different approach, if she is to take account of women's specific position. She will have to reflect on the absence of women in history, to make this absence felt, instead of simply filling the gap with an imaginary, fictionally rounded presence. Wolf does this by interpreting the Cassandra myth as denoting the beginning of women's absence. Her attempt at depicting the historical truth of the myth consists in a materialistic interpretation of the causes of the Trojan war and in a portrayal of the formation of instrumental rationality, of which the reification of women forms an integral part. Alienated utilitarian reasoning – as it has already been described by Horkheimer and Adorno in *Dialektik der Aufklärung* – and women's exclusion from history are thus given a concrete beginning by being set in a particular time and place, imaginatively portrayed as a period of transition. While the scenario is a moving fictional rendering of contemporary problems, however, it seems too neat, too definite, too concretely limited a beginning for something as complex as rationality and woman's status as an object, both of which evolved over thousands of years.[12]

Apart from transforming myth into a fairly rational account of historical reality, Wolf also tries to show psychological and Utopian elements in the mythic tale. In recapturing Kassandra's life in the form of an inner monologue, the story centres on Kassandra's self-analysis of her blind entanglement in Trojan society. Less an account of mythic, that is, phylogenetic, consciousness, this analysis must be read as an exploration of women's psychological participation in patriarchy as it takes place nowadays. The daughter's unconscious desire for her father and her brothers, her need for completion by being part of a harmonious unity, the constitution

---

12. See Thomas Mann's approach in *Joseph und seine Brüder* (Stockholmer Gesamtausgabe der Werke von Thomas Mann, 1952), where he writes about origins 'daß, je tiefer man schürft, je weiter hinab in die Unterwelt des Vergangenen man dringt und tastet, die Anfangsgründe des Menschlichen, seiner Geschichte, seiner Gesittung, sich als gänzlich unerlotbar erweisen und vor unserem Senkblei, zu welcher abenteuerlichen Zeitenlänge wir seine Schnur auch abspulen, immer wieder und weiter ins Bodenlose zurückweichen'. Mann concludes that origins are an arbitrary convention: 'So gibt es Anfänge bedingter Art, welche den Ur-Beginn der besonderen Überlieferung einer bestimmten Gemeinschaft, Volkheit oder Glaubensfamilie praktisch-tatsächlich bilden, so daß die Erinnerung, wenn auch wohl belehrt darüber, daß die Brunnenteufe damit keineswegs ernstlich als ausgepeilt gelten kann, sich bei solchem Ur denn auch national beruhigen und zum persönlich-geschichtlichen Stillstande kommen mag' (pp. 9f).

of her identity within a symbolic order which is the Law of the Father, from which she can cut herself loose only by losing her identity through the experience of madness: all these aspects are convincingly developed as the psychological determinants of her collaboration.

The Utopian element of the story consists of the idealized portrayal of a group of people practising an alternative life-style to patriarchy for a short period, and above all, of Kassandra's finally achieving complete insight into and inner freedom from patriarchy. Through her psychoanalytical monologue, using a classical, almost iambic, diction, Kassandra constitutes a model of female dissident subjectivity. Like Weil's Antigone, Wolf's Kassandra becomes the bearer of the desire for harmony between individual and society: 'Das Glück, ich selbst zu werden und dadurch den andern nützlicher – ich hab es noch erlebt' (p. 15). In Troy, however (as, by implication, in all patriarchal societies), individual and society become mortally antagonistic. Wolf's Kassandra keeps her hard-gained personal integrity by deciding to die rather than compromise. Thus she is given an important element of choice that was absent in Greek myth. By combining the teleological fatalistic pattern of Greek myth and drama with the modern conception of individual freedom, Wolf reproduces the heroic idealism which she had wanted to overcome. Kassandra's self-destructive idealism corresponds to her society's external violence, just as the story's closed form and largely linear narration corresponds to patriarchal forms of aesthetics – something for which the text has often been justly criticized, and first of all by Wolf herself in *Voraussetzungen*. I have suggested elsewhere that Wolf uses this form in a desperate attempt to make her readers see the imminent danger of the nuclear-arms race.[13] By presenting this mythic war and its opponent Kassandra in such a fatalistic way, she paradoxically wants to shock her readers into awareness and to urge them to make sure that the contemporary development towards destruction does *not* reach its logical conclusion, that the mythic pattern is finally broken. The political situation, as perceived by Wolf at the time, was too serious to allow her the freedom to play with myth; it turned Wolf's tendency to humourless German profundity into tragedy.

It is also the experience of pain before the approach of death that motivates Christa Reinig's turn to myth in *Die Frau im Brunnen*.

---

13. See Ricarda Schmidt, 'Über gesellschaftliche Ohnmacht und Utopie in Christa Wolfs *Kassandra*', *Oxford German Studies*, vol. 16, 1985, pp. 109–21, esp. p. 117.

Yet Reinig's pain and fear are not about an imminent world catastrophe; they are the 'simple' agony of the individual's approaching end. In *Die Frau im Brunnen*, a female subject reflects without pathos on her life, without attributing to it a teleological meaning. The novel consists of heterogeneous fragments which do not lose the quality of humour although they are associatively linked by the subject of death. The narrator's frustration over the limited impact of feminism and the personal – yet universally representative – experience of dissociation of meaning ('Der Himmel brach über mir zusammen' p. 114),[14] are counteracted by an imaginative construction of meaning on an entirely different level. The novel tells of the narrator's 'discovery' of a mythic pattern of naming. Discussing the *Iliad*, Celtic and other myths, and the saga of the Bohemian girls' war, the narrator uses highly idiosyncratic means to show that the names of their gods, goddesses and heroes go back to the same linguistic roots. She invents connections between apparently unrelated facts (see p. 28), and claims the existence of *one* language from which all other languages have developed, assuming that dental fricatives were at the origin of language. The narrator cheerfully acknowledges that her procedure is not rational (see pp. 29, 30, 31, 58, 66, 93, 96), yet feels highly satisfied when at the end of her manipulations she has constructed the topography of the holy mountain, that is, a theory according to which numbers lie at the origin of the names of goddesses and gods, numbers which denoted the compass-positions of the sun and moon in an early calendric system.

In fact, the narrator's procedure could be described as having the structure of mythic thinking as Ernst Cassirer has characterized it in *Philosophie der symbolischen Formen*. Cassirer states 'wie untrennbar das mythische Raumgefühl mit dem mythischen Zeitgefühl verbunden ist, und wie beide gemeinsam den Ausgangspunkt der mythischen Auffassung der Zahl bilden'.[15] On the mythic way of forming categories Cassirer writes: 'Was sich nur immer im mythischen Sinne miteinander "berührt" – mag diese Berührung als räumliches oder zeitliches Beieinander oder als irgendeine noch so entfernte Ähnlichkeit oder als Zugehörigkeit zu derselben "Klasse" oder "Gattung" verstanden werden – das hat im Grunde aufgehört, ein Vielartiges und Vielfältiges zu sein: es hat eine

---

14. See also Heinrich, *Parmenides und Jona*, p. 143: 'Denn die Existenz bedrohende Angst in unserer Situation ist . . . die vor einer allgemeinen Sinnlosigkeit.'
15. Ernst Cassirer, *Philosophie der symbolischen Formen. Das mythische Denken*, Berlin, 1925, p. 184; see also p. 125.

substantielle Einheit des Wesens gewonnen.'[16] Reinig's long-standing interest in astrology, which Cassirer classes as a form of 'mythisch-substantiellen Identitätsdenkens',[17] has perhaps attuned her to this form of thinking, which she can pursue with the same ease as she draws on the Kantian critique of reason.

The assumption that all myths are of astral origin is not in itself new.[18] Reinig's originality lies in the creative procedure of her 'discovery' of mythic naming, which denies the reader the possibility of identifying with and imitating mythic figures. Its value lies in the satisfaction of the discovery itself, in making sense of disparate fragments, in reconstructing something that seemed to be lost and scattered for ever. Despite the narrator's search for the origin of mythic names, it is the structure of the mythic pattern rather than its content that is of chief importance in the narrative connection between contemporary life and myth. This connection is of such a mediated and abstract character and touches upon so many esoteric subjects that Reinig's novel has remained outside the mainstream of feminist discussion.

Moreover, the fact that Reinig does *not* use myth to initiate a debate on normative values, that she does *not* deduce some kind of moral from her treatment of myth, *nor* project myth as a Utopian aim, documents Reinig's decentring of meaning. In her novel, life remains without the reconciliation that the recognition of positive directions provides. Yet it shows an individual's creative way of coping with such a life.

Libuše Moníková's much acclaimed novel *Die Fassade* differs in many ways from the three texts discussed so far. The style is burlesque, and myth serves as only one literary allusion among many others discernible in this novel. The main characters are male and neither they nor the neutral narrator are concerned with feminist questions. Thus the mythic allusions involve male heroic patterns: Sisyphus and Ulysses – quadrupled. Accordingly, it is only a minor adventure when one of the four Ulysseses encounters a Circe in the Taiga who turns men into reindeer. This Siberian Circe proves to be ideologically a very sound version of the old threat to men. The objects of her magic are those who do not respect the independence of the Amazonian women and, above all, Russian politicians. The didacticism which dominates large parts of the novel here appears in the guise of fantastic retribution.

In conclusion, we can claim that women's turning to myth

16. Ibid., pp. 81f.
17. Ibid., p. 85.
18. See ibid., p. 25.

which began in the mid-1970s with Christa Reinig's brilliantly provocative 'emasculation' of the patriarchal tradition and presence, culminated in Christa Wolf's *Kassandra*, the most ambitious and most widely discussed text. Its closed form, the concentration on a main character with whom author and readers identify, the attempt to provide a coherent account of contemporary problems by tracing their roots back 3,000 years, and the portrayal of a model of female dissidence, are the features which contributed to making this text easily accessible, since they follow established modes of thinking which favour linearity, identity and teleology, despite the author's express criticism of these very features. *Kassandra* also coincided with feminist thinking at the time, namely the interest in women's history, in women's everyday life, in women's special position on the edges of phallogocentrism which might enable them to become the agent of historical change. The latter assumption, however, which has inspired much of the theoretical writing by women, has not yet, as far as I can see, found a convincing literary treatment.

Women's interest in discussing moral norms via myth has also led to Weil's novel *Meine Schwester Antigone* being interpreted as a contribution to feminist writing.[19] In so far as Weil's novel dismantles a heroic model and opens up intersecting time-levels, it is in tune with modern thinking. Yet its ahistorical humanism and its reactionary concept of femininity make it a book feminists should be wary of claiming as avant-garde.

Reinig's *Die Frau im Brunnen* indicates, I think, an important change of mood. The time for depicting woman as heroically opposed to patriarchy (as Wolf had attempted it) is definitely over. The fact is that the women's movement has effected less concrete change than it had set out to do. Thus, in Reinig's *Die Frau im Brunnen* myth can no longer serve as a moral guideline for the present. But the novel shows how the creative act of making out a mythic pattern gives an individual the strength to bear a life which lacks the consolation of a meaningful pattern, and to continue exposing patriarchal behaviour and structures in her writing without any hope of fundamental changes in the near future.

Finally, Moníková's *Die Fassade* illustrates the phenomenon of postfeminism in the second half of the 1980s. Postfeminism, in reacting to shortcomings and apparent dead-ends in feminist thinking, takes some feminist insights and positions for granted and sets out to define the 'really' important issues in other areas.

---

19. See Weigel, *Stimme der Medusa*, pp. 299–303.

Thus, Moníková's novel unfolds an almost exclusively male world, while attempting to deal with national and international problems of fundamental historical importance and to draw on the great tradition of male literature. Yet, in a minor figure like Lena, the Siberian Circe of Amazonian tendency, a feminist theme is incorporated as a matter of course into the political strand of the novel, which is not concerned with feminist thinking at all. The feminist allusion gets absorbed into the purpose of a critique of Russian politics and becomes a harmless joke.

It thus seems as if women's use of myth has come full circle in just one decade: from unmasking patriarchal traditions, through the attempt to develop new role-models or to reject models, to the use of female mythic figures to serve 'larger' political purposes. Many aspects of women's working with myth have proved unsatisfactory. It is perhaps the outsider, Christa Reinig, dealing with mythic patterns rather than content, whose work indicates the direction that promises to yield the most interesting results in the future.

–17–

'Das Kapitel Mann ist beendet': 'Female Texts' by Male Authors as Critiques of Patriarchy? Stefan Schütz and Botho Strauß

MORAY McGOWAN

'Aufklärung hat keine Zukunft mehr, Weiblichkeit ist die Zukunft.'[1] Common to all the various forms of contemporary feminism is the rejection of patriarchy, which has been shown to extend far beyond the family structures and economic and political hierarchies in which it was originally identified: Dale Spender, in *Man Made Language* (1980), sees it embedded in the structures of language (the central theme of Verena Stefan's *Häutungen*, 1975); Genevieve Lloyd in *The Man of Reason* (1984), like Luce Irigaray in *Spéculum de l'autre femme* (1974), traces 'the equation of maleness with superiority' back to the Pythagoreans and shows how philosophers have 'formulated their ideals of rationality with male paradigms in mind'.[2] Many feminists concentrate their critique on the paradox of the Enlightenment: the fact that Kant implicitly and later Hegel explicitly excluded women from their model of a self-determining humanity.[3]

Thus the rejection of patriarchy links to a rejection or at least radical revision of the thought patterns and view of history handed down by and internalized as a result of the Enlightenment tradition. Feminists were suspicious of a humanism which, based on this tradition, excluded women precisely when it appeared to include them in a gender-neutral concept of humanity, and so they responded the more readily to the deconstruction of the Enlightenment

---

I am grateful to Rachel McNicholl for her critique of an earlier version of this text.
1. Friederike Hassauer and Peter Roos, 'Aufklärung: Futurologie oder Konkurs?', in Jörn Rüsen, Eberhard Lämmert and Peter Glotz (eds.), *Die Zukunft der Aufklärung*, Frankfurt/Main, 1988, pp. 40–7; here p. 40.
2. Genevieve Lloyd, *The Man of Reason*, London, 1984, p. 103.
3. See ibid., pp. 64–73, 80–5.

edifice proposed and practised by French thinkers like Jacques Derrida, Jacques Lacan or Jean Baudrillard, or by Michel Foucault, for example, who aimed to identify, and so destabilize, the construction 'man' which lies at the centre of post-Renaissance thought.[4] Feminist science fiction too, Marge Piercy's *Woman on the Edge of Time* (1979), for example, is often premised on a world-view which, as Sarah LeFanu, a leading practitioner, puts it, 'doesn't simplistically and arrogantly put humanity at the centre of the universe'.[5]

The revolt against the patriarchal Enlightenment has formal as well as thematic implications for literature: loss of faith in history produces scepticism towards linear plot and character development, both of which presuppose history as purposeful progression, and discrete individual identity as achievable and desirable. Contemporary feminism has played a crucial part in the development of an alternative aesthetic, believing, as Xavière Gauthier puts it, that if women write as men do, 'they will enter history subdued and alienated; it is a history that, logically speaking, their speech should disrupt'.[6] It is not enough for texts to assert a rejection of patriarchy; they must practise it in their form. Otherwise, like Marockh Lautenschlag's pseudo-feminist Utopian novels, *Araquin* (1981) and *Sweet America* (1983), they simply repeat patriarchal structures by inverting them.[7]

In contrast, Hélène Cixous, for example, drawing especially on Derrida and Lacan, has sought to develop a feminist aesthetic which will subvert the hierarchical oppositions which patriarchy has embedded in language and cultural values: active/passive; culture/nature; day/night; father/mother; reason/emotion; intelligence/sensitivity, etc., all of which are versions of an underlying binary male/female paradigm where male is present or at least dominant and female is excluded or at best subordinate, a paradigm summed up as phallogocentrism. Cixous – and in this she resembles Luce Irigaray – aims instead to assert multiple, hetero-

---

4. For example, Michel Foucault, *Les mots et les choses*, Paris, 1966.
5. Quoted in the *Guardian*, 22 March 1988, p. 20; see also Hilary Rose, 'Laboratory for Dreams', *New Statesman*, 6 November 1987, pp. 22f. 'Eco-feminists' see the blind anthropocentricity which has led to the destruction of other species and the despoliation of the biosphere as a direct consequence of 'patriarchal science': see for example Andrée Collard and Joyce Construcci, *Rape of the Wild*, London, 1988.
6. Quoted in Susan Bassnett, *Feminist Experiences. The Woman's Movement in Four Cultures*, London, 1986, p. 79.
7. See Sigrid Weigel, *Die Stimme der Medusa. Schreibweisen in der Gegenwartsliteratur von Frauen*, Dülmen-Hiddingsel, 1987, pp. 311f.

geneous *différance* in her texts.[8] In the following I shall refer frequently to Cixous, since the relationship of her writing to certain texts by *men* is especially interesting. I do not, however, suggest that her position in feminist aesthetics is uncontroversial, a point to which I shall return.

These various threads of the feminist reinterpretation of the crisis of the European Enlightenment as a crisis of phallogocentrism seem at first sight to come together in the opening quotation, a pronouncement by Friederike Hassauer and Peter Roos in December 1987, at a conference in Frankfurt on that characteristic theme of the 1980s, 'Zukunft der Aufklärung'. Attacking the interwoven vices of Enlightenment, Europe, technology, logocentrism and patriarchy, they argue, like Christa Wolf in *Kassandra* (1983), that the present crisis of reason is a crisis of male reason: 'Aufklärung hat keine Zukunft mehr; Weiblichkeit ist die Zukunft.'

However, such sweeping rejections are not restricted to feminist critics. Heiner Müller, for example, emphatically declared in 1982: 'Das europäische Geschichtsprinzip ist erledigt . . . Europäische Politik oder Geschichte fußt auf dem Vaterprinzip, dem paternalen Prinzip. Ich sehe in Asien das Aufgehen des mütterlichen Prinzips.'[9] This is clearly not the Asia of Taiwanese toy factories, where the exploitation process of nineteenth-century European capitalism is copied and outdone; it is not the real Third World where *The Persistence of Patriarchy*, as Peter Knauss called his recent study of modern Algeria (1987), robs women of the benefits of the revolution they helped to bring about; but rather, like 'Amerika' in much of the German literature of the 1920s, it is an idealization, in this case of something 'other' than the European civilization based on technocratic rationalism against which Müller is in revolt. Similar idealizations of the Third World are evident in the work of other First-World writers like Germaine Greer (e.g. *Sex and Destiny*, 1984), in the contemporary revival of ethnography, in the fascination with *Ursprungsmythen*: new versions of the Noble Savage as an escape from the real contradictions of technological society. In this idealization, both male and female writers link *Weiblichkeit* with a number of irrational qualities. In 1984 Gernot and Hartmut Böhme ended an essay entitled 'Currente Vernunft. Zum Projekt einer anderen Aufklärung' with a statement that appears to echo the critical reason of Horkheimer and Adorno's *Dialektik der Aufklärung*

---

8. See for example Hélène Cixous and Catherine Clément, *La Jeune Née*, Paris, 1975, pp. 115–18; see also for example, Luce Irigaray: *Spéculum de l'autre femme*, Paris, 1974; *Ce sexe qui n'en est pas un*, Paris, 1977.
9. *Gesammelte Irrtümer*, Frankfurt/Main, 1986, pp. 72f.

but actually negates it: 'Das Dunkle der Aufklärung liegt mitten in ihrem Licht. Und ins Dunkle gerückt ist alles, was den Fluß des Lebens trägt: das Weibliche wie das Kindliche, die Phantasie wie der Leib, die Gefühle und die Triebe, und vor allem die Natur.'[10]

This problematic contrast of the female and Nature to male reason or civilization is anticipated in Max Frisch's *Homo Faber* (1957), where Faber the male technocrat confronts the female, represented by Hanna and Sabine, and other forces often seen as the enemies of Enlightenment rationalism: illness, fate and, in Faber's struggle to repair an abandoned car, the jungle. The jungle, like the labyrinthine Gothic castle, is a frequent image both of the unconscious and of the female: woman as the dark continent. In criticizing Faber's misogynist fears, Frisch draws on stereotype equations of the female with fecund Nature. The jungle's lush wastefulness, celebrated by Georges Bataille as a subversive alternative to technocratic efficiency,[11] is hated by Faber for the same reason: 'Was mir auf die Nerven ging: diese Fortpflanzerei überall, es stinkt nach Fruchtbarkeit.' 'Schlamm . . . Verwesung voller Keime, glitschig wie Vaseline, Tümpel im Morgenrot wie Tümpel von schmutzigem Blut, Monatsblut'.[12] Eventually Faber, anticipating Heiner Müller, rejects the repressed, life-denying, technocratic, male-dominated First World typified by the United States, for the spontaneous, sensual, female Third World of a romanticized Cuba.

Curiously, perhaps, Frisch's stereotypes have many points of contact with Cixous's images of female textuality. Toril Moi in *Sexual/Textual Politics* describes Cixous's own writing in telling metaphors: 'a continuum that encourages non-linear forms of reading', 'a dense web . . . that offers no obvious edge to seize hold of', in short: 'a textual jungle'.[13] Cixous's own elaborations on the female text are strongly coloured by biologism and metaphysics: woman 'has never ceased to hear the resonance of forelanguage. She lets the other language speak – the language of 1000 tongues which knows neither enclosure nor death.' Cixous celebrates

---

10. *Ästhetik und Kommunikation*, vol. 15, no. 57–58, 1984, pp. 225–32; here p. 232.
11. For example, 'L'Économie à la mesure de l'univers' and 'La Part maudite', in Georges Bataille, *Oeuvres complètes*, vol. 7, Paris, 1976, pp. 9–179.
12. Reinbek, 1969, pp. 37f and 50f; see pp. 78f. Mary Daly notes Jean-Paul Sartre's equation, in *Being and Nothingness*, of slime and femaleness: Daly, *Gyn/Ecology*, London, 1979, p. 332.
13. Toril Moi, *Sexual/Textual Politics*, London, 1985, p. 102; my understanding of Cixous is indebted to Moi's outstanding book and uses Moi's English translations of Cixous. See also Karen Richter-Schröder, *Frauenliteratur und weibliche Identität*, Meisenheim, 1986, pp. 78–85.

primeval motherhood: 'in each women sings the first nameless love . . . Voice: inexhaustible milk . . . the lost mother.'[14]

This is the lost pre-Oedipal paradise evoked at the beginning of Günter Grass's *Der Butt* (1977), the best-known recent German novel by a man explicitly to explore alternatives to patriarchy. It mocks but also idealizes a prehistoric matriarchy rooted in male cravings for the 'totale Weiberfürsorge' of suckling infancy. Initially, the female in *Der Butt* is conservative, static, pre- and antirational: 'die geschichtsunlustige Weiberherrschaft';[15] the matriarch Aua's ban on representations of numbers above three implies that both the imagination and explorative, progressive reason are male qualities.[16] By the end of the novel, however, the Flounder, in accordance with his role as Mephisto, or perhaps Hanswurst, of the historical process, has abandoned the arrogant, sceptical misogyny necessary to jar mankind out of the blissful stasis of prehistoric matriarchy; history, as constructed by the Flounder and by men, is now leading to catastrophe; so, in the 1970s, the Flounder, says the narrator, is 'nicht mehr Butt' but rather 'ihr Butt'; he has allied himself to a female future. The novel's concluding paragraph identifies women as the new locus of dynamic historical change; 'Ilsebill kam. Sie übersah, überging mich. Schon war sie an mir vorbei. Ich lief ihr nach.'[17]

For Grass, locating hope for the future in the female does not however mean facile optimism: this is abundantly clear from *Die Rättin* (1986). But it is interesting that while the women's movement seems to have moved beyond the passionate separatist feminism of Mary Daly's *Gyn/Ecology* (1979) towards more tentative positions, Stefan Schütz seems to have little doubt. His novel *Medusa* (1986) provides the emphatic declaration which gives this paper its title – 'Das Kapitel Mann ist beendet' – and celebrates a supposedly female alternative.[18] It is perhaps not surprising that *Medusa*, largely written and, of course, published in the West, is not an affirmation of the GDR's undoubted progress towards the establishment of a real material basis for female emancipation; in fact it is quite the opposite.

It is not only women's writing with a GDR reference – such as

14. *La Jeune Née* (1975), quoted in Moi, *Sexual/Textual Politics*, pp. 113f.
15. *Der Butt*, Darmstadt, 1977, pp. 27, 35.
16. Prehistoric matriarchy's stress on cyclical rather than linear concepts of history is emphasized by Heide Göttner-Abendroth, *Matriarchale Mythologie*, Munich, 1980.
17. *Der Butt*, p. 556.
18. Reinbek, 1986, p. 705. Page references in the text are to this edition.

Irmtraud Morgner's *Leben und Abenteuer der Trobadora Beatriz* (1974) – that questions the extent to which socialism has overcome patriarchy. In Thomas Brasch's significantly entitled *Vor den Vätern sterben die Söhne* (1981), the GDR is experienced as a re-established, entrenched patriarchal system against which the sons struggle fruitlessly. Schütz's *Medusa* itself explicitly rejects the argument that 'die Geschichte von Mann und Frau unterliegt einzig und allein der Klassengeschichte' and that sexual oppression has therefore been eliminated by social revolution (p. 19). It thus seems to wish to contradict the argument of socialist feminists that patriarchy cannot be separated from its economic basis in capitalism.[19]

Schütz's reworking of themes from Peter Weiss's *Die Ästhetik des Widerstands* (1975–81) is especially significant. Weiss quotes a letter of Rimbaud's to the effect that hopes for historical progress lie in an end being put to the 'ewige Dienerschaft der Frauen'.[20] *Medusa* echoes the raft metaphor of Weiss's novel, and gives central prominence to the idea of the female as a crucial element of resistance and struggle (e.g. p. 53). However, *Medusa* rejects Weiss's view of the role of the subject in the historical process, and of reason as the path to a better socialist future. For Schütz, reason as a social process is one of destructive dominance, part of the social straitjacketing that robs the individual of authentic experience. 'Unser schönes Segelschiff ist zum Floß verkommen,' one figure declares (p, 87); but this raft, an image of socialism as a philosophy of hope, is rejected by Marie Flaam, Schütz's central figure, as a false, other-determined goal. She asserts her subjectivity against the faceless dictates of socialist reason, against blind obedience to historical necessity (p. 24) and the specious logic that dogmatic socialism shares with certain religions, namely that subordination is freedom (p. 27), which together produce yet another form of other-determination (p. 75). Instead she asks awkward questions and rejects opportunistic pretence.

As Marie Flaam points out in a passage which could be said neatly to summarize the argument of Genevieve Lloyd's *Man of Reason*, Marxism itself is built on the male paradigms of Western philosophy: 'Unsereins [i.e. women] ist noch nicht so lange bei Bewußtsein, wie es die Herren Männer sind, denen Platon der edle

19. For example, Zillar Eisenstein, *Capitalist Patriarchy and the Case for Socialist Feminism*, New York, 1979; Frigga Haug and Kornelia Hauser, 'Geschlechterverhältnisse', in *Argument – Sonderband 110: Geschlechterverhältnisse und Frauenpolitik*, Berlin, 1984, pp. 9–102; esp. pp. 58–64.
20. See Sibylle Cramer, 'Zum *Medusa*-Projekt von Stefan Schütz', *Merkur*, vol. 40, no. 7, 1986, pp. 598–602; here p. 601.

Prolet, und Hegel der Rekuperator als Eier im Säckchen unterm Marxschen Stössel hängen' (p. 110). However, Schütz, like Herbert Marcuse,[21] sees women's exclusion as their subversive potential: precisely through being excluded, women are not wholly enslaved to the patriarchal process. This view is comparable to that of James Tiptree Jr, a pseudonymous woman science-fiction writer, who declares in *The Women Men Don't See*: 'We live by twos and threes in the chinks of your world machine',[22] an image that evokes the early Christians waiting for Rome to crumble, or even tiny mammals huddling under ferns waiting for the evolutionary process to topple the dinosaurs.

Medusa's form, arguably, makes it a 'female' text in Cixous's sense. It is vast and diffuse, its 870 pages divided into just three sections with no other internal chapter or paragraph divisions, multiple narrative voices and frequent changes of perspective from first to third person, to *erlebte Rede* and to dialogue, often in mid-sentence. There is no obvious narrative logic or chronology, but rather instead a flowing, often unpunctuated, association of ideas, a sea of consciousness rather than a stream, which implies purposeful direction: streams are phallic, seas are womblike. As Cixous wrote in 1975: 'We are ourselves sea, sand, coral, sea-weed, beaches, tides, swimmers, children, waves ... Heterogeneous, yes.' This quotation, interestingly, is from a text called 'Le rire de la Méduse'.[23]

However, the form of Schütz's *Medusa* is its first problem. The novel presents the GDR as a rigid system of oppressive structures in which the individual is trapped, structures that are complete, closed; against this the open, diffuse form of *Medusa* is an act of resistance. However, the social specificity of the numerous short and very telling satires of the contradictions of GDR socialism is lost in the physical vastness of the text; these episodes are like a scatter of stinging jellyfish in a vast lukewarm sea. The metaphor is chosen because of a particular image in the novel. Accompanied by her alter ego, Gorga Sappho – a combination of mythical references to matriarchal prehistory and to women who have turned their exclusion and otherness into a weapon of resistance – Marie Flaam passes through a giant anus to experience the world beyond. They land in the 'Palast der Republik' in Berlin (GDR); the first stop is a

21. See Herbert Marcuse, 'Marxism and Feminism', *Women's Studies*, vol. 2, no. 3, 1974, pp. 279–88; Jürgen Habermas and Silvia Bovenschen *et al.* (eds.), *Gespräche mit Herbert Marcuse*, Frankfurt/Main, 1978, pp. 65–90.
22. Quoted in the *Guardian*, 22 March 1988, p. 20.
23. Quoted in the translation in Moi, *Sexual/Textual Politics*, p. 117.

bathroom where new arrivals to socialism wash off the 'antagonistische Widersprüche'. Immediately prior to this, the sophistry with which opportunists justify the furtherance of their own interests as 'Einsicht in die Notwendigkeit' is damned by Marie Flaam as an 'Aufenthalt im lauwarmen Wasser' (pp. 130f). This is exactly the problem with the debilitating diffuseness of Schütz's novel. Despite its author's deconstructive goal – 'ich möchte . . . die Hirnschalen aufreißen, um die Denkschablonen daraus zu entfernen' – it neutralizes its own critical insights and aggressive satires.[24]

The second problem lies in the Utopia offered by Schütz. In *Dialektik der Aufklärung*, Horkheimer and Adorno interpret the sexuality of the sirens as a direct threat to Odysseus' domination over Nature and to his return to the stability of the institutional structure from which he set out.[25] In GDR literature, from Heiner Müller's *Philoktet* (1955) onwards, the Odysseus figure has frequently stood for the pragmatic functionary who uses dialectical reasoning to divert or disarm those forces which hinder the rationalization of life and the repression of the free, libidinous subject. Odysseus, notes Helen Fehervary, is 'der Patriarch der Aufklärung, der alle diejenigen Gebiete annektiert, die seiner logozentrischen Reise in die Zukunft, sprich Revolution, im Wege stehen'.[26] In opposition to this, contemporary GDR literature uses sexuality as a metaphor which, insofar as it is functionalized for the state's purposes, signals the continuation of supposedly resolved contradictions, but which is also a potential for revolt. Thus in Schütz's play *Sappa* (1980), women abort their foetuses both as a consequence of and in revolt against the subordination of the humane to the technocratic interests of the state.[27]

In *Medusa* Maria Flaam represents 'das Unbedingte, das im Widerspruch zu jeder Dialektik steht' (p. 147) and declares: 'Dialektik ist die Erfindung des Mannes gegen die Bewegung der

---

24. Quoted in Georg Wieghaus, 'Stefan Schütz', in H. L. Arnold (ed.), *Kritisches Lexikon zur deutschsprachigen Gegenwartsliteratur*, Munich, 1978– . Sibylle Cramer's argument ('Zum *Medusa*-Projekt von Stefan Schütz') that the vastness of Schütz's text is an inherently subversive block to the remorseless course of history, producing a limbo where alternatives, the formability of history, become visible, is not, in my view, borne out by the exhausting nature of the reading experience.
25. Frankfurt/Main, 1971, pp. 29ff.
26. Helen Fehervary, 'Autorschaft, Geschlechtsbewußtsein und Öffentlichkeit. Versuch über Heiner Müllers *Die Hamletmaschine* und Christa Wolfs *Kein Ort. Nirgends*', in Irmela von der Lühe (ed.), *Entwürfe von Frauen in der Literatur des 20. Jahrhunderts*, Berlin, 1982, pp. 132–53; here p. 133.
27. Ibid., pp. 133f.

Frau' (p. 19). The philosopher Heisering displays all the dialectic refinement of the Odysseus of *Dialektik der Aufklärung* in reintegrating the subversive libido: his goal is 'die Spontaneität auf höherem Bewußtsein wieder in Anwendung zu bringen, keine zufällige mehr, sondern eine zahnradineinanderfindende, die wohin und warum bedienende Spontaneität, von einzelnen gespeist für die Gesellschaft und umgedreht' (p. 201). The first section of the text, 'Kathedrale des Ichs', is followed by one entitled 'Anabasis', a title Peter Weiss had planned for the last section of *Die Ästhetik des Widerstands*. In Schütz's 'Anabasis', the inheritance of the Enlightenment is a vast terror-machine of *Gulags*: Enlightenment reason leads, via its decay into instrumental reason, to totalitarianism. The third section, entitled in English 'Free play of love', is a celebration of free, libidinous sensuality in the spirit of Herbert Marcuse's *Eros and Civilization*.

'Free play of love' presents a great variety of discourses, perspectives, narrative and stylistic levels, beating back and forth across its theme like waves, qualifying, subverting, contradicting, enriching itself. As such it is a celebration of *différance*. However, it also relies on stereotypes: for example, a long interpolated narrative by Naphtan, Marie Flaam's husband, beneath the satire of castration anxiety, displays an aggressive reassertion of phallic sexuality:

Ach was, die Weiber haben an ihren Votzen Reißverschlüsse angebracht, und immer, wenn wir grad das bißchen Fleisch in die richtige Richtung orientiert haben, ziehn sie ihn hoch, und wieder ist ein Fetzen Fleisch dazwischen. Blutverhangene Penisse, wie lügenfette Leitartikel, die zu eitern beginnen, aus Mangel an Wirklichkeit. Handlungsarme Neurotiker, verweichlichte Brut, schimpft Pan die Kerle, mit flötentöniger Stimme . . . wie kann es wahr sein, daß Männer vor Weibern ausreißen, ob sie nicht mehr wissen, daß sie seine Flöte zwischen den Schenkeln tragen . . . sehen möchte er, bevor er nicht daran glaubt, daß sie einer schicksalhaften Evolution zum Opfer gefallen sind, das Ding seiner Erschaffung. (p. 781)

Moreover, because of this unambiguously identified male narrative, we must assume that those narratives identified as female are meant by Schütz to be understood as a genuinely female perspective, not as a satire on male projections. However, many of these female narratives too, though scornful of men's imprisonment in phallic sexuality, emphasize a female sexuality that defines itself in relation to men; most notably in grotesquely comic eulogies of the penis reminiscent of John Cleland's *Fanny Hill*.

> Oh herrliches Glied, du gerngesehener Gast meiner besucherfreundlichen Klause, sich wärmender Fremder an meinem Feuer, das nie erlöschen soll, du fügsamer Penis, wie gern umkränz ich dich mit meinem lorbeergeschmückten Schoß und tränke deine Fügsamkeit mit lodernder Feuchtigkeit aus meinem Kelch, und laß mich speisen aus deinen Hoden, himmeljauchzender Geschmack, nein, auf den ich vermag zu hoffen, der mir gerngesehen ist, will ich nicht abweisen, er soll mir, solang ich lebe, Stammgast sein. Introduktion und Hauptmahlzeit, und wenns ein sensibles Kerlchen ist, die Nachspeis auch. (p. 642)

In this male projection, the surface perspective of an active, assertive woman is contradicted by the actual sexual activity, which is structured highly traditionally: a waiting, wishing woman and an active, defining man: 'seine Hände begannen, nach den Zentren unter meiner Haut zu suchen und ließen mich erschaudern vor Geilheit, die Hügel zu ersteigen formte er das sanfte Fleisch mir, wie zwei Tongefäße, um die herum seine Finger sich drehten, als gäbe er ihnen die eigentliche Form ihrer Bestimmung zurück . . .' etc. (p. 646).

Inevitably, perhaps, given its sheer size, *Medusa* is complex and self-varying, so that it is possible to find counter-examples, as well as extensive debates on the relative merits for women and for society as a whole of co-operation between the sexes, Lysistratan bargaining, a role-reversal in which men would become merely the objects of women's sexual pleasure, or complete separation. But arguably Schütz's would-be celebration of the 'free play of love' – which is in reality no more free than the free market economy[28] – remains, for reasons we shall return to at the end of this paper, imprisoned in stereotypes.

The role of *Weiblichkeit* in the texts of Botho Strauß is equally problematic. His work shares with feminist theory the influence of French critics of humanism like Foucault, and seeks to destabilize the Enlightenment view of history as linear progress, its reductive taxonomies and its faith in the cohesive individual subject. Strauß's texts subvert Cartesian–Newtonian logic, which, as patriarchal logic, is also widely rejected by contemporary feminism, and they explore non-linear, non-hierarchic, open-edged relations between phenomena, events or persons, such as the symbiotic relationships of the story 'Marlenes Schwester' (1975). As a figure in *Der junge Mann* (1984) says: 'Jede Geschichte ist ein frevelhafter Eingriff in die schöpferische Unordnung der Lebensfülle.'[29] In *Rumor* (1980),

---

28. See Wieghaus, 'Stefan Schütz'.
29. Munich, 1984, p. 349. Page references in the text are to this edition.

Bekker experiences the 'Rede des Ganzen', the normally suppressed, disorderly discourse of life below the ordered surface, which, like the jungle in *Homo Faber*, is unmediated and unsanitized in contrast to the alienated functionality of the 'Institut Zachler'.[30] The 'Rede des Ganzen' has affinities with Cixous's pre-Oedipal 'Voice', though Strauß's critical irony still distances *Rumor* from the liturgical, celebrative tones of Cixous, and in Strauß's work up to *Rumor* one can perceive a clear Enlightenment intention: in the spirit of *Dialektik der Aufklärung*, Strauß seeks to topple the fossilized rhetoric of Enlightenment, which has become an oppressive force, and so to promote once again a genuine Enlightenment. But in a much quoted passage in *Paare Passanten* (1981) he signalled an abandonment of 'Dialektik', largely confirmed by the strong emergence of transcendental and visionary elements in his later writing.[31]

In her more radical statements like 'La sexe ou la tête' (1976), Hélène Cixous attacks 'the pervasive masculine urge to judge, diagnose, digest, name'. Theoretical analysis, she claims, is inherently repressive: 'As soon as the question "What is it?" is posed . . . as soon as a reply is sought, we are already caught up in masculine interrogation', that is, the impulse to imprison reality in rigid hierarchical structures.[32] Some of the philosophical reflections in *Paare Passanten* seem to move towards Cixous's position: 'Nicht das Aha! des Festgestellten und Durchschauten möge dem Menschen und Zuschauer entschlüpfen, sondern nur ein Ha! – staunend ein winzig Wesentliches erwischt zu haben' (pp. 185f). And in *Niemand anderes* (1987), Strauß rejects the 'Gescheitheitsvertrag der Informationsgesellschaft' in favour of 'der gedankenlose Untergrund einer großen Empfindungskraft';[33] an appeal comparable to that of Gernot and Hartmut Böhme cited above.

The formal consequences become apparent in *Der junge Mann* (1984), a novel where, as Henriette Herwig says, the reader must free him- or herself 'von der Erwartung des lineären Erzählens und des hierarchischen Begriffssystems . . . doch öffnen wird er sich nur dem, der sich zunächst in ihn verliert'.[34] This image of the text as labyrinth (which would also apply to Paul Wühr's *Das falsche Buch*, 1983), the text as a deconstructive game, has affinities to

---

30. Munich, 1980, p. 147.
31. Munich, 1981, p. 115. Page references in the text are to this edition.
32. Quoted from the English version in Moi, *Sexual/Textual Politics*, p. 111.
33. Munich, 1987, pp. 147, 192f. Page references in the text are to this edition.
34. Henriette Herwig, '"RomantischerReflexionsRoman" oder erzählerisches Labyrinth? Botho Strauß: *Der junge Mann*', in Michael Radix (ed.), *Strauß lesen*, Munich, 1987, p. 281.

Cixous's aesthetic. The narrator of *Der junge Mann* praises fiction's playfulness as a source of resistance to 'den einförmigen und zwanghaften Regimen des Fortschritts' (p. 11), suggesting, as does *Medusa*, parallels to feminist *jouissance*. He pleads for an open-edged form, to express a world which is 'voll fruchtbarer Unordnung' (p. 8); 'Wo mancher nur den glitzernden Zerfall erkennt, da sieht er viele Übergänge und Verwandlungen . . . den verschwenderischen Markt der Differenz' – a reference to Georges Bataille's theory of the creative extravagance of Nature; 'Vielfalt und Differenz aber gewähren allem Seienden den besten Schutz vor Tod und Verwesung' (p. 11). The celebration of 'Differenz' as a counter to the dead and deadening hand of binary rationalism is a characteristic feminist aesthetic position.

In this light, Strauß's treatment of female figures is perhaps surprising.[35] Let us take a short, self-contained example from *Paare Passanten*:

> Ein Mädchen in weißer Leinenhose, die weit und pumpig an den Beinen ist, eng und durchschimmernd aber um die Hüfte, so daß die hervortretenden Borten des Slips und der Schatten des Geschlechts wohl zum Dessin gehören, kommt keuchend mit einem Springseil in der Hand die Kellertreppe herauf, vom Fitting um zehn Uhr abends. Kein Blick, kein Gruß, kein Zögern, nur dieser schweißige Hauch der ertüchtigten Gliedmaßen, nur der eilige Aufsteig eines ebenso biestigen wie duldsamen, eines so geschäftigten wie gleichgültigen, so unberührbaren wie verbrauchsintensiven Narzißmus; dies mit fleischlichem Schmuck versehene Trainingsgerät, dies verkörperte Desinteresse, diese Wiederaufbereitungsanlage einer sterilen Anmut, dies Markenerzeugnis aus unseren Jahrzehnten der Verwöhnung, dieser schicke, allgegenwärtige Typ der sportlich Teilnahmslosen – ist das die Frau, die wir angeblich zum Objekt unserer Gelüste erniedrigen wollen? (p. 86)

This encounter stings the narrator to exclaim: 'Ja, wenn *Sex* töten könnte! Wenn er zumindest verwirren, verschandeln, entstellen, unbrauchbar machen könnte, was so kläglich angepaßt und ins Leere gesittet ist, und wenn er das trainierte Herz zum Auslaufen brächte' (p. 86). The violence of this reaction is alarming. However, the elements of misogynist rape-fantasy inherent in 'töten' and 'verschandeln' should not blind us to another level. The other

---

35. For an extremely perceptive and far-reaching analysis of the role of 'the female' in Strauß's work as a whole, which brings in aspects beyond the scope of this paper, see Leslie Adelson, 'Der arme Mann und "diese solidarischen Löcher". Zu Begriff und Funktion von Weiblichkeit bei Botho Strauß', in Inge Stephan and Sigrid Weigel (eds.), *Weiblichkeit und Avantgarde*, Berlin, 1987, pp. 165–86.

verbs are not penetrative, but disruptive, subversive; with them the narrator bewails the absence of the anarchic power of desire; their target is the closed, in binary terms essentially *male* efficiency and achievement-orientation, associated with the invulnerability of the woman – the opposite of Bataille's *Verschwendung*. The final image, of a wild sensuality causing the functionally disciplined heart to overflow, is profoundly Romantic. The jogger reappears in *Niemand anderes* (1987) as the athletic Atalante, whose ruthless triumph over male and female competitors is bought at the cost of 'Verzicht auf die Liebe'. Seen sociologically, this is credible enough: there are plenty of female yuppies, and indeed entrenched patriarchal structures may require women to be doubly male to succeed. But when eventually the female Homo Faber is struck down like her predecessor by illness, which threatens her ordered efficiency with chaos, the text expresses Strauß's disappointment that women do not necessarily embody the feminine qualities in favour of which he rejects the patriarchal Enlightenment (pp. 66–72).

'Der Wald', the second section of *Der junge Mann*, reads in this context like an act of revenge on the successful 'male' woman (pp. 67–107). 'Die junge Bankkauffrau' is plunged into 'die Wildnis von Gleicher Zeit', an atavistic nightmare which is 'nicht von Wegen und Fährten, sondern von unsichtbaren Strömungen und Sogkräften durchbahnt' (p. 76), a seamless sequence of horrors defying spatial, chronological and biological logic, but which all confront the rationality of her normal working existence with deeper-seated drives and anxieties and with her biological 'essence'. The woman who fails to conform to Strauß's conception of the female is punished by entrapment in the 'female' space of the labyrinth.

Other women figures in *Der junge Mann* are stereotypes: liars, sluts, whores, witches, enchantresses.[36] Leon's lover Zinth in 'Die Siedlung' is essentially a sex object, the two actresses who humiliate him in 'Die Straße' are amazonic harridans (reminiscent of the lesbian couple in *Kalldewey Farce*, 1981). The womb motif of the interpolated story 'Bernd und Bäumin' articulates archetypal male fears of women as devourers (pp. 215f). The narrator places Almut, as Schroubek does his cleaner Frau N. in *Die Widmung* (1977), on a scale of her unattractiveness for him (p. 219). 'Die Frau auf der Fähre' is a neo-Romantic *Novelle* in which Mero's fascinating beauty holds the male narrator prisoner, speared like a butterfly on the point of her memory of bliss. The interpolated narrative 'Die

---

36. See Caroline Fetscher, 'Wilhelm Meisters Wechseljahre', *Der Spiegel*, 13 August 1984, pp. 126–8.

Frau meines Bruders' plays with sado-masochistic images of lust and punishment; ejaculated sperm is 'weiße Peitschenhiebe' on the woman's face; she cleans and dresses the narrator, only to turn then, a projection of his guilt and self-disgust, into a 'kotiger Dämon' (pp. 161f). When his sympathy is aroused, it is for her as a fallen woman needing him as a knightly saviour, only for his nobility to be abused by the lascivious deceit of this lust-crazed siren, who turns out, to the dismay of the narrator, a naive seeker after peaks of mutual experience, to be a professional sex therapist, possibly just a prostitute.

In the third book, 'Die Siedlung', Strauß sketches and then rejects a seemingly postpatriarchal Utopia. Instead of the functional, binary, 'male' logic of technocratic society, the 'Syks' cultivate female characteristics and right-hemisphere intelligence in both sexes. Their goal is 'Teilhabe' in the warmth of 'der Große Schmelzfluß' of all human, natural and metaphysical knowledge, 'einberaumtsein in den Mutterkörper der Schöpfung'. Esteeming 'Schauen, Bewundern, Dienen und Preisen', they reject 'Streiten, Kämpfen, Konkurrieren' as the – clearly patriarchal – values of the establishment culture, dominated by the death wish (pp. 135–8). This community is *weiblich* in a positive sense, in its non-aggression, playfulness and taboo-free integration of the irrational (p. 123), but also in a conventionally pejorative sense: the reality of the dream of a conflict-free society is shown as a regression into a gentle, tensionless, but also flabby, boring, half-childish, half-pietistic community in which individual identity is erased (pp. 119f, 131).

Though Strauß declared in an interview in 1977 that 'jeder Mann ist auch eine Frau', *Der junge Mann* rejects an androgyny that erases contrasting opposites.[37] There are intriguing parallels between Strauß and William Blake. Not only do both at certain stages reject what Blake calls the 'mind-forg'd manacles' of reason; Strauß's critique of the Syks also seems to echo Blake's later reinstatement of a binary opposition in 'The Marriage of Heaven and Hell' (1790): 'Without contraries is no progression. Attraction and repulsion, reason and energy, love and hate, are necessary to human existence.'[38]

37. Carna Zacharias, 'Jeder Mann ist auch eine Frau', *Münchner Abendzeitung*, 11 November 1977. For a feminist critique of androgyny, see Jean Bethke Elshtain, 'Against Androgyny', in Anne Phillips (ed.), *Feminism and Equality*, London, 1987, pp. 139–59. Hassauer and Roos, in contrast, declare that 'die männliche Zukunft heißt Androgynität': 'Aufklärung', p. 47.
38. *Poems of William Blake*, ed. W. B. Yeats, London, n.d., pp. 77, 177.

Thus the form of Botho Strauß's texts has non-patriarchal elements, but his portrayal of female figures reveals a range of conventional male stereotypes which the self-irony of his texts does not fully overcome. He is sceptical towards Marcuse's faith in the potential of the 'feminine' qualities of gentleness, sensitivity, non-violence and non-competitiveness to subvert the perverted rationalism of the competitive capitalist success ethic. Strauß's portrayal of the Syks can be read as a critique of Marcuse. Yet women in his texts who do not display this femininity are a target of authorial aggression. As Leslie Adelson shows, Strauß posits an ideal *Weiblichkeit* as a Utopia with which to criticize patriarchy, but it is a Utopia from which the empirical women (as opposed to abstract constructs of the female) in his texts are excluded – of necessity since this *Weiblichkeit* is a male-occupied concept.[39]

Why do the texts of these two male writers from very different intellectual, social and political traditions demonstrate such formal and to some extent thematic affinities with the female textuality proposed by Cixous? The texts of both Schütz and Strauß contain rejections of dialectical reason, which, at least for Schütz as for Cixous, is explicitly a male category. Both authors' deep disillusion with the historical process makes them vulnerable, like Cixous, to essentialist and transcendental absolutes. Schütz and Strauß are, arguably, both in a *no-man's-land*:[40] Schütz because his Marxist upbringing, with its impelling demonstration of the contradictions of liberal-democratic capitalism, leaves him with no material alternative to the socialism he rejects as being equally irreparably flawed by patriarchy; Strauß because, having used the tools of radical negation that he acquired from his study of Adorno to undermine every Enlightenment position, he then abandoned dialectics. Schütz's alternative is the subversive power of female sexuality, Strauß's the transcendental power of love and the visonary power of art. Both, moreover, seek solace in a literary celebration of the female, thus placing themselves in a tradition in which, as Sigrid Weigel puts it, 'in einer Revision der männlichen Ordnung sich das Männliche am Stoff des Weiblichen gesundet – ein alter Traum übrigens, der sich schon bei Schlegel, Kleist, Flaubert, Marcuse u. a. findet. Der konstatierten Verwandtschaft von Sinnlichkeit, Poesie und Weiblichkeit folgt die Zusammenführung des Wunschobjekts

---

39. See Adelson, 'Der arme Mann', esp. pp. 166, 177, 182.
40. The irony is of course intentional; abandonment of entrenched male positions *need* not mean political or any other kind of impotence; the contradictions evident in the texts of these writers result from the colonization of new positions *without* the abandonment of the old ones.

Frau mit dem Wunschobjekt Text, indem sich der Mann im Text als Frau phantasiert.'[41] Weigel's essay draws attention to many points of contact between the constitution of the 'female' in the texts of Cixous and Irigaray and in texts by male writers. Cixous is one of the feminist theorists (though 'theory' is inherently suspect to Cixous as a patriarchal concept) most prone to revert to essentialism and biologism, and from whom, therefore, much recent feminist theory distances itself. On the very ground where certain male writers are laboriously pitching their tents, many women writers are decamping, recognizing that a theory of the female and of female texuality based on the binary exclusiveness of statements like 'Aufklärung hat keine Zukunft mehr; Weiblichkeit ist die Zukunft' can, as the examples of Schütz and Strauß show, be quite consistent with texts that are far from feminist and which indeed perpetuate exclusion.[42]

---

41. Sigrid Weigel, 'Der schielende Blick: Thesen zur Geschichte weiblicher Schreibpraxis', in Inge Stephan and Sigrid Weigel, *Die verborgene Frau*, Berlin, 1983, p. 109. Susan Cocalis and Kay Goodman make a similar point: 'Even in its positive variants, the Eternal Feminine, as the locus of male visions of a humanitarian utopia, coopts the subversive potential of women's oppression and denies women a positive utopian vision transcending patriarchy': *Beyond the Eternal Feminine. Critical Essays on Women and German Literature*, Stuttgart, 1982, p. 1.
42. I am grateful to Leslie Adelson for her comments on this aspect.

–18–

Botho Strauß and the Land of his Fathers: From *Rumor* to *Der junge Mann*

ARTHUR WILLIAMS

I

Botho Strauß's long novel *Der junge Mann* presents a picture of West German society caught in the deadly, dual embrace of the *unbewältigte Vergangenheit* and postmodern catalepsy. It is a society which may have one final slim chance of survival. This paper traces the way Strauß defines the nature of the problem and explores avenues which suggest possible remedies. It is a theme with which Strauß was preoccupied in his prose works in the first half of the present decade, marking them off almost completely from his theatre of both the 1970s and 1980s – although other essential ideas are common to the whole of his opus to date.

Der junge Mann[1] opens with portraits of failures: the jobless men of the 'Einleitung' and the neophyte theatre director, Leon Pracht. Thus, we know that Pracht's production of Genet's *The Maids* is doomed from the very first rehearsal. He tells us himself what he had intended and what the critics made of it. The contrast between stated intention and recorded achievement is significant – as is any inconsistency between manifesto or constitution (or *Grundgesetz*) and its achievements in practice. Even more significant is the reason for the failure; it is the exploration of this that forms the greater part of the novel's first main section, which is subtitled 'Der junge Mann', but suggests in its main heading, 'Die Straße' that Strauß

---

1. The works of Botho Strauß were all published originally by the Carl Hanser Verlag, Munich (later by dtv). The works are referred to in the text as follows (dates and references are to first editions): *Marlenes Schwester* (MS) (1975); *Rumor* (R) (1980); *Paare Passanten* (PP) (1981); *Der junge Mann* (DjM) (1984); *Diese Erinnerung an einen, der nur einen Tag zu Gast war* (E) (1985).

has started down the road of his main discussion. The scene-setting, the fashioning of the real beginnings, is crucial.

Pracht intended the play, in his interpretation of it, to present 'die Gegen-Welt, die Mythenwanderung, die Überschreitung, die Bühne als Eingangspforte zur Großen Erinnerung'. To the critics it had been 'im ganzen ein wenig bieder', the only element of surprise 'daß ein poète maudit veraltet, ein Genet staubgrau geworden sei' (DjM 32). The reason why Pracht failed in this way lay in his inability to direct his two actresses who, it becomes apparent, had sought him out, not as their dream director, but as the butt of all their malice. At the very first rehearsal their interminable chat had overwhelmed him, so that he 'kam nicht dazu, ein einziges Wort zu sagen'. Having thwarted his attempts to direct them, they turn on him with cold stares, 'so als wollten sie sagen: Nun, junger Mann, du willst hier die Führung übernehmen und bist nicht einmal imstande, uns zum Schweigen zu bringen?!' (DjM 36). The whole dilemma of Strauß's time and generation is encapsulated in this: who is capable of effective leadership, who is able to speak with a clear voice?

The humiliation of Leon Pracht in the theatre occurred in 1969 (DjM 37). By the end of the novel, some fifteen years later (DjM 347), his female tormentors have lost all influence over him: Margarethe Wirth has left the stage to marry; Pat Kurzrok is still an actress but between shows looks after her old mentor and suffers for days from 'Durchfall, erbricht sich und behauptet, sie höre Stimmen' (DjM 348).

Strauß had previously – in 1980, in *Rumor*[2] – shown a young career-woman, Grit, looking after an older man (in this case her father) while she herself suffers an all but terminal illness associated with unpleasant gastric symptoms. It was with *Rumor* that Strauß started to weave the pattern of themes and motifs which links the works under discussion here in a slowly evolving complementality and which allows us to see the later novel as the (as yet) final or penultimate statement on them.[3]

Remaining, for the moment, with Leon Pracht, 'der junge Mann' struggling to survive the cockatrice glance of modern woman, the fundamental dichotomy underlying the problematical male–female

---

2. Strauß seems to have been reluctant to categorize his prose works. *Rumor* was not called a *Roman* until it was published by Ullstein, Frankfurt/Main (1983). *Der junge Mann* was so designated only on the dustcover. The present article does not examine this question.
3. Of the later works, only the long poem *Diese Erinnerung an einen, der nur einen Tag zu Gast war* remains on this territory. Some reference is, therefore, made to it below.

relationship is soon revealed. What Pracht is looking for in his production of *The Maids* is a '*kulturelle* Definition'[4] of the figures (DjM 41); he wants his actresses to develop 'ein geschichtliches Gefühl für ihre Haltungen und ihre Körperlichkeit' (DjM 43).

This idea arises out of his comparison of sitting on a bicycle with sitting in front of the house: while the former can only evoke memories as recent as childhood, the latter 'kann unser Stammhirn reizen, kann uns aus der Geschichte entführen, bis hinter die Zeitrechnung' (DjM 43). The house is associated with a vision of himself as 'der Wächter auf der Mauer' observing a war in ancient times, and it reminds him also of when he sat with his father under the fruit trees compiling the index for the latter's book on 'Montanus'. His extensive working partnership with his father at a time when his immediate contemporaries 'zum Aufruhr riefen, überall Väter stürzen und Völker befreien wollten' (DjM 22) had taught him a great deal about secret, heretical Christian teachings full of 'weibliche Weisheit' and which referred to 'Gott die Mutter'. But Pat and Margarethe have not had this 'rein väterliche Erziehung' (DjM 21); they want only to show up his inadequacies (DjM 45). 'Sie wollen meine Ideen nicht. Sie wollen sich auf meinen Anfang nicht einlassen' (DjM 46). They cannot appreciate his burning desire to see 'die aus fernem, altem Gedächtnis durchdringenden Zeichen am *Menschen*' (DjM 51).

Pracht cannot get through to his actresses; they have totally different horizons. He, through his father, has acquired both a sense of history and, paradoxically enough, an awareness of much that would be considered proper attributes of the world of women; the two actresses have nothing of this. The book, ostensibly a journey of discovery for Leon, is an exploration of the absence, and crucially of the reason for the absence, of cultural definition and historical memory. Strauß establishes this in this first section specifically in relation to the female characters.

Indeed it is possible to construe the greater part of the novel as an attempt to conquer time (both past and future) on behalf of the female characters – Leon himself benefits from just such an experience already during his walk along the Rhine and through the streets and shops of Cologne in this first section: 'ich hatte einen Besuch auf der anderen Seite der Zeit gemacht, und als ich mich nach zwei Tagen wieder ins Theater zurückfand, da war mir als wachte ich in einem anderen Leben auf' (DjM 59). The young man who so very recently could say not a single word, has put his dual

---

4. All italics are as in the original texts.

problem of women and history into the perspective of a river landscape – and that a year and more before Heinrich Böll's valedictory tour of the political horizon in *Frauen vor Flußlandschaft*.

The idea that *Der junge Mann* may be a model for the re-education of contemporary West German women can be underpinned by brief reference to one of the several role-reversals that occur over the span of the book. The two actresses are depicted as having been allocated their role in Pracht's life, 'nicht zu meiner Unterhaltung, sondern zu meiner Weihung' (DjM 59), while they have just been compared by his mentor (and theirs), Alfred Weigert, with Bernhardt or Duse, 'nur werden sie von keinerlei Weihe mehr emporgetragen'. They had seemed initially (DjM 59) to be 'peitschenschwingende Initiationswärterinnen' (a variant on Nietzsche's exhortation to men about whips and women?), an image picked up in what Moray McGowan identifies as a session of sex therapy (DjM 156–64)[5] where the male is still to some extent under the control of the female but on this occasion administers whiplashes of sperm to the woman's face. (The scene is also reminiscent of the biblical story of Onan, for the woman is presented as a mysterious 'brother's wife'.) The transformation is completed in the synthesis of Margarethe's marriage to a manufacturer of leather goods and in Pat's strange malady, which itself mirrors both the fate of the woman in the kiosk in the 'Einleitung', who becomes decrepit and incontinent when her husband dies (DjM 13), and the lot of the strange 'brother's wife', who is soon immersed in her own excrement and embraces Leon, now almost a gallant, fairy-tale prince, 'mit moorigen Gliedern' (DjM 164).[6]

Leon's later liaison with Yossica, whom he tracks down as an all but deracinated flower of the younger generation, is a role-reversal of a different kind, of the *Knab'* in Goethe's 'Heidenröslein', since Leon plucks Yossica from the ground without hurting himself, helping her instead to recover from her disastrously split persona and enabling her to exploit her vocal talents (DjM 315f, 323ff).

Strauß is concerned, of course, not with botanical roots, nor indeed exclusively with literary roots and 'fernem, altem Gedächtnis' – although these do appear on the surface to be his primary preoccupation – as the many ancient, Middle Eastern and biblical

---

5. See above p. 276.
6. This is not the only feature at this point in the text that might remind us of Schiller's Franz Moor, who would surely have been in his element in the 'excremental culture' of the sub-title to Arthur Kroker and David Cook (eds.), *The Postmodern Scene. Excremental Culture and Hyper-Aesthetics*, 2nd edn, London, 1988.

allusions together with the host of references to German and European literature would indicate. His slowly revolving round-dance (the *Reigen* which is a constantly recurring motif in *Der junge Mann*) weaves its way through the underworld of modern German history, the urban labyrinth of contemporary society and the deadly embrace of the animation-suspending postmodern tower.

In setting himself the task of providing contemporary (West) Germany with cultural and historical perspectives, Strauß demonstrates his sensitivity to the needs of a society which was about to see its leading historians locked in what has become known as the *Historikerstreit*,[7] whose foremost newspaper would launch a section called *Zeitläufte* (a most Straussian word)[8] and where more recently no less a person than the Speaker in the Lower House of the Federal Parliament (*Bundestagspräsident*) Philipp Jenninger has split public opinion asunder with his well-meaning but atrociously timed attempt to place the Holocaust into some sort of perspective.[9] Thus it seems possible to consider Strauß – in spite of his obvious determination to match with works his words in *Paare Passanten*: 'Man schreibt einzig im Auftrag der Literatur. Man schreibt unter Aufsicht alles bisher Geschriebenen' (PP 103) – a participant in the great political debate of the decade, perhaps even a fellow-spirit with Helmut Kohl, who so often in his speeches when he first became Federal Chancellor seemed to want to place the past in new perspective by referring to himself as the first Chancellor of the postwar generation.[10]

Indeed, the passage in *Paare Passanten* continues: 'Man schreibt

---

7. While the stuff of the *Historikerstreit* was in the air from the early 1980s, the term itself is used to refer to the debate conducted in the West German press in 1986. Many of the contributions have been collected in one volume by the Piper Verlag: *'Historikerstreit'. Die Dokumentation der Kontroverse um die Einzigartigkeit der nationalsozialistische Judenvernichtung*, Munich, 1987. The concerns of the historians and often their vocabulary and perspectives are close to Strauß in the works considered in this article.
8. *Die Zeit*, 16 September 1988.
9. Jenninger's speech to mark 9 November 1938 (*Reichskristallnacht*) led immediately to his resignation. *Die Zeit*, 18 November 1988, has the text of the speech and several related articles (pp. 4–6).
10. In several speeches in October–November 1982 (see *Bulletin*, Presse- und Informationsamt der Bundesregierung, nos. 97, 99, 113, 1982, pp. 897, 913, 1033). There is no suggestion here of party-political alignment on the part of Strauß, who utterly repudiated such affiliation. See Volker Hage, 'Schreiben ist eine Séance. Der Künstler als nicht mehr junger Mann: Botho Strauß – ein Porträt', *Die Zeit*, 16 January 1987, pp. 37–8; here p. 38 (also published together with an earlier interview as 'Schreiben ist eine Séance: Begnungen mit Botho Strauß' in Michael Radix (ed.), *Strauß lesen*, Munich, 1987, pp. 188–216; here p. 215. References below are to this version).

aber doch auch, um sich nach und nach eine geistige Heimat zu schaffen, wo man eine natürliche nicht mehr besitzt.' In this sense, Strauß's work inevitably has a political dimension – a factor he acknowledged in one of his earliest prose works, the story 'Theorie der Drohung': 'kein Text existiert, der nicht Mehr über seinen Autor schreibt, als dieser von sich aus sagt; kein Text, der nicht mehr zu verstehen gibt, als der Autor selbst darunter verstanden hat – ich meine daraus folgt, daß dieses Mehr eines Textes in erster Linie von einer politischen Lektüre erschlossen werden kann' (MS 98).

II

There is no doubt that the nub of the problem facing Leon Pracht is the lack of a sense of history in the two actresses. This is why he does not know how to approach them – and one needs to know only two words of German to sense the chilling associations of his realization: 'Was mir fehlt, ist die klare Richtung für meinen Kampf' (DjM 56). He cannot get across to them that he wants them to sense the whole weight, the presence of history and culture at their backs: '"Und hinter Ihnen, Margarethe, muß auch etwas dahinter sein. Hinter Ihrem Rücken."' Margarethe's response is 'gelassen': '"Hören Sie, Leon, hinter mir ist gar nichts. Hier steh allein ich."' This provokes him to an equally chilling outburst: '"Ich bin der Lehrer, ich will es Ihnen zeigen, das geheime Reich, ich bin Ihr Führer!" rief ich wie toll und bäumte mich auf' (DjM 58).

In the Strauß plays of the period, *Der Park* (1983) and *Die Fremdenführerin* (1986), this exchange might have indicated a secret empire of the senses, here the implications are strongly social and political even though in the course of the novel they are often concealed behind a smokescreen of sensual experience. Margarethe coolly advises Leon to make do with what he has in front of him ('"Sie müssen schon vorliebnehmen mit dem, was Sie *vor* sich haben!"'), which is, of course, his actresses. What lies ahead in the novel is a journey in which Strauß confronts his characters with a new range of experience, bringing them face to face with undercurrents and events that so far have existed secretly behind their backs.

The most powerful symbol he uses in this connection is the birth out of the sleeping woman's ribs of the monstrous dwarf which is half Baudelaire and half Hitler (DjM 184f) – clothing the 'poète maudit' in the grey 'Feldherrnmantel'. Although it has to be said at once that this is not male chauvinism at work; the monster, 'Das Liebeslicht' – the title of this section (DjM 183–8) – was the result of the 'Reibung' between the man and the woman, the thinly disguised friction between the sexes (DjM 186).

The female back (likewise the eyes and the face) is one of the motifs that run throughout the book linking crucial scenes. Again, it is not used for the first time in *Der junge Mann*; it is present already in *Rumor*, where Grit's disease is located in her back: 'Die trostlose Gewißheit, daß da eine . . . Krankheit in ihrem Rücken haust, wie Schwamm am Dachbalken, und sie auf unbestimmte Weise ständig bedroht.' The idea develops here in a way which can be easily recognized later in transposed form in *Der junge Mann*: Grit believes in her semi-aware state that she is pregnant, that the growth on her back contains the fruit of evil and is about to spawn monsters upon the world (R 189f). In her nightmare state, visions of rape and abortion intermingle while she identifies the young male nurse caring for her with the father–rapist–abortionist. In order to humour her and help break the grip of the evil dream, her urine sample is taken to be tested for indications of pregnancy – by her father (R 193) – highlighting the ambivalence in a relationship which is one of the disturbing features of the book.[11]

The association of the father with the daughter's phantasmagorial pregnancy is no wilful twist of the Straussian imagination; Grit's illness seems to have been brought on by the arrival in her life of her father and may, in fact, be one indication of the virulent nature of the sickness he carries within him, that is, the psychological and emotional burden of recent German history. Bekker, although he is, like Leon Pracht, an exact contemporary of Botho Strauß, carries with him, on and at his back, a consciousness of the period and events his compatriots most want to banish to a realm beyond recall. Strauß uses literary allusion to charge Bekker and his message with significance.

Rumor opens in Zachler's 'Institut für Nachricht' which, apart from encapsulating many of Strauß's phobias in contemporary society is reminiscent of the world of the early Walser[12] – perhaps a factor which contributes to the feeling that Bekker, who in the opening words of the book 'ist tatsächlich zurückgekommen', belongs to an older generation, possibly even to that of Wolfgang Borchert, whose prefatory scene-setting to *Draußen vor der Tür* begins, of course: 'Ein Mann kommt nach Deutschland. Er war

---

11. Ambivalent relationships are a feature of all of Strauß's work from his earliest plays onwards. The examples are too numerous to list here.
12. R 7–19, esp. pp. 10–13, contain many echoes of *Ehen in Philippsburg*; the marriage of Bekker's ex-wife to a 'Häusermakler' in South Germany (p. 18) hints at the later Walser of *Das Schwanenhaus*, Frankfurt/Main, 1980.

lange weg.'[13] And as soon as Strauß has completed his own scene-setting and allows Bekker to speak for the first time in the first person, the spectre of one of Hitler's officers is conjured up: 'Aufgewachsen unter dem schweren Winterfeldzugsmantel eines wütenden Offiziers' and then a few lines later a passage which is one of the keys to the later novel:

> So erhebt sich wieder dieser Schatten mächtig über meinem Rücken und es ist, als ob das frühe Böse jetzt erst richtig wirke und mache, daß sich der enge Umlauf meiner Lebensschritte immer enger zuschließt und bald vielleicht in einem tollen Wirbel um die eigene Achse endet. Ich stehe noch einmal, ein letztes Mal gewiß, vor dem Eingang des Instituts, zu dem ich als junger Mann aus der bedrückendsten Herkunft wie zu einem Tempel der Seligen geflohen bin, von dem ich mir endlich freie Entfaltung, gute und richtige Lehre, Lebenssinn erhoffte und wo ich doch, unter Zachlers Herrschaft, in die allerschrecklichste Strafanstalt geriet, in die ein auf Selbständigkeit hoffender Mensch nur geraten kann. Vier Mal, im ganzen vier Mal in meinem Leben habe ich versucht, diesem magischem Gefängnis zu entfliehen. (R 21)

Der junge Mann is composed of an introduction and five books. Pracht escapes from his 'magisches Gefängnis' in the fourth[14] and gains his independence in the fifth – Bekker never gains his. The fourth book, 'Die Terrasse (Belsazar. Fabeln am Morgen nach dem Fest)', also shows West German society – Bekker's and Pracht's magic prison – ensnared in the evil radiation of the recent past (DjM 179–82, esp. 182) and later raises the question of burying Hitler (DjM 194, 302). If *Rumor* is the definition and initial reconnoitring, not to say reconnaissance, of the problem of contemporary West German society as a problem of the legacy of German history, and *Der junge Mann* suggests the eventual solution to it, the difference in the fates of Bekker and Pracht is perfectly logical.[15]

Bekker was, as he says, 'auf der Kippe zu Zachler zurück', on the point of re-entering the cage, when the figure of the major rose up

13. Bekker is close to Beckmann in name; he is also a latter-day 'Neinsager' who rejects pretence for the truth and finds himself locked outside society. There is an interesting comparison to be made between Strauß's transmutations of literary models to invest them with new relevance to the contemporary scene and those of Süskind, who seems simply to want to play an intellectual game and whom Stuart Parkes (p. 317 below) describes as eclectic.
14. See DjM 235, 313. The image of the cage is referred to elsewhere in this volume; see Hubert Lengauer, pp. 179f above, and Gisela Shaw, pp. 96f above; also of relevance is Juliet Wigmore, pp. 277f above.
15. The idea of the 'Strafanstalt' might suggest echoes of other works, for example, Siegfried Lenz, *Deutschstunde*, Hamburg, 1968.

again at his back for the first time in many years and 'hängt mir seinen schweren Mantel über die Schultern, daß ich mich darin wohl aufrecken möge' (R 23f). To walk tall he has to assume the mantle of the past; where this leads him immediately is into the first of five sections in the book which all open with slight variations of the same words: 'Gehen wir die Stadt hinunter' (R 25, 36, 42, 131, 194) and which all take him into areas with characteristics unmistakably drawn from and associated with the recent past. In the later novel, in keeping with many others of the decade, the characters tend to leave the town for the suburbs, the 'Rand', the 'Grenze', the 'Schwelle'. Even there, like Peter Handke's Andreas Loser,[16] they cannot escape reminders of the past – although they do gain perspectives on it.

Immediately, Bekker passes through an urban hell, a 'ganz gewöhnliches KZ, eines unter Millionen' (R 25), in which a man is subjecting his wife to a horrific beating. They are part of an eternal struggle, which Strauß describes in terms that bring together three constant preoccupations which have fundamental formal significance: 'alles gepaart, alles auf einmal, in einem einzigen, augenblicklichen, blutigen Reigen' (R 27).

The importance of the *Reigen* in *Der junge Mann* has already been mentioned. 'Das Paar' is even more fundamental to Strauß; it runs as a motif through his work from his earliest plays to his very latest ones. The third idea is less immediately obvious: the synchronism of experience. We can detect three literary models here, two of whom Strauß acknowledges by name. The one he does not name but seems often to allude to is Günter Grass, who coined the term 'Vergegenkunft' (*Ver*-gangenheit, *Gegen*-wart, Zu-*kunft*) in his *Kopfgeburten* (published, like *Rumor*, in 1980) as an attempt to come to terms with the past through a stocktaking of the present in the name of the future. The other two are Paul Valéry and T. S. Eliot, both of whom are favourite models for Strauß.[17]

Valéry provides the model for the fleeting glimpse that gives the

16. Further points of comparison between *Der Chinese des Schmerzes* as discussed by Peter Pütz above (pp. 129f) and *Der junge Mann* are the arrows that point the way, for example, DjM 68ff and 268f.
17. Günter Grass, *Kopfgeburten oder Die Deutschen sterben aus*, Darmstadt, 1980 (here 4th ed, 1983, p. 102) has many points in common with *Der junge Mann*; not mentioned elsewhere in the present discussion is, for example, the bat in Dörte's hair (p. 54), which can be related to several images in *Der junge Mann*, not least the ladybird in Almut's hair (DjM 289) and Pracht's ideas like bats in his head (DjM 153). Strauß makes several explicit references to Valéry in *Paare Passanten* (e.g. pp. 103, 108); Hage, 'Schreiben ist eine Séance', refers to both Valéry (p. 200) and Eliot (p. 209), who is mentioned by Strauß in *Diese Erinnerung* (E 59).

writer the insight into the essence of things. The Straussian *Riß* (and its many variants), that vital element captured in the tantalizing phrase 'die Einheit von Riß und Form' (PP 112), draws on the essence of French symbolist perception caught in 'le temps d'un sein nu entre deux chemises!'.[18] Strauß uses the glimpse not just to capture the essential character of what he is observing and depicting, he also exploits it as the symbol of that elusive moment of insight which creates the window from the present through the past into the future – perhaps the realization that the Third Reich, viewed from the future, will appear no more than a brief moment in history, as Belshazzar's bloody banquet does now to us (but the comparison already suggests the repetition of the common element).

Eliot had enunciated the fatalistic riddle which Strauß and his generation have to solve if they are to have a future. 'In my beginning,' said Eliot in 'East Coker', 'is my end' and 'in my end is my beginning',[19] and for Strauß the beginning that matters is all too obvious: 'Unser Älterwerden kreist in immer erweiterten Gedächtnis-Ringen um unsere einzigartige Geburtsstätte, den deutschen Nationalsozialismus' (PP 171). Undoubtedly Strauß intended the word 'Ringen' to hint both at the 'Reigen' of life and the ceaseless wrestling in and with the German memory – the latter, perhaps, holding the hopeful hint of a reference to the story of Jacob who wrestled all night with the Angel before gaining the blessing of the Lord (see PP 122).

III

For Bekker, and vitally also for Strauß, the memory, the beginning, is kept alive and has to be contended with in the very language in which recollection occurs. Strauß confronts this dilemma for the first time in an extended passage starting on page 30 of *Rumor*. Bekker upsets an elderly man in a New York bar for asexuals by speaking German. The man explains, 'daß er das Deutsch in seinem Rücken ... überhaupt nicht vertragen könne', the reason being that he cannot forget, 'und der Grund sind

---

18. The closing lines of 'Le Sylphe' in *Charmes*. Many other references to Valéry's poetry are possible; *La jeune Parque*, in particular, rewards rereading with *Der junge Mann* and Strauß's long poem in mind. See also DjM 36: 'The universe of a glimpse'.
19. The opening and closing lines of the poem. As with Valéry, Eliot's *Four Quartets* are clearly relevant.

natürlich die Lager, die deutschen'. The two vie with each other in tales about atrocities, with Bekker struggling to avoid using German and all the time worried that his accent, 'dies untergründige Deutsch in allem, was ich aussprach', might again incur the man's wrath. And here (p. 33), the analysis of Bekker's feelings is most subtle, for he is ashamed and yet not ashamed – he senses a 'widerspenstigen Stolz, ein Deutscher zu sein, und zwar, weil man hier etwas dafür tun mußte, weil es eben eine gewisse Mühe verlangte und man sein Willkommen nicht gratis kassierte.' 'Ich empfand,' he continues with a teasing twist in the tail, 'einen heftigen Stich Heimweh und Liebe zu meinem/zu einem zweifellos imaginären Land.'

Strauß, of course, does not need to be abroad to have to make such an effort; he is struggling all the time to create a home for himself, he is constantly striving to earn the right to his 'widerspenstigen Stolz' through his work as it progresses. Correspondingly, his work demands a similar effort of the reader.

The preliminary discussion of *Der junge Mann* above indicated something of the mission Strauß set himself in writing the book; there is an earlier, broader view of the same problem in *Rumor*, for Bekker's second foray 'die Stadt hinunter' (R 36) leads him first into a surreal world of frozen relics, light-wells without light,[20] obscene gestures, fear, suicide or murder and madness, but then the focus sharpens and settles on the destruction of a sense of history in the present younger generation:[21]

> Kannst du mir vielleicht einmal verraten, wie du dich bei diesen orkanartigen Lautstärken, bei diesem Punk noch mit dem Ohr und dem Geschichtssinn orientieren willst? Die Jüngsten hören sich gerade Nazischocker auf Platten an. Den Kindern geht man sowieso ans Gedächtnis. Zerfetzt das Gewebe. Die Schule zuerst. Statt Geschichte und Entziffern der Kulturen lernen sie vernünftig fernzusehen. Die Schule! Hand in Hand mit den täglichen Löscharbeiten des Fernsehens, dieser dicke weiße Löschkalk, der in den Kindern jeden Brand von Gier und Ach

---

20. The repetition of the word 'Licht' on R 37f and elsewhere seems to suggest Goethe's dying words. The allusions to Goethe are altogether too numerous for any attempt to be made to plot them here.
21. Hamish Reid, p. 63 above, reminds us of Walter Scheel's warnings to this effect. With similar concerns in mind Scheel also said, 'eine Demokratie ist immer auf dem Wege zu sich selbst' (Tübingen University, 8 October 1977; see *Bulletin*, Presse- und Informationsamt der Bundesregierung, no. 98, 1977, p. 897) which together with Alfred Weigert's 'wir sind immer auf dem Weg, hinter die Dinge zu kommen' (DjM 55) allows an intriguing dual perspective on Strauß's work.

erstickt. Ich sage dir: ein, zwei Generationen noch, und es werden vollkommen erinnerungsfreie Menschen durch ihr Schicksal schweben. Die werden alles vergessen haben. Nach uns werden sie alles vergessen, was einmal war . . . Dummer Zauber Geschichte. Was war das? (R 38f)

The idea of a new generation of 'Nazis' gains in definition in *Der junge Mann* where Yossica, in a passage reminiscent of Thomas Mann's *Mario und der Zauberer*, in a trance uses words that strike fear into the heart of Leon: 'auf einmal bekam ich es doch mit der Angst. Ich glaubte aus diesem jungen Geschöpf das Anwehen eines alten Unheils, eines geschichtlichen Fluchs viel eher zu verspüren als eine Jugend- oder Wohlstandsnot.' Yossica had said of her peers:

'Jugend, die kannst du dir schenken. Alle von 16 bis 25 sind sie Nazis. Die meisten werden ja auch Jungunternehmer. Die sehen praktisch keinen Ausweg mehr und machen sich selbständig. Dafür brauchen sie aber innerlich viel Stärke und Brutalität. Woher nehmen? "Ausländer raus" und so, das sind bleibende Sachen, die liegen in Deutschland so sicher in der Luft wie saurer Regen. Da bedienst du dich, wenn du irgendwas durchstehen mußt.' (DjM 197)

In a country where suddenly the far Right has started to win seats in *Land* elections and the granddaughters of Nazi criminals feel the need to speak out against the new racism aimed at Turkish *Gastarbeiter* in Berlin, Strauß's concern is no literary artifice.[22]

As we shall see below, Strauß also explored this pattern of ideas in *Paare Passanten*. In *Rumor*, his angst culminates in a vision of a world of computers and microchips which in the words, spoken on the telephone by Zachler, whether imagined by Bekker or actual, will become reality:

Freiheit vom 19. Jahrhundert! . . . fordern wir . . . jetzt, am Ende des zwanzigsten, endlich . . . mit einer großen Aufbäumung . . . ins nächste Zeitalter hinüber, auf frische Erkenntniswiesen getragen, wo es nun endlich heißt: die Ganze Sammlung denken, sich auf dem Flecke strecken und um und um verteilen, was wir an Gütern, Geist, Geschichte schon gesammelt haben. Wahrscheinlich ist es längst genug.

22. West Berlin elections of 29 January 1989 when the Republican Party won 7.5 per cent of the vote (see *Die Zeit*, 3 February 1989, pp. 1–4), the Frankfurt municipal elections (12 March 1989) when the NDP recorded 6.6 per cent and, more recently, the elections for the European Parliament (18 June 1989) when the Republikaner polled 7.1 per cent on average across the whole Federal Republic (14.6 per cent in Bavaria). See also the article on Francesca Frank 'Legacy of a Nazi grandfather', *The Independent*, 30 January 1989, p. 12.

Wahrscheinlich haben wir jetzt so ziemlich alles an der Hand und mehr kommt nicht hinzu. (R 39f)

Surely this is the monstrous vision of the future that motivates Botho Strauß: he has at his back an *unbewältigte Hitler-Vergangenheit* while ahead lies the apparently totally system-tamed world of microchip and computer, the latter posing as an antidote to the problematical inheritance of the former, but ignoring the dilemma rather than resolving it. This would be a future with nothing of Germany in it – and nothing of art.

Two sections in *Der junge Mann* explore these ideas in some detail. 'Die Siedlung' shows a people of the future who are no longer capable of real creativity; they can only take apart and reassemble existing objects (DjM 142f), they seek to by-pass language as a means of communication (DjM 148), and they keep an empty magic cage which for them houses all the essence of the evil spirits that bind them together as a people (DjM 140f). 'Die Geschichte der Almut' brings us face to face with a team of modern art-restorers who have mastered all the latest technological aids available to them but have no sense of the power of the past in the works of art they restore; their education has been 'führerlos' (DjM 280), their teamwork seems to hold out the prospect of an age of new .'Unschuld, gemischt aus Vergeßlichkeit und Perfektion' (DjM 283), but they would not be equipped to cope should the giants from the past begin to stir again (DjM 280). We can recognize characteristics initially attributed to Pat and Margarethe in both the 'Synkreas' and the art-restorers; Strauß is exploring variations on his main theme that the West Germans of today have as yet been provided with no substantial means of defence against the re-emergence of the evil from the past on the next stage of its round-dance.

For Strauß, as he indicated in the continuation of the New York scene in *Rumor*, there are no ready-made answers, but the question exists – and it exists in the language, with the very idea that there is something definable as German:

> Daß das Deutsch in diesem einzigartigen Vernichtungswerk nicht untergegangen war, daß es einem Hitler nicht gelungen war, auch das Deutsch noch mitzuverheizen . . . dies ganze Deutschsein trotz Hitler erfreute mich im Innersten, während ich oben auf englisch lallte und stotterte, und ich schämte mich auch nicht, daß wir ausgerechnet über das Lager lallten und stotterten, fand es am Ende gar des Unaussprechlichen würdig, daß wir in einem schweren, scherzlosen Rausch immer dasselbe zum selben Thema sagten, why? (R 33)

These are areas which are explored with greater clarity in *Paare Passanten*. They are developed less clearly in *Rumor* because they become confused, in the book's lack of focus, with the 'Rumor' Bekker senses in the town, 'der noch gehört werden will' (R 42). It leads him into the undercurrents of history, but also into the labyrinthine 'Lügenwelt der Beziehungen' (R 47, 161) – the omnipresent theme of Strauß's theatre. The 'Lügenwelt' is apparent both in the lives Bekker observes and in the ambivalent development of his own relationship with his daughter (from father/daughter through surrogate husband/wife to mother/child). The interfusion and confusion of these levels is complete when Bekker repeats the words 'Rumor, Narr und Frau' (R 65ff) pointing at the rumblings in the gut of contemporary West German society, at himself and, to her confusion, at Grit. And Grit, the representative of modern young womanhood, is shown to have been affected by the 'Rumor' also at the level of her most intimate personal relationship, with Joseph (her live-in lover).

The key passage, a discrete section on pages 52–3, opens: 'Risse, Rumor, Gewalt und Unrast, plötzliche Stöße von ungebändigtem Leben unter deinen Sohlen' and ends

> Ein unbewußtes Stutzen vor dem, was war und was sich anbahnt, erlebt auch Grit und kann mit Joseph und seinen schlaffen Entzücken nichts mehr anfangen. Es hat sich etwas in ihr abgespalten und sie sagt mit einem Mal, arglos und fest entschlossen: 'Ich suche jemanden mit Kräften, die ich noch gar nicht kenne. Jemanden, der mal eine ganz andere Sprache spricht.'

She is caught on the threshold between the world Yossica fears and that of *Der Park*, the other route that Strauß explores in his attempt to diagnose the sickness afflicting his age. However, we must forgo any further discussion of the 'Lügenwelt der Beziehungen' and follow Bekker as he teeters on the brink of insanity, struggling with the language and the existential dilemma it holds for him.

In Austria, surrounded by German with which he cannot identify, he offers a passionate anticipation of the paradoxical words from *Paare Passanten*: 'Es schafft ein tiefes Zuhaus und ein tiefes Exil, da in der Sprache zu sein' (PP 101), when he bursts out: 'Bloß raus hier! Raus aus der Sprache! . . . Bin ein Patriot, weiß aber nicht, an wen soll ich mich wenden. Aber wo ist zu meiner Treue der Herr?' (R 78). His sallies 'die Stadt hinunter' become successive explorations of the dilemma posed by German history and the need for its expression in the German language. He sees people cut off from the development of the real Germany in soundproof cabins created by the level of welfare they enjoy (R 95). It is an image which foreshadows the end of the book when Bekker, almost certainly mad by now, soliloquizes on local radio from 'der schalltoten Bude' (R 195).

Bekker's is a voice crying in the wilderness, and when he communes with the soul of the dead officer–father (R 196) he is very close to Strauß for whom 'Schreiben ist eine Séance'.[23] He is close, as the sequence progresses, also to further ideas of crucial importance in *Paare Passanten*, *Der junge Mann* and the later long poem *Diese Erinnerung an einen, der nur einen Tag zu Gast war*. Bekker, first described as a 'Bauchredner' (R 195), becomes a 'rumorender Nachtwächter' and sees himself as he wanders down the street as 'Sänger und Gutteil schweigende Mehrheit dazu' (R 198). The long poem draws much of its inspiration from the image of the poet as at once 'Sänger' and 'Wächter' (E 20f); *Der junge Mann* and *Paare Passanten* both reach their point of greatest hope in the figure of a singer who represents the real silent majority – both are women.

The liberating act of singing could never be performed by contemporary West German women – at least not as Strauß depicts them; the singer at the end of *Paare Passanten* is not German, she is Russian, and she is not in Germany, she is in Venice, a city protected by its water-dependence from the history-erasing influence of more modern means of transport (PP 202–4).[24] It is hardly surprising, then, that when Strauß introduces the 'Bankkauffrau' to the 'Besitzer der Deutschen' and a hint of a rapprochement is achieved, it is in an aquarium (DjM 85).

IV

The interrelated questions of historical consciousness and modern, high-welfare, high-tech, low-fidelity society are a central concern in *Paare Passanten*. In the first section, 'Paare', where Strauß depicts modern couples totally lacking in depth of feeling and attachment in a society which does all their caring for them, he soon points out the root of the problem: 'Die Leidenschaft, das Leben selbst braucht Rückgriffe (mehr noch als Antizipationen) und sammelt Kräfte aus Reichen, die vergangen sind, aus geschichtlichem Gedächtnis.

---

23. See Hage, 'Schreiben ist eine Séance', p. 209.
24. There is also a clear reference to Thomas Mann's *Der Tod in Venedig* in the description of a figure seen (or not seen) in Venice in 1969 shortly before his death (Adorno).

Doch woher nehmen . . .? Dazugehörig sein in der Fläche der Vernetzung ist an die Stelle der zerschnittenen Wurzeln getreten: das Diachrone, der Vertikalaufbau hängt in der Luft' (PP 26) – a state which anticipates so many of the situations depicted in *Der junge Mann* and which he sees as a direct consequence of the Third Reich:

> Verwunderlich wäre es, doch nicht mehr undenkbar, wenn eines fernen Tages, aus der Anderen Zeit heraus, das deutsche Dritte Reich nicht vornehmlich nach seinem blutigen Formgefühl beurteilt würde, mit dem es die Schrecken der Diffusion im ersten Massenzeitalter beseitigte, sondern vielmehr erinnert würde als das erste, alles in die Verirrung treibende Beben, als der Erste Ruck vor dem langsam gewaltigen Aufbruch in eine 'geschichtslose' statische Epoche. (PP 182f)

These are precisely the effects Strauß seeks to resist by his excursions in *Der junge Mann* into both past and future. He attempts it by crossing the threshold of the unconscious and the dream. And he is not being simply esoteric; his concerns are not other-worldly. Memory and deep, healthy dream-sleep simply mark his beginnings. 'Braucht man aber nicht die Erinnerung zur Gesundheit des ganzen Organismus, wie man auch im Schlaf den Traum nötig braucht?' (PP 178f) is an idea which leads via a mention of Nietzsche's hate for German anti-Semitism, the result of their 'Selbstanglotzung', to a discussion of the treatment of Turkish *Gastarbeiter* in Berlin. Strauß's fear is as plain as the passage is powerful:

> Eine schier unentrinnbare, wesenstiefe Unredlichkeit und Unfreiheit durchzieht die gesamte sogenannte Vergangenheitsbewältigung, die halbe Aufklärung und halbe Verherrlichung des nationellen, des deutschen Untergrunds in jedem von uns; diese trostlose Ambivalenz, diese nie zu erstattenden inneren Reparationskosten insgesamt könnten im Zusammenhang einer tatsächlichen Verschlechterung der materiellen Lebenslage sehr schnell dazu führen, daß die gekrümmte deutsche Seele sich heftig aufreckt, den unverdaulichen Ballast, das Phantasma einer untilgbaren Schuld einfach von sich schüttelt und sich vom Bösen kuriert, indem sie nun aufs neue das Böse will und tut. Und wieder zuerst damit beginnt, gegen die Fremden im Land ihr Gift zu versprühen. (PP 180f)

While Strauß portrays the total immersion of his compatriots in the present, and particularly in the perennial wash of the media, as a conscious attempt on their part to escape the grip of history – 'Nur der Tod der Geschichte selbst kann uns befreien, nur die Erledigung der Erinnerung durch die totale Gegenwart der Massenmedien, in der alles bloß Erscheinung, bloß ästhetisches Vorüberziehen ist' (PP 171) – he himself lives in a different world, his 'einziges wahres Erlebnis von Zeit ist das einer schwankenden Synchronität' (PP 97). The role of the poet and of the work of art is to resist the destruction of historical memory, for 'nichts könnte jetzt vorbildlicher wirken als die Begabung, mit *seiner* Zeit zu brechen und die Fesseln der totalen Gegenwart zu sprengen' (PP 105); the poet must evoke twilight zones in which immediate surroundings lose their harsh concrete presence (PP 116f) and so preserve his contemporaries 'von der totalen Diktatur der Gegenwart' (PP 111).[25]

The question of recollection deprivation is related to women in *Paare Passanten* (PP 49–53), albeit without reference to specific German dimensions – although the reference to the 'Großmutter, die erzählende Alte' (PP 53) must raise echoes of at least Günter Grass and the opening to *Die Blechtrommel*. The final words of this section, 'Wie wird es künftig sein, wenn die Mütter sich zu erinnern beginnen?', are less a question than a conundrum, and *Der junge Mann* is the appropriately open-edged response to it.

Here, in *Paare Passanten*, Strauß sketches an area of difference between men and women in relation to memory as a factor of creativity. It opens with the reported question (posed by a woman) of 'woher Frauen, künstlerisch tätige, ihre schöpferische Kraft ('Kreativität') beziehen', for motherhood turns women at one stroke from children into adults: 'Aber der Kindheit geraubt . . . das hieße doch: den Nährboden der Erinnerung zerstört. Und ohne Erinnerung sei keine Kreativität' (PP 50). Strauß himself questions this reasoning but does reflect on the differences he observes between male and female recollection. He has listened to women reminiscing: '[Sie] taten dies nicht im Sog eines Verlustempfindens . . . sie erinnerten sich *an* etwas, sie erinnerten es nicht und entsannen sich nicht.' This is superficial recall, and it causes him to reflect, 'Hat man wirklich den Frauen die Macht des Erinnerns gebrochen? Und waren es die geborenen Kinder, die das taten?' (PP 51).

A feminist might reply to this 'Mann hat'; Strauß is less direct. He seeks the answer in the role of women in the traditional family

---

25. The play *Trilogie des Wiedersehens* (1977) explores something of this idea: 'Wo ein Bild ist, hat die Wirklichkeit ein Loch. Wo ein Zeichen herrscht, hat das gezeichnete Ding nicht auch noch Platz' and 'jedes große Bild schafft sich sozusagen seine eigenen Realismus-Begriffe' (dtv, 3rd ed, Nördlingen, 1985, p. 42).

where, responsible for the education and care of the children, women had to look to the future and be completely selfless: 'Die Selbstlose war aber auch notwendig die Erinnerungslose, nur der Egozentriker erinnert sich stark.' Men are not robbed of childhood by their children; a man possesses 'in seinem Sohn gewiß noch mehr als in seiner Tochter das Zeug zur schönsten Selbstbesinnung'. His own father had tried to implant in him 'seine frühen Erinnerungen, seine verlorene Zeit' by dictating them to him – 'es war ein ausgesprochen autoritäres Erinnern' which drew him out of the sphere of the mother into his father's past (PP 51f).[26]

We are on precisely the ground Strauß delineates in *Der junge Mann*: 'er [wollte] meine Lenkung und Bildung nicht der Mutter überlassen, sondern drängte sie viel zu früh von mir und verschloß mich eifersüchtig in seiner Obhut' (DjM 21). The summary Strauß offers in *Paare Passanten* is cogent: 'So war Erinnern nicht nur tatsächlich eine Technik männlicher Kreativität, es war auch das Privileg der männlichen Vorherrschaft in der Familie. Der Geist der Herkunft wurde in erster Linie vom Vater dargestellt' (PP 52). And while this latter sentence is a clear link in the chain from *Rumor* to *Der junge Mann*, the passage that immediately precedes it places a first foot on the territory of what Strauß later terms a 'RomantischerReflexionsRoman' (DjM 15):[27]

> Und das begriffslose Kind erfuhr durch die herrschaftliche Temperament des väterlichen Erinnerns früh, allzu früh von der Kritik und dem eigentlichen Mangel der zuhandenen Wirklichkeit, deren reichliche Verlockungen es sich doch gerade erst zu erschließen begann . . . Im Ursprung der sentimentalen Kritik waren Sehnsucht und Erinnerung, Hoffnung und Heimweh noch in einem Glutkern miteinander verschmolzen. Später erst sonderte die abkühlende Vernunft die Elemente einer sozialaufklärerischen Vorwärts-Schau von denen eines vernunftwidrigen, 'kranken' Rückkehrdrangs – eine vielleicht niemals wahre Scheidung. (PP 52)

In the 'Einleitung' to *Der junge Mann* (DjM 7–16), the men who (quite incredibly) call to the author, '"Komm her! Erzähl uns was!"' are young, younger even than the author (in their mid-thirties); and yet – a result of drink and unemployment – they suffer

---

26. Strauß claims not to be an autobiographical writer (Hage, 'Schreiben ist eine Séance', p. 208), nevertheless these descriptions do seem to carry distinct autobiographical traits.
27. Cf. Henriette Herwig, '"RomantischerReflexionsRoman" oder erzählerisches Labyrinth?', in Radix (ed.), *Strauß lesen*, pp. 267–82.

from totally warped memories which yet seem typical for all Germans: 'Ihnen, den Trinkern und aus der Zeit Gerutschten, diesen einsamen, geschüttelten Männlein, die gar nichts wissen und stets behaupten, ihre besten Freunde seien alle bei Stalingrad gefallen, dreht sich ohnehin die Geschichte im Kopf herum, und sie sprechen einfach an einem deutschen Gemurmel mit, das, weit älter als sie selbst, ungestört unterhalb der Zeit dahinrinnt.' They are younger versions of Bekker, their perceptions have 'die subjektive Emphase, die leidgeborene, "kranke", mit der der Vater in seinen "besten Mannesjahren" sich erinnerte' (PP 53); their time is completely out of joint. They have lost even the inquisitive interest of children who ask the time simply to get a closer look at a stranger (DjM 7).[28] Everywhere time is the problem. The *Volk ohne Raum*, in common with the rest of humanity, have conquered space, but they are totally lost in time. Even the appearance of the 'Mittdreißiger' defies precise dating: they are locked into the 1950s by their quiffs and their jargon, and their faces wear 'die Maske eines unkenntlichen Alters' (DjM 8).

Such young men do not possess the qualities and vision Strauß needs as he seeks to break through the walls of history and contemporary media-bound society. If there is any potential force that can achieve this, it seems more likely to lie in their female coevals and juniors whose stories, when they are able to tell them, will be 'überlieferte oft mehr als selbsterlebte' (PP 53).

However, the shift to female perspectives alone will be insufficient – an additional shift in perception is needed to give a clear view. The inspiration Strauß draws on here is again outlined in *Paare Passanten*:

Eine Lehre kam uns (Entwurzelten) vom Orient herüber, daß zwar das 'Rad der Geschichte' nicht aufzuhalten und zurückzurollen sei, daß es aber sehr stabile menschliche Daseinsformen gebe, in denen das 'Rad der Geschichte' selbst eine vollkommen untergeordnete Rolle spielt. Und diese Lehre wurde uns gerade zu dem Zeitpunkt erteilt, da unsere eigene Kultur mitsamt ihrem Zwangssystem der wirtschaftlichen Überentwicklung und Überentfaltung in eine akute Krise der Geschichtsbesinnung geriet. Daher empfingen wir – mit dem besonderen Signal der Geiselnahme der Amerikaner – eine tief reichende Mahnung aus den politischen Tagesnachrichten: in der Herkunft des Menschen liegen große Epochen (und liegen möglicherweise große Epochen bereit zur Wiedergeburt), die sich durch Gleichmaß, Dauer, Überlieferung, Ebene, Einfachheit

28. The motif returns towards the end of the book when Ossia claims that even the curiosity about strangers has disappeared (DjM 370).

und Antimaterialismus von all dem unterscheiden, was die Dynamik des Industriezeitalters uns seit der Französischen Revolution als Geschichtsbild eingehämmert hat. Wenn der Aufstieg der Herkunft gerade dort sich vollzieht, wo das Eis der neueren Geschichte und des Fortschritts am dünnsten ist, dann mag dies vor allem mit den geistigen Traditionen des Islams zusammenhängen. (PP 181f)

It is an idea which bore fruit not only in *Der junge Mann*. *Der Park*, *Die Fremdenführerin* and *Diese Erinnerung an einen, der nur einen Tag zu Gast war* all depend for their effect on a sense of being transported in time and space to the cradle of Western culture with its balance of Graeco-Roman, Judaic and Arabic roots.

The above quotation from *Paare Passanten* hints at the spiritual traditions of Islam, immediately conjuring images of minarets and the timeless calling of the faithful to prayer. The minaret is the arrow of time set vertical; and it is not cut off at the base from its cultural roots. We are in the time-free, towered world of the intercalated tales of *Der junge Mann*. That the tower as a symbol has implications with roots also in other religions is a fact not missed by Strauß: his 'Turm der Deutschen' (DjM 77ff) is a veritable Tower of Babel, and there is plenty of evidence throughout the book to suggest the influence of the Graeco-Roman god Priapus. He may have stood model for the first story within the novel, 'Der stehende Liebespfeil', and he is certainly the forebear of the 'Dauererregung' (DjM 249) we encounter in the 'ruhmloses, giftiges Männlein' in 'Die Händlerin auf der hohen Kante' (DjM 126), of the 'starrer Vorsprung' in 'Die Frau meines Bruders' (DjM 161) and of the painful, 'priapische Säule' in 'Die Frau auf der Fähre' (DjM 240), where Leon, although apparently translocated both geographically and in time to areas close to those of Thomas Mann's *Joseph und seine Brüder*, to some extent apes Felix Krull – but without Krull's miraculous performance.

V

'Der stehende Liebespfeil', with which the first main section of *Der junge Mann* ends, shows two female and two male athletes waiting to be called into the arena; they are 'Ersatzleute am Rande des Sportfelds'. In an unmistakable reference to *Katz und Maus*, given the situation in terms both of the location and of the structure of the book, one of the men standing behind the women watches 'die auf- und absteigenden "Mäuse" ihrer Schulterblätter' (DjM 62). Just as

Grass had his narrator Pilenz set the cat on Mahlke's mouse and his *Novelle* in motion, so Strauß now sets his exploration of the lost roots and identity of contemporary West Germany in motion. His athletes are called onto the track, their task to set records by making up for lost time: 'Da begeben sich die leichten Nachläufer, die späten Ersatzleute hinunter zum Start und ziehen schlafwandelnd über die verschossene, mondhelle Aschenbahn Runde um Runde, erstreben Rekorde in einer Leistung, die nach dem Zeitmaß des Säumens berechnet wird' (DjM 64). Had they not been called to the start, the women would have turned their backs from the 'Hintermänner' and faced them – Strauß himself underlined the consequence: 'Diese aber sähen nicht länger über die weibliche Schulter dem Kampf entgegen – sie sähen dann nur noch *bis ans* Auge der Frau' (DjM 63). Backs, faces, eyes – the motifs are familiar. And already Strauß holds out the hope of escape from the fate of being frozen for ever into the stare that never penetrates below the surface; he sets them off on the round after round of the *Reigen* that makes up his novel. Significantly, it is the women who are now in the forefront; it is the women who lead off in their encircling movement to break the spell both of the horizontal trajectory of the 'Zeitpfeil' and of the vertical stasis of the 'Liebespfeil'.

It can be no surprise, then, that what follows is predominantly an exploration of the shape and shaping of contemporary West German society which seeks to uncover the perspectives and powers that forced women into the position they are in. Even in the sections of the novel that are apparently about men or are narrated by men, the ultimate focus is the fate of women. This pattern is obvious in 'Der Wald', the story of the 'Bankkauffrau', a modern young woman successful in business who finds herself in a nightmare world of a German forest laden with biblical allusion. It is less obvious in the next section, 'Die Siedlung (Die Gesellschaftslosen)', where the first-person narrator is obviously male, but is never mentioned by name (unless the reference on page 160 to 'die Pracht der letzten Dinge' is seen both as an oblique hint at his identity and his ability to identify with the other gender),[29] and where the whole is an exploration of a future world in which the male-dominated society of today has been replaced by a community in which the

29. Strauß cleverly interchanges and neutralizes gender using pronouns; the strange 'Frau meines Bruders' becomes 'wer' then 'er' and later 'das Wesen' and 'es' (DjM 161f). In the scene where the older Mero seduces Leon (before they have said a single word to each other), the roles are completely reversed: she dictates the stages of love-making, he experiences a female orgasm (DjM 225ff). See also Juliet Wigmore, pp. 214–6 above, and Moray McGowan, pp. 271–8 above.

qualities of the right side of the brain, the female side, hold exclusive sway. When the book moves on to its main section, 'Die Terrasse (Belsazar. Fabeln am Morgen nach dem Fest)', the society suspended on the threshold of both the palace and the new day is unambiguously that of contemporary West Germany dislocated in time and cultural setting. Four of the seven figures here are female, and while two of the women hardly contribute to the discussion and the 'fables', two of the men ('der Wieder-Nietzsche' and 'der Moderne') are shown to be locked in intellectual conflict, virtually cancelling each other (DjM 181–218), and Leon, clearly identified again, tells a tale in which the liberation of men is gained indirectly from a male act of will, the immediate outcome of which is the integration of the whole woman ('Die Frau, auf der Fähre'). This is followed by one of the two stories which have a female first-person narrator, 'Die Geschichte der Almut' – arguably the most significant section in the book as a whole. Just how significant is indicated by its effect on the men: 'Jeder von uns drei Männern, die wir unsere Bekundungen bereits vorgebracht hatten, erkannte nun wohl, daß diese Frau ihn an Tiefe des Drangsals und Klugheit des Gefühls zweifellos übertraf. Wenngleich sie auch nur von einem einzigen traurigen und unabänderlich traurigen Standpunkt aus ihre Geschichte erzählt hatte. Doch in ihrem Nachhall konnten wir vorerst nur schweigen' (DjM 193).

It is the men who are silenced – and in the silence the voice of the young Yossica at last makes itself heard. It is a 'sachter Gesang'; not a song complete in itself, but 'eine vor sich hin gesungene, eintönige Melodie, gleichsam ohne Anfang und ohne Ziel', a poem in which she calls to her friend to seek her out. She is 'wie geschaffen / Für den Ausschau haltenden Mann!' (DjM 193). Leon, although Almut has perceptively described him as the 'Erotiker aus Entsagung' (DjM 250), had presented himself as the 'Säumiger Sucher' (DjM 182), and it is he who must find and rescue Yossica from her fate as a flower head without a stem, in need of a little soil, a new beginning. Yossica, the representative of the younger generation, breaks through all the fixations, she is 'das kostbar Wenige . . . nur noch Antlitz und Stimme' (DjM 316). It is her call which reaches Leon the moment before the cortège of West German society, the product and prisoner of a past which is not yet its past, following the coffin containing the 'Kadaver des größten Frevlers und schlimmsten Deutschen' (DjM 296) sweeps the other postwar figures along with it, leaving him caught for a moment in the balance. He is forced to leave his vantage point, but he is now aware that he must avoid being drawn into the centre of the maelstrom, becoming again 'untergemischt' (DjM 305).

It is during Leon's escape and search for Yossica, which reads like a heady mix of *Dungeons and Dragons*, *Pacman* and *Star Wars*,[30] when his passage seems about to be blocked by a slow-moving giant tortoise with 'der schlimmste Deutsche' on its back (DjM 309), that he does something West Germany has not yet been able to do: dodges by and races on faster than ever. Then when he reaches a victory arch only to find himself in another hallucination, he loses all composure – breaking out of himself and out of the magic cage: 'Nun ertrug ich's nicht länger. Ich kam außer Fassung. Ich tobte in meinem Strahlenkäfig, ich schrie und trat aus gegen das Holodrom. Und wollte es nicht weichen, dann eben weg mit mir! Lieber der leibliche Tod als diese synthetische Ewigkeit!' (DjM 313). The way is clear not only for the discovery of Yossica but also for his self-discovery and his rejection of the world of the post-modern tower. 'Lieber der leibliche Tod als diese synthetische Ewigkeit!' might be the vicarious cry of the poet for his people.

Yossica, when he finds her, might have been plucked from Grass or Goethe. She is a modern 'Kopfgewächs' desperately in need of rebirth, but her eyes have distinctly classical powers: 'Dann traf mich ihr tiefer, lebensdunkler, unbeirrbarer Blick und durchdrang mich ruhig. Wir traten langsam einer aus des andern tiefster Erinnerung hervor.' He kisses her mouth, closing his hitherto unsparingly open eyes. 'Ich schloß die Augen . . . Ich war der Aufstehend-Aufatmende; einer, der sich nach langer, langer Zeit von seiner Warte erhob, vom Dasitzen losgekommen und von seinen noch ungetanen Schritten unwiderstehlich angezogen. Keine Absicht, nur Gesicht' (DjM 388).

Every word is in place – Leon now has sight, he has vision, his wait is over, the future beckons: he will be able to guide (significantly as 'Anleiter und Ratgeber' (DjM 362), not as 'Führer') the much younger Yossica, who has been thrown out of the garden (DjM 322) but who can sing all the better for that – her voice now carries further (DjM 323).

What then follows in the book is the final break with Ossia, the name by which Alfred Weigert has become famous. This final section, 'Der Turm', includes a long review and discussion of the man's art and attitudes which can be interpreted broadly as Strauß's reflections on the state of contemporary writing. Ossia is past it; Leon has moved on. So much is clear. It is equally clear that Ossia

---

30. Strauß refers explicitly to the latter two (DjM 9, 366, 383) and to *Monopoly* (DjM 218). It is possible that the computer game exercises a much wider influence over the form of the novel than can be explored here.

is caught in a world starved of real humanity and that he is incapable of progressing beyond the stage of drafting plans; he is suspended in constant, mutually exclusive beginnings (DjM 378). It is less clear precisely what or whom Ossia himself represents: the very name is a musical term which allows the performer to designate an alternative section or passage – perhaps inviting the reader to see Ossia as a symbol for Strauß himself, or for some other figure, possibly the generation of Böll and Grass.[31]

When he leaves the world of Ossia, now no longer the old Alfred Weigert, Leon is simply glad. Strauß does not offer a manifesto for the future; it would ill become him to do so when he has consistently rejected all forms of *Gleichschaltung* throughout his work. What he has done is much more challenging than this. On the way, he has dared to suggest it is time to bury Hitler, and, if this cannot be done effectively, he has shown that the Antic Hitler can be circumvented. And he has set a goal that women be given the chance of self-fulfilment in future, typically encapsulating this in a striking image. In the hotel Leon had watched a mother and daughter skating on the artificial pond; they represent something West German women have been denied. Leon's attention focuses on the mother:

> Dies waren wohl keine Landsleute von mir. Aufrecht und weich, bot die junge Frau den Anblick einer modernen bürgerlichen Schönheit, an der Stil und Körpergeist als das Erbe einer langen, unzerstörten Familiengeschichte hervortraten. Weder Puppe noch Dame, sondern eine rätselhaft gelöste Erscheinung, in der äußere Anmut, Herkunft, weiblicher Stolz sich unbeschwert vereinten, so wie es in unserem tiefbehinderten Land wohl niemals möglich wäre. (DjM 384)

Thus Strauß reminds us of the object of his explorations in *Der junge Mann*, the nature and possible consequences of the 'Behinderung'.

VI

Strauß does seem to offer an answer which lies in the re-creation of

---

31. There is much about Ossia, who 'tingelt' through society (DjM 335) and collects 'Augenblicke' (DjM 360), to suggest Hans Schnier, and Strauß acknowledged that Böll impressed him (Hage, 'Schreiben ist eine Séance', p. 201). We must not forget the ideas Strauß explored in 'Theorie der Drohung' and which recur here (self-quotation); in his play *Kalldewey Farce* (1981) he also provides alternative endings.

a healthy relationship between male and female, and he shows how this had hitherto been precluded by male prejudices, fetishes and adolescent pudeur. If these can be overcome, women will be in a better position to find a new balance which will set them at peace with themselves. Strauß seeks to aid the removal of these obstacles to women, which arise out of and also give rise to disabilities in men, by exposing them. Thus the most damning depiction of male prejudice is associated with a character called Reppenfries, who is described as a 'Denker-Sanitäter' and is accused by his wife's sister of simply taking things apart without being able to put them together again; she refers to him as 'ein Wieder-Nietzsche, ein Abermals- und Nochmals-Nietzsche, ein Nietzsche, wahrhaftig von der allertraurigsten Gestalt!' (DjM 199). These words link him to the passage from *Paare Passanten* about Turkish *Gastarbeiter* and to Yossica's words about the 'Nazis' of the younger generation. Significantly, it is Reppenfries who hypnotized her. Here, misogyny triumphs, blinding him to the message of Yossica's words and leading him, when his wife suggests he might do some real first-aid work and free them of his 'krankhafte Lästerreden', to round on her with the most soul-crushing words in the book:

'Du bist', versetzte ihr kalt der Sanitäter, 'nicht würdig der Sprache, die dir über die Lippen kommt. Dir fehlt im tiefsten die moralische Berechtigung, in deutscher Sprache zu sprechen. Welchen Nutzen hat es denn gehabt, daß du mir so lange zuhören durftest? Ich bin es doch wohl nicht gewesen, der frech und unwissend dahergeredet hat. *Ich* erkenne die Autoritäten an. Ich gehorche dem größeren Geist. Ich folge dem, dessen Erfahrung reicher ist als die meine. Du aber? Du willst dich *selber* behaupten, doch damit behauptest du leider Gottes nichts Besonderes.' (DjM 200)

And Strauß does not hesitate to point up the effect of this monstrous assault. It brings to her eyes 'der Einbruch des Unversöhnlichen, aber auch blankes Entsetzen, Zukunftsangst' and to her lips the completely false expression 'Du bist unausleidlich' – but her whole soul is packed into it. Small wonder that Strauß had to invent a new term, given the enormity of what he had just set down on paper.[32]

The other divide between men and women, the one which is potentially superable (if only by several sessions of sex therapy), is

---

32. Strauß does something similar in *Paare Passanten* (p. 46): 'ein unheimlich schönes Mädchen, das alle Jungens ganz aufreißend (!) finden.'

represented by Leon, who is locked into a state of priapism because he cannot reconcile the public eroticism of the female back and the inhibiting purity displayed in private by the female face and eyes: 'Dürfen wir überhaupt von wahrer Vereinigung sprechen, solange sich unsere Vergnügungen vor der Schwelle der Keuschheit abspielen, solange das Antlitz als Wärter des Rückens, die Huldigung als Zensur der Lust empfunden wird?' (DjM 246f). We know that Leon's state can be overcome because he does triumph over it as a result of his experiences in the book. And as he progresses, he is able, by an act of will in each case, to help two female figures to a better future. His last glimmer of willpower (DjM 236) leads to his breaking Mero's hold on him and she, segmented by name as well as by nature, at last finds peace with her younger self. Yossica, also because of an act of defiance on Leon's part (DjM 313), recovers from the devastations of her severed state.

The changes in Mero and Yossica indicate the route to salvation for the female characters; it leads through stages of rejuvenation and rebirth. One figure stands out here as the exception: Almut, whose story as she herself points out, is realistic: 'So will ich Ihnen . . . anschaulich aus einer Gegend des Lebendigen berichten' (DjM 250). The contrast between her tale and the story of the 'Bankkauffrau', which plays almost in its entirety in the mythic realm of dream, is instructive, for the reborn 'Bankkauffrau' is in the end united with a complementary male partner. Similarly, Leon will find his appropriate female companion not in Almut, from whom he wanted a response (DjM 221), but in the much younger Yossica.

At the end of her story the 'Bankkauffrau' is able to draw on all the experience she has gathered during her immersion in 'Gleiche Zeit' in the womb-like world of the German forest. Thus her newly created memory and identity (she has been born again) carry an awareness of the dual nature of the 'Besitzer der Deutschen', his kind eyes and his ferocious, moustached carp yaw, which enables her to tame the nightmare hunter-lycanthrope and ensures that her liaison with him (now revealed as Wolf-Dieter Gründe) works. 'So befand sie sich denn im Besitz der beiden höchsten Mittel, die dem Menschen verbleiben, um sich bis zuletzt gegen sein unabwendbares Schicksal zu erheben: die verschwenderische Liebe und die unerschrockene Tatkraft' (DjM 107). Together they can realize his plans for the future – which she can guide because, in her dream, she has been there before (DjM 106).

How different is the linear story of Almut, who, like her generation – and it is Strauß's own – is cut off from the past by the poor restoration of the 1950s,[33] lacking any real identity and strength of her own. Almut's apprenticeship to her father, a restorer of local (Regensburg) wall-paintings and frescoes, had hidden her 'erste Mädchenblüte' under 'dem groben, männlichen Arbeitszeug' (DjM 255). He had made her aware of the 'Augen der Vergangenheit' (DjM 257) but had died prematurely, leaving her to face the labyrinth alone, her 'Einweihung' incomplete (DjM 259).

Her lack of identity has its effect on her private life. She is completely subservient and her 'fiancé' makes her 'eine unwerte Person' (DjM 267). Strauß is developing the image of a second-class citizen. Clearly he has the first principle of the *Grundgesetz* in mind ('Die Würde des Menschen ist unantastbar'), placing his Almut very close to Heinrich Böll's Katharina Blum. We are dealing with images, the dignity of the individual and the law.

Almut is brought before the courts because she attacks an American abstract painting with a pair of nail-scissors. The image it presented had seemed to her to threaten her very existence. The law has no category it can easily apply here; it attempts to place her outside its purview – and succeeds. It cannot comprehend the nature of the existential challenge she faced and therefore tries to demonstrate her 'Schuld*unfähigkeit*' (DjM 271), in the end letting her go unpunished for social reasons – she has lost her job, and her fiancé has ditched her. Nobody takes her seriously. At this point she becomes involved with the modern team of art-restorers mentioned above (p. 291). Eventually she challenges their lack of awareness of the 'Augen der Vergangenheit', and they, who recognize her problem as a lack of awareness of her own 'Würde' (DjM 276f), give her a simple task to perform on her own – the restoration of a fresco that had been originally restored in the 1950s to the wrong model. Up on the scaffolding, she suddenly feels herself to be 'eine Frau bald in ihren mittleren Jahren, zum ersten Mal vollkommen allein an einer solch erhöhten Stelle' (DjM 287). However, her experiences count for nothing – even the apparent rejuvenation of the return to the years of her girlhood when she first joined the team had given her nothing of lasting value. Once she has cleaned off the 1950s image she feels faint: 'Wie ein erloschener Spiegel sah es mich an! Es war weg. Vor mir war nichts – und ich war nichts' (DjM 288). The dream she then experiences does nothing to help: she sees herself reflected in the eye of a giant Kafkaesque ladybird – 'eine entsetzliche, zerstückelte Gestalt' (DjM

---

33. Julian Preece, pp. 322 and 326 below, draws our attention to Grass's views on 'die falschen Fuffziger'.

290). She capitulates and ends up sitting outside a café in the 'Nebenstraße der Nebenstraßen' looking at the sooty shadow left behind on a wall by an old explosion (DjM 292).

There is a poignancy as well as a realism about the story of Almut, 'die Niedergeschlagene', which is not found elsewhere in the book. She stands as a deeply sympathetic symbol of the visible effects of the most recent past on the present. Strauß depicts a member of a *verlorene Generation* defined as much by sex as by age. He does it in the name of the future, in order that in Yossica's generation the wounds of the past might be healed. He does it also to save a society which 'ernährt sich vom Tod ihres größten Frevlers' (DjM 181) before the final *stretta* (DjM 119), the final 'Kehraus' (DjM 302) brings the round-dance of West Germany's destiny to the catastrophic end Strauß fears.

VII

Strauß seems also to hint at the end of an era in art; Leon Pracht puts the world of Ossia behind him. In his own work, Strauß moved on immediately from the 'RomantischerReflexionsRoman', a truly poetic novel, to a long poem, *Diese Erinnerung*, which might reward comparison with aspects of Eliot or Valéry. However, even here, as has been suggested above, he remains the poet who is 'Sänger' and 'Wächter' of things German. The poem contains a nostalgic backward glance which yet holds out hope for the future as it highlights an aspect of the *unbewältigte Vergangenheit* not addressed directly in the earlier works – the division of Germany.

Bin ich denn nicht geboren in meinem Vaterland?

'Jena vor uns im lieblichen Tale' – sah ich's nicht früh
und ging mit dem Vater am Ufer von Saale und Unstrut?

Wann war das und wo?

Kein Deutschland gekannt zeit meines Lebens.
Zwei fremde Staaten nur, die mir verboten,
je im Namen eines Volkes der Deutsche zu sein.
Soviel Geschichte, um so zu enden?

Man spüre einmal: das Herz eines Kleist und
die Teilung des Lands. Man denke doch: welch ein Reunieren,
wenn einer, in uns, die Bühne der Geschichte aufschlüg!

> Vielleicht, wer deutsch ist, lernt sich ergänzen.
> Und jedes Bruchstück Verständigung
> gleicht einer Zelle im nationalen Geweb,
> die immer den Bauplan des Ganzen enthält.
> (E 47f)

This is no banner-carrier or prophet of *Wiedervereinigung*; his choice of 'Reunieren' is deliberate, not clumsy.[34] Just as Strauß the novelist anticipated so much of the *Historikerstreit* and associated developments, here Strauß the poet born in Naumburg an der Saale (where Nietzsche spent the years of his decline in his sister's care) anticipates the sentiments of a son of Halle an der Saale – Hans-Dietrich Genscher: 'Die DDR ist der Teil Deutschlands, in dem in Halle an der Saale mein Geburtshaus steht, in dem ich aufgewachsen bin, in dem ich zur Schule ging, in dem ich die Universitäten in Halle und Leipzig besuchte – hier ist mein Vater, hier sind meine Großeltern begraben – hier habe ich meine Heimat.' The speech goes on to address the issue of the division of Germany: 'Das Verhältnis der beiden deutschen Staaten zueinander ist bestimmt durch die gemeinsame Geschichte, die gemeinsame Sprache, die Mitverantwortung für das Überleben der Menschheit.' These are feelings, one senses, from which Strauß would not dissent. And we might conclude that Mr Genscher would identify with Botho Strauß in his poetic endeavours, since towards the end of his speech he speaks of responsibility:

> Unter größerer Unsicherheit handeln und für größere Sicherheit sorgen – das ist 'Das Prinzip Verantwortung', das der Philosoph Hans Jonas als 'Versuch einer Ethik für die technologische Zivilisation' vorgelegt hat. 'Noch für das Unbekannte im voraus mitzuhaften', so sagt Jonas, 'ist bei der letztlichen Ungewißheit der Hoffnung gerade eine Bedingung handelnder Verantwortung: eben das, was man den Mut zur Verantwortung nennt.' Diese Haftung gegenüber allen künftigen Generationen müssen wir akzeptieren.[35]

The novels of Botho Strauß in the 1980s leave us in no doubt that he has shouldered his responsibilities for future generations unequivocally and consistently.

---

34. Rolf Michaelis ('Königsweg oder Holzweg', *Die Zeit*, 21 June 1985, p. 45) takes Strauß severely to task for his choice of vocabulary in the poem.
35. Speaking in Potsdam in June 1988 (*Bulletin*, Presse- und Informationsamt der Bundesregierung, no. 83, 1988, pp. 785–91; here pp. 785, 786, 791).

−19−

The Novels of Patrick Süskind: A Phenomenon of the 1980s

STUART PARKES

In his introduction to *The Name of the Rose* dated 5 January 1980, Umberto Eco compares the intellectual climate of that time with the atmosphere of ten years earlier. He no longer sees 'a widespread conviction that one should write only out of a commitment to the present, in order to change the world.' It is now possible for 'the man of letters (restored to his loftiest dignity) . . . [to] write out of pure love of writing'.[1]

It may well be that the work of Patrick Süskind arises from a similar feeling. It certainly contrasts with that of previously dominating figures like Böll, Grass and Walser, who, despite their uneasiness in that role, must ultimately be regarded as writers who, at least at times, have hoped to influence if not change the world. In fact, a considerable proportion of German literature in the 1960s and 1970s must be regarded as 'committed' in the sense that Eco uses the term, including the work of Michael Ende, the name that dominated the best-seller lists of the Federal Republic in the early 1980s until the arrival of Patrick Süskind. Ende's *Die unendliche Geschichte* is certainly far removed from social or critical realism but in its attitude to technical rationality, it can easily be linked with the developing alternative and Green movements of the late 1970s and early 1980s.

In the case of the kind of committed writers mentioned above, the critic is often able to refer to articles, interviews or simply signatures under manifestos or resolutions in the attempt to interpret his subject. This is not possible with Süskind. Despite (or because of) his success, he has been unwilling to give interviews or utter an opinion on particular subjects. The biographical details that are generally available are also few. He is the son of the late W(ilhelm) E(manuel) Süskind, the writer and journalist best

---

1. U. Eco, *The Name of the Rose*, London, 1984, p. 5.

known for his collection of essays on language *Aus dem Wörterbuch des Unmenschen*. His penchant for French settings can be explained by his having studied history in Aix-en-Provence. Beside this lack of biographical information, there are few minor publications to refer to. A prose piece 'Das Vermächtnis des Maitre Mussard' consists of the first-person death-bed writings of Mussard, a historical figure mentioned in Rousseau's *Confessions*, who is suffering from the delusion that the world is being taken over by sea shells.[2] There is a connection here with the novels, namely the theme of the individual ruled by an obsession, as will be seen later. Otherwise, Süskind has worked as a scriptwriter, particularly on the television series about a Munich gossip columnist *Kir Royal*, in which Franz Xaver Kroetz played the major role (and incidentally expressed himself happy to be reaching a larger audience than he had ever done as a dramatist). Finally, it is interesting to note that Süskind, on the evidence of an article that appeared in 1986, is unwilling to reveal literary influences. It is entitled 'Amnesie in litteris', by which he means the inability to recall anything he has read. The tone of the piece is ironic and it is, of course, impossible to take the claim of amnesia too seriously. What is more interesting, however, is the scepticism shown towards reading as an enlightening, educative activity. Süskind refers to his 'Resignation über die Vergeblichkeit allen Strebens nach Erkenntnis'[3] and is only willing to concede that literature may affect consciousness 'auf so unmerklich-osmotische Weise, daß es des Prozesses nicht gewahr wird'.[4] This too is clearly far removed from the conventional conception of the committed writer.

One is, therefore, forced to concentrate almost exclusively on Süskind's main works, of which there are three, the two prose works *Das Parfum* and *Die Taube* and the play *Der Kontrabaß*, which preceded them and was a considerable theatrical success in the early 1980s, enjoying a production at the National Theatre. Although it is not strictly relevant to a discussion of the novel in the 1980s it is worthy of a brief mention, as it shares the theme of the isolated individual already referred to. It is in fact a play for a single character, the double bass player of the title. He is unhappy with the instrument he plays: 'Der Kontrabaß ist das scheußlichste, plumpeste, unelegranteste Instrument, das je erfunden wurde. Ein

---

2. P. Süskind, 'Das Vermächtnis des Maitre Mussard', *Neue Deutsche Hefte*, no. 149, 1976, pp. 62–79.
3. P. Süskind, 'Amnesie in litteris', *L80*, no. 37, March 1986, p. 32.
4. Ibid., p. 34.

Waldschrat von Instrument.'[5] Moreover, he finds the security of his existence in the world of subsidized music boring, an interesting contrast to the worrying insecurity that afflicts many artists in Britain. Generally, he comes across as a fairly crude figure – the phrase 'mir ist das wurscht' provides a leitmotif within his complaints – and in many respects he seems a kindred spirit of Qualtinger's Herr Karl. Particularly revealing is his attitude towards women. He is convinced of their inferiority: 'Die Frau spielt ja in der Musik eine untergeordnete Rolle'[6] but is still plagued by sexual fantasies. He links his frustrations with the instrument he plays: when entertaining women in his small flat, he is inhibited by its bulky presence. Because of its size it cannot be hidden anywhere. To sum up, *Der Kontrabaß* is an amusing, well-sustained piece of theatre which in its concentration on an unhappy individual prefigures the two major prose works.

The first of these, *Das Parfum*, which appeared in 1985 and quickly established Süskind as a best-selling writer, deals with a very different kind of individual from the frustrated musician. It is, as the sub-title succinctly puts it 'Die Geschichte eines Mörders'. The plot can be outlined very quickly: Jean-Baptiste Grenouille is a man who gives off no odour and is distinctly unattractive to his fellow human beings. At the same time, he is blessed with a highly developed sense of smell. Because of this he determines to become a perfumer. The novel largely recounts the foul deeds he commits in pursuit of his ambition to create the perfect perfume, for which he needs to distil the natural scent of beautiful young virgins. These girls are the victims of his murders. When he applies the ultimate perfume to himself, he is initially able to make himself loved but is finally torn limb from limb by a mob of criminals who are overcome by the power of his aroma.

The first thing to say about *Das Parfum* is that it is in no way a psychological study of crime or obsession in the sense that such a study might concentrate on the role of childhood or other formative influences in the development of a criminal personality. Grenouille is presented as an inhuman monster from birth. That he survives his mother's attempts to get rid of him and that she is executed for this only underlines his inhuman nature and the malign influence he has on all who come into contact with him. Rather than seeking to explain, Süskind expresses Grenouille's wickedness only in literary terms by the image of the 'Zeck' (tick),

---

5. P. Süskind, *Der Kontrabaß*, Zurich, 1984, p. 49.
6. Ibid., p. 43.

comparing him throughout to such a creature. As a monster who simply commits evil deeds, Grenouille is a product of Süskind's literary imagination just as much as nineteenth-century creations like Frankenstein arose out of the Romantic imagination. Indeed, the idea of a man without an odour is reminiscent of Chamisso's creation of Peter Schlemihl – the man without a shadow. This unreality is underlined by the factor already referred to: that a horrible end is invariably the fate of all those whose path Grenouille crosses, not least of those who seek to exploit his skills. For instance, when he has left the employment of the Parisian perfumer Baldini, whom he has helped to riches, the man's house collapses into the Seine before he can enjoy any of these gains. Such an incident clearly belongs to the world of the fairy-tale or horror story.

By contrast, the second prose work *Die Taube* has more in common with *Der Kontrabaß*, where the musician's difficulties are explicable in social and psychological terms. In this work, the isolated individual is the doorman at a Paris bank. He is a totally passive figure who wishes to avoid all the unforeseeable challenges of life by following an unchanging routine both in his tiny flat and at his work. This plan is dashed by the arrival of the pigeon of the title. The bird has somehow got into the block of flats where the porter Jonathan Noel lives and, not least because of the mess it makes, represents to him a chaotic interruption to the pattern of his life. This unexpected event is of course reminiscent of the world of the *Novelle*, although Süskind does not classify his work as belonging to that genre. Suffice it to say that the pigeon's arrival is enough to make Noel run away in fear. He has an unhappy day at his work, tearing his trousers – another unprecedented event – before seeking refuge in a cheap hotel. There is, however, a kind of happy-end to *Die Taube*. Noel finally feels able to return to his flat and when he does, there are no traces of the pigeon's visit left.

Die Taube concentrates on the mentality of a person who has decided to opt out of life but is challenged by its threatening manifestations. In addition to the pigeon, there is the disorderly figure of the clochard who shits in public. As with the pigeon, shit is a symbol of the disorder Noel fears. Süskind, however, does not just express Noel's distress through symbols. He concentrates on the feelings of his protagonist in a generally convincing way. He does this at times by using a style comparable to that of Martin Walser, whose novels abound with descriptions of inadequate characters. The following description of Noel is a good example of the effective way Süskind portrays his character: 'Er kam sich wie verkrüppelt vor, wie die Karikatur eines Wachmanns, wie ein Spottbild seiner selbst. Er verachtete sich. Er haßte sich in diesen Stunden.'[7] Here Süskind uses a direct style, very different from the more expansive style of *Das Parfum*, which will be considered below. What is more, he advances social and psychological reasons for Noel's condition. During the war, he had to flee from the Germans who killed his parents. He was brought up by an uncle, who in turn forced him into military service in Indo-China and then into an unsuccessful marriage. It is these experiences that have led him to the conclusion 'daß auf die Menschen kein Verlaß sei und daß man nur leben könne, wenn man sie sich vom Leibe hielt' (p. 8). In an original, if somewhat precious, compound Süskind describes him as a 'Marionettenmenschmaschine' (p. 84). These childhood events are recalled later. On the day Noel's mother was taken away, there was a great thunderstorm and a similar storm occurs following his flight from his flat. After it has abated he plucks up the courage to return. It is to be regarded, therefore, as a purifying event that, at least in part, releases him from his trauma. Although the attempt by Süskind to introduce a psychological dimension is beyond dispute, the question of how far such a release is credible remains. A number of critics have raised this point[8] and it must be conceded that this aspect of the book seems too brief and simplistic. Its strength lies rather in the portrayal of Noel as an obsessed individual.

Even if it is somewhat unsatisfactory, there is a clear social and political dimension to *Die Taube*. Whether *Das Parfum* possesses anything similar is without doubt the major question that has to be asked of the novel, so that it can finally be decided if Süskind is in any sense a committed writer. The relevance of perfumes and smells – Süskind dwells at length on the stench of eighteenth-century Paris – to the present age when unpleasant smells are suppressed by deodorants and other products of the chemical industry was pointed out by reviewers at the time of its first appearance.[9] As part of this theme, Süskind makes great play of the

---

7. P. Süskind, *Die Taube*, Zurich, 1987, p. 75. Page references in the text are to this edition.
8. See R. Krämaer-Badoni, 'Gewitter des Unheils, Gewitternder Heilung', *Die Welt*, 28 March 1987.
9. See M. Fischer, 'Ein Stänkerer gegen die Deo-Zeit', *Der Spiegel*, 4 March 1985. It is also interesting to note that a history of smell was published by the French historian Alain Corbin a few years before *Das Parfum*: A. Corbin, *Le Miasme et la Jonquille. L'odorat et l'imaginaire social, 18e – 20e siècles*, Aubier-Montagne, 1982 (English-language edition: *The Foul and the Fragrant: Odour and the French Social Imagination*, trans. by Miriam Kochan, Leamington Spa, 1986).

two meanings of the phrase 'jemanden nicht riechen können' when describing the inhuman monster Grenouille who gives off no odour. It is said that during his childhood other children could never 'riechen' him, whilst the final set of murders he commits follow the recognition that he cannot 'riechen' himself. At this level, *Das Parfum* would seem to be little more than ironic poking fun at one of the foibles of the present time. There remains, however, the question of the hideous murders and whether they are meant to recall the hideous murders of history, most particularly recent history.

There is certainly a case for interpreting *Das Parfum* in this way. It is Grenouille's ambition to become the greatest perfumer of all time, an aim that echoes the characterization of Hitler as the greatest leader of all time. One of the major scenes in the novel invokes the phenomenon of mass hysteria, which has been such a feature of modern totalitarian societies. When Grenouille is finally captured and about to be executed for his crimes, he covers himself with his ultimate perfume, the product he has distilled from the bodies of his victims. The result is that the assembled crowds not only enter upon an unbridled orgy, but also that they begin to feel love for the person whose blood they were shouting for a few moments earlier. If this is reminiscent of the world of mass rallies and the like, then the descriptions of Grenouille's motives recall the personalities of modern-day dictators. He holds his fellow human beings in contempt, not least in the moment of his greatest triumph. Thus it is said of him at the planned execution: 'Grenouille stand und lächelte . . . Aber es war kein Lächeln, sondern ein häßliches zynisches Grinsen, das auf seinen Lippen lag und das seinen ganzen Triumph und seine ganze Verachtung widerspiegelte.'[10] What is more, Grenouille is an ascetic, who in his obsession has no time for the normal pleasures of the world.

Another interesting point is that Süskind frequently expresses Grenouille's obsession in aesthetic terms. It is said to be the search for an aesthetic principle, whilst the process of distilling the victims' odour is found particularly satisfying by Grenouille because it represents 'eine künstlerische Technik' (p. 273). Is Süskind then writing allegorically about politics and art? Again one might think of the case of Hitler, the failed painter turned politician. However, in the final analysis, it is difficult to take any political dimension too seriously. Reviewing the novel for *Neue Deutsche Hefte*, Jürgen P. Wallmann says that *Das Parfum* might find two types of reader,

---

10. P. Süskind, *Das Parfum*, Zurich, 1985, p. 304.

those who just want entertainment and those who see a political allegory. He concludes: 'Auf ihre Kosten kommen sie beide.'[11] Against this, it could be argued that a political or any other kind of statement in a work of art should not be quite so arbitrary or gratuitous, should go beyond a series of vague allusions. Comparing *Das Parfum* to *Die Blechtrommel*, as a number of critics do, Joachim Kaiser rightly notes a lack of what he calls 'Menschliches' and 'Verbindliches'.[12]

If critics have been at odds about the content of *Das Parfum*, there has been general agreement about its stylistic qualities. What is immediately remarkable is the way the story is told by an omniscient narrator. There is no trace of the phenomenon of the unreliable or inadequate narrator that became a feature of so many works of the 1960s, for instance, Johnson's *Das dritte Buch über Achim* or Grass's *Hundejahre*. *Das Parfum* begins in accordance with the techniques of the traditional story-teller: 'Im achtzehnten Jahrhundert lebte in Frankreich ein Mann . . .'. This sovereign style continues throughout, with Süskind displaying total control of his material. Given the all-knowing, somewhat aloof narrative viewpoint, it is not surprising that with the exception of one interpolated dialogue there is little direct speech, although it must be pointed out that this is understandable in the light of Grenouille's uncommunicative character. Instead, the novel is marked by a series of virtuoso linguistic *tours de force*, one example of which is the use of adjectives in this passage describing a perfume created by Grenouille: 'Es war keine Spur ordinär. Absolut klassisch, rund und harmonisch war es. Und trotzdem faszinierend neu. Es war frisch aber nicht reißerisch. Es war blumig, ohne schmalzig zu sein. Es besaß Tiefe, eine herrliche, haftende, schwelgerische, dunkelbraune Tiefe – und war doch kein bißchen überladen oder schwülstig' (p. 79). This passage consists essentially of a series of antitheses, marked by the use of assonance (frisch, reißerisch: blumig, schmalzig) and alliteration (herrlich, haftende). There is a whole series of different ways of expressing contrast 'trotzdem', 'aber nicht', 'ohne zu', 'doch'. Twice adjectives come in threes – the classic number.

At the same time, there is an ironic dimension to this passage in the way it deliberately seems to recall the language of advertising. Several of the adjectives, for instance 'frisch', 'blumig' and 'herrlich', obviously belong to the vocabulary of advertising, although only in the phrase 'faszinierend neu' does the overall tone lapse into the

---

11. J. P. Wallmann, 'Patrick Süskind, *Das Parfum*', *Neue Deutsche Hefte*, no. 186, 1985, p. 384.
12. J. Kaiser, 'Von Flottheit und Phantasie', *Süddeutsche Zeitung*, 28 March 1985.

banality of the typical advertisement. Otherwise, Süskind is playfully modifying and enhancing a specific type of linguistic register.

The overall sense of the author's control can be seen in the following passage, which describes the commercial skills of Grenouille's employer in the town of Grasse – a widow: 'Mit bewegenden Worten schilderte sie den Herren ihre Situation als alleinstehende Frau, ließ sich Angebote machen, verglich die Preise, seufzte und verkaufte endlich – oder verkaufte nicht. Parfümierte Pomade, kühl gelagert, hielt sich lange' (p. 223). The change of direction provided by 'verkaufte nicht' at one level is a surprise for the reader but with hindsight, it can be seen as the confirmation of the business acumen implied before. The terse final sentence underscores everything. Such a passage is again marked by ironic distance, something that, along with verbal humour, is a major characteristic of Süskind's style. A good example of this humour is the following short passage, marked by different usages of the verb 'haben', characterizing Grenouille's situation as he begins his final quest for the perfect perfume: 'Er hatte einen Geruch, er hatte Geld, er hatte Selbstvertrauen und er hatte es eilig' (p. 209).

These examples will serve to show something of Süskind's stylistic talent. What is more, the stylistic control is complemented by a clear structuring of the novel with the more hectic first and third parts centring on Grenouille's career as a perfumer and the second providing a kind of quiet intermezzo, as it describes the period when he retreats from society and lives as a hermit. A short fourth part describes his death. It is these aesthetic factors that substantiate the claim that Süskind is no mere writer of trivia but someone to be taken seriously.

It is also necessary to ask whether his success is based solely on his talents as a stylist, coupled with the imaginative ability to create a good story or, one might say particularly with reference to *Das Parfum*, a good yarn. These are skills that will no doubt always be in demand, but it is also useful to look at Süskind's work in relation to a phenomenon that is much discussed at the moment – namely postmodernism. An exact definition of this term is generally acknowledged to be difficult, especially in the case of literature. It is, however, accepted by most critics that Eco's *Name of the Rose* is the postmodern novel *par excellence*. In it the hero and his companion, deliberately a kind of medieval Holmes and Watson duo, try to interpret clues and signs in their investigations of a series of murders. Their world though is not that of Conan Doyle, whose hero is capable of solving all mysteries and restoring order in every sense of the word. Eco's hero, significantly named William Baskerville, concludes at the end of the novel that 'there is no order in the universe',[13] whilst the narrator, appropriately the Watson figure, does not know if what he has written 'contains some hidden meaning, or more than one, or many, or none at all'.[14] This might be said of *Das Parfum* and, to a lesser extent, of *Die Taube*. As already shown, they are anything but clear statements.

Another factor that is held to be typical of literary postmodernism is a tendency to incorporate echoes of other writing. Thus Frank Lucht entitles an essay on postmodernism: 'Erkennen Sie die Melodie?' and there are certainly melodies to be recognized in the case of Süskind. The overall conception of *Die Taube* with a doorman as the main character is reminiscent of Kafka, albeit with a very non-Kafkaesque kind of happy ending. On the stylistic level, as already seen in the example of the use of the language of advertising, echoes abound. The start of *Das Parfum* seems to recall that of Kleist's *Michael Kohlhaas*, whilst the description of Grenouille's imagined feelings of greatness during his period of isolation from society is based on the feelings of God the creator in Genesis: 'Und als er sah, daß es gut war und daß das ganze Land von seinem göttlichen Grenouillesamen durchtränkt war, da ließ der Große Grenouille einen Weingeistregen herniedergehen' (p. 161). Elsewhere there are different kinds of echo. It is said of Grenouille at one stage: 'Jetzt sei seine Langmut zuende' (p. 115), a sentiment expressed more directly by Hitler. It is in fact a kind of eclecticism that characterizes *Das Parfum*. In a narrative supposedly set in the eighteenth century, there are such words as 'Chuzpe', 'Arbeitsteilung', 'Rationalisierung' and even 'Berufsverbot', whereas elsewhere the style seems to be deliberately archaic, as in the following comparison which is made when Grenouille reaches his place of retreat: 'So wie ein Schiffbrüchiger nach wochenlanger Irrfahrt die erste von Menschen bewohnte Insel ekstatisch begrüßt, feierte Grenouille seine Ankunft auf dem Berg der Einsamkeit' (p. 154). Such a passage may well come close to what Lucht sees as a further characteristic of postmodern writing, namely 'inszenierte Naivität im Bewußtsein, daß man heute so eigentlich nicht mehr schreiben kann'.[15]

If it is correct to connect Süskind with the current literary expression of postmodernism, this would explain part of his success. However, there is another, probably related factor, especially

13. Eco, *The Name of the Rose*, p. 492.
14. Ibid., p. 501.
15. F. Lucht, 'Erkennen Sie die Melodie?' in Volker Hage (ed.), *Deutsche Literatur 1986: Jahresüberblick*, Stuttgart, 1987, p. 304.

in the case of *Das Parfum*, namely the narrator's cosy relationship with his readers. Thus the second paragraph of the novel begins by contrasting the eighteenth century with the present: 'Zu der Zeit, von der wir reden, herrschte in den Städten ein für uns moderne Menschen kaum vorstellbarer Gestank' (p. 5). Later there is a similar reference to 'Uns heutigen Menschen, die wir physikalisch ausgebildet sind' (p. 129), as opposed to the ignoramuses of earlier years. Although there may be a touch of irony here – there are many present-day ignoramuses as far as physics is concerned – it is still fair to maintain that Süskind does not seek to challenge the reader with his account of the past in *Das Parfum*, as most serious historical novelists do. The reader is taken into the narrator's confidence and is not asked serious questions about, for instance, mass murder. This relates to the postmodern aspect of Süskind's writing in the sense that by incorporating and intermingling various historical ages and kinds of writing, he is also failing to differentiate between them. In this, he appeals to readers at a time when, unlike the 1960s, radical questioning does not seem to be fashionable. One also wonders about the appeal of *Das Parfum* with its murders of women to those who do not react favourably to the phenomenon of female emancipation.

The implication of the above is that Süskind belongs in the realm of trivial or, as one critic puts it, 'middle-brow' literature.[16] That he has made the top hundred in the list of British paper-back best-sellers, albeit well below the Jeffrey Archers of this world, might seem to confirm this, quite irrespective of the fact that it is a translation from the German. It would, however, be wrong to overlook the world-wide success of *Das Parfum* or to accept without further ado the comforting axiom that anything that sells in large quantities must be inferior writing. It is therefore necessary to consider possible reasons why Süskind's novel has achieved such phenomenal international success among a whole range of readers.

The major reason is quite simply that Süskind tells a good story well and in a manner that appeals to contemporary readers with their interest in history or at least a delight in celebrating historical anniversaries such as three hundred years of the Glorious Revolution or two hundred years of the French Revolution. In an article published in early 1988, Hauke Braunhorst contrasts the present neo-conservative ideological climate with the Utopian ideals of philosophers from Kant to Adorno. He says of contemporary thinkers: 'Sie propagieren die allgemeine Abschaffung des

---

16. B. von Matt, '"Midcult"', *Neue Zürcher Zeitung*, 9 April 1987.

Allgemeinen, arbeiten theoretisch am Verfall von Theorie und denken das Denkverbot.'[17] If one accepts the contention that this is an age of paradoxes where distinctions are blurred and nearly everything is arbitrary, a claim made elsewhere in this volume under the phrase 'anything goes' (see p. 32 above and p. 345 below), then *Das Parfum* fits in very well with such an ethos. It provides through its author's varied knowledge and use of allusion intellectual stimulation without the requirement to consider fundamental questions. Süskind writes about murders in such a way that it is not necessary to feel moral revulsion in relation to the perpetrator or pity in relation to the victim. There is scant need to differentiate or examine in detail either characters or events. It is a relief to be confronted with horrors that, unlike Auschwitz, genocide in Kampuchea or massacres in China, provide solely a source of diverting entertainment.

17. H. Braunhorst, 'Die Unverzichtbarkeit der Utopie', *Frankfurter Rundschau*, 23 January 1988.

– 20 –

Literature and the End of the World: Günter Grass's *Die Rättin*

JULIAN PREECE

> Man frage nicht, was all die Zeit ich machte.
> Ich bleibe stumm;
> und sage nicht warum.
> Und Stille gibt es, da die Erde krachte.
> Kein Wort, das traf;
> man spricht nur aus dem Schlaf.
> Und träumt von einer Sonne, welche lachte.
> Es geht vorbei;
> nachher wars einerlei.
> Das Wort entschlief, als jene Welt erwachte.
> Karl Kraus[1]

Die Rättin is a duel of words and stories between the last survivor of the human race, the fictional narrator, Grass, and his dreamed partner, spokeswoman of the rat population, the erstwhile companions and now successors of mankind. It is unclear at times, even to the narrator, who is actually dreaming whom and what is fact and what fantasy, until in the final sections of the book the postholocaust world of the rat gradually swallows up the human fictions, one by one.[2] The dialogue construction of the novel is founded on this clash between the cold, sardonic reportage of the She-Rat, explaining the rationale to the pre- and posthistory of 'der Große Knall', and the fantasies and fictions of her human interlocutor:

---

1. Karl Kraus, 1933, in Hans Wollschläger (ed.), *Das Karl–Kraus–Lesebuch*, Zurich, 1980.
2. The narrator is dependent upon her from the beginning of his long dream, as she can decide which of the stories is to be dreamt next: 'Was halfen mir mein Nein, mein Ich bin, Ich bin immer noch; Ihre Stimme hielt den Oberton, siegte: Weg sind sie, weg!' (p. 29). On another occasion she unceremoniously dismisses his interventions: 'Verzisch dich in deine Geschichten' (p. 297). All references are to Günter Grass, *Werkeausgabe in zehn Bänden*, ed. Volker Neuhaus, 10 vols., Darmstadt, 1987 (*Die Rättin*, vol. 7).

'Schluß! sagt sie. Euch gab es mal. Gewesen seid ihr, erinnert als Wahn' (p. 7). 'Aber ich bin doch da! rief ich. In meiner Raumkapsel: ich. Auf meiner Umlaufbahn: ich. In deinen und meinen Träumen: ich, du und ich!' (p. 251).

After the recent deaths of Johnson, Böll, Weiss and Andersch, Günter Grass, who last year (1987) celebrated his own sixtieth birthday, is very much a senior voice (if not yet grand old man) of West German letters. His generation has witnessed the history of the Federal Republic from its beginnings in the aftermath of the Third Reich, and in his work the sense of historical continuity, of the past weighing down upon the present, has always been prominent. His unbroken attachment to his home town of Danzig/Gdansk makes this historical legacy and the partition of Germany and Europe all the more poignant. It is the postwar situation of the 1950s, 'das gesamtdeutsche Fälscherwerk', to which the causes of the final war are to be traced and for this reason Grass returns to motifs and characters from this period. In the historical scheme of things the twentieth century represents the climax in the horrible cycle of human violence: 'Jadochja! Hungernde, brennende, dann schwimmende, gleich darauf abgeknallte Menschen. Und Menschen, die andere Menschen hungern, verbrennen, absaufen ließen und zusahen, wie die wenigen Menschen, die an Land kamen, von Menschen glattweg abgeknallt wurden' (p. 60). This cyclical conception of history ('Alles, was stattfindet, findet wiederholt statt') threatens to rob the novel of real political punch, however, and blurs the historical specificity of the atomic hic et nunc.

The She-Rat, speaking in the future, refers to the period we are now living in as the 'Zwischenkriegszeit'[3] and then later modifies even this view: 'Den ersten, den zweiten Weltkrieg und den von ihresgleichen vorweggenommenen dritten faßt sie zu einem einzigen Kriegsgeschehen zusammen, das, nach ihren Worten, folgerichtig mit dem großen Knall endete' (p. 204).

History, with Germany at the centre of it, has always been the primary material of Grass's novels; it is not just the tale of the Flounder now which reaches its terrible but predictable end, but that of Oskar Matzerath as well. Grass remains true to his begin-

---

3. In *Kassandra*, Christa Wolf already writes of the 'Vorkriegszeit' referring to her own *Kassandra. Vier Vorlesungen. Eine Erzählung*, Berlin (GDR), 1983. For essays on other recent accounts of the end of the world see Gunter Grimm, Werner Faulstich and Peter Kuon (eds.), *Apokalypse. Weltuntergangsvisionen in der Literatur des zwanzigsten Jahrhunderts*, Frankfurt/Main, 1986, esp. Wolfgang Ignée, 'Apokalypse als Ergebnis eines Geschäftsberichtes. Günter Grass' Roman *Die Rättin*', pp. 385–401.

nings and to an ethic derived from the years of the *Gruppe 47*; literature in *Die Rättin* is still placed in the service of the Enlightenment. If in the Danzig works he created a literary memorial to the perversions of Hitler's Germany, he now attempts a similar task for the imminent threat of world destruction. The obvious contradictions inherent in writing about the future are made a theme of the book.

This is Grass's most overtly political book since *Aus dem Tagebuch einer Schnecke* and it shares some of the latter's weaknesses. The inherent pitfalls of 'committed literature' and the *roman à thèse* are that the author is 'preaching to the saved' and that the literary form does not quite do justice to its political content. The fables and stories may depoliticize their themes by wrapping them up in a new mythology and thus mystifying the historical causes. Grass's latest novel by no means escapes these dangers. Like the earlier book, *Die Rättin* treats political themes – environmental and nuclear destruction, the hubris of industrial civilization – which have also been the subject of journalistic articles and political speeches. It is the fictional counterpart to the author's major political concerns of the early 1980s, and the media industry – press, TV and video – exerts an influence on the style of the book.

The language of the press and radio is parodied and the media-oriented Newspeak of politicians exposed as something which distorts and trivializes catastrophe, transforming it into consumer information, as if it were no different from proposals for tax reforms. Each of the major threads of the narrative is made into a video by the now sixty-year-old Oskar Matzerath, and the narrator has the ability to flash back and forth in time, choosing his story, just as if he were changing television channels. This method serves to highlight the problem of the suitability of the literary means to their monumental theme and with the introduction of the 'smurfs' in the final section, the problem becomes acute.

In his novels Grass has frequently preferred image, allegory and fable to a developed, reflective argument. Thus the 'Mehlwürmer' episode in *Hundejahre* is employed to represent the *Wirtschaftswunder* of the 1950s and thus the 'Niobe' chapter in *Die Blechtrommel* presents the rise of fascism in parable-like terms – albeit in the latter case the open-ended parable of absurdist literature.[4] This technique separates his work from that of the earlier generation of modernist

---

4. On Grass and the parable of the Absurd see Dieter Stolz, 'Der frühe Grass und die Literatur des Absurden (1954–9)', *Germanica Wratislawiensia*, Mikrofiche no. 6, 1988, pp. 229–378, also Werner Frizen, '*Die Blechtrommel* – ein schwarzer Roman', *Arcadia*, vol. 21, 1986, pp. 166–89.

novelists, Mann, Musil and Broch, all of whom dealt explicitly with political themes, and particularly the rise of fascism, in far broader, more totalizing ways. The dangers for Grass are that the poetic means are not quite sufficient to their task, that historical and political processes are reduced to simplified forms, to inadequate schemata, and that his critical analysis remains woefully superficial.[5] These dangers are overcome in *Die Blechtrommel* and *Katz und Maus* through the hypostasization of the narrative perspective ('authorial' or 'personal'?) and the consequent ambiguity of the narrative personae. It is allayed in *Der Butt* by means of irony and a dialogic structure. The construction in *Die Rättin* is by no means didactic, however, and general problems of political literature and media are a central theme; principally the power of the word and the image (a writer's only tools) in conflict with the seemingly inexorable march of history towards oblivion.

There are too many stories wanting and waiting to be told, crowding the page and the narrator's mind – 'Lauter Geschichten, die ihr Ende suchen' – fragments which have to be narrated even though the End has already occurred. Evidence for a lack of clarity and chronology are the jumbled chapter headings, where nothing has priority over anything else; Hänsel and Gretel are as significant as world politics. These are stories of the past, 'eine verpfuschte Schöpfung' and Noah's Ark, the Pied Piper of Hamelin, plague and the apocalyptic fears of the Middle Ages, imaginary stories from the Grimm fairy-tales and the galaxy of resurrected characters from Grass's earlier work. Yet the structure is loose and devoid of any genuine plot and tension, as the only real link between the stories is the narrator's dream of his rat partner. A major criticism of *Die Rättin* is that the parts do not quite add up to the whole. 'Abschiednehmen' is the title of one of the poems, and in the more elegiac verses this is precisely what Grass is doing, taking personal leave, however reluctantly, from his literature and his world.

In *Aus dem Tagebuch einer Schnecke*, he explains that, 'ein Schriftsteller ist jemand, der gegen die verstreichende Zeit schreibt' (vol. 4, p. 400); literature is conceived of here as a meditation on the past, on the catastrophe and guilt of the last war. The narrative simultaneity of reports from the 1969 election campaign and the account of Hermann Ott and the Danzig Jews indicates the contem-

---

5. Ignée's remark that 'Sie [the She-Rat] den Kern des Übels erfaßt hat' is surely exaggerated praise in this respect. See Ignée, 'Apokalypse', p. 394.

porary significance of this past. Brandt and Kiesinger are both images of political forces which have historical antecedents: when the former political exile (Brandt) defeats the former Nazi Party member (Kiesinger), the snail – the symbol for slow but inexorable progress – scores a famous victory. The 'Prinzip Zweifel', which is the author's and the snail's own, is already a revision of Bloch's 'Prinzip Hoffnung', but it gives way in *Kopfgeburten* to the bleaker image of Sisyphus. This Sisyphus is an illustration of political resistance who treats his political responsibility as a gesture of defiance and existential necessity. Now even he is redundant. The term 'Vergegenkunft' is invented in *Kopfgeburten* in order to characterize the playful and provocative treatment of narrative time in the work of the 1970s and to attack critics who had suggested that his fleeing into the past in *Der Butt* was a flight from reality. In *Die Rättin*, however, by means of dreaming and inventing fictions, Grass is writing no longer against the past but against the future; against the ending to end all endings and all meanings.

This is fiction against the Bomb; 'weil ich durch Wörter das Ende aufschieben möchte' (p. 13). It is also the account of the failure of this attempt, of the powerlessness of words and literature in the face of human folly and blindness.[6] Orbiting the earth in his capsule, the narrator can do nothing but keep on inventing and imagining stories, as he himself becomes an ever-paler figment of the She-Rat's imagination and his grip on reality becomes ever weaker – ('Könnte es sein, daß beide / die Ratte und ich / geträumt werden und Traum / dritter Gattung sind?' p. 382). The consequent distance from his readers is symptomatic of the writer's powerlessness and the pointlessness of his writing. In his dreamed speech to the Bundestag he must thank his audience for their 'beredte Abwesenheit'. The intimation is that nobody is even listening any more.

This failure of literature is the failure of the Enlightenment and of 'die Erziehung des Menschengeschlechtes', a phrase which is mentioned in the very first sentence. It is a multi-media parable account of the 'Dialektik der Aufklärung', which Oskar, the She-Rat and the narrator together concoct. In his essays and speeches of this period Grass returns to the theme of the failure and poverty of the Enlightenment project; 'Ich, ihr Untertan, will, daß ihre herrschende Vernunft

---

6. The despairing cries of Oskar and the She-Rat could be the author's own: 'Hätten die Hühner warnend eckige Eier gelegt, hätte der Mensch das Würfelei Fortschritt genannt, höhnte sie; und er donnerte, . . . Müssen Flüsse bergauf fließen und Berge kopfstehen, damit ihr begreift?' (p. 300).

endlich Untertan der geschundenen Natur wird.'[7] This battle for supremacy is played out in *Die Rättin*.

Jean Paul's 'Rede des toten Christus vom Weltgebäude herab, daß kein Gott mehr sei'[8] becomes the sermon of the She-Rat from the 'Müllberg herab', piles of rubbish being all that is left of human civilization, 'Restbestände menschlicher Historie'. The rats are not the only would-be enlighteners: Oskar Matzerath, now the impresario of the Post Futurum video company, the brothers Grimm, the minister and secretary of state for 'mittelfristige Waldschäden', the artist Malskat with his fake Gothic friezes and the evil stepmother's 'Zauberspiegel' all proffer didactic advice, predict the future, issue warnings and use their various artistic media as a means of education. Malskat, whose forgeries combine religious and apocalyptic motifs from the Middle Ages with fables from mysterious, forgotten bestiaries, gives himself up and is punished with a prison sentence. Ulbricht and Adenauer, on the other hand, the great political counterfeiters, remain in office and prepare the way towards Armageddon: 'Ach, hätte man seine Bilder, zumal er die Wahrheit ans Licht brachte, doch stehen lassen und den wahren Schwindel, der nie eingestanden wurde, die Machwerke der Staatsgründer außer Kraft gesetzt' (p. 401). The different types of truth and falsehood in art and reality are illustrated in this parable of 'die falschen Fuffziger', as 'die andere Wahrheit' of art is ignored by society. Correctly interpreted Malskat's pictures could have acted as a warning to humanity. The problem is that the didactic tone of Oskar's video and of the She-Rat's lectures (delivered either from a pulpit or in front of a blackboard) becomes that of Grass's text and the effect is inevitably rather flat. Grass harangues his readers just as his narrator is harangued by his rat partner.

The advice and explanations come now too late; the time has passed when the march towards the end could have been halted. Here lies the difference with *Der Butt*, where, after the horrific crescendo of the 'Vatertag', there is offered the movement towards a possible future, the Utopia of the female principle. The She-Rat takes over the role of the Flounder and continues his history, explaining in schematic and naive form how human history devel-

---

7. 'Der Traum der Vernunft. Rede zur Veröffentlichung der Verstaltungsreihe "Vom Elend der Aufklärung" in der Akademie der Künste, Berlin', 1984, in *Gesammelte Werke*, vol. 9, pp. 886–91; also 'Ist das noch Aufklärung?', ibid., pp. 907–10.
8. Jean Paul, *Blumen-, Frucht- und Dornenstücke oder Ehestand, Tod und Hochzeit des Armenadvokaten F. St. Siebenkäs im Reichsflecken Kuhschnappel*, 1796–97. The speech alluded to is the first 'Blumenstück'.

oped with apparent inexorability, towards the final explosion. The model for historical representation is the video film and 'es war einmal' fairy-tale; world history from Noah to the final explosion is presented in a tone and style reminiscent of animal fables of both La Fontaine and Walt Disney. There is no internal contradiction in this hybrid mixture: 'Keines der allerneusten Medien, das nicht im Märchen seinen Ursprung hätte' (p. 254).

Rats have been from the very beginning the partners but also the antithesis and persecuted 'Other' of mankind, always associated with doom and disease and living off the plentiful refuse civilization has always provided: 'Von Anbeginn Haß und der Wunsch vertilgt zu sehen, was würgt und Brechreiz macht' (p. 9). They survived both the Great Flood and 'der Große Knall' by burying themselves in the ground and have been present at every major historical event and calamity. Unlike human beings, however, they know how to adapt and when to abandon a sinking ship, and this they have done with great regularity – the She-Rat's version of history reads at times like a list of maritime disasters. The principle of 'das Rattige' (whether the Jews or the unidentified enemy) has dominated human history and the cry, 'Die Ratten sind unser Unglück', resounded from the Black Death down to Auschwitz. Hitler is a latter-day incarnation of the Pied Piper.[9]

The principal weakness of *Die Rättin* lies in the attempt to give an explanation of why human history arrives at the point of its own destruction. The theory which constitutes this parabolic account (the message or *Aussage* of the parable) is simple to the point of banality, even though underlaid with irony. This strand of the narrative reaches back to Noah and to the Creation – it was rat droppings which indicated the recession of the waters and it is from the rats that human beings are originally descended – and continues via the revised version of the Pied Piper legend to the genetically constructed 'Watsoncricks' of the posthuman world. The idea is that man has denied the rattishness within himself and that only when man and rat come together does humanity have a chance of survival; 'Es wird der Homo Sapiens an der Gattung Rattus Norvegicus genesen' (p. 175). The children of Hamelin perish because

9. In a lecture initially given in Israel, 'Wie sagen wir es den Kindern?' (vol. 9, pp. 755–70), Grass explains his indebtedness to Heine's *Der Rabbi von Bacherach* for *Aus dem Tagebuch einer Schnecke*, which he at one point planned as a continuation of the Heine fragment. In *Die Rättin*, motifs in the Hamelin episodes linking the plague and the medieval pogroms to the rats and the wandering flagellants seem to be borrowed in part from Heine's text. The poem 'Es war einmal ein Land, das hieß Deutsch' also has discernible echoes of Heine's *Deutschland, ein Wintermärchen*.

they seek social and sexual union with the rats (which the punks, shortly before 'Ultimo' try to emulate) and are punished by the frightened authorities. Once this union has been achieved through progress in the practical application of genetics, all will be well: 'Das krumme Holz, von dem der Philosoph Kant sagte es bilde den Menschen unabänderlich ab, kann, wir wissen es, endlich gestreckt werden' (p. 175). The parallels with the basic fable of *Der Butt* are obvious, but whereas the earlier novel undermined and questioned its feminist thesis and erected a polyphonic dialogue of narratives and ideologies upon its skeletal framework, here the analysis of the 'verstiegener Mensch' goes almost unchallenged. Grass has moved away from the polyphony of *Der Butt* back to the unidimensional allegory of *Aus dem Tagebuch einer Schnecke*.

Die Rättin is a summation of the failure of political, enlightened literature, which the emasculation of the imagination has caused, and of the victory of those forces against which Grass has pitted himself in his political career. Yet the tone of resignation is still suffused with a nuance of hope. The Utopian moment which was explicit in *Der Butt* glimmers still at the end of *Die Rättin*, when the rats steal the old Solidarity badge (kept as a fetish in the posthuman world) and rebel against their new exploiters the 'Rattenmenschen' or 'Watsoncricks'.[10] The Utopia of the women's city of Vineta, a lost Atlantis in the Baltic, the Utopia of the fairy-tale figures in their still green and burgeoning forest and even the post-human societies of rats and 'Watsoncricks', the dreamed of genetical amalgam of man and rat, offer alternative realities which may yet be realized. Utopia is either projected back into the past to Vineta, a motif left over from *Der Butt* and which is interwoven with three important strands of the text, or it is banished to the cartoon kitsch of the Grimms' fairy-tale forest. The rat children of Hamelin are a grotesque prefiguration of the (false) Utopia of the 'Rattenmenschen', prefiguring both the punks and the post-human 'Watsoncricks'. In the Malskat paintings, which link the three rat children (who are christened after the three Magi) explicitly to the lost city of Vineta, we have perhaps a debased 'ästhetischer Vorschein' (Bloch) of this Utopia, which, as Damroka explains, failed for reasons all too familiar – the matriarchal Vinetan order is over-

---

10. The parallel between the pigs in Orwell's *Animal Farm* and the 'Watsoncricks' is clear, as both come to resemble more and more the human beings they had initially replaced and thus betray the revolutionary or Utopian hope placed in them. The sevenhundredth anniversary of the Pied Piper is also 'Orwells Jahr' (1984): 'Orwells Jahrzehnt 1 + 2' in vol. 9, pp. 775–89, 844–53. Both Orwell and Heine are placed by Grass in the tradition of the Enlightenment.

thrown by the invaders from Hamelin. The posthuman development of the rats and 'Watsoncricks' is thus already presaged in the fate of Vineta.

Otherwise the Utopian motif is a series of missed opportunities and failures, 'ihr hättet und ihr hättet'. The failure of humanist politics, of the Flounder and of the Enlightenment rehearses the fate of the male principle in *Der Butt* ('So erinnern wir den verstiegenen Menschen: immer höher hinaus, immer steiler erdacht . . . Seht wie zerknautscht sein Fortschritt zu Fall kam', p. 12) and is the basis of the novel's fable, repeated in a series of variations. The verse passage in Chapter 5 expresses this central idea.

> Unser Vorhaben hieß: nicht nur, wie man mit Messer
> und Gabel, sondern mit seinesgleichen auch,
> ferner mit der Vernunft, dem allmächtigen Büchsenöffner
> umzugehen habe, solle gelernt werden
> nach und nach.
>
> Erzogen möge das Menschengeschlecht sich frei,
> jawohl, frei selbstbestimmen, damit es,
> seiner Unmündigkeit ledig, lerne, der Natur behutsam,
> möglichst behutsam das Chaos
> abzugewöhnen.
>
> Im Verlauf seiner Erziehung habe das Menschengeschlecht
> die Tugend mit Löffeln zu essen, fleißig den Konjunktiv
> und die Toleranz zu üben,
> auch wenn das schwerfalle
> unter Brüdern.
>
> Eine besondere Lektion trug uns auf,
> den Schlaf der Vernunft zu bewachen,
> auf das jegliches Traumgetier
> gezähmt werde und fortan der Aufklärung brav
> aus der Hand fresse.
>
> Halbwegs erleuchtet mußte das Menschengeschlecht
> nun nicht mehr planlos im Urschlamm verrückt spielen,
> vielmehr begann es, sich mit System zu säubern.
> Klar sprach erlernte Hygiene sich aus: Wehe
> den Schmutzigen!
>
> Sobald wir unsere Erziehung fortgeschritten nannten,
> wurde das Wissen zur Macht erklärt

> und nicht nur auf Papier angewendet. Es riefen
> die Aufgeklärten: Wehe
> den Unwissenden!
>
> Als schließlich die Gewalt, trotz aller Vernunft, nicht aus der
> Welt zu schaffen war, erzog sich
> das Menschengeschlecht zur gegenseitigen Abschreckung.
> So lernte es Friedenhalten, bis irgendein Zufall
> unaufgeklärt dazwischenkam.
>
> Da endlich war die Erziehung des Menschengeschlechts
> so gut wie abgeschlossen. Große Helligkeit
> leuchtete jeden Winkel aus. Schade, daß es danach
> so duster wurde und niemand mehr
> seine Schule fand.

The mixture of the quirky and personal with the serious is typical of the Grass lyric and of *Die Rättin* in particular. Thus reason is the almighty tin-opener, tolerance and the subjunctive are made grammatically equivalent. The recurrence of the watchwords 'Erziehung', 'Menschengeschlecht', 'Vernunft' and 'Aufklärung' betrays the preoccupation with Lessing, whose essay stands almost metonomically for the intellectual movements of the eighteenth century. In the penultimate stanza a continuity between these efforts and the policy of deterrence and mutually assured destruction (MAD) is established. The reason and education of the Enlightenment represent the beginning of the path which leads down towards annihilation. A scheme of historical development is, however, only grafted on to a concept of history which remains at bottom absurd, beyond human control and understanding. The Goya etching *The Sleep of Reason Begets Monsters* is cited as a parallel to Lessing in order to characterize the ambiguous and threatening potential of a civilization founded solely on reason. Real political insight is, however, wanting and an essentially historical process is presented via images which are flat and unidimensional: the 'Wehe!' exclamations, for instance, render the divisions between East and West in trite terms.[11]

Literature, with the *Märchen* as an image of the imaginative and humane potential of literature, provides 'die andere Wahrheit' to the world of reason. Without this counter-balance humanity cannot

---

11. For an analysis of this tendency in Grass's earlier work see Gertrude Cepl-Kaufmann, *Günter Grass. Eine Analyse des Gesamtwerkes unter dem Aspekt von Literatur und Politik*, Kronberg, 1975.

survive and the death of the world will follow the death of the forests, 'denn mit den Wäldern . . . sterben auch die Märchen'. Consequently the fairy-tale figures are the only ones to offer resistance to the political blindness of the country's leaders – 'doch in Grimms Wäldern wächst der Widerstand' – and a delegation sets off for Bonn to capture the government. Fact and fantasy are in open conflict and for a brief while the *Märchen* are in control – 'Die Märchen haben die Macht ergriffen!' Their power is shortlived, however, and their Utopian refuge, laden with all the Romantic associations only a German forest has, is bulldozed and the government rescued.[12] The ending, and it has to be a happy one – this is a fairy-tale! – is imaginary, wishful thinking, as the two children Hänsel and Gretel flee to the only place left to them – the past – and find everything in the forest just as it always was and always should be.

The false idyll of this ending is immediately made relative to the world of harsh fact: 'Wem aber der rückgewendete Schluß des stummen Films vom sterbenden Wald und vom Ende der Märchen zu verheißungsvoll, von Hoffnung geschönt und nicht böse genug ist, der möge, rät unser Herr Matzerath, die Zeitung aufschlagen und lesen, bis daß ihn Zorn überkommt, was des Kanzlers Experten zu sagen haben' (p. 423).

In a similar way the women sailors of the 'Neue Ilsebill', feminist inheritors of the spirit of *Der Butt*, are poised between two realities: the polluted Baltic Sea, which is the object of their scientific investigation, and the dream, inspired by the Flounder, of the lost city of Vineta. Their captain Damroka still holds secret confabulations with the fish, but the fish himself never comes to speak in the book as his mission has failed and is all but over.[13] At the moment the women actually enter the city, heralded by siren-like singing of jellyfish, the final unthinkable explosion occurs. The terror of the fact once again triumphs over fantasy, but one cannot but admire the sober economy with which Grass describes their demise: 'Nie gesehenes Licht. Sie sind geblendet. Hitze haucht sie verzehrend an. Sie vergehen. Wo ich hindeute, suche, ist nichts mehr' (p. 293).

Grass spares us the horrific details of suffering and obliteration,

---

12. The forest is very much a parodied, artificial backcloth, a painted idyll of the Biedermeier period, which links it both to the Biedermeier of the 1950s and to the 'restaurierte Restauration' of the present decade. The *Bundeskanzler* is an obvious caricature of Helmut Kohl.
13. 'Hier haben wir Anfang der siebziger den Butt gefangen . . . Lauter Hoffnungen und wunderschöne Versprechungen. Wurde nichts daraus. Alles nur Quallen, die schrumpfen, sobald du sie anguckst' (p. 65).

radiation sickness and fire storms. There is no account of what happens to human beings – they simply cease to exist. The exception is the narrator who refuses to grasp what has happened and continues to tell his stories. His account of Oskar's sixtieth birthday, in itself a witty satirical vignette, can be no more than a dream because Oskar, together with all his family, has already been wiped out in Gdansk. The narrator has no other recourse, however, except to continue 'als ob' and he thus skirts around the all-important issue of how literature can take the nuclear holocaust as its subject.

The blind ruthlessness of industrial exploitation which has caused the poisoning of the forests is still a fit subject for satire. Grass is at his most trenchant when he has the Chancellor's entourage drive past painted boards depicting a still blossoming nature and hiding the acid death of the trees behind them. Even the neutron bomb, the weapon which kills people but leaves buildings intact, lends him opportunity to vent his regulated hatred. In his imaginary address to the Bundestag, his satire is reminiscent of the classic form of Swift's *Modest Proposal*, praising the new weapon as the only means to rescue centuries of European culture – but a satire of nuclear death itself?

The author's refuge in fairy-tales, imaginary stories and dreams indicates the difficulties a realist author faces in giving meaning to something which is meaningless. *Die Rättin* is the drama of the confrontation between the word and nothingness and in this confrontation lie both the strengths and the failings of the book. Grass had wanted initially to give *Der Butt* the sub-title 'ein Märchen'. The 'es war einmal' fairy-tale form is a constituent narrative principle in the novel, as it was already in *Die Blechtrommel*, where it is used precisely to represent the most horrific and brutal aspects of National Socialism. He employs flights of fantasy in order to escape from a narrow social realism and to lend Oskar's fictional autobiography an exemplary and all-encompassing validity. The allegorical parable of 'Niobe' and more particularly the chapter 'Glaube Hoffnung Liebe', with its nursery-rhyme refrains of 'der himmlische Gasmann' and 'ein leichtgläubiges Volk', have the most inhuman acts of National Socialism as their subject. This grotesque *Kontrafaktur* of a simple form was a controversial method but the chapter has become one of the most celebrated episodes.[14]

---

14. The literary form is in this case only apparently of a simple naivety – see Patrick O'Neill, 'Musical Form and the Pauline Message in a key chapter of *Die Blechtrommel*', *Seminar*, vol. 10, 1974, pp. 298–307.

There is literary continuity in Grass telling parables of the Third Reich and fairy-tales of the nuclear holocaust. What distinguishes *Die Blechtrommel* from *Die Rättin*, however, is its attention to the realist detail, the precise social milieu and its characters, all of which act as a counter-weight to the fantastical aspects. The realist, factual side and the author's famous 'Sucht zum Gegenstand' are all but completely lost in *Die Rättin*, as if, in the face of world annihilation, the author's grip on reality has been fatally weakened. The claim that the dream 'entblößt die Wirklichkeit' is sadly no longer true and Oskar's explanation for the absence of more factual information rings rather hollow: 'Der Mensch hat das Dokumentarische satt. Soviel Wirklichkeit ermüdet. An Tatsachen glaubt ohnehin niemand mehr. Nur noch Träume aus der Trickkiste bringen stimmige Fakten' (p. 77).

The man-made apocalypse, a uniquely modern phenomenon, is a subject to which Grass has returned again and again in his novels. From the Danzig works and the catastrophe of the Third Reich via *Örtlich betäubt* (the use of napalm in the Vietnam war) to *Der Butt*, with its never-ending cycle of slaughter and persecution which culminates in the monstrous perversion of the 'Vatertag', he has sought to give historical disaster literary form. What Adorno criticized in Brecht's *Der aufhaltsame Aufstieg des Arturo Ui*, a play which tells of the rise of Hitler in parodic and parabolic form, may provide a clue as to why *Die Rättin* is ultimately an unsatisfying account of this greatest and lowest of all subjects; namely that the theory or 'die Lehre' is inadequate and grotesquely insufficient to its subject. Adorno's criticism was that the true terror of fascism was 'eskamotiert' and that, 'dem politischen Engagement zuliebe wird die politische Realität zu leicht gewogen: das mindert auch die politische Wirkung'.[15]

This dilemma never becomes a subject of reflexion in *Die Rättin*. Grass reacts to the threat of nuclear extinction in the only way he as a writer knows how: by telling stories. The book is a mixture of satire, essay, fiction and lyric and it demonstrates the historic powerlessness of these forms, and indeed of all discourse, to alter the movement towards destruction. Yet, like Sisyphus, Grass will

---

15. T. W. Adorno, 'Engagement', in *Noten zur Literatur*, Frankfurt/Main, 1974. David Dowling discusses the 'grotesque inappropriateness of the response' of most science-fiction novels dealing with atomic destruction. While no one would doubt the seriousness of Grass's intention, telling fairy-tales, conversing with a rat and giving a potted history of the world is just such an 'inappropriate response'. David Dowling, *Fictions of Nuclear Disaster*, London, 1987.

continue in his work, which has become almost a compulsion, driven by 'Ängste vorm leeren Papier' (p. 183). His alternative to writing, 'stottern und aus dem Text fallen', would be an admission of final defeat which is not yet necessary. It is only in his fiction, after all, that the world ceases to exist. In the world outside the fiction there are still listeners and they have time to respond; Grass thus ends on an ambivalent note which keeps alive a flickering hope. Were it not for this hope his parables and satire would have been pointless, if not impossible. The narrator assures the She-Rat that given another chance humanity will do everything better, in emulation of the harmonious rat society: 'Ein schöner Traum, sagte die Rättin, bevor sie verging' (p. 456).

−21−

German Literature on the Threshold of the Twenty-First Century: A Critic's Perspective

MARTIN LÜDKE

I

'Gestern wird sein, was morgen gewesen ist.' This familiar sentence, which only appears paradoxical when we read it for the first time, opens what is one of the great tales written in the second half of our century: *Das Treffen in Telgte* by Günter Grass.[1] Its subject is the *Gruppe 47*, the association of writers which was founded by Hans Werner Richter and which shaped West German literature after the Second World War before collapsing in 1968 as a result of internal contradictions, the onslaught of Peter Handke in 1966 and the influence of the student movement. But this story is set three hundred years in the past in the last year of the Thirty Years' War. There, in Telgte, a little town between Münster and Osnabrück, writers, critics and publishers meet to read from their manuscripts, to discuss them and, 'vom Rande her', to contribute a 'politisches Wörtchen' in those chaotic times. Everybody who is anybody makes the adventurous journey to be there: Grimmelshausen and Gryphius, Paul Gerhardt and Hofmannswaldau, Logau and Zesen and, not Hans Werner Richter, but Simon Dach, who had invited them so long ago. As Grass says: 'Unsere Geschichten von heute müssen sich nicht jetzt zugetragen haben. Diese fing vor mehr als dreihundert Jahren an. Andere Geschichten auch. So lange rührt jede Geschichte her, die in Deutschland handelt.'[2]

It is a beautiful and sad story, a German story, that Grass tells here. It is fiction, of course, for these events did not happen at that

---

Translated by Arthur Williams and revised by Sarah Brickwood and Arthur Williams.
1. Darmstadt, 1979, p. 7.
2. Ibid.

time, in 1647. They did happen in 1947, but what happened in 1947 is transported back three hundred years. This is literary history, therefore, set in motion by Günter Grass.

II

In 1935, in his essay 'Die Macht des Wortes', Heinrich Mann reflected on the relationship between literature and history when he said: 'Was eine Gesellschaft oder ein Jahrhundert werden, weiß die Literatur im voraus – oder niemand weiß es.'[3] Forty years later, with a modesty born of the experience of more recent history, Peter Härtling offered the contrasting insight: 'Die Literatur trägt nach, sie eilt selten voran.'[4] The two positions stand in sharp contradistinction: the visionary confidence of Heinrich Mann; the backward glance of Peter Härtling.

Yet, on closer examination the conflict dissolves. Arthur C. Danto, for example, claims: 'Wenn die Zukunft offen ist, kann die Vergangenheit nicht endgültig verschlossen sein.'[5] This implies that if logically we are denied a knowledge of the future then, in principle, this knowledge is also denied us of the past. For the future is the premise of the past. Thus the Copernican view of the world appears as the logical precondition for the understanding of the Ptolemaic view, even though it is not the historical precondition. Or more simply: the Second World War appears as the precondition for the understanding of the First. The First World War, in the German-speaking world as in the English-speaking world, only got its name as a result of the Second; before that it was simply called the *Weltkrieg* and the Great War.

III

Historical knowledge (even if only in the limited field of literary history), secure statements, reliable prognoses about the past as it emerges, are all, as we see, beset with difficulties. And yet perhaps it is precisely within the possibilities of literature to vault over such

---

3. Heinrich Mann, 'Die Macht des Wortes', *Die Neue Weltbühne*, vol. 4, no. 10, 7 March 1935, p. 285.
4. Elisabeth and Rolf Hackenbracht (eds.), *Peter Härtling: Materialienbuch*, Darmstadt, 1979, p. 7.
5. Arthur C. Danto, *Analytische Philosophie der Geschichte*, Frankfurt/Main, 1974, p. 314.

difficulties.

Let us suppose it is the year 2006. On 21 February of this year an article appears in *The New New Yorker* under the title 'Bohemia on Sea', a report by Timothy Taylor about his latest trip to Europe. Apart from a small troop of two hundred soldiers in Berlin, the American forces have withdrawn from Europe. West European towns are teeming with Russian tourists who have long since made themselves at home here. Like the Japanese now, they have become a common sight. The European Community, throttled by its own bureaucracy, is capable only of feeble resistance to the special requests and self-seeking of the regions. The private motorcar can be used only in exceptional circumstances and with special permission. The great cities have atrophied to become nothing but gigantic pedestrian zones, etc., etc.

Speculation? Indubitably. But for literature this is also a possibility of the kind that Hans Magnus Enzensberger has explored in his most recent book *Ach Europa!*:[6] a report, a travelogue, an essay and a fiction which, at the end, depicts present wishes, hopes and fears as having materialized as reality.

IV

German literature on the threshold of the twenty-first century. Let us attempt the experiment of taking this factual observation as a fiction. Let us undertake the paradoxical venture of a look back from the future – for example, from the year 2006.

This will earn for us, first of all, the objection that this is wild speculation. I fully accept this and will therefore set it immediately to one side. Then, more positively, we gain a sort of platform which allows us to see at least a little way beyond the ends of our noses. A vantage point of this kind is essential, since the situation in the 1980s is anything but clear. It was to remove such difficulties that the concept of postmodernism was launched. Only there is, as the champions of this concept themselves have to admit, not even a remotely acceptable definition of it. As Huyssen and Scherpe correctly observe: 'Das vieldeutige Phänomen der Postmoderne läßt sich Mitte der 80er Jahre nicht oder noch nicht in einer Definition bändigen.'[7] The idea of postmodernism, it seems to me, is less a concept than a cipher for a mood which grows essentially

6. Frankfurt/Main, 1987, p. 449.
7. Andreas Huyssen and Klaus R. Scherpe (eds.), *Postmoderne: Zeichen eines kulturellen Wandels*, Reinbek, 1986, p. 10.

out of negation. The normative forces of modernism have disappeared. The claims that particular orientations and methods alone are valid have simply evaporated. Schools which once competed, which once denied each other the right to exist, have long since come together in peaceful co-existence. Of course we still have experimental literature, but it no longer has the progressive pathos of the avant-garde. The 'Tod der Moderne', this bold and pithy phrase, is therefore hardly open to dispute. However, so far no heir has become apparent. It is impossible, it seems to me, to take stock of postmodernism – for the very reason that it is as yet totally unclear whether there is anything for it to inherit. For modernism, as a term, embraced much more than the concept of an epoch in the history of art and literature; modernism was founded in the philosophy of history and consequently it was also determined by social theory.

The dynamism of modernism was guaranteed by the interlinking of aesthetics, social theory and the philosophy of history. This made it possible to label art and literature as 'Vorschein' (Bloch); similarly one might refer to Adorno's phrase that art is the social antithesis of society to define art as that Utopian area in which a non-identity can develop within a situation of universal pressure to create an identity. In brief, the aesthetic energy of modernism was drawn constantly from social developments.

When Habermas today demands the continuation of the 'unvollendeten Projekts der Moderne' and notes with good reason that the self-enlightenment of the Enlightenment will not be advanced by getting rid of the latter, this may still have implications in terms of cultural policy but hardly any at all in terms of aesthetics. In the introduction to their survey of the situation, *Postmoderne. Zeichen eines kulturellen Wandels*, Huyssen and Scherpe indicate the problem without pursuing it further:

> Im Zeichen der Postmoderne erhebt sich die Frage, ob und wie ein kultureller Gesamtzusammenhang westlich-kapitalistischer Gesellschaften in den 80er Jahren auszumachen und zu artikulieren ist. Der Prozeß der gegenwärtigen gesellschaftlichen Veränderung kann, wie immer benannt (postindustrielle Gesellschaft, Konsumgesellschaft, Vergesellschaftung durch die elektronischen Medien, Reproduktions- und Simulationsgesellschaft, technologische Gesellschaft), doch recht genau beschrieben werden. Zweifelhaft ist jedoch unter dieser Voraussetzung die kulturelle Noch- oder Nachmoderne, ihre eher obsolete, zeitgemäße oder zukunftsträchtige Funktionsbestimmung.[8]

8. Ibid., p. 8.

A Critic's Perspective

What appears to me above all to be doubtful is whether we can in any way keep a firm hold on the 'Gesamtzusammenhang westlich-kapitalistischer Gesellschaften in den 80er Jahren'. What Peter Bürger once described as the 'Institution Kunst',[9] that is, the continual attempt by modernism to vault the barrier between art and life, has meanwhile, in paradoxical fashion, been realized.

It is paradoxical because the term 'Institution Kunst' embraces two conflicting tendencies. While Bürger's reflections could still be understood as a continuation of Adorno's aesthetic theory, that is, while Bürger (at least implicitly) clung to the distinction between art and culture industry, today this distinction can no longer be upheld: our daily life itself has been extensively aestheticized, the boundaries are fluid and, to be somewhat provocative, nobody nowadays can say where *Warenästhetik* ends and *wahre Kunst* begins. On the other hand, art today can no longer be defined as the social antithesis of society: it has become quite the opposite, a social system alongside many others and, in keeping with this, conciliatory toward what was once termed the whole. The Utopian revolutionary momentum which propelled modernism is petering out in the modestly dimensioned definitions of its function. In this process the autonomy of art has become at once complete and redundant.

It is therefore hardly surprising that no heir to modernism has so far come forward. The inheritance has long since been divided up. What modernism once was, what its dialectic entailed above and beyond the simple aesthetic expression of societal developments, has been subdivided into its various parts and these have been, as it were, deposited in different social systems. It is possible that 'das unvollendete Projekt der Moderne' may yet be carried forward, but only in those social systems which still have energy reserves at their disposal.

So we come back to the question: what is to be gained by a glance back from the future – let us say (to join forces with Enzensberger again), from the year 2006? Above all, we gain a vantage point, a perspective which allows us to reach out beyond the catalogue of negations. It is easy to list all the things that are no longer possible, and above all everything that is no longer valid. The same is true for everything that enjoys postmodern liberty, that has been released from its historical and social ties, that is no longer prohibited. In poetry, every gentle blossoming of young love bursts out in verse, sonnets are again in vogue – and *Novellen*.

9. *Theorie der Avantgarde*, Frankfurt/Main, 1974.

The whole of tradition is freely available. We have been here before, in the early nineteenth century. And it was out of the latter that modernism developed.

V

Wie nun aber die Kunst in der Natur und in den endlichen Gabieten des Lebens ihr Vor hat, ebenso hat sie auch ein Nach, d.h. einen Kreis, der wiederum ihre Auffassungs- und Darstellungsweise überschreitet. Denn die Kunst hat noch in sich selbst eine Schranke und geht deshalb in höhere Formen des Bewußtseins über. Diese Beschränkung bestimmt denn auch die Stellung, welche wir jetzt in unserem heutigen Leben der Kunst anzuweisen gewohnt sind. Uns gilt die Kunst nicht mehr als die höchste Weise, in welcher die Wahrheit sich Existenz verschafft. [Ist einmal] der vollkommene Inhalt vollkommen in Kunstgestalten hervorgetreten, so wendet sich der weiterblickende Geist von dieser Objektivität in sein Inneres zurück und stößt sie von sich fort. Solch eine Zeit ist die unsrige. Man kann wohl hoffen, daß die Kunst immer mehr steigen und sich vollenden werde, aber ihre Form hat aufgehört, das höchste Bedürfnis des Geistes zu sein.[10]

This quotation has become well-known, even notorious as Hegel's theory of the end of art. And yet Hegel never said anything about the end of art; in fact, he said quite the opposite: 'Man kann wohl hoffen, daß die Kunst immer mehr steigen und sich vollenden werde', etc. But Hegel did refute the idea of art as an agent of cognition, or at least he understood art as only a very imperfect mode of cognition.

For my purposes, the conclusion to be drawn from this is that once the perfect content has emerged in perfect artistic form and thus, in Hegel's view, the history of art has run its course, henceforth the whole panoply of tradition is freely available, just as it is today to postmodernism.

Moreover, it is set free by the bravura treatment of the philosophy of history in the Hegelian system, in which the course of world history is set down as the unfolding of reason in reality. It is only with the suspicion that reason has in fact become real and reality rational, that aesthetics has subsequently developed a new and previously unheard-of thrust.

Odo Marquard, the Gießen philosopher who enjoys his reputa-

---

10. Hegel, *Ästhetik*, ed. Friedrich Bassenge, vol. 1, West Berlin, 1985, p. 110.

tion as a sceptic, who calls himself a 'Transzendentalbelletrist', and who, with such strange neologisms as 'Inkompetenzkompensationskompetenz' and above all his 'Abschied vom Prinzipiellen', has become something of a philosophical hoarding for the marketing of the postmodern, pointed out a remarkable circumstance in an early essay entitled 'Kant und die Wende zur Ästhetik' (1962). In his opinion, philosophy which advanced into the realm of aesthetics was not interpreting art in order to understand art, but rather in order to understand the world. It did not interpret the artist in order to understand the artist, the genius for whom, as Kant said, Nature provided the norm, but rather in order to understand mankind. Consequently, the turn to aesthetics meant the emergence of the following conviction: 'also dies: daß die Ästhetik seit dem Ende des 18. Jahrhunderts und dem Anspruch nach bis heute zur diensthabenden Fundamentalphilosophie wird'.

The turn to aesthetics belonged in the context of the 'Abkehr von der (exakten) Wissenschaft als dominierende Macht'. More precisely: aesthetics was used as a way out, 'wo das wissenschaftliche Denken nicht mehr und das geschichtliche Denken noch nicht trägt'. This is Marquard's thesis: 'Der Zug zur Ästhetik entsteht aus der Hemmung des Verlaufs der Wende von der Wissenschaftsphilosophie zur Geschichtsphilosophie.'[11] Moreover, because of this – the conclusion is obvious – Hegel could quite happily bid farewell to aesthetics. For this same reason aesthetics came back into play precisely when Hegel's philosophy of history was established.

Starting with Lukács's *Theorie des Romans*, and including Benjamin, Bloch and Adorno, the great visions of social theory in our century had always come in the guise of aesthetics. Every attempt to find a historical opening to the Utopian reservoir of modernism had succeeded only in burying this approach all the more deeply. In the end, art appeared as the locum tenens for the subject of history. Viewed thus, Marquard's thesis is seen to lack clarity, for we are completely justified in reading Adorno's aesthetic theory (1970) as the most rigorously logical explication of his philosophy of history.

The dilemma of the 1980s, the so-called postmodern era, stems directly from the separation of the philosophy of history from aesthetics. Postmodernism regards the philosophy of history in the same way as Hegel was regarded very shortly after his death: as a 'toter Hund'.

Even Jürgen Habermas, who took up the intentions of Critical

---

11. Odo Marquard, 'Kant und die Wende zur Ästhetik', *Philosophisches Jahrbuch*, no. 70, 1962, pp. 232ff.

Theory most determinedly and pursued them further, admits that his idea of 'unversehrter Intersubjektivität', as 'Vorschein von symmetrischen Verhältnissen freier reziproker Anerkennung', could not 'zur Totalität einer versöhnten Lebensform ausgemalt und als Utopie in die Zukunft geworfen werden'.[12] In other words: the attempt to account more scientifically for the Utopian element in critical thought has reduced it to little more than a heuristic idea.

Thus, viewed with Enzensberger from the year 2006, Marquard's old thesis could yet prove helpful: where historical thought does not bear fruit, aesthetics is used to provide a solution. For where powerful changes cut massively into life hopes are eclipsed by fears: what the future holds must appear uncertain, while, by contrast, the breaking down and decay of traditional forms are (at least) foreseeable. Such fears are clearly discernible even within the passionate espousal of progress in Goethe's *Faust*. The path from Kant to Hegel led bourgeois society across the threshold of the Industrial Revolution.

The 1980s mark an altogether analogous threshold between epochs, with similar tremendous acceleration in development. There is therefore virtually no call for philosophy of history, at least not of the optimistic variety. Visions of decline and destruction are accordingly all the rage. Anything expected by way of prognosis is expected of aesthetics. 'Was eine Gesellschaft oder ein Jahrhundert werden, weiß die Literatur im voraus – oder niemand weiß es.'[13]

VI

Reinhard Lettau has provided an amusing illustration of the difficulties we experience today even with basic geographical (and ideological) orientation. Lettau had climbed onto the flat roof of his house in San Francisco with a friend in order to gain a good view of the city and it had occurred to him 'daß hinsichtlich der Bezeichnungen der Himmelsrichtungen neue Überlegungen angestellt werden müssen'. During the roof-top conversation his friend had casually mentioned some of the qualities of the Western world and pointed as he did so out at the Pacific – in the direction of Russia and China.[14]

12. Jürgen Habermas, 'Die Einheit der Vernunft in der Vielfalt ihrer Stimmen', *Merkur*, vol. 42, no. 1, 1988, p. 14.
13. Mann, 'Die Macht des Wortes', p. 285.
14. Reinhard Lettau, *Zur Frage der Himmelsrichtungen*, Munich, 1988, pp. 7ff.

A Critic's Perspective

Henceforth, so I fear, every attempt to find a fixed point of view and to define it will have to take account of the observations made by the two friends:

> Wenn Du in den Westen zeigst, zeigst Du dann nicht in den Osten? Den Osten rief er, haben wir schon im Osten! Ist es dann nicht ungünstig für Euch, entgegnete ich, an beiden Küsten von Osten umgeben zu sein? Der wirkliche Osten, wenn ihr ihn sucht, ist im Westen, während der Westen, von dem ihr sprecht, weit im Osten entfernt ist![15]

The difficulties of orientation are no less apparent in the values and structures of society. A few key concepts will serve to highlight some relevant areas of change: the work ethos of middle-class society; spare time and leisure; the personal computer; information technology; electronic media; videos; the book of the film – and the printing industry, the book-market, literature?

If we return once more to the future, we may assert without fear of contradiction that books which were once important have disappeared from view again together with the cause they were bound up with (often too closely). The significance of Peter Schneider's little story *Lenz*, particularly in its double reference to the tradition of great bourgeois literature, Büchner and Lenz, was inevitably greatly overrated. *Lenz* signalled the end of the student movement and the beginning of what at the time was called 'neue Innerlichkeit', 'neue Subjektivität'. Schneider articulated the spirit of the day – as did Peter Sloterdijk barely fifteen years later. And Hochhuth's dramas which relate to a particular historical situation, his *Juristen* for example, are also disappearing into history without a trace, like the events that occasioned their writing.

It is easy to add to the catalogue: bestsellers, like Simmel's *Doch mit den Clowns kamen die Tränen*; world bestsellers, like Patrick Süskind's *Das Parfum*; the little surprise successes, such as Thorsten Becker's *Die Bürgschaft*; the short-lived fashions and trends; the private myths; the confessions born of experience; the so-called 'father books', even if they are by Peter Härtling and Christoph Meckel. In every case we are in danger of speculating wrongly, of making a mistake. For this reason alone it is not worth continuing the list.

---

15. Ibid., p. 7.

VII

From the historical distance which Enzensberger's fiction, the year 2006, allows us, we can, however, recognize clearly three loosely interrelated elements:

(1) the death of modernism;
(2) the end of postwar literature, or rather the generation change in German literature that has become definitive in the 1980s;
(3) the change in the 'general literary climate', that is, the loss of Utopia entailed by the substitution of aesthetics for philosophy of history.

Modernism drew its energy, as I have said, from the philosophy of history, the idea of progress. Its central category was the 'New'. We can still find convincing evidence for this in the development of the young Handke. Following the model developed by the Russian formalists, literary progress was regarded as the result of formal innovation, which in its turn was directed against the established way of seeing things. Thus literature, not by dint of any critical content it might hold but by dint of its form, could be understood as a protest against the development of society, specifically by means of the precisely directed negation.[16]

It was precisely this claim that came to be thoroughly questioned in the 1960s – and not without good grounds. The catchphrase of the 'death of literature', as we have seen, has had a long and honourable life, but in fact it only testified to the diminishing power of negation. In the very concept of art, as Adorno said, there is already 'das Ferment beigemengt, das ihn aufhebt'.[17] But Adorno kept firmly to his view of the function of art as official *Statthalter*. So long as the way to real change was barred, there could be no dispensing with the social antithesis of society and consequently with art.

The students at that time saw things differently. And their frontal attack on the foundations which legitimized bourgeois literature was not without its consequences, even if not the desired ones. Among other things, the massive criticism accelerated the erosion of modernism. Paradoxically, the pronouncement that art was dead

---

16. See Martin Lüdke, 'Plädoyer gegen die Weinerlichkeit', *Literaturmagazin*, no. 15, 1985, pp. 113ff.
17. Cf. *Ästhetische Theorie*, Frankfurt/Main, 1970, pp. 11ff.

A Critic's Perspective

drew its life from the idea of progress which provided the grounds for this diagnosis.

Postmodernism, as the epitome of lost commitment, therefore appears to me also to result from the criticism that modernism lacked commitment. The catchphrase 'Anything goes. Alles ist möglich. Alles erlaubt' also undermines the distinction between art and culture industry. With no traditions out of reach, with form and means ranked side by side, in times of peaceful coexistence between once competing trends, everything has become equivalent (*gleich–gültig*). And is it a coincidence that this process of the erosion of modernism coincides with a generation change in German literature?

Probably every generation is inclined to overestimate the significance of its own epoch. Yet there are historical differences, phases of – to use Thomas Mann's solid middle-class description of his own epoch – 'Kulturkrise and Zeitwende'. The significant authors of our postwar literature, Andersch and Böll, Hans Werner Richter and Arno Schmidt, Max Frisch und Dürrenmatt, were unable, because of the historical experience that had shaped them, to understand literature simply as literature. They had to see themselves, sometimes even against their will (Arno Schmidt is a case in point), as representatives of a middle-class public. They made their contribution, to use an expression at once simple and emotive, to the creation of democratic conditions.

Many of this generation are now dead, others are old and perhaps tired. Even so, the degree to which they, as a generation, have fallen silent can be explained, in my view, only by a change in the 'general literary climate', to wit: the replacement of philosophy of history by aesthetics. As long as the erosion of modernism was in progress, literature could draw energy from the difference between concrete significance and self-appraisal, in fact from a fiction. This illusion has been destroyed – again by the protest movement of the 1960s. In the 1980s the producers of literature have become aware of its marginal position.

At the same time, art has achieved something for which the scope was strictly limited in modernism by the rigorous definition of art as the social antithesis of society: art (together with literature) has firmly established itself as a social system in its own right but – again paradoxically – in so doing has burst asunder all its limitations. Many spheres of life have been aestheticized, while the sphere of aesthetics has lost all commitment and – being therefore indifferent (*gleichgültig*) – coats daily life with slime.

Martin Lüdke

VIII

'Ich glaube nicht an normale Erzählungen,' wrote Gert Jonke, at that time still very young, in his *Glashausbesichtigung* (1970). 'Ich kann nur an Erzählungen, die durch andere Erzählungen unterbrochen werden, glauben.'[18] With these apparently innocuous, in fact extremely significant sentences Jonke took his leave of experimental literature in order to use experimental techniques in his presentation of experience (in books such as *Der Ferne Klang* and *Schule der Geläufigkeit*). And the same path was trodden by the young Peter Handke from his *Die Hornissen*, *Der Hausierer* and *Publikumsbeschimpfung* up to his *Wunschloses Unglück*. Since then, apart from one or two screenplays and film scripts, Jonke has produced very little. By contrast, Handke's production has come in a steady stream: new books which admittedly no longer seek each in turn to secure new ways of looking at things through new means, but seek on the contrary to secure a traditional way of seeing. Impressed among others by the French metaphysician of the object, Francis Ponge, Handke became increasingly sceptical about modernism's belief in progress. His cycle *Langsame Heimkehr* describes this process programmatically. Like *Der Chinese des Schmerzes*, this cycle sets out to be both a story about real things and a poetics, setting out the reason for the story. In this Handke is still bound to the modern. But he also reaches back deliberately to before modernism, for example, to Stifter's 'sanftes Gesetz'. Botho Strauß, incidentally, in *Der junge Mann*, also takes up premodern, Romantic positions for similar motives, even if his reasons differ in detail.

IX

The heated debates about Botho Strauß and Peter Handke, viewed from the year 2006, have long been gathering dust in the archives of literary history.

The results of these discussions, for example, Handke's story *Die Wiederholung*, will live on; one might say, for a 'postmodern reason'. What in the 1980s hastened to call itself postmodern, lusting after the spirit of the times, has long since been dumped on the great rubbish tip of history, at the foot of which nobody now stands, not even a Benjaminian angel. Handke used the licence of postmodernism, the free availability of all tradition, to secure a firm footing in the present for himself.

18. Gert F. Jonke, *Glashausbesichtigung*, Frankfurt/Main, 1970, p. 24.

X

'Gestern wird sein, was morgen gewesen ist.' This means, so Grass thought, 'Unsere Geschichten von heute müssen sich nicht jetzt zugetragen haben. Diese fing vor mehr als dreihundert Jahren an. Andere Geschichten auch. So lang rührt jede Geschichte her, die in Deutschland handelt.'[19]

If – and this is an open question which I should be glad to leave open – good grounds could be found to substantiate this sentence, we should soon have to reckon with another change in the 'general literary climate'. Every departure from matters of principle has so far always been a leave-taking for a limited period of time. And the times, as Bob Dylan knew, they are a-changing.

---

19. Grass, *Das Treffen in Telgte*, p. 7.

Notes on the Contributors

Sarah Brickwood is a graduate of the University of Cambridge who recently completed the Postgraduate Diploma in Interpreting and Translating in the Department of Modern Languages of the University of Bradford. She is currently converting the Diploma to an MA prior to commencing work for a doctorate.

Gordon Burgess is a graduate of London University and completed his doctorate at the University of Aberdeen, where he is now Lecturer in German. He has published on German literature from the seventeenth to the twentieth centuries and on the use of computers for literary analysis and language teaching. He has made particular studies of Wolfgang Borchert and Wolfgang Koeppen.

Christa Hartwig teaches in the Sektion Sprach- und Literaturwissenschaft at the Martin-Luther-Universität, Halle, where she studied at both undergraduate and postgraduate levels. From 1986 to 1988 she taught in the German Department of the University of Leeds.

David Jenkinson is Principal Lecturer in German at Goldsmiths' College in the University of London. He has published widely, in particular on Hans Henny Jahnn, Hofmannsthal, Hauptmann, Brecht, Grass, Arnold Zweig, Heinrich Mann, Christa Wolf and Hermann Kant. He also translates and is currently preparing a book on *Brecht's Major Plays* sub-titled 'the socialist vision'.

Martin Kane is Senior Lecturer in German and European Studies at the University of Kent at Canterbury. He is the author of a study of George Grosz and Ernst Toller, *Weimar Germany and the Limits of Political Art*. He has written a number of reviews and articles on contemporary East and West German literature. He is also a contributor to Keith Bullivant (ed.), *After the 'Death of Literature': West German Writing of the 1970s* (Berg, 1989).

Brian Keith-Smith is Senior Lecturer in German at the University of Bristol, where he has taught for twenty-nine years. His extensive list of publications shows a wide interest in twentieth-century writers, especially Lothar Schreyer and Hugo von Hofmannsthal. He is a contributor to Lothar Huber (ed.), *Franz Werfel: An Austrian Writer Reassessed* (Berg, 1989). His current research interests include Friederike Brun, German Women Expressionists, Johannes Bobrowski and Ilse Aichinger.

Hubert Lengauer studied at the University of Vienna and taught briefly at the University of Naples before joining the staff of the Institut für Germanistik of the Universität für Bildungswissenschaften in Klagenfurt. He has published widely on Austrian literature of the nineteenth century, the turn of the century and, his most recent research, the postwar period.

Martin Lüdke is one of the Federal Republic's foremost and most prolific literary critics. He was for a time Professor für Neuere Deutsche Sprache und Literatur at the J. W. Goethe-Universität, Frankfurt, and has been visiting professor at a number of American universities. He is a regular contributor to *Der Spiegel*, *Die Zeit* and the *Frankfurter Rundschau* as well as to a number of radio and television programmes. He was a cofounder of the journal *Ästhetik und Kommunikation*. He is currently preparing a book for publication on *Leitfaden im Labyrinth. Literatur an den Rändern der Moderne*.

Moray McGowan studied at the University of Newcastle and also holds a doctorate from Hamburg University. He has taught at the Universities of Siegen, Kassel, Lancaster, Hull and Strathclyde, where he was codirector of the Contemporary German Studies programme. He has published numerous articles on modern German literature, including contributions to Keith Bullivant (ed.), *After the 'Death of Literature'* (Berg, 1989), and a major study of *Marieluise Fleißer*. He is now Professor of German at Sheffield University.

Norbert Mecklenburg is Professor of German Literature in the Institut für Deutsche Sprache und Literatur at the University of Cologne. His publications include the following major works: *Kritisches Interpretieren* (1972), *Naturlyrik und Gesellschaft* (1977), *Erzählte Provinz* (1982) and *Die grünen Inseln* (1986).

Stuart Parkes graduated at Oxford University before completing his PhD at Bradford University. He is now Senior Lecturer in German at Sheffield City Polytechnic. He has published a number of articles on modern German literature and society. In 1986 he published *Writers and Politics in West Germany*.

Malcolm Pender is Senior Lecturer in German at the University of Strathclyde where, after undergraduate study at Cambridge University,

Notes on the Contributors

he gained his PhD. He is particularly noted for his work on German–Swiss literature and contemporary East and West German literature. He has published major books on *Max Frisch: His Work and its Swiss Background* and *The Creative Imagination and Society: The German–Swiss 'Künstlerroman'* (since Keller) and is a contributor to Keith Bullivant (ed.), *The Modern German Novel* (Berg, 1987); he is currently co-editing a collection of essays on contemporary German–Swiss prose writing.

Julian Preece is currently working on the final stages of his doctoral thesis on the treatment of history in the novels of Günter Grass. He is the Laning Junior Fellow at the Queen's College, Oxford University.

Peter Pütz is Professor für Neuere Deutsche Literatur at the Rheinische Friedrich-Wilhelms-Universität, Bonn. He is particularly noted for his publications on Nietzsche, Thomas Mann and the drama of the Enlightenment (*Die Zeit im Drama*, 1977, and *Die Leistung der Form. Lessings Dramen*, 1986). Recently he has made a special study of the work of Peter Handke.

J. H. Reid studied at the Universities of Glasgow and Frankfurt and taught at the University of West Berlin before joining the University of Nottingham, where he is currently Reader in German. He has an impressive list of publications on twentieth-century German fiction, including a volume on the twentieth-century German novel (with E. Boa) and two books on Heinrich Böll, the second of which, *Heinrich Böll – A German for his Time* (1988), was published by Berg and has received wide critical acclaim. His new volume, *Writing Without Taboos: The New East German Literature*, was published by Berg in 1990.

Andrea Reiter studied at the University of Salzburg, where she completed her PhD in 1984. At the time of the Bradford conference she held a fellowship from the Österreichische Forschungsgemeinschaft at the University of Southampton where, after a brief period of teaching in Salzburg University, she is now a Research Fellow working on the memoirs of concentration-camp survivors. She has published a book on the computer analysis of a contemporary right-wing Austrian journal and articles on Franz Kafka, on the use of computing in literary analysis and on the prose and poetry of a group of contemporary right-wing writers in Austria.

Ricarda Schmidt studied at the Universities of Hanover and Hull. She gained her PhD at Hanover University in 1981, and has taught English and German at the Universities of Hanover, Salford, UMIST, Osnabrück, Caen and Southampton. She has published several articles and reviews on German and Anglo-American women's writing and on Critical Theory.

Notes on the Contributors

Her book on *Westdeutsche Frauenliteratur in den 70er Jahren* was published in 1982. She is now lecturer in German at Sheffield University.

Ralf Schnell is currently spending some time as Visiting Professor of German Literature in the Keio University, Tokyo, where the 1990 IVG Congress is to be held. At the time of the Bradford conference he was Außerplanmäßiger Professor für Neuere Deutsche Literaturgeschichte at the University of Hanover. His research ranges through literary theory, cultural policy (in both the Federal Republic and the GDR) and culture and literature during the Third Reich (*Literarische Innere Emigration 1933–45*, 1976). In 1986 he published *Die Literatur der Bundesrepublik. Autoren, Geschichte, Literaturbetrieb*. The publication of a volume on 'literary irony in the nineteenth century' is expected in late 1989.

Gisela Shaw is Senior Lecturer in German at Bristol Polytechnic. She studied at the Universities of Mainz and Bonn, where she was awarded her D. Phil. for a thesis on the reception of Kantian philosophy in Great Britain. She also has a BA from Kirksville, Missouri, where she was a Fulbright student of American literature and history, and an M. Phil. from Bath, for a thesis on East German literature. She has published on philosophy and GDR studies.

Roland Smith lectures in the Modern Languages Department of the University of Bradford, where he gained both his MA and his PhD having studied originally at the University of London. He is a specialist in GDR studies and has published particularly on the Church in the GDR.

Juliet Wigmore lectures in German in the Department of Modern Languages at the University of Salford. She pursued her undergraduate studies at the University of London and went on to complete higher degrees in both London and Kent. She has published on Ingeborg Bachmann, Theodor Storm and Feminist Writing in West Germany and is a contributor to Keith Bullivant (ed.), *After the 'Death of Literature'* (Berg, 1989).

Arthur Williams is Senior Lecturer in German Studies at the University of Bradford. After an early article on Thomas Mann, the subject of his postgraduate work at Keele University, he changed from the study of literature to the study of West German society and has published on social policy and the media, in particular the governance of broadcasting (*Broadcasting and Democracy in West Germany*). Since 1985 he has returned to literature, with particular reference to the contemporary West German novel.

Select Bibliography

Acker, Robert and Marianne Burkhard (eds.), *Blick auf die Schweiz. Zur Frage der Eigenständigkeit der Schweizer Literatur seit 1970*, Amsterdam, 1987
Adorno, Theodor W., *Eingriffe*, Frankfurt/Main, 1963
——, *Ästhetische Theorie*, ed. Gretel Adorno and Rolf Tiedemann, Frankfurt/Main, 1970
——, *Noten zur Literatur*, Frankfurt/Main, 1974
Argument – Sonderband 110: Geschlechterverhältnisse und Frauenpolitik, Berlin, 1984
Arnold, Hans Ludwig (ed.), *Kritisches Lexikon zur deutschsprachigen Gegenwartsliteratur*, Munich, 1978–
——(ed.), *Bestandsaufnahme Gegenwartsliteratur. Bundesrepublik Deutschland, Deutsche Demokratische Republik, Österreich, Schweiz*, Munich, 1988
Aspetsberger, Friedbert and Hubert Lengauer (eds.), *Zeit ohne Manifeste. Zur Literatur der siebziger Jahre in Österreich*, Vienna, 1987
Ayac, Gürsel, Viktoria Rehberg and Sara Sayin (eds.), *Izmirer Colloquien. Die Schweizer Literatur der Gegenwart*, Izmir, 1987
Bachmann, Dieter (ed.), *Fortschreiben. 98 Autoren der deutschen Schweiz*, Zurich, 1977
Bakhtin, Mikhail, *Die Ästhetik des Wortes*, Frankfurt/Main, 1979
Barry, Peter (ed.), *Issues in Contemporary Critical Theory*, London, 1987
Bassnett, Susan, *Feminist Experiences. The Woman's Movement in Four Cultures*, London, 1986
Benjamin, Walter, 'Geschichtsphilosophische Thesen', in *Illuminationen. Ausgewählte Schriften*, ed. Siegfried Unseld, Frankfurt/Main, 1961
——, 'Über den Begriff der Geschichte', *Gesammelte Schriften*, eds. Rolf Tiedemann and Hermann Schweppenhäuser, Frankfurt/Main, vol. 1, pt 2, 1974
Bernhard, Hans Joachim, et al., *Geschichte der Literatur der Bundesrepublik Deutschland*, Berlin (GDR), 1983
Biermann, Wolf, *Mit Marx- und Engelszungen*, Berlin, 1968
Blumenberg, Hans, *Arbeit am Mythos*, Frankfurt/Main, 1979
Bormann, Alexander von (ed.), *Sehnsuchtsangst. Zur österreichischen Literatur der Gegenwart*, Amsterdam, 1987
Botond, Anneliese (ed.), *Über Thomas Bernhard*, Frankfurt/Main, 1970

Select Bibliography

Brandstetter, Alois (ed.), *Gegenwartsliteratur als Bildungswert*, Vienna, 1982
Brecht, Bertolt, *Über Realismus*, Frankfurt/Main, 1971
Bullivant, Keith, *Realism Today. Aspects of the Contemporary West German Novel*, Leamington Spa, 1987
——(ed.), *The Modern German Novel*, Leamington Spa, 1987
——(ed.), *After the 'Death of Literature': West German Writing of the 1970s*, Oxford, 1989
Bürger, Christa (ed.), *Zerstörung, Rettung des Mythos durch Licht*, Frankfurt/Main, 1986
Bürger, Peter, *Theorie der Avantgarde*, Frankfurt/Main, 1974
Cassirer, Ernst, *Philosophie der symbolischen Formen. Das mythische Denken*, Berlin, 1925
Cepl-Kaufmann, Gertrude, *Günter Grass. Eine Analyse des Gesamtwerkes unter dem Aspekt von Literatur und Politik*, Kronberg, 1975
Cixous, Hélène and Catherine Clément, *La Jeune Née*, Paris, 1975
Cocalis, Susan and Kay Goodman, *Beyond the Eternal Feminine. Critical Essays on Women and German Literature*, Stuttgart, 1982
Collard, Andrée and Joyce Construcci, *Rape of the Wild*, London, 1988
Corbin, A., *Le Miasme et la jonquille. L'odorat et l'imaginaire social, 18e–20e siècles*, Aubier-Montagne, 1982
Daly, Mary, *Gyn/Ecology*, London, 1979
Danto, Arthur C., *Analytische Philosophie der Geschichte*, Frankfurt/Main, 1974
DDR-Literatur '83 im Gespräch, Berlin (GDR), 1984
Dowling, David, *Fictions of Nuclear Disaster*, London, 1987
Durzak, Manfred, *Gespräche über den Roman. Formbestimmungen und Analysen*, Frankfurt/Main, 1976
Eagleton, Terry, *Literary Theory. An Introduction*, Oxford, 1983
Eco, Umberto, *The Name of the Rose*, London, 1984
Eisenstein, Zillar, *Capitalist Patriarchy and the Case for Socialist Feminism*, New York, 1979
Engelberg, Ernst, *Bismarck: Urpreuße und Reichsgründer*, Berlin (GDR), 1985
Foucault, Michel, *Les mots et les choses*, Paris, 1966
Fowler, Roger, *Linguistic Criticism*, Oxford, 1986
Frank, Manfred, *Der kommende Gott. Vorlesungen über die Neue Mythologie*, Frankfurt/Main, 1982
Fries, Ulrich, *Uwe Johnsons 'Jahrestage'*, Göttingen, 1989
Gaus, Günter, *Wo Deutschland liegt. Eine Ortsbestimmung*, Munich, 1986
Geppert, Hans Vilmar, *Der 'andere' historische Roman*, Tübingen, 1976
Görtz, Franz Josef, Volker Hage and Uwe Wittstock (eds.), *Deutsche Literatur 1987. Jahresüberblick*, Stuttgart, 1988 (and subsequent volumes; see also Hage)
Göttner-Abendroth, Heide, *Matriarchale Mythologie*, Munich, 1980
Grimm, Gunter, Werner Faulstich and Peter Kuon (eds.), *Apokalypse.*

Select Bibliography

Weltuntergangsvisionen in der Literatur des zwanzigsten Jahrhunderts, Frankfurt/Main, 1986

Gumbrecht, Hans Ulrich and Ursula Link-Heer (eds.), *Epochenschwellen und Epochenstrukturen im Diskurs der Literatur- und Sprachhistorie*, Frankfurt/Main, 1984

Habermas, Jürgen, *Der philosophische Diskurs der Moderne*, Frankfurt/Main, 1985

——, *Eine Art Schadensabwicklung. Kleine Politische Schriften IV*, Frankfurt/Main, 1987

——, (ed.), *Stichworte zur 'Geistigen Situation der Zeit'*, 2 vols., Frankfurt/Main, 1979

Habermas, Jürgen, Silvia Bovenschen, et al. (eds.), *Gespräche mit Herbert Marcuse*, Frankfurt/Main, 1978

Hackenbracht, Elisabeth and Rolf Hackenbracht (eds.), *Peter Härtling: Materialienbuch*, Darmstadt, 1979

Hage, Volker (ed.), *Deutsche Literatur 1981 [1986]. Jahresüberblick*, Stuttgart, 1982 [1987] (see also Görtz, et al.)

Hegel, Georg W. F., *Ästhetik*, ed. Friedrich Bassenge, Berlin (FRG), 1985

Heinrich, Klaus, *Parmenides und Jona. Vier Studien über das Verhältnis von Philosophie und Mythologie*, Basel, 1982

Hildesheimer, Wolfgang, *'Das Ende der Fiktionen'. Reden aus fünfundzwanzig Jahren*, Frankfurt/Main, 1984

Hirdina, Karin, *Günter de Bruyn. Leben und Werke*, Berlin (GDR), 1983

'Historikerstreit'. Die Dokumentation der Kontroverse um die Einzigartigkeit der nationalsozialistische Judenvernichtung, Munich, 1987

Hörisch, Jochen and Hubert Winkels (eds.), *Das schnelle Altern der neuesten Literatur*, Düsseldorf, 1985

Horkheimer, M. and T. W. Adorno, *Dialektik der Aufklärung*, Frankfurt/Main, 1971

Hurrelmann, Bettina, Maria Kublitz and Brigitte Röttger (eds.), *Man müßte ein Mann sein. . . ? Interpretationen und Kontroversen zu Geschlechtertausch-Geschichten in der Frauenliteratur*, Düsseldorf, 1987

Huyssen, Andreas and Klaus R. Scherpe (eds.), *Postmoderne: Zeichen eines kulturellen Wandels*, Reinbek, 1986

Irigaray, Luce, *Spéculum de l'autre femme*, Paris, 1974

——, *Ce sexe qui n'en est pas un*, Paris, 1977

Jurgensen, Manfred (ed.), *Bernhard. Annäherungen*, Berne, 1981

——, *Deutsche Frauenautoren der Gegenwart*, Berne, 1983

——, *Women, Writers, Women Writers – An Alternative History of German Literature*, Queensland, 1984

Kaufmann, Hans (ed.), *Über DDR-Literatur. Beiträge aus fünfundzwanzig Jahren*, Berlin (GDR), 1986

Kemper, Peter (ed.), *'Postmoderne' oder der Kampf um die Zukunft*, Frankfurt/Main, 1988

Klussmann, Paul Gerhard and Heinrich Mohr (eds.), *Deutsche Misere einst*

Select Bibliography

und jetzt: Die deutsche Misere als Thema der Gegenwartsliteratur: Das Preußensyndrom in der Literatur der DDR, Bonn, 1982

Kocka, Jürgen and Thomas Nipperdey (eds.), *Theorie und Erzählung in der Geschichte*, Munich, 1979

Koselleck, Reinhart, W. J. Mommsen, Jörn Rüsen and Heinrich Lutz (eds.), *Formen der Geschichtsschreibung*, Munich, 1982

Kraft, Martin, *'Schweizerhaus'. Das Haus-Motiv im Deutschschweizer Roman des 20. Jahrhunderts*, Berne, 1971

Kroker, Arthur and David Cook (eds.), *The Postmodern Scene. Excremental Culture and Hyper-Aesthetics*, 2nd edn, London, 1988

LaCapra, Dominick, *Geschichte und Kritik*, Frankfurt/Main, 1987

Lämmert, Eberhard (ed.), *Romantheorie*, Cologne, 1975

Lerchi, Fredi (ed.), *Vorschlag zur Unversöhnlichkeit*, Zurich, 1984

Lloyd, Genevieve, *The Man of Reason*, London, 1984

Lotman, Yuri M., *Die Struktur literarischer Texte*, Munich, 1972

Lühe, Irmela von der (ed.), *Entwürfe von Frauen in der Literatur des 20. Jahrhunderts*, Berlin, 1982

Lukács, Georg, *Der historische Roman*, in *Werke: Probleme des Realismus III*, vol. 6, Darmstadt, 1965

Lützeler, Paul M. (ed.), *Deutsche Romane des 20. Jahrhunderts. Neue Interpretationen*, Königstein, 1983

Mann, Thomas, *Schriften und Reden zur Literatur, Kunst und Philosophie*, vol. 2, Frankfurt/Main, 1968

Markolin, Caroline, *Die Großväter sind die Lehrer. Johannes Freumbichler und sein Enkel Thomas Bernhard*, Salzburg, 1988

Matt, Peter von, *Das verlorene Monument*, Frankfurt/Main, 1985

Mecklenburg, Norbert, *Erzählte Provinz*, Königstein, 1982

——, *Die grünen Inseln*, Munich, 1986

Menge, Marlies, *Die Sachsen – das Staatsvolk der DDR*, Munich, 1985

Mittenzwei, Ingrid, *Friedrich II. von Preußen. Eine Biographie*, Berlin (GDR), 1980

Moi, Toril, *Sexual/Textual Politics*, London, 1985

Müller, Harro, *Geschichte zwischen Kairos und Katastrophe. Historische Romane im 20. Jahrhundert*, Frankfurt/Main, 1988

Niederhauser, Rolf and Martin Zingg (eds.), *Geschichten aus der Geschichte der Schweiz nach 1945*, Darmstadt, 1983

Panoke, Helga, *Erwin Strittmatter. Lebenszeit*, Berlin (GDR), 1987

Pezold, Klaus (ed.), *Entwicklungstendenzen der deutschsprachigen Literatur der Schweiz in den sechziger und siebziger Jahren*, Leipzig, 1984

Phillips, Anne (ed.), *Feminism and Equality*, London, 1987

Piltz, Georg, *August der Starke: Träume und Taten eines deutschen Fürsten*, Berlin (GDR), 1986

Pulver, Elsbeth (ed.), *Zwischenzeilen. Schriftstellerinnen der deutschen Schweiz*, Zurich, 1985

Pütz, Peter, *Peter Handke*, Frankfurt/Main, 1982

Select Bibliography

Quandt, Siegfried and Hans Süssmuth (eds.), *Historisches Erzählen. Formen und Funktionen*, Göttingen, 1982

Radix, Michael (ed.), *Strauß lesen*, Munich, 1987

Reid, James H., *Heinrich Böll. A German for his Time*, Oxford, 1988

——, *Writing Without Taboos: The New East German Literature*, Oxford, 1990

Richter-Schröder, Karen, *Frauenliteratur und weibliche Identität*, Meisenheim, 1986

Roberts, David, and Philip Thomson (eds.), *The Modern German Historical Novel: Paradigms, Problems, Perspectives*, Oxford, 1990

Rönisch, Siegfried (ed.), *DDR Literatur im Gespräch 1985*, Berlin (GDR), 1986

Rüsen, Jörn, Eberhard Lämmert and Peter Glotz (eds.), *Die Zukunft der Aufklärung*, Frankfurt/Main, 1988

Schabert, Ina, *Der historische Roman in England und Amerika*, Darmstadt, 1981

Schaeffer-Hegel, Barbara and Brigitte Wartmann (eds.), *Mythos Frau. Projektionen und Inszenierungen im Patriarchat*, Berlin, 1984

Scheunemann, Dietrich, *Romankrise*, Heidelberg, 1978

Schiffer, Werner, *Theorien der Geschichtsschreibung und ihre erzähltheoretische Relevanz*, Stuttgart, 1980

Schlesier, Renate (ed.), *Faszination des Mythos. Studien zu antiken und modernen Interpretationen*, Basel, 1985

Schlosser, Horst D. and Hans D. Zimmermann (eds.), *Poetik. Essays über Ingeborg Bachmann, Heinrich Böll, Wolfgang Hildesheimer, Uwe Johnson, Christa Wolf ... und andere. Beiträge zu den Frankfurter Poetik-Vorlesungen*, Frankfurt/Main, 1988

Schmidt-Dengler, Wedelin, *Der Übertreibungskünstler. Zu Thomas Bernhard*, Vienna, 1986

Schmitt, Hans-Jürgen and Godehard Schramm (eds.), *Sozialistische Realismuskonzeptionen. Dokumente zum 1. Allunionskongreß der Sowjetschriftsteller*, Frankfurt/Main, 1974

Schnell, Ralf, *Die literatur der Bundesrepublik. Autoren, Geschichte, Literaturbetrieb*, Stuttgart, 1986

Schoenberg, Arnold, *Style and Idea. Selected Writings*, ed. Leonard Stein, London, 1975

Schöne Albrecht (ed.), *Akten des VII. Internationalen Germanistik-Kongresses. Göttingen 1985*, Tübingen, 1986

Schriftsteller der Gegenwart: Erwin Strittmatter. Analysen, Erörterungen, Gespräche, Berlin (GDR), 1980

Schuscheng, Dorothee, *Arbeit am Mythos Frau. Wirklichkeit und Autonomie in der literarischen Mythenrezeption Ingeborg Bachmanns, Christa Wolfs und Gertrud Leuteneggers*, Frankfurt/Main, 1987

Seghers, Anna, *Über Kunstwerk und Wirklichkeit. Die Tendenz in der reinen Kunst*, Berlin (GDR), 1970

Select Bibliography

Seibert, Ingrid and Sepp Dreissinger, *Die Schwierigen. Portraits zur österreichischen Gegenwartskunst*, Vienna, 1986

Seiler, Bernd W., *Die leidigen Tatsachen*, Stuttgart, 1983

Sotriffer, Kristian (ed.), *Der Kunst ihre Freiheit. Wege der österreichischen Moderne von 1880 bis zur Gegenwart*, Vienna, 1987

Stegmüller, Wolfgang, *Hauptströmungen der Gegenwartsphilosophie*, vol. 1, Stuttgart, 1978

Stephan, Inge and Sigrid Weigel, *Die verborgene Frau*, Berlin, 1983

——(eds.), *Weiblichkeit und Avantgarde*, Berlin, 1987

Strittmatter, Eva, *Briefe aus Schulzenhof*, Berlin (GDR), 1979

Tate, Dennis, *The East German Novel. Identity, Community, Continuity*, Bath, 1984

Wehler, Hans-Ulrich, *Das Deutsche Kaiserreich: 1871–1918*, Göttingen, 1973

——, *Entsorgung der deutschen Vergangenheit?*, Munich, 1988

Weidenfeld, Werner (ed.), *Die Identität der Deutschen*, Munich, 1983

Weigel, Sigrid, *Die Stimme der Medusa. Schreibweisen in der Gegenwartsliteratur von Frauen*, Dülmen-Hiddingsel, 1987

Williams, Ingrid K. J. (ed.), *GDR: Individual and Society*, Conference Proceedings, Ealing College of HE, London, 1987

Wilpert, Gero von, *Sachwörterbuch der Literatur*, Stuttgart, 1969

Wittgenstein, Ludwig, *Philosophische Untersuchungen*, Werkausgabe, vol. 1, Frankfurt/Main, 1984

Index

Note: a number of items in this index have been deliberately kept broad in order not to create distinctions that would be artificial in the present context. Thus, for example, 'women' refers to women's writing, women's situation in society, women's issues etc, and 'history' includes philosophy of history and historiography as well as the treatment of history in the novel.

academic novel, 1, 5, 6, 135–52
Adenauer, Konrad, 326
Adorno, Theodor W., 149, 277, 318, 333, 338, 339, 341, 344
Aeschylus, 250, 256
   Oresteia (458 BC), 17
Amis, Kingsley
   Lucky Jim (1954), 79
Andersch, Alfred, 12, 13–14, 18, 19, 20, 322, 345
   Winterspelt (1974), 13–14, 18
Arbeiterroman, 161
Archer, Jeffrey, 318
Aue, Hartmut von, 145
August the Strong, 61, 71, 73
Austrian novel, 169–86
autobiography, 2, 5, 73, 93, 148, 169, 174, 177, 187, 188, 189, 191, 204, 206, 254, 332

Bach, Johann Sebastian, 187
Bachmann, Ingeborg, 239
Bahro, Rudolf, 111
Bakhtin, Mikhail, 41, 43
Barthes, Roland, 40, 253
Bataille, Georges, 266, 273, 274
Baudelaire, Charles, 284
Baudrillard, Jean, 9, 15, 264
Bauernroman, 161
Becker, Jurek
   Bronsteins Kinder (1986), 4
Becker, Thorsten
   Die Bürgschaft (1985), 343
Beethoven, Ludwig van, 190, 195, 196, 198
Benjamin, Walter, 9, 12, 17, 46, 341, 346
Berger, John, 183

Bernhard, Thomas, 6, 101, 131, 187–207
   Watten. Ein Nachlaß (1969), 190
   Der Ignorant und der Wahnsinnige (1975), 189, 191
   Die Ursache. Eine Andeutung (1975), 204
   Der Keller. Eine Entziehung (1976), 188
   '*Monologe auf Mallorca*' (1981), 197
   Beton (1982), 189, 190, 197
   Ein Kind (1982), 203
   Wittgensteins Neffe. Eine Freundschaft (1982), 190
   Der Untergeher (1983), 189, 190, 206
   Alte Meister (1985), 189, 194, 199–205, 207
Biermann, Wolf, 71, 111, 225
Bismarck, Otto von, 3, 41, 63, 64, 65
Blake, William, 276
Bloch, Ernst, 18, 325, 328, 338, 341
Böhmer-Schlegel-Schelling, Caroline, 61
Böll, Heinrich, 1, 4, 302, 305, 309, 322, 345
   Frauen vor Flußlandschaft (1985), 2, 282
Böni, Franz, 157, 158
bondage, 162, 211, 213, 214, 215
Borchert, Wolfgang
   Draußen vor der Tür (1947), 285
Born, Nicolas
   Die erdabgewandte Seite der Geschichte (1976), 2
Brahms, Johannes, 192
Brandstetter, Alois, 4, 142–8, 149
   Die Burg (1986), 4, 142–8, 151
Brandt, Willy, 324, 325

Index

Brasch, Thomas, 111, 223
  Vor den Vätern sterben die Söhne (1981), 268
Braun, Volker, 61, 66
  Großer Frieden (1976), 69
  Hinze-Kunze-Roman (1985), 64
Brecht, Bertolt, 41, 46, 104, 181, 247, 252
  Der aufhaltsame Aufstieg des Arturo Ui (1941), 333
  Die Geschäfte des Herrn Julius Cäsar (1957), 72
Broch, Hermann, 324
Bruyn, Günter de, 64, 77–89
  Der Hohlweg (1963), 77, 78
  Buridans Esel (1968), 77, 78, 79, 80, 81, 82, 88, 89
  Preisverleihung (1972), 77, 78, 79, 80, 88, 89
  Das Leben des Jean Paul Friedrich Richter (1976), 77
  Märkische Forschungen (1978), 77, 79–80, 87, 89
  Neue Herrlichkeit (1984), 64, 82–7
  Frauendienst (1986), 77
Büchner, Georg, 343
  Lenz (1839), 110, 112, 121
Bürger, Peter, 339
Burger, Hermann, 156
  '*Die Leser auf der Stör*' (1970), 155
  Schilten (1976), 157, 164
Byron, George Gordon, 6th Baron, 115

campus-novel, 135
Camus, Albert
  L'Étranger (1942), 98
Cassirer, Ernst
  Philosophie der symbolischen Formen (1925), 259–60
Celan, Paul, 199
Chamisso, Adelbert von, 312
Chaucer, Geoffrey, 246
Cixous, Hélène, 264–5, 266, 269, 273, 274, 277–8
Clausewitz, Karl von
  Vom Kriege (1832–7), 19
Cleland, John
  Fanny Hill (1748–9), 271
Critical Theory, 341

Damm, Sigrid, 69
  Vögel, die verkünden Land (1985), 61
Dante Alighieri

Divine Comedy (1300–21), 74
Danzig (Gdansk), 64, 322, 323, 324, 333
Derrida, Jacques, 9, 264
Diderot, Denis, 64
Disney, Walt, 327
documentary, 10, 13, 14, 19, 20, 32, 40, 43, 109, 112, 333
Döblin, Alfred
  Wallenstein (1920), 32
Dorfgeschichte, 165, 167
dream, 94, 103, 123, 130, 148, 226–8, 230, 255, 276, 285, 294, 304, 305, 321, 324, 325, 331, 332, 333
Dürrenmatt, Friedrich, 155, 345
Dylan, Bob, 347

Ebersbach, Volker
  Caroline (1987), 61
Eco, Umberto
  The Name of the Rose (1984), 3, 309, 316
Eichendorff, Joseph von, 125
Eliot, T. S., 287, 288, 306
Elsner, Gisela, 210
Ende, Michael
  Die unendliche Geschichte (1979), 309
Enlightenment, 2, 26, 263–6, 271, 272–3, 275, 277, 323, 325, 329, 330, 338
Enzensberger, Hans Magnus, 2, 339, 342, 344
  Der Untergang der Titanic (1978), 74
  Ach Europa! (1987), 337
Ernst, Gustav, 172
  Frühling in der Via Condotti (1987), 180–2
Eue, Dieter
  Ketzers Jugend (1982), 225

fantasy, 137, 138, 216, 227–31, 233–4, 255, 274, 321, 331, 332
father, 4, 18, 34–6, 39–40, 45, 54, 62, 81, 82, 84, 94, 100, 116–19, 127, 158, 163, 177–8, 239, 245, 257–8, 264, 280–1, 285, 292, 293, 296, 305, 343
female, 1, 16, 17, 23, 71, 72, 78, 85, 87, 214, 215, 233, 254, 258, 259, 261, 262, 263–78, 280–2, 285, 297, 298, 300, 303, 304, 318, 326
feminist, 6, 22, 66, 140, 209–11, 233, 236, 241, 250, 260–2, 263–5, 268, 272, 274, 278, 295, 328, 331

Index

Feuchtwanger, Lion, 66, 69–70, 72
  Jud Süß (1925), 70
Feyl, Renate, 5, 61, 62, 64, 140–2
  Idylle mit Professor (1986), 5, 61, 64, 140–2, 146, 151
Fian, Antonio, 175, 182, 184, 185
Flaubert, Gustave, 11, 22, 277
  Bouvard et Pécuchet (1881), 10
Fleißer, Marieluise, 210
Fontane, Theodor, 11, 81
Foucault, Michel, 264, 272
Frankenstein, 312
Frederick II, 3, 62, 63, 64, 65, 69
Frederick II of Sicily, 61
Frederick William I, 62, 68, 69
Fremdarbeiter, 158, 159, 160, 161, 162
Freytag, Gustav, 73, 177
Frisch, Max, 2, 156, 168, 345
  Stiller (1954), 154, 155, 165
  Homo Faber (1957), 266, 273
  Wilhelm Tell für die Schule (1971), 154
Fühmann, Franz
  Saiäns-Fiktschen (1981), 72

Ganz, Raffael
  Im Zementgarten (1971), 162
Gastarbeiter, 215, 290, 294, 303
Gaus, Günter, 225
Geiser, Christoph, 158, 167
Genet, Jean
  The Maids (1947), 279, 281
Genscher, Hans Dietrich, 307
Gerhardt, Paul, 335
German–Swiss novel, 153–68
Glaser, Peter, 173
Goebbels, Josef, 247
Goethe, Johann Wolfgang von, 14, 81, 82, 89, 115, 121, 148, 150, 248, 282, 301
  Torquato Tasso (1790), 170
  Römische Elegien (1795), 181
  Faust (1808 and 1832), 62, 66, 342
  Dichtung und Wahrheit (1811–14), 53
Gorki, Maxim, 49
Gottsched, Johann Christoph, 62, 64, 140, 141, 142, 150
Gottsched, Luise Adelgunde Victorie, 61, 140
Gould, Glenn, 191
Goya, Francisco José de, 330
grandmother, 39, 53, 82, 83, 86, 87, 295
Grass, Günter, 1, 2, 4, 12, 39, 130, 267, 287, 295, 299, 301, 302, 309, 321–34, 335, 336, 347
  Die Blechtrommel (1959), 295, 315, 323, 324, 332, 333
  Katz und Maus (1961), 298, 324
  Hundejahre (1963), 315, 323
  Örtlich betäubt (1969), 333
  Aus dem Tagebuch einer Schnecke (1972), 323, 324–5, 328
  Der Butt (1977), 12, 267, 324, 325, 326, 328, 329, 331, 332, 333
  Das Treffen in Telgte (1979), 335
  Kopfgeburten (1980), 287, 325
  Die Rättin (1986), 1, 2, 12, 130, 267, 321–34
Graves, Robert, 17
Greer, Germaine, 265
Grimmelshausen, Hans Jakob Christoffel von, 335
Grundgesetz, 279, 305
Gruppe 47, 4, 323, 335
Gryphius, Andreas, 335
Günderrode, Karoline von, 61, 70, 238
Gutzkow, Karl Ferdinand, 11

Habermas, Jürgen, 338
Härtling, Peter, 336, 343
Handke, Peter, 4, 6, 123–33, 147, 169, 170, 287, 335, 344, 346
  Die Hornissen (1966), 346
  Publikumsbeschimpfung (1966), 346
  Der Hausierer (1967), 346
  Die Angst des Tormanns beim Elfmeter (1970), 123, 124
  Wunschloses Unglück (1972), 169, 346
  Die Stunde der wahren Empfindung (1975), 123
  Langsame Heimkehr (1979), 123, 131, 346
  Die Lehre der Sainte-Victoire (1980), 126
  Über die Dörfer (1981), 128
  Der Chinese des Schmerzes (1983), 4, 123–33, 346
  Phantasien der Wiederholung (1983), 128
  Die Wiederholung (1986), 170, 346
  Die Abwesenheit (1987), 169
  Nachmittag eines Schriftstellers (1987), 169
Harich, Wolfgang, 65
Haslinger, Josef, 172, 176, 178, 182, 183–4, 185
  Der Tod des Kleinhäuslers Ignaz Hajek

Index

(1985), 178, 183–4
Politik der Gefühle (1987), 185–6
Hauff, Wilhelm, 81
'Haus-Motiv', 157, 158, 160, 166
Haydn, Josef, 192
Hebel, Johann Peter, 104
Hegel, Georg Wilhelm Friedrich, 12, 26, 176, 263, 340, 341, 342
Heidegger, Martin, 199
Heimatroman, 161
Hein, Christoph, 4, 61, 62, 68, 77, 91–105
  Der fremde Freund (1982) = *Drachenblut* (1985), 68, 92, 93–9, 100, 101, 102, 103, 105
  Die wahre Geschichte des Ah Q (1984), 100, 103
  Horns Ende (1985), 4, 62, 92, 93, 95, 99–104, 105
Heine, Heinrich, 121, 138
Heinisch, Paul, 178
Herder, 82
Herodotus, 27, 235
Heym, Stefan
  Der König Davids Bericht (1972), 72
  'Mein Richard' (1976), 112–14
Hildebrandslied, 144
Hildesheimer, Wolfgang, 1, 12, 20–1, 22
  Mozart (1977), 20
  Marbot (1981), 20
historical novel, 3, 4, 5, 6, 7, 11, 14–15, 21, 30, 32, 37, 40, 45, 61–75, 318
Historikerstreit, 3, 31, 39, 63, 283, 307
history, 2, 3, 5, 9–27, 29, 30–3, 34, 35, 36–47, 88, 99, 100–1, 128, 142, 149, 152, 157, 178, 183, 253, 255, 257, 261, 263–4, 267, 272, 281–6, 288, 289, 292–4, 297, 314, 318, 322, 324, 326–7, 330, 336, 338, 340–6
Hitler, Adolf, 55, 64, 284, 286, 291, 302, 314, 317, 323, 327, 333
Hochhuth, Rolf
  Die Juristen (1979), 343
Hölderlin, Friedrich, 81
Hoffmann, E. T. A., 148
Hoffmann-Reicker, Klaus
  Teufelsbünder (1982), 73
Hofmannswaldau, Christian Hofmann von, 335
Holthusen, Hans Egon
  Indiana Campus. Ein amerikanisches Tagebuch (1969), 136

Homer, 125, 235, 250
  Iliad, 17, 240, 259
  Odyssey, 17
Honecker, Erich, 63
Horkheimer/Adorno
  Dialektik der Aufklärung (1971), 257, 265, 270, 271, 273

identity, 20, 22, 24, 64, 65, 94, 103, 111, 117, 136, 167, 191, 223, 225, 227, 249, 250–1, 254, 258, 260, 261, 264, 276, 292, 299, 304–5, 338
Inglin, Meinrad
  Schweizerspiegel (1938), 157
Innerhofer, Franz, 172
  Schattseite (1974), 177
  Schöne Tage (1974), 177
  Die großen Wörter (1977), 177
  Der Emporkömmling (1982), 177, 178

Jaeck, Hans-Peter
  Kammerherr und König. Voltaire in Preußen (1987), 61, 73
Jaeggi, Urs, 173
Jean Paul, 27, 81, 82, 89, 326
Jelinek, Elfriede, 209–19
  Die Liebhaberinnen (1975), 212
  Die Klavierspielerin (1983), 209, 210, 211–17, 219
  Oh Wildnis, oh Schutz vor ihr (1985), 209, 211, 217–19
Jenninger, Philipp, 283
Johnson, Uwe, 4, 12, 23–5, 29–47, 315, 322
  Mutmassungen über Jakob (1959), 29
  Das dritte Buch über Achim (1961), 315
  Jahrestage (1970–83), 23–5, 29, 30, 32, 44, 45, 46, 47
  Heute neunzig Jahr (fragment), 29, 42
  Versuch, einen Vater zu finden (1988), 4, 5, 29–47
Jonke, Gerd
  Glashausbesichtigung (1970), 346
  Der Ferne Klang (1979), 346
  Schule der Geläufigkeit (1985), 346
Joyce, James
  Ulysses (1922), 23
Jünger, Ernst, 12, 14–16, 22, 23
  Auf den Marmorklippen (1960), 16
  Eumeswil (1977), 14–16, 22

Kafka, Franz, 317
  Das Urteil (1916), 144

Index

'Josefine, die Sängerin oder das Volk der Mäuse' (1919), 148
Das Schloß (1926), 151
Kant, Hermann, 65, 77, 238
  Die Aula (1965), 72, 82, 240
  Der Aufenthalt (1977), 62, 240
Kant, Immanuel, 247, 260, 263, 318, 328, 341, 342
Kauer, Walther
  Spätholz (1976), 165
Keats, John, 249
Keller, Gottfried
  Der Grüne Heinrich (1854–5 and 1879–80), 180
  Martin Salander (1886), 159
Kerenyi, Karl, 17
Kiesinger, Kurt Georg, 324, 325
Kleist, Heinrich von, 61, 70, 104, 230, 238, 277, 306
  Michael Kohlhaas (1810), 317
Kluge, Alexander, 10, 12, 14, 19–20, 32
  Schlachtbeschreibung. Der organisatorische Aufbau eines Unglücks (1978), 19–20, 32
  Die Patriotin (1979), 14
Köhlmeier, Michael
  Spielplatz für Helden (1988), 170
Kohl, Helmut, 3, 283
Kraus, Karl, 186, 321
Kreisky, Bruno, 174
Kroetz, Franz Xaver, 310
Künstlerroman, 213, 217
Kunert, Günter, 66, 230

Lacan, Jacques, 264
Laederach, Jürg, 9
La Fontaine, 327
Lautenschlag, Marockh
  Araquin (1981), 264
  Sweet America (1983), 264
Lenin, Vladimir Ilich, 40
Lenz, J. M. R., 61
Lenz, Siegfried, 1, 21–2, 23
  Heimatmuseum (1978), 22
  Exerzierplatz (1985), 21–2
Lessing, Gotthold Ephraim, 330
Lettau, Reinhard
  Zur Frage der Himmelsrichtungen (1988), 342–3
Leutenegger, Gertrud, 156, 157, 158, 163–8
  'Das verlorene Monument' (1979), 157
  Vorabend (1980), 164
  Leb wohl, Gute Reise (1984), 163
  Kontinent (1985), 163–8
Lewin, Waldtraut, 61, 69–70, 72, 73, 74
  Federico (1984), 61, 66, 69–70, 72, 74
Lodge, David, 149
Logau, Friedrich Freiherr von, 335
Lukács, Georg, 11, 67–8, 69, 70, 71, 341
  Der historische Roman (1937), 67–8
Luther, Martin, 3, 27, 63, 65
Luxemburg, Rosa, 42

Machiavelli, Niccolò, 251
Mahler, Gustav, 192
male, 6, 71, 72, 78, 85, 214, 215, 233, 235, 254, 256, 260, 262, 264–8, 271, 272, 275, 276, 277, 278, 280, 282, 284, 285, 295, 298–300, 303, 304, 329
Mann, Heinrich
  'Die Macht des Wortes', 336
  Henri Quatre (1935 and 1938), 3
Mann, Thomas, 9, 22, 37, 82, 121, 257, 324, 345
  Buddenbrooks (1901), 191
  Mario und der Zauberer (1930), 290
  Joseph und seine Brüder (1933–42), 3, 298
Marcuse, Herbert, 269, 271, 277
  Eros and Civilization, 271
Maron, Monika, 6, 221–34
  Flugasche (1981), 222–30, 231, 232, 233
  Die Überläuferin (1986), 222, 227, 230–4
  'Deutsch-deutscher Briefwechsel' (1987), 221, 222
Marquard, Odo, 340–2
Marx, Karl, 9, 27, 63, 71, 173, 240
matriarchy, 267, 269, 328
May, Karl, 81
Meckel, Christoph, 343
Mecklenburg, 24, 34, 35, 36, 37, 38, 39, 41
media, 18, 19, 111, 174, 182, 293, 294, 297, 310, 323, 324, 325, 326, 343
Meier, Gerhard, 158, 167
Mendelssohn, Felix, 190
Mengele, Josef, 114, 116–18
Meyer, E. Y., 155, 157, 167
  In Trubschachen (1972), 161
  Die Rückfahrt (1977), 154

Mitgutsch, Anna
  Züchtigung (1985), 178
modern, 4, 11, 18, 30, 31, 32, 35, 39, 40, 43, 44, 45, 47, 68, 73, 82, 97, 99, 110, 142, 143, 146, 147, 154, 159, 161, 163, 165, 168, 174, 176, 182, 190, 192, 197, 206, 219, 240, 258, 261, 265, 280, 283, 291, 292, 293, 299, 300, 301, 302, 305, 314, 318, 323, 333, 338–41, 344–6
Molière, 121
Moníková, Libuše
  Die Fassade (1987), 254, 260–2
Morgner, Irmtraud, 5, 66, 268
  Leben und Abenteuer der Trobadora Beatriz nach Zeugnissen ihrer Spielfrau Laura (1974), 6, 268
  Amanda (1983), 66, 70
mother, 20, 84, 85, 94, 140, 169, 177, 178, 211–13, 215, 228, 264, 267, 292, 295–6, 302, 311
Mozart, Wolfgang Amadeus, 187, 190, 191, 192
Müller, Heiner, 61, 64, 265, 266
  Philoktet (1955), 270
  Leben Gundlings Friedrich von Preußen Lessings Schlaf Traum Schrei (1977), 62
Müntzer, Thomas, 63
Muschg, Adolf, 7, 155, 156, 157, 165
  Gegenzauber (1967), 157
  Albissers Grund (1974), 156
  Baiyun oder die Freundschaftsgesellschaft (1980), 7, 165
music, 6, 173, 187–207, 211–15, 302, 311–12
Musil, Robert, 324
myth, 2, 5, 6, 16, 17, 18, 70, 74, 125, 131, 154, 157, 163, 245, 253–62, 265, 269, 280, 304, 323, 343

national literatures, 6, 9
Nazi, 4, 55, 110, 119, 132, 157, 254–5, 289–90, 303, 325
'Neue Subjektivität', 2
Neumann, Gerd, 222, 224
  Schuld der Worte (1979), 221, 224
Neutsch, Erik, 77
  Drei Tage unseres Lebens (1969), 66
  Der Frieden im Osten (1987), 62
Nexø, Martin Andersen, 49
Nietzsche, Friedrich, 65, 71, 128, 132, 138, 239, 282, 294, 300, 303
Novalis

  Heinrich von Ofterdingen (1802), 125
  Novelle, 51, 92, 93, 95, 99, 101, 102, 105, 136, 183, 275, 299, 312, 339

Pascal, Blaise, 190
patriarchy, 71, 163, 210, 211, 215, 218, 219, 256–8, 261–2, 263–78
Pedretti, Erica
  Valerie oder Das unerzogene Auge (1986), 165
phallogocentrism, 261, 264, 265
Plenzdorf, Ulrich, 250
  Die neuen Leiden des jungen W. (1973), 66, 240
pornography, 211, 214, 215
postfeminism, 261
postmodernism, 3, 6, 7, 9, 15, 30, 31, 32, 47, 253, 279, 283, 301, 316–17, 318, 337–9, 340, 341, 345, 346
postpatriarchy, 276
Professorenroman, 135
Proust, Marcel, 49
Prussia, 27, 41, 61, 62, 63, 64, 65, 68, 69, 71, 77, 80, 81, 88

Ransmayr, Christoph
  Die Schrecken des Eises und der Finsternis (1984), 170
realism, 5, 20, 32, 37, 87, 156, 163, 171–2, 174–6, 180, 184–5, 211, 217, 221, 222, 227, 230, 231, 306, 309, 332
Redl, Thomas, 172
Reger, Max, 189, 190, 199, 200
Reinig, Christa, 254, 258–60, 261, 262
  Entmannung (1976), 254
  Die Frau im Brunnen (1984), 254, 259, 261
Richter, Hans Werner, 335, 345
Rilke, Rainer Maria, 138, 149
Rimbaud, Arthur, 268
role of the writer, 169, 170, 175, 176
Rousseau, Jean Jacques
  Confessions (1782), 310

Sakowski, Helmut
  Wie ein Vogel im Schwarm (1984), 64
Sand, George, 11
satire, 38, 40, 41, 43, 141, 146, 147, 156, 209–19, 269, 270, 271, 332, 333, 334
Scharang, Michael, 172, 182
  Charly Traktor (1973), 178
  Harry. Eine Abrechnung (1984), 178, 183

Index

Scheel, Walter, 63
Schiller, Friedrich, 65, 82
Schlegel, Friedrich von, 277
'Schlüsselerzählung', 235, 236, 238
Schmidt, Arno, 9, 345
Schneider, Hansjörg
  Lieber Leo (1980), 158
Schneider, Peter, 4, 107–22, 343
  Lenz (1973), 108, 110, 115, 120, 343
  ... und schon bist du ein Verfassungsfeind (1975), 109, 110, 115, 120, 121
  Atempause (1977), 107
  Die Botschaft des Pferdekopfs und andere Essais aus einem friedlichen Jahrzehnt (1981), 108
  Der Mauerspringer (1982), 108, 110–14, 115, 120, 121
  Vati (1987), 4, 107, 108, 110, 113, 114–22
  Deutsche Ängste (1988), 120–2
Schoenberg, Arnold, 190, 192, 193, 197, 206
Schopenhauer, Arthur, 190
Schütz, Stefan, 267–72, 277, 278
  Sappa (1980), 270
  Medusa (1986), 267–72, 274
Schutting, Jutta, 178
Scott, Walter, 3, 11, 30, 68
Seghers, Anna, 238
Shakespeare, William, 65, 121, 136, 138, 246
Simmel, Johannes Mario
  Doch mit den Clowns kamen die Tränen (1987), 343
Sloterdijk, Peter, 343
socialist realism, 11, 66, 77
Sophocles, 255
Sorbs, 53, 54, 58
Späth, Gerold, 167
Stade, Martin, 61, 62, 68–9, 71, 73
  Der König und sein Narr (1975), 62, 68–9, 73
  Der närrische Krieg (1981), 61, 71, 73
Stefan, Verena
  Häutungen (1975), 5, 263
Sterchi, Beat, 158–62, 165
  Blösch (1983), 158–62, 164, 165, 167, 168
Strauß, Botho, 4, 6, 272–8, 279–308, 346
  'Marlenes Schwester' (1975), 272
  'Theorie der Drohung' (1975), 284
  Die Widmung (1977), 275

Rumor (1980), 273, 280, 285–92
Kalldewey Farce (1981), 275
Paare Passanten (1981), 273, 274, 283, 290, 292–8, 303
Der Park (1983), 284, 292, 298
Der junge Mann (1984), 272, 274, 275–6, 279–306, 346
Diese Erinnerung an einen, der nur einen Tag zu Gast war (1985), 279, 298, 306–7
Die Fremdenführerin (1986), 284, 298
Niemand anderes (1987), 273, 275
Strittmatter, Erwin, 5, 49–59
  Ochsenkutscher (1951), 50
  Tinko (1955), 50
  Der Wundertäter (1957–80), 50, 62
  Ole Bienkopp (1963), 50
  Die blaue Nachtigall oder der Anfang von etwas (1972), 51, 52
  Meine Freundin Tina Babe (1977), 52
  Selbstermunterungen (1981), 52, 59
  Der Laden (1983–7), 5, 49–59
  Grüner Juni (1985), 53
Strittmatter, Eva
  Briefe aus Schulzenhof (1979), 50
Struck, Karin
  Klassenliebe (1973), 5
Süskind, Patrick, 3, 309–19, 343
  'Das Vermächtnis des Maitre Mussard' (1976), 310
  Der Kontrabaß (1984), 310–11, 312
  Das Parfum (1985), 3, 310, 312, 313–19, 343
  'Amnesie in litteris' (1986), 310
  Die Taube (1987), 310, 311–13, 317
Süskind, W. E., 309
  Aus dem Wörterbuch des Unmenschen (1968), 310
Swift, Jonathan, 332

Third Reich, 1, 4, 34, 39, 62, 288, 294, 322, 333
Tocqueville, Alexis de, 11

Ulbricht, Walter, 66, 71, 326
Utopia, 140, 148, 170, 244, 245, 257, 258, 260, 264, 270, 276, 277, 318, 326, 328–9, 331, 338, 339, 341, 342, 344

Valery, Paul, 136, 152, 287, 306
Vergangenheit, 29, 31, 67, 279, 287, 291, 305, 306, 336
Vesper, Bernward

Index

Die Reise (1977), 2
Virgil, 125, 130, 235
Voltaire, 61, 62

Wagner, Richard, 187
Waldheim, Kurt, 3, 185
Walser, Martin, 1, 135–40, 285, 309, 312
  Ein fliehendes Pferd (1978), 136, 138
  Brandung (1985), 1, 135–40, 151
  Jagd (1988), 1
Walser, Robert, 163
Walter, Otto F.
  Die ersten Unruhen (1972), 156
  Die Verwilderung (1977), 7
Walther, Joachim, 61, 62, 71, 73
  Bewerbung bei Hofe (1982), 61, 62, 66, 71, 73, 74
Weber, Max, 251
Webern, Anton, 206
Weil, Greta
  Meine Schwester Antigone (1980), 254–6
Weiss, Peter, 12, 23, 25–6, 240, 268, 271, 322
  Die Ästhetik des Widerstands (1975–81), 23, 25–6, 240, 268, 271
Wieland, Christoph Martin, 81
Wilhelm II, 41
Winkler, Josef, 177
  Der Leibeigene (1987), 171
Wittgenstein, Ludwig, 9, 190
Wolf, Christa, 5, 12, 16–18, 22, 23, 55, 61, 68, 70, 71, 72, 73, 74, 77, 130, 235–52, 254, 256–8, 261, 265
  Der geteilte Himmel (1963), 238, 245
  Nachdenken über Christa T. (1974), 18, 238, 244
  Kindheitsmuster (1977), 55, 62, 68, 240, 250
  Kein Ort. Nirgends (1979), 18, 61, 70, 71, 74, 238, 250
  Kassandra (1983), 5, 6, 16–18, 22, 70, 72, 130, 235–52, 254, 256–8, 261, 265
  Voraussetzungen einer Erzählung: Kassandra (Frankfurt Lectures) (1983), 9, 17, 235, 236, 238, 239–40, 241, 244, 247, 250, 256, 258
  Störfall (1987), 247
Wolfgruber, Gernot, 172, 177, 178–80
  Verlauf eines Sommers (1981), 178
  Die Nähe der Sonne (1985), 177, 178, 179–80
women, 5–6, 18, 22, 70, 140, 142, 146–7, 155, 158, 210–11, 214–15, 217, 222, 228, 231, 235, 236, 239–40, 245, 246, 250, 253–7, 260–2, 263–9, 272, 275, 277–8, 280, 281–2, 285, 292, 293, 295–6, 299–300, 302, 303, 311, 318, 328, 331
Wühr, Paul
  Das falsche Buch (1983), 273

Zeller, Michael
  Follens Erbe. Eine deutsche Geschichte (1986), 148–52
Zenker, Helmut, 172
Zesen, Philipp von, 335
Zorn, Fritz
  Mars (1977), 155
Zweig, Arnold, 82